Political Traditions in Foreign Policy Series

KENNETH W. THOMPSON, EDITOR

Power and Progress

American National Identity, the War of 1898, and the Rise of American Imperialism

Paul T. McCartney

LOUISIANA STATE UNIVERSITY PRESS

BATON ROUGE

DESIGNER: Andrew Shurtz
TYPEFACE: Berthold Walbaum Book
TYPESETTER: G&S Typesetters, Inc.
PRINTER AND BINDER: Edwards Brothers, Inc.

LIBRARY OF CONGRESS CATALOGING-IN-PUBLICATION DATA

McCartney, Paul T., 1969–
   Power and progress: American national identity, the War of 1898, and the rise of
American imperialism / Paul T. McCartney.
     p. cm. – (Political traditions in foreign policy)
   Includes bibliographical references and index.
   ISBN 0-8071-3114-8 (cloth: alk. paper)
   1. United States–Foreign relations–1897–1901. 2. Spanish-American War, 1898.
3. Imperialism. 4. United States–Territorial expansion. I. Title. II. Series: Political
traditions in foreign policy series.
E713.M38 2005
327.73'009'34–dc22

                     2005008050

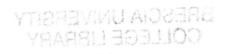

To my son, Tyler John New, who makes me proud

Contents

Acknowledgments

This book was a long time in the making, and it would never have become a reality without the tremendous help I have received from others. Foremost among those to whom I owe thanks are Martha Derthick and Kenneth Thompson. Professors Thompson and Derthick have been mentors to me in the fullest sense of the word. They have been unusually close and perceptive readers of many thousands of pages of drafts, offering both support and criticism of my work when needed and teaching through their example what clear thinking and clear writing entail. More broadly, I learned from them what it means to be a scholar and teacher, and I will always try to model my career on their examples, laboring in the recognition that even as I fall short of the ideal they represent, at least I will fall in the right direction.

James Ceaser and William Lee Miller also read various drafts of this work in its entirety and provided crucial feedback that clearly improved its argument. Wilson Carey McWilliams generously read several chapters and guided my research in new and better directions. Edward Rhodes, Daniel Tichenor, and Susan Lawrence variously read chapters, taught me how to do research, and gave me opportunities to test my ideas before sharp and insightful audiences. All of these individuals, especially Professor Lawrence, helped me to develop professionally as both a teacher and researcher. I would also like to thank the individuals at Louisiana State University Press, who not only helped to bring the project to fruition but also became partners in the process. In particular, Lee Sioles and Dennis Marshall deserve special mention for providing countless suggestions and corrections that invariably improved the quality of the manuscript.

Various individuals and institutions provided crucial assistance, both financial and emotional, during the preparation of the manuscript.

The H. B. Earhart Foundation and the Institute for the Study of World Politics provided funding at critical points of the project, while the Miller Center of Public Affairs provided not only financial assistance but a haven of good people. My students at Rutgers University often gave me helpful feedback on my ideas and generally kept me on my toes for three years. It was a pleasure to teach them.

My family rarely understood why I persisted in pursuing the strange career of an academic, but they stood by me nonetheless. My mother, Jane, my brothers, Joe and Damian, and my sister, Allison, helped keep me relatively normal. I have also drawn inspiration from the members of my family who are not here to read this book, though I wish they were: my father, John, and my sisters Jean and Mary. Please, everyone, fill out your organ donor cards. My son, Tyler John New, to whom this book is dedicated, makes it all count.

As one might expect, my thinking on this project evolved constantly, in part due to my conversations with insightful and patiently accommodating friends. Among those who let me bounce ideas off them are John Dinan, Pat Dunn, Michael Fitzpatrick, James Staab, Steve Tauber, and Leslie Urofsky. I know I have left out many others, and to them I send a blanket thank-you. My father-in-law, Jeremy Millett, happens to be a political theorist and an expert on many of the themes covered in this book. Fortunately, he is also a willing reader, able wine educator, and raiser of wonderful daughters. One of those daughters, my wife, Alison Millett McCartney, deserves the most credit for helping me to complete this project. First off, she lived with me for many of the years I worked on it. Enough said. But she is also a professor, and I shamelessly exploited her proximity, expertise, and editing savvy. Above all that, though, I owe her the highest debt of gratitude just for her being *her*. Life is good.

Introduction

AT THE DAWN of the twenty-first century, foreign policy has once again become a central preoccupation of the American people. After a decade of prosperous complacency, the terrorist attacks of September 11, 2001, jolted public opinion to a renewed appreciation of the importance of international affairs, and the government's response has been vigorous. For the first time since the cold war ended more than a dozen years ago, the United States has shown a clear focus and sense of purpose in eliminating foreign threats and forcefully establishing an international environment amenable to American interests and values. As part of the effort to undermine hostile forces that might contribute to global terrorism, the administration of President George W. Bush controversially elected to invade Iraq in order to oust the dictator Saddam Hussein and implant democracy in the troubled Middle East. In one of his many speeches explaining American goals, he declared, "The establishment of a free Iraq in the heart of the Middle East will be a watershed event in the global democratic revolution. . . . The advance of freedom is the calling of our time. It is the calling of our country. From the Fourteen Points to the speech at Westminster, America has put our power at the service of principle. We believe that liberty is the design of nature. . . . It is the right and capacity of all mankind."[1]

Americans remain deeply divided about whether the war against Iraq was justified, and skepticism abounds about the real reasons for starting it, but the sincerity of the Bush administration—both in seeking to democratize Iraq and in believing that doing so is consistent with American principles—seems real, whatever other motives might have contributed to the decision to initiate hostilities. The aggressive doctrine of preventive intervention that Bush invoked to justify the invasion, coupled with his drive to alter the domestic governance of a foreign state, has been widely interpreted as signaling a new and dangerous era in American foreign policy. According to the new logic, the United States will no longer wait for threats to manifest themselves; nor will it idly tolerate brutal dictators of relatively weak regimes openly rejecting American leadership and values while fostering conditions that may some day result in new terrorist attacks. Instead, the United States will unilaterally intervene in other countries when it deems conditions warrant such action, using its military supremacy to spread its values and enhance national security. It is this assertiveness that has been widely regarded as introducing the new era in U.S. foreign policy.

A closer look at American history, particularly the era that launched both the twentieth century and the emergence of the United States as a world power, should lead us to question whether the U.S. war against Iraq represents as radical a departure from American tradition as this conventional wisdom suggests. Certainly, America's current unilateralist militarism signals a strategic departure from recent history; on the other hand, the War of 1898 foreshadowed current U.S. foreign policy in important ways, and a careful examination of it can help us to make sense of some of the issues presently facing the nation. In particular, the two conflicts demonstrate how the United States defines itself through its foreign policy by melding the ideological and cultural sources of its identity with the practical exigencies of international relations. This book offers a comprehensive analysis of the nexus of foreign policy and nationalism that shaped the transforming events of 1898–99. Its findings suggest that a full and proper understanding of contemporary foreign policy requires that we pay greater attention to America's nationalist logic, which seems naturally to invite an imperialist posture based in benevolent arrogance.

More specifically, this book systematically describes America's cultural milieu in 1898 and explains how it structured the thinking of American policy makers during the wars and colonial expansionism that took place at that time. At the same time, it demonstrates how the War of 1898 and its consequences contributed in overlooked but decisive ways to the development of American national identity. As this book makes clear, foreign policy and national values can be mutually and reciprocally influential, with a significant development in either one likely to find reflection in the other. Such was certainly the case in

1898. Before the War of 1898, the United States was a strong but mostly self-absorbed nation; afterwards, it was a globally active "power" in possession of colonial territories at the far end of the Pacific Ocean and with a markedly increased influence in the affairs of its immediate island neighbors. For this reason, Woodrow Wilson wrote in 1902, "[n]o war has ever transformed us quite as the war with Spain transformed us. We have witnessed a new revolution. We have seen the transformation of America completed."[2]

Americans in 1898 grappled with the significance of their nation's new policies, and inspired debates both on the streets and in the corridors of power revealed a nation engaged in serious reflection about its identity and its mission. As Robert L. Beisner wrote in 1968, the war and its aftermath "provoked a major crisis of belief and attitude that caused men . . . to inquire into more general questions about the makeup of American society, the future of American democratic institutions, and the nation's future role in international affairs." It was, Beisner concluded, "one of the most exacting and thorough examinations of the basic principles of American government and society in our history."[3]

The United States had complex motives for starting the war, and the fact that there were no clear security interests immediately at stake has made it difficult for subsequent generations to agree on what its reasons really were. Some scholars have identified economic motives as driving the movement to war, while others have been persuaded by the argument that the United States intervened exclusively for noble, humanitarian purposes. Still other studies have claimed that the yellow press, the collective restlessness of the American people, or the machinations of an expansionist cabal were responsible for the American decision to attack Spain. Further complicating historical understanding of American motives was the territorial expansion that ensued from the war, which has colored most subsequent analyses of it.

For most of the country at the time, territorial expansionism was an unexpected consequence of the campaign, and many segments of the American public fiercely opposed it, including Mugwumps, Populists, and others who for their own reasons simply disagreed with the proposition that the United States should become an imperial power. Despite their resistance, a peace treaty that included clauses annexing the Philippine Islands, Guam, and Puerto Rico passed the Senate, and the islands became U.S. territories. While hostilities were raging over the summer, moreover, in a separate action the United States also acquired Hawaii, and after the war, through the Platt Amendment, it maintained control of Cuba as well. For better or worse, the War of 1898 resulted in the United States becoming an imperial power. As historian Akira Iriye put it, "The globalization of America had begun," and a scholarly cottage industry attempting to explain how exactly this transformation in American foreign policy and national identity took place has been growing ever since.[4]

A brief survey of the major explanations that have been given for these events will help to illuminate this book's argument. In many ways, this work synthesizes existing accounts: the wide range of interpretations that have been offered regarding the events of 1898 are frequently more complementary than historians and political scientists have admitted. On the other hand, the present book emphasizes the role played by American culture and ideology in shaping American policy makers' perceptions of their policy options, and this position often forces my text to one side or another of existing debates. By distinguishing this book from representative existing accounts, with particular attention given to a few of the most recent studies of the conflict, the following overview of the scholarship surrounding the war, while not intended to be comprehensive, will clarify for the reader the assumptions and arguments that animate this text.[5]

One important set of studies posits that Americans fought against Spain and expanded U.S. boundaries after the war primarily to enlarge the nation's economic power. Some scholars have argued, for instance, that while the American people and their congressional representatives agitated for war against Spain for noble, humanitarian reasons, President William McKinley instead used the war as an opportunity for the United States to begin an economic-imperialist program.[6] Both the prosecution and settlement of the war, according to this view, reveal that McKinley's economic motives in safeguarding the investments of big business trumped in practice the more laudatory intentions of the American people. By strengthening American business interests in this way, McKinley hoped to augment the overall power and prestige of the United States.[7]

A related line of argument is that the war was manufactured in an effort to ease domestic pressure from agitated agrarian and labor groups who were dangerously dissatisfied with their economic situation.[8] Americans, under a cloud since the Depression of 1893, were eager to embark on a crusade on behalf of the oppressed Cuban population because it took their minds off their own problems, and they were also willing to expand American territory and power after the war was over because they believed that doing so would alleviate their own difficulties.[9] Enhancing American economic opportunity in this way served both to distract and to allay a dangerously discontented population while shifting the worst symptoms of economic distress to the inhabitants of other lands.

Two new studies develop this economic-imperialist approach further. The first is Matthew Frye Jacobson's *Barbarian Virtues*, which argues that racism was mixed with America's economic imperialism. This caused Americans to view the inhabitants of the lands they conquered as nothing but a cheap, expendable source of labor and yielded a frankly exploitative colonialism. The United States would conquer other people, destroying them if necessary (Jacobson even suggests in places that Americans *wanted* to harm the nonwhites they encountered) in order to generate wealth for itself.[10] Somewhat related to this analysis, but with more focus on America's Cuba-centrism, is Louis A. Pèrez Jr.'s *The War of 1898*. Pèrez's explicitly revisionist study argues that the United States intervened in the Cuban–Spanish War, with the goals of allowing American investors to extract the island's resources and preventing Cuban freedom, only when it believed that the Cubans were about to win independence for themselves. At the same time, Americans invented a myth of humanitarian purpose as a way to mask their real, imperialist goals and reinforce their belief in themselves as being a good and noble people.[11]

Jacobson's analysis is useful for highlighting the influence of racism and economic interests on American policy (the first of which is discussed at length in this book), but it is ultimately limited by taking as binary approach to American motives as that taken by Americans themselves in 1898, with equally distorting results. American economic interests were never pursued nearly as vigorously in the conquered lands as should have been the case had economic materialism been the overriding motivation; nor would the United States have invested so heavily in developing the conquered lands. A more textured and nuanced understanding of both American character and purpose is therefore needed to understand American ambitions properly; as in other studies that offer a primarily economic interpretation of American actions, Jacobson too casually dismisses or ignores geopolitical, humanitarian, pragmatic, and other motives.

The present book shares much in common with Pèrez's study insofar as both are interested in demonstrating how Americans used the events of 1898–99 to construct a new identity for themselves. Pèrez argues that Americans actively sought to craft an interpretation of their foreign policy in 1898–99 that would redound to their honor, and that they subsequently incorporated this newly generated interpretation into their identity. This book makes precisely the same case, and for this reason it will henceforth use the outdated appellation Spanish-American War rather than the more appropriate War of 1898 to show its emphasis on how Americans perceived their own actions. The two analyses differ, however, in crucial respects. Most importantly, Pèrez does not appear to regard American expressions of humanitarian intent prior to the war as being in any way sincere, and he downplays in general the role of norms in dictating behavior. Second, his argument that American leaders believed that the Cubans were on the verge of victory seems slightly overdrawn. In reality, much evidence indicates that Americans believed that the crisis in Cuba was never going to end: Spanish stubbornness and Cuban incompetence, Americans thought, would together guarantee perpetual chaos on the island.

Overall, the two books take a too-narrow view of how Americans thought, and they are thus unable to imagine that Americans can be both greedy racists and humanitarian pragmatists at the same time. The national identity that Americans were articulating in 1898 was not a fiction but a reality that influenced how they approached their foreign-policy making, for both good and ill. Americans were far from being angels in 1898 (or today, for that matter), but by the standards of the day they were not especially demonic, either. One limitation of primarily economic arguments is that they imply that only certain kinds of states pursue their economic interests on the world stage—namely, rapacious, dangerous, exploitative states. That is simply untrue: the reality is that *all* states compete for position in the global economy, and states that fail to do so not only suffer economically but also risk losing their geopolitical position. The United States is and has been unexceptional in seeking to secure and advance its national economy through its international relations. This observation, on the other hand, does not mean that economic gain is the exclusive or even overriding foreign-policy motivation of the United States; moralism, the basic pursuit of security, and various other concerns also figure prominently in American foreign policy. One purpose of this book is to invite a less-Manichean understanding of American nationalism and foreign policy by illustrating how Americans in 1898 mixed noble motives with destructive and hateful belief systems.

Another set of studies argues quite differently that American expansionism in 1898 was a simple case of geopolitical opportunism. One element of this argument is that American imperialism was engineered by a handful of important, influential political leaders, including Theodore Roosevelt and Henry Cabot Lodge, among others, who manipulated President McKinley to adopt their "large policy."[12] The major recent representative of this line of analysis is Warren Zimmerman's *First Great Triumph*. His main argument is that America's movers and shakers at the end of the nineteenth century envisioned a new role for the United States as one of the world's leading powers. They sought to enhance America's existing geopolitical advantages by building an isthmian canal that would facilitate American shipping and by building a first-rate blue-water navy. This vision required the acquisition of naval bases that would link Caribbean approaches to the proposed canal and extend across the Pacific to East Asia.[13] Closely related to this argument is Fareed Zakaria's in *From Wealth to Power*. Zakaria's "state-centered realism" holds that, like all states, the United States expanded its political interests overseas in the 1890s once its state capacities allowed it to do so. His book spells out a theory of international relations that posits that states seek to expand their power relative to other states in order to pursue their interests, but do so only when their power is sufficiently centralized and well-administered to allow them to make proper use of their productive capacities. Only after America had fully recovered from the division and destruction of the Civil War and harnessed its resources, Zakaria argues, was it prepared to pursue a robust foreign policy that included overseas expansion.[14] Almost as soon as it was able to do so, in short, the United States acted like other leading world powers by conquering the lands that would secure its geopolitical position and allow it to project its power overseas.

Like arguments based on the presumption of economic imperialism, this approach must also be regarded as incomplete. First, Zimmerman's account relies on a depiction of McKinley as a weak leader that no longer is supportable, as Lewis L. Gould's studies make clear.[15] There is little question that the members of Zimmerman's Large Policy group generated the geopolitical rationale for expansion that McKinley pursued; nor is there any doubt that their governmental positions enabled them to enjoy unusual influence in his administration. But it is also clear that McKinley was a strong leader with an independent mind, and the course of imperialism upon which he led the United States reflected goals and values distinctive to his leadership style. Specifically, McKinley was more of a moralist than his Large Policy peers, and he explicitly sought to conform American policies to the idea of American mission—a topic discussed below. Likewise, Zakaria's account does not explain why the Spanish-American War was the trigger that sparked the period's most significant expansion. Why, for instance, did it take a humanitarian crisis to rouse the United States from its (relatively) isolationist slumber? Why had the United States not simply seized Cuba, Puerto Rico, and the Philippines, not to mention other available territories, five or ten years sooner (or later, for that matter)? Although realists such as Zakaria convincingly demonstrate how power capacities tend to yield certain behaviors by states, they are unable—they do not try—to explain specific foreign policies. Thus, Zakaria cannot explain why Americans saw an actionable opportunity for expansion into Cuba and the Philippines in 1898 but not, for instance, in 1893, when the country's capacity was essentially the same.[16]

When one considers that the colonial policies pursued by the United States exceeded in scope and ambition the recognized requirements of geopolitics, it becomes clear that neither Zakaria's state-centered realism nor Zimmerman's Large Policy imperialism can fully explain American foreign policy during this episode. Ultimately, while these security-power arguments provide potent explanations for American behavior up to a point (as the term *power* in this book's title indicates), and while they also introduce a set of significant considerations that mitigate the Manichean perspective of the economic-imperialism approach, they ultimately suffer from their own version of the latter's materialist limitations. Though it is clearly the case that on some occasions the United States will act in exclusive pursuit of its economic interests and that on others it will engage in behavior driven solely by security concerns (and that most often it will pursue goals defined by some combination of the two), these materialist perspectives ignore the role that norms play in policy making. When a state has a certain set of material interests, be they economic, geopolitical, or otherwise, that state can almost always choose among several policy options to achieve its interests. Which course that state will pursue will be determined in part by its culture. Moreover, the material interests the state defines as important in the first place are likely to be defined to some degree by priorities derived from the state's culture and identity. Finally, on some occasions a state may pursue policies that have no relationship to material interests but that express that state's culture and values.

As these observations should indicate, it would be incorrect to regard this book as rejecting any of the analyses summarized above, except regarding the relatively minor points that were highlighted. Instead, this book should be seen as offering a framework for filling in the gaps between them and elucidating the moral logic followed by the United States. It augments, but does not necessarily challenge, existing accounts of 1898. Although there are many permutations on each school of thought that this overview does not address, there does remain one final body of scholarship.

This other approach insists that the events of 1898 reflect mostly the vagaries of historical contingency, holding that both the war and American imperialism were to a large degree unavoidable. Scholars following this approach suggest that a series of historical accidents shoved the process forward despite any one person's or group's goals.[17] This approach draws attention to three sets of incommensurate political conditions that together made war practically unavoidable: a Spanish political situation and ideological perspective that made the relinquishment of Cuba impossible, a Cuban insurrection that was unalterably committed to achieving complete independence from Spain, and a frenzied state of American public opinion—stoked by the yellow press and quickly reflected in Congress—that insisted that Spain stop oppressing the Cuban population.[18] On this line also, the postwar expansion resulted from an unusual series of unexpected developments, beginning notably with Dewey's unexpectedly thorough victory at Manila. Rather than reflecting a consciously preplanned course of action, America's postwar colonial adventurism found post hoc rationalizations being invoked to justify and secure a string of unanticipated military successes.

This perspective also can benefit from the cultural analysis supplied in this book. Clearly, the constellation of forces at play in 1898 greatly increased the likelihood of war, as these accounts argue, but only because Americans read the events both as creating a moral imperative to act and as inviting an assertion of Great Power status. The yellow press could move the public to call for war in 1898 only because there were elements of pride and moralism prominently available in the national culture that it could manipulate. Likewise, Dewey's victory would in any context have been regarded as impressive, and any triumphant power would have sought to parley it to strategic advantage in the global arena. It is less clear, however, that another state would have interpreted their admiral's victory as signaling Providence's desire for it to become a great power and initiate a novel, messianic colonization program to uplift the region's inhabitants. At each juncture of the process of foreign-policy making, in other words, Americans approached their options through a cultural prism that clearly disposed them to favor some policies over others. This worldview, by interacting with circumstances in 1898 that seemed uniquely tailored to appeal to it, yielded both the Spanish-American War and the territorial expansion that was its most noteworthy consequence.[19] American foreign policy may have seemed inevitable, but it would have gone in some very different directions had its leaders followed the dictates of a different normative matrix.

The approach followed in this book fits with and draws from an existing model that has been used to interpret both American national identity and U.S. foreign policy—the idea of American mission. The idea of American mission expresses American national identity in a distinctly operative fashion by insisting that U.S. foreign policy should reflect the nation's norms and values, ideally defined. The belief that the United States has a special role to play in world affairs and human history has been shared throughout American history both by the makers of U.S. foreign policy and by the American people. Some Americans have held to an exemplarist model of the mission, believing that the United States should change the world through the power of its example, while others, called vindicationists, prefer a more assertive engagement with the world.[20] The underlying assumption shared by both groups is that the United States has been especially entrusted with the responsibility to improve the world. As a result of this missionary component of American national identity, U.S. foreign policy has often involved not only the pursuit of the national interest, materially understood, but the sometimes strenuous promulgation of American values to the world.[21]

By presenting the first intensive exploration of how the idea of American mission shaped the initiation and settlement of the Spanish-American War, this book accomplishes two important goals. First, it provides fresh insight into a transformative moment in the development of both U.S. foreign policy and American national identity. Other scholars of the Spanish-American War have referred in more or less detail to how the idea of America's mission influenced American behavior during this episode, but no previous study has offered a sustained analysis of the war and its settlement using the idea of American mission as its primary interpretive framework. By focusing in detail on this dimension of the Spanish-American War, I am able in this book to achieve a richer interpretation of the moral, cultural, and ideological dimensions of the episode than is attempted elsewhere.

Second, this book represents the first thorough case-study analysis of the idea of American mission itself. Other studies of the concept either examined several cases or provided expansive overviews of U.S. foreign policy. This book complements these analyses by allowing the reader to discern how the idea can infiltrate the policy-making process at every level, and it examines the application of it in much greater detail than is otherwise available. Furthermore, it is the only examination of the idea of American mission to draw extensively on the insights of social theory, which enables a more systematic analysis of the cultural dimension of the idea than is otherwise available. By demonstrating how the idea permeated American culture and shaped American national identity and foreign policy in 1898, I am able in this project to provide important evidence supporting the argument that the idea of American mission can significantly influence American leaders as they formulate U.S. foreign policy.

To empirically ground its analysis, this book focuses on two significant but distinct policy debates related to the war. The first regarded the terms by which the United States would fight Spain. The second was the famous debate about whether to include in the war's peace treaty a provision annexing the Philippine Islands. These two policy debates, each of which operated on very concrete levels, with important and identifiable repercussions obviously attaching to them, are here deconstructed to reveal the underlying cultural assumptions that patterned Americans' decision making. The specific norms that emerged in these debates may be subsumed under two general categories: "power," and "progress." When the United States indicated a desire to be regarded as a peer of the world's leading states, this was an expression of the "power" norm. Likewise, when it acted in conscious accord with social Darwinist assumptions, which posited that only the most "fit" nations survive, it also obeyed the imperatives of power. The norms dictating appropriate behavior for a world power, therefore, derived both from the international community (whose membership was at the time restricted to the states of Europe and Japan) and from an emerging cultural consensus built upon social Darwinism.

In following social Darwinian dictates, the United States also displayed fidelity to the norm of "progress." As a theory explaining how individuals and societies advance through human history, social Darwinism was unafraid to rank people and communities accordingly. Thus, those who possessed power were by definition more "advanced" than those who did not, and they deserved their power as a result. Progress was even more prominently expressed, however, in the racial, religious, and democratic theories that were current in 1898–1900. Anglo-Saxons were regarded by white Americans as being the most advanced race, and so it was deemed important to preserve as far as possible the "progressive" characteristics of the nation that their exclusive maintenance of power provided. Religious progressivism, meanwhile, was enunciated in the form of liberal Protestant millennialism. A considerable segment of the American people, including most elected officials in the federal government, believed that human history was progressing steadily toward a new and better age, the kingdom of God, and they further believed that their nation had been anointed by God to lead the world in the accomplishment of this biblical goal. Finally, Americans were certain that their nation embodied by far the most advanced and sophisticated political order in human history—indeed, the most perfect order that perhaps could ever be established by man. Each of these normative constructs—relating to social Darwinism, race, religion, liberal nationalism, and international stature—were deemed central to American national identity, and so Americans ineluctably oriented their foreign policy according to them.

This book also demonstrates how Americans gave concrete definition to the abstract terms (e.g., freedom, democracy, equality) by which they have historically defined themselves. It shows how ideals have meaning only within cultural contexts, and it also reveals how Americans develop their identity in part through their foreign policy. Some will argue that analyzing debates as this book does can yield misleading results, either because the speakers are engaging in intentional obfuscation or because the normative interests being expressed are epiphenomenal to the "real"—that is, material—interests. This book disagrees, and the wide range of evidence it offers, much of it drawn from the Pamphlets of American History series,[22] should persuade the reader that at least some of the arguments made in defense of American policy were sincere, no matter how profanely illogical they might seem to us today. Moreover, even if appeals to collective values are mere rhetoric or propaganda, that rhetoric nonetheless reveals a great deal about the norms, prejudices, and self-understandings of the intended audience.[23] As Michael H. Hunt noted, "Public rhetoric is not simply a screen, tool, or ornament" but is "rich in symbols and mythology and closely constrained by certain rules. To be effective, public rhetoric must draw on values and concerns widely shared and easily understood by its audience."[24]

By analyzing the nature and structure of the arguments that Americans made to defend their policy preferences in 1898–99, this book reveals the cultural frameworks that constrained and channeled American decision making. During those years, American national identity achieved a newly globalized reification that both reflected and informed its new imperial posture, and we are living in its shadow even today. This book, in short, makes some different but interrelated arguments about American national identity and U.S. foreign policy, and the lessons it holds about the Spanish-American War are still applicable today—perhaps, unfortunately, *too* applicable.

CHAPTER ONE

Culture, National Identity, and the Idea of American Mission

DURING THE Spanish-American War, Americans chose certain foreign policies over others because their national values disposed them to view those options as more attractive than the alternatives. For example, American leaders in 1898 were not forced to declare war against Spain in quite the same way that later leaders were compelled to respond to the Japanese attack on Pearl Harbor in 1941. Nor was there any irrefutable necessity to include colonial acquisitions in the peace treaty settling the conflict, especially since doing so led immediately and not unexpectedly to the far more costly Philippine-American War. Materialist accounts of American decision making during these junctures help us to understand some of the forces that drove American policy makers to settle on their chosen courses of action, but ultimately they fail to explain the full logic of U.S. actions. Simply acquiring Filipino coaling stations, for example, would have been cheaper, easier, and far less likely to spur a Filipino insurgency than insisting on control of the entire archipelago, and it would have satisfied the American interest in facilitating access to the eastern Pacific and its promising Chinese market. Yet the United States chose in the face of clear and convincing counterarguments to turn the islands into its first formal colony. In order to account more completely for U.S. policies favoring war and expansion during this episode, therefore, one needs to understand how the mindset of the American people and their leaders conditioned them to regard some options as preferable to other, equally viable, courses of action. This understanding can come only from a careful reading of the interplay between American values and prevailing notions of the proper place of the United States in world affairs, which in turn were based on contemporary, mainstream cultural interpretations of American national identity.

This chapter develops the theoretical framework of the book's overall argument. It does so in a series of distinct but interrelated discussions. First, it briefly summarizes the school of international relations theory with which this study is most consonant, constructivism (or the sociological approach), before discussing social theory more generally. As part of this discussion, crucial terms are defined and the cultural basis of nationalism is elucidated. Next, the chapter outlines the origins of American nationalism, and in particular the origins of the idea of American mission. This discussion by no means comprehensively summarizes the nature and sources of American nationalism, but it does highlight the bases of American nationalism's universalistic and moralistic tendencies. Two features of America's nationalist tradition bear a special relationship to the idea of American mission: American civil religion and Enlightenment liberalism. They accordingly receive focused attention.

Finally, the chapter ties these discussions together to show how culture and ideology fuse in American nationalist thought to yield a distinctly American style of foreign policy. Cultural dynamics of particular relevance to 1898–99 are discussed at length in the next chapter; this chapter places into their proper context both those cultural dynamics and the specific arguments made during the period's major foreign-policy debates.

CONSTRUCTIVISM, SOCIAL THEORY, AND NATIONALISM

The underlying logic of this book's argument, that agents are guided in their actions by internalized cultural expectations, reflects the sociological, or "constructivist," school of international relations (IR) theory. Constructivism draws attention to the normative contexts within which a leader defines his or her state's national interests and analyzes how a state's identity helps to shape its goals. Without question, all states seek security as their primary goal, and they try therefore to increase their material power relative to other states. Most schools of IR theory, notably realism, neorealism, and, in a different way, neoliberalism, have developed systematic ways of measuring states' efforts to increase their power on the world stage. Left out of these theories, however, is any explanation of why different states pursue different types of goals, especially foreign policies that are not clearly related to immediate security interests, or why they interpret their economic or security interests as requiring some sorts of actions but not others.[1] For example, a state may at some point engage in humanitarianism, a behavior that bears no necessary relationship to security, and the "rules" governing acceptable humanitarian interventions may change over time, also for reasons having little or nothing to do with material interests.[2] Furthermore, when states are confronted with strategic choices that more clearly relate to the materialist concerns that most IR theorists find controlling, such as those concerning security or economic interests, they generally have available several options, and attention to material concerns will not necessarily lead analysts or decision makers to choose the "correct" one.

A more fruitful understanding of strategic thinking takes account of the power of ideas. As Judith Goldstein and Robert O. Keohane explain, "Ideas serve the purpose of guiding behavior under conditions of uncertainty by stipulating causal patterns or by providing compelling ethical or moral motivations for action. Ideas can be broad or narrow; they can stipulate what is right and wrong, provide new social visions, or merely suggest what economic policy will steer a nation toward increased wealth. New ideas may even lead—even if not immediately—to a significant change in the constitution of interests."[3] Ideas and values, in other words, not only constitute nonmaterial motivations for action (as in the case of humanitarian interventions), but they can also channel or reconstitute those objectives. Moreover, these ideational influences do not exist in free-standing form but more typically interlock into systems of thought and cultural worldviews. Sociologists and anthropologists have developed rigorous ways to explain how cultures shape individuals' perceptions and constrain their rationality, and constructivism applies their research models to the study of international relations. It systematically addresses dimensions of the foreign-policy decision-making process that other theories simply do not attempt and thus rounds out our understanding of international relations in useful ways.[4]

While the cultural approach to foreign policy represents a new synthesis of cultural analysis and IR theory, it is important to remember that its fundamental insights were also part of classical realist theory and that the logics of realism and constructivism are not inherently contradictory. As Hans J. Morgenthau wrote in 1948 in the realist standard *Politics among Nations,* for instance, "[Power's] content and the manner of its use are determined by the political and cultural environment." The focuses of classical realism and the cultural approach to foreign policy, however, are quite dissimilar. Whereas constructivism seeks to explain how the norms affecting foreign policy are created and how each state develops its own identity-based style of conducting its foreign affairs, Morgenthau's realism is more concerned with uncovering generalizable principles of international conduct; it thus warns against allowing cultural biases to interfere with the rational pursuit of power. (In his evaluation of the American style of foreign policy, for instance, Morgenthau did not argue that cultural or ideological forces were irrelevant to American foreign policy, but that they had been *too* relevant. And, he argued, it was precisely the moralistic bent of American culture that most qualified or prevented the realization of the moral goals in its foreign policy.) Most subsequent realist and neoliberal thinkers, however, most notably those writing after Kenneth Waltz outlined his elegant structural model in *Theory of International Politics,* have come to reject any suggestion of culture's relevance to international relations. Constructivism is therefore a necessary corrective to the monolithic materialism and structuralism of contemporary IR theory, although an important fusion of realism and constructivism, Henry R. Nau's *At Home Abroad,* offers a promising approach to synthesizing the insights of the respective theories.[5]

By applying the insights of sociological theory, one can readily observe how U.S. foreign policy in 1898 was made by men whose behavior was shaped in significant ways by their particular understanding of American national identity. Had they understood the nature and purpose of the United States by reference to another set of norms, they would have responded differently to the circumstances confronting them. By gaining a clearer understanding of both the relationship between, on the one hand, national identity and constructivist theory and, on the other, the intellectual roots of American national identity, the reader will be better equipped to recognize the significance of the arguments that different actors made during the various debates covered later in the book.

A proper apprehension of the deep structure of the cultural dynamic underlying U.S. foreign policy in 1898 requires a basic grasp of the process by which societies acquire their dominant worldviews. The standard account of this process is Peter Berger's model of the social construction of reality, in which individuals and the social realms they inhabit–including, for example, their families, nations, or religions–interact with each other in an ongoing, reciprocal dynamic. Environmental factors influence human behavior, but individuals, in exercising their free will, help in turn to shape their environment. In other words, people and their societies both shape each other in constitutive ways, so that it is impossible to understand one without knowing the other. Through acculturation, people encounter their social worlds as "given": the cultures into which they are born define their sense of reality. But it is important to bear in mind both that the "givens" that exert this power are themselves the product of human action and intention and also that each individual in the normal course of living helps to mold their form and meaning.[6]

To demonstrate, crudely, what this means, think of a family as an example of a minisociety. Parents socialize their children by encouraging behavior that they regard as "good" and by punishing behavior that they consider to be "bad." They speak to their children in whatever language is native to them and live according to the (usually unspoken) household rules that structure day-to-day life–such as, everyone does chores in the evening. A child born into this family will encounter the rules of the family as realities that are simply "there." Boy or girl, the child will naturally conform its behavior to them. If the family speaks Spanish, the child will speak Spanish, and she will also habituate herself to the family's daily routines and come to regard households that do things very differently as being strange. But her very existence in turn changes the structure of the family, since she will only imperfectly conform to the household's existing practices. If she has a physical disability or a willful personality that makes it difficult for her to do the required chores, for example, family rules will have to shift slightly to accommodate her condition–perhaps by creating a categorical exemption in the case of a disability or devising persuasive new punishments in the case of willfulness. Because of the existence of the child and its unique qualities, in other words, the rules and practices of the family will be subtly different than they were before the child was born.

So it is with all individuals in every type of social group. Now, the influence that each person has on the nature and structure of her group will vary enormously according to any number of variables, including the group's size (a family is much more malleable, for example, than the Roman Catholic Church or China), the strength and position of the person or her ideas, the rigidity of the society, and so forth. The important thing to remember in this regard, however, is that those social worlds—everything about them—are made of people, by people, and for people. By the same token, those same people are made of, by, and for the cultural systems that they inhabit. In short, neither people nor the cultural worlds they inhabit are abstractions, but coexist inextricably in complex systems of interdependence.

Thus, cultures, identities, and norms—three terms that will be defined shortly—are not as rigidly deterministic as ideological interpretations of human behavior argue. There is no historical inevitability inherent in the sociological model, no Marxist dialectic or Hegelian end of history. There is change, however, and a revolution is not necessary for it to occur (although revolutions will do the trick, too). Instead, cultures typically evolve naturally but almost imperceptibly over time. Despite their changeability, however, cultures are durable and help to stabilize societies by providing them with cohesion and purpose. Once we recognize that our social worlds combine in delicate balance elements of both stability, which we need in order to avoid the existential terror of anomie, and change, we can recognize the strength and value of human agency in social life. We are not, in other words, helpless before the tides of history. Rather, we constitute its flow.[7]

At this point it is possible to present a more rigorous summary of social theory. Its primary principle is that people play an ongoing role in creating the symbolic universe that gives meaning and purpose to their experiences. On the most basic level, people cannot survive without society, as Aristotle observed when he called man a "social animal." Tarzan is a myth, not an option. Social theory builds on this fact in describing how humans, through various forms of social conditioning, both internalize and contribute to the frameworks through which they receive truth and meaning. Social theory holds, furthermore, that people cannot make sense of their experiences without society, since the means by which they understand and interpret the world around them—language, paradigms, analytic categories—emerge from and reflect socialization and education. Furthermore, as Hume first argued, the act of interpretation is inescapably normative, because people's values and prejudices will inevitably shape their encounters with reality. In other words, the sociological perspective rejects the notion that people ever live their lives and deal with others from a Rawlsian "original position"; rather, they always inhabit any number of social contexts, which provide them with their moral and epistemological vantage points.

The interpretive frameworks, or "structures," that a man has learned, which derive from his social contexts, by their very nature delimit the ways that he thinks. The man cannot think outside of language, for instance, nor can he unilaterally escape the heritage of his race, gender, or nationality. To a considerable degree, these social categories make him who he is, irregardless of whether he chooses to accord them this power. It is of course possible to learn a new language or join a new religion (especially in the United States), but to do so takes not only an unusual conscious effort but also, in the absence of genius, the availability of an attractive alternative structure. In addition, one does not unlearn those worldviews that one has already incorporated into one's thought processes.[8] Of course, it rarely crosses most people's minds that they should or even can reject the structures that organize their thinking and their lives; as Louis J. Halle observed, "This dependence on abstractions to which we have given our allegiance makes us instinctively resist any knowledge of existential realities that tend to discredit them."[9] Or, in Andrew Greeley's more simple formulation, "One is constrained to be loyal to that which defines what one is."[10]

To define the first of our three terms, then, a *culture* is the overall framework of meaning that a given social group has constructed to define, structure, and give purpose to its world. A culture is comprehensive—nothing escapes its purview, material or ideational, and everything is defined by its terms, including "others," who are defined as somehow not fitting within the framework as it members have chosen to constitute it. In international relations, a statesman will inevitably respond not only to exogenous material imperatives such as threats or other crises but also to impulses deriving from the state's political culture and the various racial, religious, and other norms that formed his or her outlook on life. In other words, factors that shape the way that leaders perceive their situations can play an important role in determining the kind of foreign-policy choices that their states will make. In addition, each leader is also a member of a special society composed of international actors who, like any social group, construct and follow rules that reflect their shared identity. Actors in the international system, on this understanding, constitute a society of their own, one replete with rules, protocols, identities, and other accoutrements of mutual intelligibility.[11]

Identity is a characteristic of an actor that defines him, her, or it (as in a nation's identity or a neighborhood's identity) and that both constitutes and prescribes the conduct and beliefs appropriate to the actor. An identity is culturally defined, and it is incorporated into the very essence of the moral agent who bears it. As Alexander Wendt puts it, "To have an identity is simply to have a certain idea about who one is in a given situation."[12] Sometimes, one's racial identity matters most, sometimes one's religious identity is most relevant, and sometimes it is one's national identity that will be most important to defining not only how one will act in a given situation, but how one will be treated by others (if the identity is known). An identity is not simply a composite of one's behaviors but a source and method of providing coherence and purpose to those behaviors.

Embedded in an identity are *norms,* which might be considered the building blocks of cultures. Norms tell us how we should act, and they shape our behavior in two basic ways: constitutively and prescriptively. Constitutive norms tell us what kind of conduct is appropriate to and definitive of a given identity or culture. One who rides horses, lassoes longhorns, and wears a Stetson is likely to be a cowboy, while someone who engages is none of these behaviors is almost certainly not a cowboy. Horse riding, lasso throwing, and Stetson wearing are therefore among the constitutive norms of cowboyhood. Prescriptive norms, meanwhile, tell us what we "ought" to do in any given situation. They regulate and guide our actions. Thus, if our cowboy comes upon a villain who is trying to steal his livestock, the code of cowboy honor will require him to do something assertive and probably physical to protect his animals and punish the villain in the black hat. In other words, prescriptive cowboy norms will tell him what kinds of things he should do in that situation, as well as what choices he must never make (e.g., run away).

Clearly, constitutive and prescriptive norms exist on a continuum, a point made more obvious when we consider how rarely one chooses, afresh, suddenly to adopt a completely new identity, with its concomitant norms. Ordinarily, we unconsciously refer to norms when seeking to "do the right thing." In our earlier discussion of the rules that families follow, those "rules" are examples of what I am now calling norms. Norms permeate a culture and need not be formally defined to be controlling, but they can also become embodied in institutions or acquire a coercive dimension and become laws. As Peter J. Katzenstein writes, "Norms that are institutionalized matter in particular because they more easily find expression in law and culture. Institutionalized norms express a world view that influences behavior not only directly, by setting standards for appropriateness of behavior, but also indirectly, through selective prefabricated links between values that individuals or collectivities habitually rely upon to address specific problems."[13]

To summarize the analytic perspective from which this book will proceed, people assign meanings to events, conditions, and all other phenomena that they encounter according to the norms and intellectual constructs learned during their acculturation. Truth and value are established within these symbolic parameters and are institutionalized as people seek to stabilize and propagate them as organizing principles for their societies and their lives. This process lies at the heart of all kinds of human activity, including the way that nations, for example, are conceived and how their deeper relationship with the identities of their members is established. This process also accounts for the symbolic value that individuals attach to their groups' (including their nations') actions and the ways that religious, racial, and other beliefs can become intertwined with nationalist sentiments and with each other.[14] The specific cultural and normative content of American national identity thus can be expected to color the perceptions of American leaders and to incline them to construct policies rooted in the norms of that identity. In fact, as later chapters will show, when Americans consciously grappled with the meaning and substance of their identity in 1898–1900, they engaged in an unusually explicit act of cultural construction, and they did so through their foreign policy. Before moving on to that discussion, however, it will be helpful to spend a moment analyzing in more depth the nature and origins of national identities, which are of particular significance to international politics.

Nationalism exists when a particular social group believes that it is in some way fundamentally different from all other groups of people in the world. In extreme cases, nations interpret their collective experiences (real or imagined) in such a way that they cannot imagine themselves legitimately sharing a state with anyone else, and instances of unfulfilled nationalist aspiration often lead to violence. Nationalism's political dimension is a product of the international state system, reflecting not only the state system's method of clustering populations into distinct and autonomous political units but also its manner of conferring the legitimacy of sovereignty on those communities that become states. The nation thus occupies a place in our symbolic discourse that is distinctly structured by its relationship with the state. Drawing on this connection, Anthony Giddens goes so far as to argue that "A 'nation' . . . only exists when a state has a unified administrative reach over the territory over which its sovereignty is claimed."[15]

A nation is more than that, however. Nationalist sentiment is of necessity neither functionalist nor rational, but rather is rooted in the basic human need to feel that one is part of something transcendent, something that innately confers dignity on its members. Even if it is true, as commonly held, that nationalism emerged only after the French Revolution, the concept was able to spread and gain global legitimacy as an organizing principle for human societies because it touched on this universally felt need. In criticizing the prevailing view of nationalism as a modern phenomenon related exclusively to the modern state, therefore, the medievalist Adrian Hastings argues that nationalism as a source and reflection of collective identity long predates the state. Nevertheless, it remains analytically useful to confine our use of the term *nation* to those situations when this general cultural dynamic is structured around real or aspirative sovereign communities—but only as long as we bear in mind the universality of the culture/identity dynamic that nationalism expresses.[16]

As the last section argued, people by nature construct cultures and communities with which they intuitively identify. Nationalism exists when these identities become self-conscious in a way that demands political manifestation, either through the creation of a new state (as was the case of Germany in the nineteenth century and in the many instances during the massive wave of twentieth-century decolonization) or through the reorientation of existing state cultures, as typically occurs during ideological revolutions or nationalistic revivals. To understand the *identity* of a given nation, the essential object of examination is the underlying *culture* upon which each particular nationalism rests. How a nation asserts itself politically–whether in terms of its espoused values, its treatment of nonnational ethnic groups that reside within the state, or in any other way–will reflect the culture that underlies and to a considerable degree justifies its very existence. This is no less true of the American nation than it is of others.

The remainder of this chapter and the next focus on the sources and normative implications of American national identity, showing that the manner by which Americans have described their nation has led naturally to the sentiment that the United States has a mission to the world, broadly conceived. In particular, a staple of American national identity is that the United States is the most advanced country on earth, with both special insight into the best way to organize human affairs and a destiny to change the world along those lines. Embedded in this identity are foreign-policy implications that are not always clearly recognized but that have had an important influence on the country's global relations; this particular normative matrix is called "the idea of American mission."

AMERICAN NATIONALISM AND THE IDEA OF AMERICAN MISSION

In *America's Mission,* Tony Smith explains how the idea of American mission has shaped U.S. foreign policy in the twentieth century. Smith argues that the idea of American mission reflects the belief that, as Kant argued, democracies will not go to war against one another. Acting on this belief, the shapers of U.S. foreign policy have steadfastly encouraged other states to adopt liberal democratic norms. Woodrow Wilson's commitment to make the world "safe for democracy" after World War I epitomized this effort, but Smith argues that America's greatest success came at the end of World War II with the conversion of Germany and Japan to the U.S. model. Subsequent administrations have continued to pursue the goal of establishing a liberal world order. President Eisenhower, for instance, described "our purposes abroad" as including "the establishment of universal peace with justice"; President Carter declared that, "[b]ecause we are free, we can never be indifferent to the fate of freedom elsewhere"; and President George H. W. Bush defended a vision of "a new world order, where diverse nations are drawn together in common cause to achieve the universal aspirations of mankind–peace and security, freedom, and the rule of law." In short, Smith argues, American statesmen in the twentieth century have reliably sought the extension of democratic government around the world as part of a broad effort to establish a lasting peace that is consistent with American values.[17]

America's motives in seeking the spread of democracy around the world run deeper and further than the enhancement of national security, however. There can of course be no doubt that national security is the paramount goal of U.S. foreign policy, as it is with all states. Nor is there any question that when the United States seeks to foster democracy abroad, it believes its actions to be consistent with its security interests. But the United States has always viewed itself as more than just another country, and this self-perception has sometimes influenced the conduct of its foreign relations in a way that bears little direct relation to national-security concerns. Moreover, it is surely no coincidence that it has been the United States, rather than, say, Germany or Russia, that has engaged in an activist, democratizing foreign policy. In other words, Americans have sought to universalize liberal democratic values and institutions not only because their extension serves its national-security interests but also because it has held those values and institutions to be *good*. This position underlines why realists such as Hans Morgenthau, Henry Kissinger, and John Mearshimer have been uncomfortable with the idea of American mission, since it can turn foreign policy from a rational pursuit of the national material interest into a moral crusade.[18]

The enduring appeal of foreign-policy arguments that draw on the idea of American mission, which have appeared in some form since the administration of George Washington, is its relationship to America's nationalist ideology. As Edward McNall Burns put it, "One of the principal clues to knowledge of America is the sense of mission which has run like a golden thread through most of her history." The mission idea reflects and engenders an optimism in the American people that has both undergirded their accomplishments and instilled them with arrogance. It captures Americans' self-perception as being an exceptional people with a distinctly productive and progressive national character. The American idea of mission, in short, is a style of describing the national character that has special implications for U.S. foreign policy. It is a nationalist construct, but its norms directly implicate the peoples of the world by positing for the United States a duty to universalize its values for the good of both itself and others. This intentional spreading of American values around the world has as its ironic and unintentional goal the undermining of another staple of American nationalism—one that putatively underlies the mission itself—American exceptionalism.[19]

American exceptionalism is a familiar way of characterizing American national identity that Seymour Martin Lipset, its most able theorist, claims is an empirically measurable fact rooted in the ideological nature of American nationalism. Lipset argues that, "[i]n Europe, nationality is related to community, and thus one cannot become un-English or un-Swedish. Being an American, however, is an ideological commitment. It is not a matter of birth. Those who reject American values are un-American." The ideological nature of American national identity distinguishes the United States from other nations, which tend to define themselves ethnically and as historical communities with distinct claims on their lands. By contrast, the belief that the United States is an exceptional nation defined by a creed is inherently normative. As Daniel Bell noted, exceptionalism connotes "being exemplary ('a city upon a hill'), or a beacon among nations; or immune from the social ills and decadence that have beset all other republics in the past; or . . . exempt from the historical course of 'social laws' of development which all nations must eventually follow." Embedded in Americans' belief in their exceptionalism, therefore, is a presumption of superiority, usually moral, that imparts to them the right and capacity to lead other nations. That superiority has sometimes been asserted to reflect the biological excellence of the American population—Charles Darwin offered such a rationale—and at other times has been identified with the American political system. Throughout their nation's history, however, Americans have been happy to ascribe excellence to themselves by reference to whatever rationale was handy.[20]

Some critics of the idea of American exceptionalism hold that the nation's experiences hold no special lessons for others since Americans act and react to the same forces that shape the behaviors of all people.[21] Given the obvious merit of the argument that Americans, as human beings, respond to the same compulsions as other people, how, then, did Americans develop their clear sense of peculiarity? Four features of the American experience seem to underlie the notion that the United States is a special nation with a uniquely important destiny: its origins, geography, religious heritage, and Enlightenment heritage. Certainly, these attributes do not exhaust the sources of American national identity, but they have been instrumental to the sense that the United States is exceptional and that it has a mission to the world, and they therefore merit special attention.

The Founding Moment

More than any other country, both America and its identity have been constructed wholesale, and underlying the formative act was a sense of purpose, a belief that there was a reason for creating the new country. When "making" the United States, the founders merged many different and often incompatible intellectual currents, including Enlightenment beliefs about the perfectibility of man, Protestant values that inordinately represented the influence of the New England descendants of the Puritans, the British common-law tradition, a belief in racial hierarchy, and a Graeco-Roman tradition that stressed the fallibility of man and that inclined the founders to load the government they created with safeguards against the abuse of power by limited and corruptible men. Despite (and perhaps because of) an obsessive concern with corruption, however, America's nationalist revolt against Great Britain was imagined to be fraught with truly revolutionary implications, and the founders declared that their purpose was not only to attain justice for themselves but also to usher in a new era in human history, in which people could rule themselves.[22]

When Thomas Paine declared, "We have it in our power to begin the world over again," therefore, he spoke for a generation.[23] The "createdness" of the United States and the fact that ideas and not ethnicity were used to justify that creation lie at the heart of American national identity. According to Albert K. Weinberg, "The fundamental premise of the mission idea was that, as John Jay said in 1777, Americans were the first people favored by Providence with the opportunity of choosing rationally their forms of government and thus constructing upon them respect for the 'great and equal rights of human nature.'"[24] In short, the underlying spirit attending the founding of the United States, including the very fact that it was "founded," suggested to Americans that the country they were building was a new kind of enterprise, an experiment of global-historical relevance. As Theodore Roosevelt declared in his 1905 inaugural address, "To us as a people it has been granted to lay the foundations of our national life in a new continent. . . . Upon the success of our experiment much depends, not only as regards our own welfare, but as regards the welfare of mankind."[25] Of the philosophical traditions noted above that shaped the culture and political ideals of the founding fathers, two–Enlightenment rationality and Protestant Christianity (at least some variants thereof)–supplied the fledgling nation most directly with its sense of mission. (Although American Protestantism tends to take a dim, pessimistic view of human nature, it has also been heavily influenced by millennial beliefs.)[26] The geographical isolation and material abundance of the United States reinforced the optimistic currents of these worldviews.

The territory of the United States and the seemingly providential[27] way that European colonizers first discovered and settled it played perhaps the most obvious role in encouraging Americans to think that their new nation was destined to be somehow different from others:[28] the fact that God had kept the rich bounties of the New World hidden from Europeans for so long suggested to Americans that there was a reason why *they* had been the ones to inherit the bounty it provided.[29] Colonel David Humphreys, George Washington's protégé and an eventual minister to Spain and Portugal, captured this sentiment when he wrote, "America, after having been concealed for so many ages from the rest of the world, was probably discovered, in the maturity of time, to become the theater for displaying the illustrious designs of Providence in its dispensations to the human race."[30]

Under the influence of a biblical worldview, Europeans from the first days of colonization referred to the United States as "the promised land."[31] The Puritans in particular discerned special meaning in the discovery of and their migration to the New World. They did not understand history linearly, but as the repetition of archetypal events described in the Bible, so that one understood one's world by reference to the biblical passages that most closely approximated one's experiences. Given this epistemology, the parallels between the Puritans' transatlantic journey and various biblical passages seemed too striking to be coincidental. The Separatists' "terrifying experience" of crossing the Atlantic Ocean, for example, clearly mirrored Noah's task of starting mankind anew after the Flood, while Exodus told them that the corrupted Europe that they were leaving behind was Egypt and that they were the new chosen people.[32] It seemed self-evident from these passages that the Puritans had found not just a new tract of land, but the "New Israel," where redemptive history would reach its full promise—and that they were the elect, whom God had chosen as the instruments by which to accomplish his purposes.[33]

The colonists' belief that North America was a new Eden rested not only upon a religiously influenced interpretation of the continent's discovery but also upon its amazing trove of natural resources. As John Jay wrote in the *Federalist Papers:*

> Providence has in a particular manner blessed [America] with a variety of soils and productions and watered it with innumerable streams for the delight and accommodation of its inhabitants. A succession of navigable waters forms a kind of chain round its borders, as if to bind it together; while the most noble rivers in the world, running at convenient distances, present them with highways for the easy communication of friendly aids and the mutual transportation and exchange of their various commodities.[34]

The frontier and the image of the American West as a land of boundless promise reinforced Americans' conviction that they inhabited a special land. Being buffered by a vast ocean that the European armies could traverse only with great difficulty was signally beneficial for the security and durability of the developing republic, and the people of the United States knew it.[35] Expansive land provided an outlet for restless individuals searching for economic opportunity,[36] so much so that some thinkers, such as William Graham Sumner, attributed America's success to its geography, which could (at least for the then-foreseeable future) exempt individuals from Malthusian and Ricardian laws of struggle, as much as to its political institutions.[37] Awareness of the vast extent of their natural resources and amazement that those resources were lying there just waiting to be plucked by their forefathers contributed to Americans' sense that theirs was a nation for which Providence had in view a special destiny.[38]

Of course, the land that the European colonizers discovered and settled was *not* uninhabited, and its resources were already being used by the original inhabitants. Because these indigenous people were inconsistent with the Europeans' plans and because the Europeans were profoundly racist, the Native Americans were marginalized out of existence, both mythically and in practice. Through force of will and culturally induced blindness to the reality of previous, rightful occupants of a land that otherwise fit their vision, the Europeans persuaded themselves that the myth of original discovery was in substance true, and this worldview allowed them to preserve for themselves and their descendants the sense of destiny that followed from it. As later chapters will show, Americans have continued to demonstrate this well-honed ability to corrupt their ideals with racism in order to maintain in their self-understanding the mythic purity that their special destiny required.

Within the existing worldview of the Europeans, however, the geographic circumstances attending the birth and development of the United States *were* uniquely auspicious, but it was the religious traditions of the American people and the influence of Enlightenment values on their leaders that inclined Americans to interpret these conditions to mean that their nation had a special destiny. The religious interpretation, which posited a divine purpose for both the land and the settlers who would "civilize" it, appeared first, in the early colonial period, and it peaked around the founding era.[39]

CIVIL RELIGION, NATIONAL IDENTITY,
AND AMERICAN MISSION

Both American exceptionalism and the idea of American mission began as religious ideas, and even today they relate unmistakably to the American civil religion. This is not an accident. Americans have always been by Western standards an unusually religious people, and it was only to be expected that they would merge their religious and nationalist sentiments. Of peculiar importance to the development of American national identity, particularly its civil-religious dimension, was the legacy of the Puritans. John Winthrop articulated the earliest version of the idea of American mission before the Puritans had even finished their journey to the shores of the New World when he famously declared, "For we must consider that we shall be as a city upon a hill, the eyes of all the people are upon us."[40] As noted above, the Puritans interpreted their migration from Europe as an event of literally biblical proportions, and their worldview conduced them to regard their project as figuring centrally into Providence's grand historical design. Ernest Lee Tuveson explains in his important study *Redeemer Nation: The Idea of America's Millennial Role* that, by the time that American colonization had reached the stage of secure flourishing, the "idea that history is moving toward a millennial regeneration became not only respectable but almost canonical." Moreover, mankind's regeneration was linked in the Protestant mind directly with the Reformation itself. The pope, according to millennialist Protestants, was the anti-Christ, and his reign marked the period of Satan's ascendancy that immediately preceded man's final movement toward the kingdom of God.[41]

In order for Reformed nations to progress to the next stage in millennial history, therefore, they had to cleanse their societies of Roman Catholicism. The English Puritans were unusually driven to accomplish this task, and their nation's Anglican establishment never seemed to match their standards for institutional or doctrinal purity (hence, their sobriquet, Puritans).[42] The Puritans obsessed over England's corruption because closely related to millennial historicism was the notion of elect nationhood. As humanity advanced toward its utopian consummation, the elect or chosen people whom God had predestined to save would lead the way. By the time of Elizabeth's reign, English national identity had merged with Protestantism.[43] The Puritans subscribed fervently to the British conception of elect nationhood, but they soon regarded this status as devolving specifically upon *them*, since the larger society of which they were a part had failed to cleanse itself satisfactorily of corrupting "Romish" influences.[44]

The extremists among them, the Separatists, therefore left to start over again across the Atlantic. After they had settled in North America, the physical isolation of their New World experiment reinforced their sense of spiritual distinctness, and they grew convinced that they were *the* elect–that they formed Augustine's City of God.[45] More moderate Puritans, led by John Winthrop, soon followed the Separatists to establish "New England" colonies as well; they shared the Separatists' conviction that they had been chosen by God to lead in the regeneration of mankind.[46] As Cotton Mather wrote in 1702, "'Tis possible that our Lord Jesus Christ carried some thousands of reformers into the retirements of an American desert on purpose that . . . he might there (*to* them first, and then *by* them) give a specimen of many good things which he would have his churches elsewhere aspire and arise unto."[47] In a 1799 sermon, another preacher argued, "It has been often remarked that the people of the United States come nearer to a parallel with Ancient Israel, than any other nation upon the globe. Hence, 'Our American Israel,' is a term frequently used; and common consent allows it apt and proper."[48]

But the Puritans were merely one sect among many in colonial American society, and they were by no means the only colonists to contribute to the development of American national culture and identity. Yet they exerted disproportionate influence in large part due to their focused dedication to nation building. Unlike the other colonists, the Puritans came to America as a self-conscious community, and they were among the first to sever their Old World allegiances and identify themselves primarily with the New World. In addition, they held their mission in inordinately high esteem, so that, to a degree unique among American colonists, they institutionalized and transmitted their identity to future generations and thereby supplied to them a historical memory with nationalist significance.[49] Finally, they practiced a limited form of democracy (what Sidney Mead called a "democracy of the Saints"),[50] thereby helping to establish a democratic culture on American soil while ensuring that their social structures would not be rendered obsolete by the wave of social-contract democratic theory that would captivate the founders of the United States. Uniquely among American colonists, in short, the Puritans strove to create a sense of collective identity in North America, and their sense of exceptionalness and mission came as a result to be deeply embedded in the structure of American national consciousness.[51]

The religious dimension of American national identity—America's civil religion—is not, however, the same as Puritanism. Rather, America's civil religion includes a historical dimension that is as important as its religious elements: the civil religion serves as a means of interpreting the collective, signature experiences of American history within a transcendent framework.[52] The two most significant events to give substance to America's civil religion were the Revolutionary War and the Civil War. Each conflict was interpreted both at the time and subsequently in lofty metaphorical terms: the first would redeem from the corruption of the Old World (as one preacher of the time announced, "Our independence will redeem one quarter of the globe from tyranny and oppression, and consecrate it the chosen seat of truth, justice, freedom, learning, and religion"), while the second would purify Americans of their own collective sins. Both wars, the second in particular, were cast in an apocalyptic light, indicating that in American civil religion, the *nation* itself is venerated as a community of biblical significance.[53]

American civil religion's theological dimension, according to Robert N. Bellah, is rooted in the "common elements of religious orientation that the great majority of Americans share . . . [that] have played a crucial role in the development of American institutions and [that] still provide a religious dimension for the whole fabric of American life, including the political sphere."[54] It is a cultural construct that unites the patriotic sentiments of the mainstream of American society with their religious beliefs.[55] Its normative foundation in the "religious orientation" of "the great majority of Americans" marks it as having a family relationship with what Jaydeva Uyangoda called "majoritarian nationalism," a hierarchical arrangement in which the national culture in fact is the culture embodied by the majority community, with little input from minority subcultures.[56] Historically, this has meant that it is an admixture of nationalism and Protestantism.[57]

America's civil religion emerges on solemn or ceremonial occasions, when society's deep-seated religio-cultural values come to the surface and are made explicit. The most important of these are inaugural addresses, when the civil religion's "main priest," to use Martin

Marty's term, articulates his vision for the country. These addresses invariably include religious imagery, most often imagery that is consistent with Protestant beliefs and that is evocative of the civil-religion's central motifs, such as "chosen nation" or "Providential destiny." George Washington set the precedent for imbuing inaugural addresses with religious imagery, declaring in his first address, for instance: "No people can be bound to acknowledge and adore the Invisible Hand which conducts the affairs of men more than those of the United States. Every step by which they have advanced to the character of an independent nation seems to have been distinguished by some token of providential agency." Likewise, Thomas Jefferson asked in 1805 for "the favor of that Being in whose hands we are, who led our fathers, as Israel of old, from their native land and planted them in a country flowing with all the necessaries and comforts of life; who has covered our infancy with His providence and our riper years with His wisdom and power." In 1857, James Buchanan expressed confidence that Providence would not allow the dissolution of the Union "until it shall have been peacefully instrumental by its example in the extension of civil and religious liberty throughout the world." Other than Washington's twelve-line second inaugural address, which he used to emphasize that the presidency was not an elective monarchy, and James Madison's second inaugural address, civil-religious phrases like these adorn every single inaugural address in American history. Their invocation during the ritualistic transfer of political power indicates the strength of association between American nationalism and the nation's civil religion, and their form demonstrates that, if only at the symbolic level, the Puritans' legacy is still with us.[58]

The United States, in short, has a vibrant civil religion, which expresses both the common denominator of the nation's mainstream religious values and the distinctive history of the American people, and it merges these strands into a nationalist philosophy. It allows Americans to express in the language of transcendence the belief that the United States is an exceptional country and that the American people have a providential destiny. Its existence—even more, its strength—explains substantially how a crusading moral spirit attaches to American nationalism and how the people of the United States define themselves in part by reference to their mission. There is also, however, a secular-ideological foundation of the idea of American mission, the Enlightenment, which has in fact been more directly important than Puritanism to the form and functions of the United States government. Enlightenment theories created a parallel version of the Puritan idea of mission from a completely independent, even antagonistic, perspective, by positing that a new era in human history was dawning that was to be characterized not by the reign of the saints, a Christian utopia, but by universal freedom and equality, a humanistic utopia. America's founding fathers were neither Puritans nor blind disciples of the Enlightenment (although Thomas Jefferson and Benjamin Franklin were leading philosophers of what has been called the American Enlightenment), but they shared in the philosophies of progress that each of those belief systems embraced and hoped that the nation they founded would be instrumental in humanity's advance, whatever its destination.

THE ENLIGHTENMENT AND AMERICAN NATIONAL IDENTITY

The Enlightenment was an intellectual movement centered in Europe that emphasized the goodness and rationality of humanity. According to its political vision, individuals should be restored to their natural freedom—after they were fitted to use it effectively—in order that the human race could achieve its full potential. Enlightenment thinkers boldly rejected the enforced "superstitions" that were propagated by inherited institutions, especially religious ones, and believed that truth could be found only when people applied their innate reason to the natural world around them. For them, the scientific method was the only path to wisdom. Enlightenment thinkers therefore encouraged the establishment of social and political conditions that would enable all men (and their arguments were frequently gendered despite their universalist logic) to apply their rational faculties to the world around them, believing that progress would then become the law of humanity.[59]

The Enlightenment worldview, particularly its moral prescriptions, rested on an optimistic view of human nature. Believing that human rationality naturally will follow universal laws unless clouded by the darkness of man-made superstitions, Enlightenment thinkers considered reason to be the only proper foundation of morality. The universe, they held, operates according to natural law, and so does the human mind. Thus, by learning truth only by encountering an external nature with which it is consonant, the human mind, acting in accordance with rational principles, will tend naturally to act harmoniously with nature, and people will behave morally. The Enlightenment's perspective on institutionalized religion, by contrast, was that it was an obstacle to truth, and hence to morality. Baron d'Holbach presented the case most starkly in 1772:

> Fatigued with an inconceivable theology, ridiculous fables, impenetrable mysteries, puerile ceremonies, let the human mind apply itself to the study of nature, to intelligible objects, sensible truths, and useful knowledge. . . . To learn the true principles of morality, men have no need of theology, of revelation, or gods: They have need only of reason. They have only to enter into themselves, to reflect upon their own nature, consult their sensible interests, consider the object of society, and of the individuals who compose it; and they will easily perceive, that virtue is the interest, and vice the unhappiness of their kind. Let us persuade men to be just, beneficent, moderate, sociable; not because the gods demand it, but because they must please men. Let us advise them to abstain from vice and crimes; not because they will be punished in the other world, but because they will suffer for it in this.[60]

Enlightenment thinkers also assumed basic human equality, holding that, although individuals are unequal in talents, they share in the ability to reason. This equal possession of reason meant that a just society must offer equality of opportunity, so that a society's elites are selected meritocratically, not on the basis of aristocratic or religious membership. In order for individuals to behave morally, moreover, it is necessary that their minds be educated and freed from the debilitating restraints imposed by unenlightened systems of thought. Freedom (at least from unenlightened authority) thus was a necessary precondition for thinking and action. In the political realm, this meant that an individual must freely consent to live under the authority of his or her government.

Thomas Hobbes first articulated the theory of social contract that explained how this could be possible, but his theory retained a commitment to monarchical government. John Locke was dissatisfied with the limited freedom of the Hobbesian model, and, in a more purely Enlightenment fashion, he defended a framework of government that would be limited in scope and accountable to the people and that would base its laws on the will of the majority. Only a republican government, he reasoned, could adequately and without corruption protect a man's property consistently with his natural freedom and equality. Locke thus spelled out the basic formula for modern liberal government.[61]

The unfettered enjoyment of one's natural liberty envisioned by liberal theory was certainly treated as an end unto itself, but its ultimate purpose was progress. Condorcet argued, for instance, that "nature has set no limit to the realization of our hopes. . . . [Therefore] we can entertain a hope *that is almost a certainty* . . . of the absolute perfection of the human race [and we may] . . . extend such hopes to the intellectual and moral faculties" (emphasis added).[62] Science, by producing a gradual accretion and refinement of knowledge, would provide the means of this progress, but, as a new discipline, it required the abandonment of past practices and institutions that were not supportive of its worldview. In particular, nationalism and religion were insufficiently rationalistic and should be regarded as obsolete. They needed to be replaced in a new world order that both built upon and fostered the natural freedom and equality of mankind, without regard for the anachronistic distinctions of existing social and political practices. As Turgot wrote in 1750, "(M)anners are gradually softened, the human mind takes enlightenment, separate nations draw nearer to each other, commerce and policy connect at last all parts of the globe, and the total mass of the human race, by the alterations of calm and agitation, of good conditions and of bad, marches always, although slowly, towards still higher perfection. . . . The time has come. Emerge, Europe from the darkness that covered you!"[63] This, then, was the hope and vision of the Enlightenment: a new beginning in history, when government and society would be founded on a new set of principles and values that would enable humanity at last to attain perfection, in conditions of freedom, equality, and justice.

In France, where these ideas were most fervidly embraced, the opprobrium of well-entrenched beliefs, institutions, and practices necessitated a complete social and political revolution. The sanguinary realization of this frenzied idealism in 1789 ultimately did in fact catapult France's old order, but the chaos, mass executions, and capstone Napoleonic imperium shattered the movement's utopianism and provided a cautionary lesson for some Enlightenment adherents.

The situation in North America, a continental tabula rasa, however, was different, and Enlightenment optimism sustained itself by keeping focused on the American project. Given the racist denial by North American Europeans of the value of existing indigenous societies, it was possible for them to conceive of the "New World" as providing a perfect chance to create a model of liberal government without having to deal with inconvenient social realities, as the French had been forced to do with such disastrous results. The United States could serve as a pristine and unencumbered Enlightenment experiment. European Americans generally shared in this disposition, and they eagerly subscribed to the Enlightenment's esteem for their mission.[64] As Wilson Carey McWilliams explains, "America was the redemptive land which had escaped European corruptions and recovered the liberty of nature. Free to experiment with the new social and moral teachings, America was 'the first lodge of humanity,' and from her example might arise the freedom and brotherhood of man."[65]

For Enlightenment thinkers, the United States offered a literal break from the past and an opportunity to launch humanity's new start. For these optimists, on both sides of the Atlantic, the United States promised to be the instrumentality by which man's highest hopes could be realized. Because it lacked a feudal tradition, it could quietly and without great convulsions institute Locke's model of government and society. Lacking as well a history of dominance by an overarching religious establishment (although the colonies were peppered with local ones), Americans were also saved the necessity of overcoming any deeply entrenched institutionalized "superstitions." And as noted above, America's geography and founding moment seemed to confirm the impression that it presented the ideal opportunity for putting into practice the values of the new era. Still, it took conscious effort to integrate the radical Enlightenment worldview into America's national identity, and despite the efforts of the most politically important and unreconstructed American Enlightenment thinker, Thomas Jefferson, the United States never did embrace the Enlightenment's utopianism without serious reservations.[66]

Jefferson's most familiar Enlightenment tract is, of course, the Declaration of Independence, the document in which he justified the separation of the American colonies from Great Britain not only by referring to the colonists' several specific grievances against King George III but also by appealing to the principle of natural rights and to Locke's theory of social contract. Jefferson's framing of the colonists' motives according to these justifications placed their struggles within a liberal framework, and, as the new nation matured and became more secure, the Declaration came to be regarded as the official statement of American political philosophy. When given the task of drafting the United States' nationalist declaration, in other words, Jefferson took the opportunity to conjoin symbolically the nation with Enlightenment principles. However, Jefferson alone did not infuse into the developing American national consciousness an Enlightenment outlook. A general equality of conditions—relative of course to European standards of the time—characterized the society not only in theory but in fact, and the fundamental American/Enlightenment ideals of liberty, equality, and progress were firmly entrenched as American cultural norms by the time Jefferson wrote the Declaration. He simply articulated them in a starkly compelling way, inviting their permanent veneration as part of America's defining text.

Thus, Americans incorporated Enlightenment values into their identity, but only ambiguously. It was too much to ask them to apply fully the Enlightenment's universalist ambitions to their peculiar experiences; after all, a philosophy that denies any fundamental distinctions among men, particularly those based upon nationality, cannot be embodied with integrity within any discrete political entity.[67] National loyalty requires more than a vague sense of shared humanity, and Americans certainly possessed a clearer sense of themselves as people than that. Rogers Smith, noting the dilemma inherent in founding and sustaining a liberal-democratic (i.e., Enlightenment) state, argues that the United States satisfied the fundamental requirement of having a reason for independent existence by defining the nation ascriptively—as being comprised of white, Anglo-Saxon, Protestant, heterosexual males. Those not possessing these biological and cultural qualities thus were excluded from membership in the formal political community for much of the nation's history. In this way, American leaders elided the basic dilemma of liberal-democratic citizenship by premising membership in the American nation by an entirely different set of criteria than those recommended by Enlightenment ideals. America's leaders, according to Smith, "solved" the dilemma of fostering a particularistic political loyalty consistently with a universalistic creed by refusing to confront the dilemma at all and by resorting instead to the tried-and-true method of identifying the political community by reference to ascriptive characteristics. This dimension of American national identity will be examined more in the next chapter.[68]

Even within the confines of their liberal worldview, however, with all its universalist pretensions, Americans managed to persuade themselves to accept another solution, albeit a compromise, to the challenge of justifying the independent existence of their particularistic political community. That solution was American exceptionalism. The United States would serve as the *model* demonstrating how liberal democracy could work in practice. Americans would form a special community, one that took the best elements of their Old World heritages and made them more broadly appealing and relevant in a polyglot society.[69] And since this community was founded not in utopia but in a preexisting society of nations, with real-world constraints on what it could feasibly accomplish, it needed to establish prudent limits on its goals: it could not strive right away to be a world-encompassing brotherhood of man.

But it was enough to inspire particularistic loyalty among the American people to remind them that they were conducting the first modern experiment in self-government, the results of which would be decisive for all mankind. There was more than enough pride to be had in that goal. As Alexander Hamilton famously put the matter at the outset of the *Federalist:*

> It has been frequently remarked that it seems to have been reserved to the people of this country, by their conduct and example, to decide the important question, whether societies of men are really capable or not of establishing good government from reflection and choice, or whether they are forever destined to depend for their political constitutions on accident and force. If there be any truth in the remark, the crisis at which we are arrived may with propriety be

regarded as the era in which that decision is to be made; and a wrong election of the part we shall act may, in this view, deserve to be considered as the general misfortune of mankind.[70]

According to its nationalist myth, therefore, the United States is a particularistic community that happens also to be of universal significance. It embodies the universal within itself. James H. Moorhead explains: "Chief among [America's] contradictions has been the ascription of universal significance to the inherently limited experience of a single nation. Perhaps . . . the difficulty is endemic to any mythology of a chosen people. Unless the myth places that people at the center of a sacred cosmos, it loses its power to inspire or to bind."[71] Americans could feel bound to their liberal-democratic order, in other words, because its success would validate them as a people and demonstrate that they are, indeed, special.

The American project, then, was to be defined not only by the ideals of the Enlightenment but by their successful implementation in the flawed circumstances of reality.[72] Among the founders' concerns was the need for institutional safeguards that would protect and not merely assert man's natural rights; they were not overly optimistic that liberty's promise would be readily achieved. The founders in particular were deeply mistrustful of human nature. (As James Madison famously wrote, for example, "But what is government itself but the greatest of all reflections on human nature? If men were angels, no government would be necessary.") They knew that if they were to make their democratic experiment last, they had to make Faustian bargains with man's baser interests. Inherent in America's political philosophy, therefore, was a clear rejection of one of the European Enlightenment's central tenets: the perfectibility of man. The founders instead built into the very structure of American government, tacitly but unmistakably, the acknowledgement that it is unavoidable that men will try to do evil things to each other.[73]

This pessimism that one finds embedded in America's governmental institutions owed much to the nation's deep religiosity, which was marked among the founding fathers by the dark strains of Calvinism. Their continuing loyalty to religious ideas and institutions made them ambivalent toward the full flowering of Enlightenment thought and doubtful, to say the least, of the possibility that individuals could be perfected in this world.[74] But their ambivalence mostly rested on their stern rejection of sentimental idealism; in their scrupulous attention to the lessons of the past, particularly those found in the histories of Greece and Rome, the founders learned that devotion to ideals yields only the despotism of those ideals' champions. Ideas come from people, and people, not ideas, wield power. For progress to take place in reality, and not merely in the utopian fantasies of philosophers, people must compromise with people and seek limited ends. Progress is a gradualist enterprise. As Kenneth W. Thompson wrote, "Not ultimate ends but immediate political proposals are the stuff of politics." This was the understanding of the founders. Alexander Hamilton thus excoriated the French for their Revolution, founded as it was on the explicit rejection of religion and the bloody quest to found a worldly utopia. And Hamilton was not alone in his criticism of the French; the horrors that their utopian ambitions unleashed became instrumental in turning the American mind decisively against the use of revolutionary means to pursue justice and confirmed to Americans that their distrust of human nature and of utopian ventures was warranted.[75]

Despite these grave misgivings, however, Americans did not abandon the Enlightenment, nor did they lose faith in themselves as the nation chosen to reform the world. To the contrary, the initially precarious but gradually strengthened bond in the American national identity between Enlightenment idealism, Puritan election, and Graeco-Roman-Calvinistic pessimism yielded a certain confidence that Americans had learned how to achieve their mission in a piecemeal but sustainable way. As the United States not only survived but flourished, its self-confidence grew. Progress, if not perfection, was proven by the American experiment to be possible so long as societies remained vigilant to the realities of the world and the need to compromise with those realities. According to its nationalist myth, therefore, the United States came legitimately but ironically to represent "progress" by enmeshing in its principles a decidedly antiprogressive realism, but it always acted with an Enlightenment gleam in its eye.

Americans have also retained, in a form similarly strengthened by successful experience, their self-perception as the universal nation. In the United States, by following James Madison's simple but remarkably effective model of "interest checking interest," unprecedented diversity has been contained within a single political system by balancing conflicting ambitions within a liberal framework.[76] Thus, national unity and fellow feeling have been nurtured not by blandly (and impossibly) denying the differences between Americans, but by imagining that the quality "Americanness" holds a transcendent value big enough to accommodate whatever internal differences exist among the people. Once again, it bears repeating that America's experience has never come terribly close to approximating this ideal. Different segments of American society have, in fact, enjoyed a formally privileged status in American social and political institutions, while others have been radically excluded from meaningful participation in American life. But American nationalism had demanded the collective imagination to deny this history and maintain the hope, which is posited as a reality, that pluralism in equality actually does characterize the national culture.[77] American national identity is thus premised upon the belief that the nation is "universal" as measured by the theoretical applicability of its principles and in comparison to the particularities of its population. It is bigger, more inclusive, and more significantly purposeful than any individual or group who belongs to it. On the world stage, however, whether the national myth is accurate or not, the United States cannot help but be a particularity, however universal its pretensions. It is but one state among many. This tension finds expression in the idea of American mission, which expresses the universalist ambitions of a particularistic state.

THE IDEA OF AMERICAN MISSION AND U.S. FOREIGN POLICY

The foreign policy of the United States builds on the normative assumption that the U.S. national interest is at minimum consistent with and sometimes constructive of global welfare. Culturally rejecting zero-sum logic, Americans believe that they help others when they help themselves. Even more, U.S. foreign policy often interpolates a tendency to change other societies in directions that the United States deems fit.

Yet, this attitude has not ordinarily resulted in an aggressively crusading spirit, such as Napoleon's or Hitler's; instead, the progressive mission pursued by the United States in its foreign policy has, characteristically, tended in the main to be conceived incrementally, by carefully weighing the opportunities for change with the realities of American power. This approach has led Americans to formulate the major goals of their foreign policy by reference to values and ideals rooted in their identity as an exceptional nation with a destiny to mankind, but American realism has also led the country to pursue its goals prudently so that the United States might remain in the forefront of man's steady and stumbling progress.

In practice, the cumulative effect of the idea of American mission on U.S. foreign policy has been to combine altruism with acquisitiveness. Americans seek to spread their political principles abroad not only to "improve" other peoples—and this benevolence is often sincere, if sometimes misdirected—but also because doing so expands American power.[78] Because they have conceived of their country as the objectification of universally meritorious values, advocates of the idea of American mission argue that America's interests are on some level coterminous with mankind's. Thus a writer in 1899 could describe the conquest of the Philippines as the islands' "liberation" since the imposition of American values upon the Filipino society could only make the Filipinos more free and civilized. If the Filipinos resisted this obvious blessing, then it only meant that they were unable to comprehend the opportunity that Americans were providing them—all the more evidence that they needed our guidance.[79] By merging the U.S. national interest with the improvement of other countries, the idea of American mission allows the United States to arrogate global power and influence while seeming to act not just for itself, but also on behalf of weaker countries.

Globally extending the influence of American values (while maintaining control over their implementation) has the added benefit of enabling the United States to fulfill its dual mandate to God and freedom. Given this logic, it is difficult to conceive of a situation in which the United States, in seeking to extend its influence, could act in a way that proponents of the idea of American mission would regard as illegitimate.[80] According to America's nationalist mythos, in short, the United

States can justifiably increase its power and prestige on the world stage consistently with its mission, because, unlike any other nation-state, it is representative of beneficent, universalist values. The idea of American mission thus embodies the foreign-policy implications of America's "exceptional" qualities. Whatever their goals, the makers of U.S. foreign policy have maintained the myth of American mission by consistently invoking it as providing the normative standard on which to base the country's actions and measure its successes in global affairs. Moreover, it has been particularly manifest during crucial turning points in American geopolitical history, demonstrating that when the country consciously defines its role in the world, it hearkens both to geostrategic calculations and to the values that are believed to underlie and justify the nation and its purpose.

Regrettably, this attitude has frequently embodied corrupting arrogance more than a generous spirit of universalist altruism. Even more dismaying, the hostility to nonwhites that has always been a part of American national identity has also proven to be durable. Neither flaw, however, communicates the necessary spirit of the idea of American mission. American national identity has been slowly evolving—its religious culture is strikingly more tolerant than that of the founders, for example, and African Americans are now citizens, rather than slaves—and this evolution has usually been in a direction that brings it closer to its ideals.[81] Ultimately, of course, the quest to attain America's ideals is impossible, as the founders recognized (but we may have forgotten), since there will always be humans, not angels, directing the nation's progress.

During the Spanish-American War, Americans followed a national self-consciousness clearly reminiscent of both the Puritans and the *philosophes,* and they acted with a realist's attention to the changing patterns of world power. Paradigmatically, the Spanish-American War embodied the full spirit of the idea of American mission—including its assertion of American exceptionalism, its concern for the well-being of (some) others, its misguided belief that the only solution for the problems of those "others" was to force them to submit to the "benevolent" control of the United States, and its drossing of naked self-interest with capacious claims of national virtue. The idea of American mission does indeed represent the spirit of the United States: proud, hopeful, friendly, and, like any human endeavor, flawed. When kept within the fragile bounds of cultural humility and realist prudence, it is good when the idea of American mission influences U.S. foreign policy, because, however corrupt we may be as a nation, it is better to strive to improve the lives of others, and through that effort to improve ourselves, than to regard others exclusively through the prism of selfish instrumentalism.

CHAPTER TWO

American Cultural Constructs in the 1890s

THE NORMS AND concepts that structured American national identity in the 1890s were tightly interwoven in an ideological paradigm centered on the idea of progress. "Progress" often implies *telos*, a purposive direction that channels and imparts meaning to history's flow, and for reasons explained in the preceding chapter, Americans in the 1890s believed that their nation was destined to lead humanity to the achievement of its collective teleological purpose. They often described the historical process in quasi-Hegelian terms, wherein the human race progresses as "enlightened" civilizations replace their more "primitive" precursors, either from within, through natural evolutionary development, or from without, through conquest.[1] Americans presumed themselves to be humanity's vanguard, the cutting edge of social evolution. They also thought themselves to have a particular responsibility to bring others up to the standards of American civilization, both to share the blessings of their superior civilization and also to fulfill the nation's destiny to transform the world into a paradise of universal liberty—the kingdom of God.

The American cultural understanding of progress built on four conceptual foundations: evolutionary theory (usually a modified version of Darwin's theory of natural selection), racism, liberal Protestantism, and nationalist liberalism. Evolutionary doctrines—the neophyte of this foursome—provided scientific legitimation for Americans' other, more longstanding, beliefs and thus became an organizing principle of American culture. At the same time, racism experienced a vicious renaissance in the 1890s, and contemporary theories of ethnicity endorsed racial hierarchy as both natural and necessary. The third cornerstone of the 1890s American ideology of progress was the firm belief shared by many Americans, including many of those in power, that the United States was the new Israel, chosen to lead the way to the coming kingdom of God. Finally, the liberal ideology at the core of America's political culture and institutions buttressed the normative progressivism of American culture not only through its own logic but also by merging with American nationalism. This nationalizing of liberal thought–conceiving of the nation as the very embodiment of liberal values–led Americans to believe that anything their country did was ipso facto both liberal and progressive. These four strands of American thought were intricately interconnected and interpreted as being mutually reinforcing, which made it difficult for Americans to discern inconsistencies among them, often with pernicious results. This chapter examines each of these four cultural frameworks, considering both their ability to structure social norms and their relevance to U.S. foreign policy.

EVOLUTIONARY THEORY AND AMERICAN CULTURE

Evolutionary doctrines fed into the egoistic side of the idea of American mission. As Julius W. Pratt noted in his influential 1936 work *Expansionists of 1898*, the Darwinian hypothesis of evolution through natural selection provided "philosophic backing" for preexisting American beliefs in the nation's inherent excellence.[2] It was the missing piece of America's ideological puzzle, and it became an orthodoxy, with few exceptions, for members of both the scientific and religious communities.[3] Darwin's theory of natural selection, which was commonly invoked by reference to Herbert Spencer's popular phrase "survival of the fittest," held that the weak members of a species are weeded out due to the incompatibility between their inherited characteristics and the environment into which they are born, so that only a species' strongest representatives survive and propagate. In his second book, *The Descent of Man*, Charles Darwin expanded his theory of natural selection to encompass not just biological evolution, but evolution within and between human societies. In the book, Darwin explicitly endorsed the idea that the United States, as the strongest civilization, was at the apex of the evolutionary process when he wrote, "There is apparently much truth in the belief that the wonderful progress of the United States, as well as the character of the people, are the results of natural selection; for the more energetic, restless, and courageous men from all parts of Europe have emigrated during the last ten or twelve generations to that great country, and have there succeeded best." Darwin's interpretation of America's success fit into the broader pattern of civilizational evolution that he defined, wherein favorable biological characteristics among the population yield greater national power: "Obscure as is the problem of the advance of civilisation, we can at least see that a nation which produced during a lengthened period the greatest number of highly intellectual, energetic, brave, patriotic, and benevolent men, would generally prevail over less favoured nations."[4]

Social Darwinism was a worldview accepted by the most important thinkers in the late nineteenth century, including theologians (Asa Gray, Henry Ward Beecher, Josiah Strong, Washington Gladden), political scientists (John Fiske, Alfred T. Mahan, John Burgess), sociologists (William Graham Sumner, Lester Ward, Albion Small), and philosophers (William James, John Dewey). In the newly created discipline of anthropology, which was then called ethnology, Franz Boas stood alone outside the Darwinian-evolutionary orthodoxy. Acceptance of evolutionary theory as a worldview, and not just a theory explaining biological diversity, was practically universal. As one sociologist described his discipline's theoretical premises:

> Social Science, like all other sciences, does not rest with the mere collection, verification, and collation of facts derived from the study of man in his relations with his fellows; it searches beneath these facts for the general principles which underlie and account for them. These principles, when scientifically discovered and verified, are regarded as *laws of evolution* and deductive inferences logically drawn from them are strictly justifiable according to the scientific method. . . . Having clearly recognized these general principles underlying all actual progressive tendencies in society, the deduction from them of rational rules of conduct is the only reasonably and genuinely scientific mode of procedure. (Emphasis in the original)[5]

Given the consensus among the educated classes, it is unsurprising that scholarly and political debates at that time tended to take place according to the terms of social-evolutionary theory.

One major component of the evolutionary worldview—whether in Darwinian or Lamarckian form[6]—was the notion that the universe flows ever onwards, that history is marked by progress and dynamism. The key to successfully negotiating one's way in the world is thus to discern the direction in which the cosmos is moving and to follow that course. Because evolution spelled out the scientific principles according to which history flowed, it became in effect a blueprint for understanding the nature and direction of progress. It was a silver bullet. As such, it could be employed in support of a broad array of theories and policies.[7]

For instance, evolutionism, particularly Darwinism, had become integrated into moral philosophy by the 1890s, as evidenced in the best-selling writings of the English social philosopher Benjamin Kidd. In his books, Kidd argued the necessity of conforming human behavior to the progressive laws of nature, writing that "[p]rogress everywhere from the beginning of life has been effected in the same way, and it is possible in no other way. It is the result of selection and rejection." He continued, "Progress is a necessity from which there is simply no escape, and from which there has never been any escape since the beginning of life. . . . This orderly and beautiful world which we see around us is now, and always has been, the scene of incessant rivalry between all the forms of life inhabiting it–rivalry, too, not chiefly conducted between different species but between members of the same species."[8] The world, in other words, is constantly progressing to more advanced stages because all forms of life compete with each other for supremacy, and those who opt out of this competition for supremacy simply die off: they lose, and the future comes to be shaped by the winners. As a result, the choice confronting moral agents is between fighting to define the future and passively marginalizing oneself to insignificance. Overall, Darwinism's tacit normative message was that "good" qualities abet survival, which was often misinterpreted to mean that power is interconnected with virtue and that the possessors of power are by definition virtuous.[9] This normative dimension of Darwinism had a bracing effect on those looking for insight into social, political, and moral matters.

As far as defining a posture toward the world, therefore, social Darwinism had much to say. But what sorts of political prescriptions followed from its proactive, fight-for-survival depiction of biological, social, and moral life? To demonstrate the enormous flexibility and pervasiveness of the Darwinian worldview, consider the philosophies of two very different American thinkers, William Graham Sumner and Brooks Adams. Sumner, a sociologist at Yale University, was exceptionally popular, but his popularity ebbed markedly over the course of the 1890s, reaching its nadir after the professor expressed his opposition first to the Spanish-American War and then to its expansionist settlement. Due to his fierce antistatism and obsessive commitment to the Protestant work ethic, his name has become associated with laissez-faire individualism and libertarianism.[10] Sumner, whose ideas fit generally into the Jeffersonian tradition of American political thought, vociferously opposed the expansionism that followed the Spanish-American War because he was sure it would lead to the kind of governmental centralization that he saw as the root of injustice. Brooks Adams, on the other hand, was more of a Hamiltonian thinker whose evolutionary theories did not emphasize survival of the fittest *individuals,* as Sumner's did, but the survival (and ultimate decay) of civilizations. Adams's understanding of societal evolution, in fact, held governmental centralization to be a necessary precursor to progress. Each of these thinkers drew from the same well of Darwinian competition to produce their distinctive and often diametrically opposed theories of human society.

Sumner is remembered today for his stark, cold commitment to the idea of survival of the fittest and concomitant opposition to governmental intervention on behalf of any group in society, including the destitute. The Darwinian roots of his thinking are evident in the following passage, whose theme is repeated frequently in Sumner's works: "The whole retrospect of human history runs downwards towards beast-like misery and slavery to the destructive forces of nature. The whole history has been one series of toilsome, painful, and bloody struggles, first to find out where we were and what were the conditions of greater ease, and then to devise means to get relief. Most of the way the motives of advance have been experience of suffering and instinct."[11] Sumner argued, simply, that life was hard by its very nature and that individuals, who usually recognized this obvious fact as a result of their life experiences, worked in order to ameliorate their conditions. Since for Sumner "survival of the fittest" hinged on individual initiative, it thus was a less deterministic philosophy than it was for other thinkers of his time. It was deterministic to the extent that industry and ambition are heritable characteristics or that natural talent and intelligence abet success. Nevertheless, individuals always could *choose* their behaviors and thereby maintain some control over their life's fortunes. Thus, one who was fit to survive worked hard and was self-reliant and one who did not work hard was not fit to survive. As he put it, "There is no device whatever to be invented for securing happiness without industry, economy, and virtue."[12]

The central political lesson that Sumner drew from this position was that state interference in the natural order was inherently unjust. "The truth is," he wrote, "that the social order is fixed by laws of nature precisely analogous to those of the physical order."[13] Those who achieved comfort and security through their own initiative deserved to enjoy the fruits of their labor. State interventionism, Sumner held, could have no other effect than to deprive these individuals of their gain and then to redistribute it to those who had not earned it. Either the government helped a few wealthy plutocrats through "jobbery" and subsidies or, in socialist schemes, it aided the underclass, whose moral unfitness rendered them undeserving of the help. In no circumstances did it ever seem to benefit the "Forgotten Man," the thrifty hard worker who funded government's programs. A government to Sumner is thus "robbery made lawful."[14] Justice is best achieved in its absence, when the deserving are able through their own effort to find their proper, natural place in the social order and the undeserving, rather than surviving off the labors of the fit, die off. As he wrote, "The law of survival of the fittest was not made by man and cannot be abrogated by man. We can only, by interfering with it, produce survival of the unfittest."[15] (Sumner did endorse, however, *voluntary* support of the "weak" and cooperative efforts to ameliorate the condition of the downtrodden that did not involve the state.)[16] William Graham Sumner's social Darwinism, in short, defended extreme libertarianism with forceful simplicity, and it reflected the Episcopalian ethos of a former minister.

On the other hand, Brooks Adams, a member of *that* Adams family, in his *The Law of Civilization and Decay* concocted a comprehensive theory uniting everything from photosynthesis to politics to poetry.[17] Adams's family name helped him win the ear of influential men, most notably Theodore Roosevelt, and made him a very influential if somewhat eccentric thinker in the early twentieth century.[18] Adams laid out his thesis in the book's preface, where he explained, "The theory proposed is based upon the accepted scientific principle that the law of force and energy is of universal application in nature, and that animal life is one of the outlets through which solar energy is dissipated." Continuing, in an argument that somehow evokes Darwin, Locke, Marx, and principles derived from Newtonian physics, he wrote:

> Starting from this fundamental proposition, the first deduction is, that, as human societies are forms of animal life, these societies must differ among themselves in energy, in proportion as nature has endowed them, more or less abundantly, with energetic material. . . . Probably the velocity of the social movement of any community is proportionate to its energy and mass, and its centralization is proportionate to its velocity; therefore, as human movement is accelerated, societies centralize. Whenever a race is so richly endowed with energetic material that it does not expend all its energy in the daily struggle for life, the surplus may be stored in the shape of wealth; and this stock of stored energy may be transferred from community to community, either by conquest, or by superiority in economic competition.[19]

In other words, economic strength is a form of the stored energy that is basic to human life (as well as the whole universe), and it is associated with social centralization.

Adams did not detect a smooth, upward trajectory of economic centralization and development in his reading of history, however, but one of cycles of civilizational advancement and decline. A civilization, upon reaching the height of its centralization and economic success, will begin to waste its excess energy by stratifying its economy—turning its excess energy on itself, in a purely economic form—leaving itself vulnerable to conquest by others. "[W]hen a highly centralized society disintegrates, under the pressure of economic competition, it is because the energy of the race has been exhausted. Consequently, the survivors of such a community lack the power necessary for renewed concentration, and must probably remain inert until supplied with fresh energetic material by the infusion of barbarian blood."[20] Adams's gloomy assessment of his own time was that the peak of European and American civilization had already been attained.[21] European civilization was set to decline, the barbarians ready to storm the gates.

While Adams never abandoned completely the comprehensive theory of human history presented in *The Law of Civilization and Decay*, the United States's invigorating success in the Spanish-American War seemed to temper his pessimistic outlook somewhat. He began his second book, *The New Empire:* "During the last decade the world has traversed one of those periodic crises which attend an alteration in the social equilibrium. The seat of energy has migrated from Europe to America. . . . In 1789 the United States was a wilderness lying upon the outskirts of Christendom; she is now the heart of civilization and the focus of energy."[22] Adams attributed America's ascension to its scientific expertise, which enabled it to adapt productively to its environment and circumstances. Whereas Adams had previously regarded the law of civilizations' rise and decline to be, in essence, a natural law over which man had no control, he now conceived of man as having, at least potentially, the ability to conform himself consciously to the flow of history. In particular, Adams now encouraged outward growth—imperialism— as a means of sustaining the dynamism characteristic of civilizations on the rise.

Perhaps Adams altered his thinking because it was now *his* country that was at the apex of global civilization, and he did not wish to believe that a collapse was inevitable, as his theory in its initial form had described. Predictably, Adams urged governmental centralization to capture the extraordinary "velocity" of the times, and he encouraged expansion quite brazenly as a means of extending and securing the nation's power. Hoping that his "scientific" analysis of history would help his leaders chart the wisest course in national policy, Adams strove to ensure that his nation would remain the "fittest" and that it would survive.[23] Sharing the company of powerful and like-minded men, Brooks Adams became in the first two decades of the twentieth century an important figure in American political and intellectual life.

Examining the directly contrasting theories of Brooks Adams and William Graham Sumner in this way, it becomes clear that the evolutionary worldview could be accommodated to almost any political program. Where Sumner strenuously defended individualism and the sharp reduction of governmental power as the keys to civilizational

advancement, Adams was equally adamant that greatness and prosperity, but most of all, progress, could only result from government
centralization and expansion. On the one hand, social Darwinism's
ability to undergird such diverse theories suggests that its flexibility
implied little independent explanatory power. On the other hand, this
capaciousness demonstrates the authority that social Darwinism possessed at the turn of the century. It therefore seems odd to argue that
the worldview of social Darwinism had little or no impact on the events
of 1898.

Nevertheless, some historians remain unimpressed. James A. Field
Jr., for instance, wrote a scathing assessment of the scholarship surrounding turn-of-the-century American imperialism, in which he included this argument: "The standard ideologists who are alleged to
have infected the American people with the disease of Darwinist expansionism were few in number and of doubtful leverage, and the standard quotations from their works are selective and unrepresentative."[24]
He adds, "Faced with a foot-dragging Senate, and lacking both suitable
movers and shakers and evidence in party platforms and presidential
messages, the convention has been to fall back on Fiske and Strong, on
the Omaha *Bee*, on the social thought of Harry Thurston Peck, and on
the improbable (or at least highly irrational) desire of farmers for a
China market to absorb the surplus."[25] Responding to Field's arguments, Walter LaFeber, in an otherwise highly unsympathetic response
(since his own research was part of the disreputable canon savaged by
Field), noted his agreement with Field on this point: "The long misplaced emphasis on Social Darwinism is certainly an example of such
mistaken conventional wisdom. [Many historians] pointed out long ago
that Social Darwinism was more a rationale for, than a cause of, American expansionism."[26] Robert L. Beisner, undertaking the same task as
LaFeber, also rejected much of what Field had to say while finding
common ground here: "Most of the critical parts of his essay—most notably his devastating assault on those attributing great influence to Social Darwinists and other intellectuals—are persuasive."[27] Clearly, social
Darwinism holds little promise for one seeking to understand American foreign policy during this episode. Or does it?

Two considerations attenuate the criticisms noted above. First,
contrary to what Field asserted, there is very ample evidence that the

ideological positions defended by John Fiske, Josiah Strong, and others *were* shared by the "movers and shakers." Despite Field's claims, presidential speeches do in fact indicate either that William McKinley accepted the essential substance of the sorts of arguments reviewed in this chapter or that he believed that the main body of the American people (to whom he gave these speeches)–and not just Beisner's "intellectuals"–would be persuaded by them. Moreover, in the lengthy pre- and postwar debates in both the House and the Senate, in which *every* member was allotted time to make clear his position on the subject as well as his reasons, the repetition of themes relating to providential, national, and racial destiny was so frequent as to be almost numbing.

These observations lead to the second consideration that appears to have been downplayed by Field, LaFeber, and Beisner–that evolutionism was a central concept in American culture and thus would have shaped people's perceptions of events, if only indirectly. The argument that these three authors reject seems to go something like this: A handful of prominent intellectuals and publicists spun theories relating to national destiny that drew on evolutionary dogmas and social Darwinian paradigms. Politicians such as Theodore Roosevelt and Henry Cabot Lodge read their works, were suitably impressed, and attempted under their influence to engage in an imperialist program. In short, ideas were the cause and policies were the effect of American expansionism. Few ideas, however, have as directly traceable an effect on any action as this syllogism suggests. There are always intermediating circumstances that lend ideas their persuasive power, and these intermediaries thus can be expected to acquire a more direct explanatory value than the ideas on their own. For example, the Declaration of Independence, or its reading, did not "cause" the American Revolution. Political and economic grievances held by the colonists against England seem more directly important to the events of the 1770s. Does that mean, however, that the ideas expressed in the Declaration are of no value to understanding the nature of the Revolutionary War or its consequences? Some historians would indeed hold that the ideas were in fact irrelevant to the events. Most would acknowledge, however, that the concepts of equality and liberty expressed in the document were important in shaping the way that the colonists interpreted the nature, importance, and solution to their conflict with England.

Likewise, the prominence of evolutionary ideas in American thought and culture, on every level, strongly suggests that they intrinsically shaped the way that Americans reacted to the events of 1898. They were neither merely a rhetorical overlay nor an ex post facto rationale given to obscure "truer" motives. To hold that they were is to argue that people think outside of the cultural and ideological constructs that form the way they perceive their world. Much evidence suggests that evolutionary and providential theories were part and parcel of the very thought processes of the individuals who made American foreign policy in the years around 1898.[28] If American thought and culture were characterized by a Christian, progressive approach to interpreting events, then it seems unlikely that foreign policy decisions made during these years, by members of that culture, would be made according to different rationales.

In fact, evolutionary theory, particularly Darwinism, acted as the foundation supporting America's cultural framework during the 1890s, including its more sordid qualities. It justified American superiority in a way that both science and religion could countenance, while its progressive view of history resonated with a long-standing American ethos. It also could be used to legitimate racism (as its most infamous manifestations in Nazi and Fascist ideology demonstrated), and it helped American leaders to restrict, on a scientific basis, formal membership in American civilization to Anglo-Saxons, as the next section explains.

AMERICAN CONCEPTIONS OF RACE IN THE 1890S

Racism at the end of the nineteenth century was structured and legitimated along Darwinian lines, but it rested on much older assumptions. These earlier views found their way into the evolutionary matrix by ranking races hierarchically while also assigning to each race distinguishing characteristics, with the higher races inevitably possessing characteristics of a nobler and more "moral" quality than those of lesser races. These attributes fitted whites to occupy a paternalistic role over inferior races.[29] Anglo-Saxons, for example, were regarded as the most evolved race (say, a ten on a scale of one to ten) followed by the next-best-developed race (usually the Germans, or "Teutons," who would rate a nine), and so on down the scale. They were also believed uniquely to possess the capacity for enlightened self-rule, which the "lower" races were constitutionally unable to emulate.[30] Evolutionary theory provided scientific formulas and language to demonstrate the biological roots of these capacities, thus providing scientific reinforcement of the hierarchical nature of societal racism.

It is important to point out here that the justifications used to defend racial discrimination derived from the research of the social-scientific establishment, not the rantings of fringe groups. For example, anthropology was institutionalized as an academic discipline by John Wesley Powell, the head of the Bureau of American Ethnology, and his work aimed steadfastly at proving that each race occupied a different rung on the evolutionary ladder, with whites on top and blacks at the bottom. W. J. McGee, head of the American Anthropological Association, insisted that racial and cultural differences mandated white paternalism over inferior dark-skinned races. Despite the predominance that Franz Boas's cultural relativism would eventually come to have in the discipline, during the 1890s in popular, scholarly, and political thinking, the theories of Powell, McGee, and other evolutionary anthropologists comprised the standard canon of social truth on matters relating to racial differences.[31]

This research was important for confirming and thereby sustaining the continued viability of what Rogers Smith calls "ascriptive Americanism," a feature of America's political ideology that defined the United States as a white, Anglo-Saxon nation.[32] Smith calls the last three decades of the nineteenth century "the era of the militant WASP," when the Democrats (still the party of the South) "trumpeted their belief in America as a white Christian nation," and Republicans, though more divided, "insisted that whoever might be included as Americans, the Protestant and Anglo-Saxon character of the national culture had to be not just preserved but enhanced."[33] During this period, numerous immigration laws were passed to prevent "inferior races" from becoming U.S. citizens.[34] For example, in 1896 Henry Cabot Lodge proposed a literacy test to restrict immigration (President Grover Cleveland vetoed it); its goal was to keep racial minorities from entering the country. In the course of defending the proposed legislation, Lodge referred to the theories of Gustave Le Bon, a noted proponent of racial essentialism.[35]

Lodge argued that each race was characterized by "an indestructible stock of ideas, traditions, sentiments, modes of thought," "an unconscious inheritance" that was the "soul of a race."[36] These differences, Lodge argued, represented the gradual accrual of thousands of years' worth of inherited characteristics. By arguing that races with the "wrong" characteristics must be excluded from citizenship, Lodge clearly meant to suggest that the United States was, and must remain, an Anglo-Saxon nation.[37]

Literacy tests and other means were employed not only to structure the immigrant pool but also to disenfranchise blacks who were already in the United States. Even by American standards, it was a troubled time in American race relations, marked by three significant developments: the disenfranchisement of black voters, the establishment of legal segregation, and a sharp increase in lynchings. Blacks were stripped of the vote during these years at an alarming rate—between 1896 and 1904, for example, the number of black registered voters in Louisiana fell from 130,334 to 1,342.[38] This decline in black voters was not an accident. As Congressman John Williams (D-Miss.) boasted:

> We have succeeded in disenfranchising the worst portion of the colored population of the State of Mississippi by subjecting them, as well as white people, to an educational qualification, and as nearly all of the white men can read and write, and as very few negroes can, notwithstanding the fact that the schools are now and have been open to them for thirty years, we manage to secure for the electorate a majority safe for white supremacy and civilization. . . . And if I am the only Democrat in this House, I shall stand for white supremacy in Hawaii, when that question comes up, as I have stood for it in Mississippi. . . . I shall vote for those provisions of the scheme which make for a white man's supremacy.[39]

Literacy tests were not the only means used to take the vote away from blacks in the 1890s. Among the schemes used were white primaries and poll taxes, and grandfather clauses were enacted to allow whites who failed to meet these requirements to continue to vote.[40] The U.S. Supreme Court, by refusing to acknowledge the racial purpose and effects of this chicanery, acquiesced in the transformation of the Southern electorate into a practically all-white body.[41]

The Supreme Court provided a more proactive defense of the proposition that the United States was a white nation in its prosegregation decision in *Plessy v. Ferguson* in 1896.[42] Government-sanctioned segregation had begun only in 1887, when Florida mandated separation of the races on trains. Prior to the passage of Florida's law, segregation, at least in the Old Confederacy, was uncommon.[43] Even after Southern states began passing these laws, however, many train companies refused to enforce them because they did not want to offend blacks—who constituted a sizeable portion of their clientele—and also because they considered the laws' enforcement to require needless expense. Nevertheless, some prominent African Americans brought test cases to court in hopes of overturning the laws.[44] The Supreme Court chose instead to establish the precedent used to justify segregation laws, which afterwards were passed with ever-increasing frequency during the era of the Spanish-American War. Segregation attained full legitimacy, legally and socially, during the 1890s.

Not only were blacks disenfranchised and segregated during the 1890s, they also became subject to unprecedented mob violence. No longer protected by their value as property, as they were, invidiously, before the Civil War, or by Northern troops, as they were immediately after it, blacks found themselves increasingly vulnerable to widespread informal violence that was countenanced by the silence of the government. The Ku Klux Klan rose to prominence in the 1880s, and lynching became a common practice. In one high-profile episode, ten blacks were lynched in Wilmington North Carolina in 1898 after "'the best elements' of the local white population organized an armed mob" in response to the efforts of some local blacks to run for government office.[45] President William McKinley gave no acknowledgment of the incident. Goldwin Smith, a retired Oxford professor, commented on the state of affairs:

> When hatred of a race has mounted to such a pitch that the people of one race go out by thousands to see a man of the other race burnt alive, and carry away his charred bones or pieces of his singed garments as souvenirs; when they even photograph and phonograph his dying agonies; how can it be hoped that the two races will ever form one commonwealth? Can it even be hoped that they will ever

dwell side by side in peace? . . . President McKinley, while he was preaching the love of law to the Filipinos with fire and sword, stood in the midst of a country where lawless lynching was going on, yet could not venture to protest.[46]

Edward A. Johnson, a contemporary black historian, observed with exasperation that "often there seems no effort even to put the Negro in any particular place save the grave, as many of the lynchings and murders appear to be done either for the fun of shooting some one, or else with extermination in view. There is no attempt at reason or right. The mob spirit is growing–prejudice is more intense. Formerly it was confined to the rabble, now it has taken hold of those of education, and standing."[47]

The example of Thomas Dixon, a pastor who each month published his sermons in a journal, shows the new spirit of 1890s American racism. Dixon may have been the most popular preacher in the United States in 1898. Though a Southerner, his Baptist ministry was in New York City, where his congregation was larger than that of any other Protestant minister in the country.[48] In one sermon, entitled "A Friendly Warning to the Negro," Dixon explained in clear, social Darwinist language his understanding of blacks' status and future in the American nation:

> Before us looms up in the dawning century a mighty republic of three hundred millions of people–Anglo-Saxon people, with Anglo-Saxon government and Anglo-Saxon rulers. The Negro is a vanishing quantity in our national life. As we move toward our great future he becomes less and less important. . . . The Negro who believes that the Anglo-Saxon race fought the [Civil War] in order to help him should re-read history. White men never have fought one another in behalf of the Negro, and they are not going to do it in the future. . . . The blackest day for the Negro was the day he became a voter in the South. . . . It transformed the South into a seething furnace of race hatreds. It forced the Southern white man to become a corrupt politician to save his own civilization. . . . The result has been a threat to the progress of the Republic. . . . The mission of the African is not to govern the Anglo-Saxon. It is time the negro knew this.[49]

Clearly, racism's violent resurgence in the 1890s had become associated with a reassertion of the belief that the United States was an Anglo-Saxon nation—a belief that could only have repercussions for a foreign policy that found America overseeing largely nonwhite territories.

At the end of the nineteenth century, the distinction between nations and races was blurred. Ethnic homogeneity was presumed for ideological reasons to exist within each nation-state—even though few believed that to be the case in actuality—and the character of each nation-state was explained in terms of its representative race. From this belief emerged two kinds of conclusions. The first, racial essentialism, was that racial differences were permanent and that the status of the races within global civilization was therefore fixed. The second held that racial *capacities* were essentially equal, but that evolutionary development put some races far ahead of others. Proponents of the second view considered "lesser" races to be at least theoretically capable of catching up to the "higher" races, including their ability for self-rule, but they deemed this capacity to be latent and probably generations of development away from being realizable. Both positions led, at least for the short term, to acceptance of white racial paternalism over "backward" civilizations.

Some of those who held the former position argued that the United States should, as a matter of duty, assume Kipling's "White Man's Burden" and share its genius for government with less fortunately endowed races. As one of the founders of the discipline of political science, John W. Burgess, explained:

> [B]y far the larger part of the surface of the globe is inhabited by populations which have not succeeded in establishing civilized states; which have, in fact, no capacity to accomplish such a work; and which must, therefore, remain in a state of barbarism or semi-barbarism, unless the political nations undertake the work of state organization for them. This condition of things authorizes the political nations not only to answer the call of the unpolitical populations for aid and direction, but also to force organization upon them by any means necessary, in their honest judgment, to accomplish this result. There is no human right to the status of barbarism.[50]

The corollary of there being no human right to barbarism, of course, was that there *was* such a right for civilized people to rule over barbarians. A more chilling articulation of the belief that the capacity for self-government depends on one's race came from Representative Williams:

> Individual accomplishment is skin deep, Mr. Chairman; hereditary traits, tendencies, and capabilities are inbred to the marrow of the bones. Why, Mr. Chairman, you could shipwreck 10,000 illiterate white Americans or Englishmen or Scotchmen, of whom not one knew a letter in a book, on a desert island, and in three weeks they would have a fairly good government, conceived and administered upon fairly democratic lines, based upon popular sovereignty, defective, perhaps, but protecting, at least, these three things—their liberties, an approximate equality of opportunity among all men, and the sanctity of their wives, their daughters, and their homes. You could shipwreck an equal number of American Indians, every man of who was a graduate of Hampden-Sidney or Carlisle, or 10,000 Negroes, every one of whom was a graduate of Harvard University, and in less than three years they would have retrograded governmentally to the old tribal relations, half the men would have been killed and the other half would have two wives apiece.[51]

One of the more influential proponents of the second view was Benjamin Kidd, the Englishman mentioned above, whose enormously popular effort to explain religion according to evolutionary theory also provided readers with what became a widely cited and authoritative accounting of national differences.[52] Kidd insisted that moral virtues underpin an individual's or group's ability to engage in self-government, and his evolutionary perspective inclined him to the position that each race possesses such virtues only in a manner and extent commensurate with their level of evolution. Religious leader Washington Gladden, in a pamphlet advocating the extension of American rule over Cuba, cited Kidd's account of Latin Americans' capacity for self-government to support the claim that only Anglo-Saxons were sufficiently virtuous to exercise democratic government:

> [T]he general prevalence of those qualities which distinguish peoples of low social efficiency has been like a blight on the whole region. In nearly all of the republics in question the history of government has been the same. Under the outward forms of written

laws and constitutions of the most exemplary character, they have displayed a general absence of that sense of public and private duty which has always distinguished peoples who have reached a high state of social development. Corruption in all branches of the government, insolvency, bankruptcy and political revolutions succeeding each other at short intervals, have become the normal incidents of public life–the accompanying features being a permanent state of uncertainty, lack of energy and enterprise amongst people, and general commercial depression.[53]

Gladden hastened to add: "These remarks do not apply to Chile or the Argentine Republic, both of which are to a considerable extent populated by Europeans."[54]

Since the art of self-government had received its most refined and perfect development in the United States, many came to attribute this accomplishment to the *race* of America's founders and leaders, and in this way racism and liberal democracy were conjoined. The impenetrability of racist attitudes, in short, often meant that other beliefs had to bend to conform to its logic, rather than vice versa. Race relations have always been an embarrassment for the United States, but even by America's dismal standards the decade of the 1890s stands out in the country's postslavery history. The number of lynchings reached an all-time high during these years as whites in the South rebelled against the vestiges of Reconstruction and the descendants of Northern abolitionists lost their interest in defending African Americans. Still, while racial constructs figured prominently in American thinking in the 1890s, so, too, did constitutional and religious norms, and neither of these were consistently interpreted as supporting racism. Sometimes, the universalist values espoused in both managed to countervail racist assumptions; indeed, they have served as the main source of norms capable of eroding racism's iron grip on American culture.

AMERICAN RELIGIOUS CULTURE IN THE 1890S

The Reverend James Marcus King declared what was widely accepted as fact in 1898 when he wrote, "By historic origin and precedent, by principles of legislative action, by the character of our fundamental institutions, by judicial decisions and by the genius of our civilization, we are a Christian Nation."[55] By *Christian,* King meant, in particular, *Protestant,* and in critical ways the United States in the 1890s *was* a Protestant nation. To be sure, Americans could and did accurately claim that they protected the religious freedom of a greater diversity of religious beliefs than had any previous (or contemporary) political order.[56] But they could not credit themselves with maintaining a truly religiously pluralist society since the overwhelming majority of Americans belonged to Protestant sects, the culture embodied Protestant values, and the laws enforced Protestant norms.[57]

In the 1890s, not only were most American citizens Protestants,[58] but the Supreme Court had not yet interpreted the Constitution in a way that would prevent society from preferring the religious beliefs of the majority. In 1833, for instance, Supreme Court Justice Joseph Story wrote in his definitive *Commentaries on the Constitution,* "It is impossible for those who believe in the truth of Christianity as a divine revelation to doubt that it is the especial duty of government to foster and encourage it among all the citizens and subjects."[59] In 1889, moreover, the Supreme Court, in *Davis v. Beason,* while upholding Congress's denial of polygamists' (Mormons') right to vote, casually invoked Christian standards to evaluate the conduct in question: "Bigamy and polygamy are crimes by the laws of all civilized and Christian countries. . . . Probably never before in the history of this country has it been seriously contended that the whole punitive power of the government, for acts recognized by the general consent of the Christian world in modern times as proper matters for prohibitory legislation, must be suspended in order that the tenets of a religious sect may be carried out without hindrance."[60] In *Reynolds v. U.S.,* which held that actions stemming from religious belief were not protected by the Constitution, the Supreme Court also suggested that there was a connection between enforceable Christian morality and Anglo-Saxonism, writing that "[p]olygamy has always been odious among the Northern and Western Nations of Europe and, until the establishment of the Mormon Church, was almost exclusively a feature of the life of Asiatic and African people."[61] Since, in the First Amendment, the clauses relating to establishment and free exercise formally prohibited such religious favoritism, the above examples from the national level demonstrate how cultural norms influence legal interpretation.

On the other hand, while the United States government has never been able to make a law "respecting an establishment of religion," the states did have this power, leading, in the early years of the republic, to the forging of formal bonds between state governments and the dominant religion of their citizens. Given the nation's religious demographics, it is unsurprising that every state's formally established religion had been either Protestantism or some general form of Christianity.[62] Even after the formal disestablishment of religion at the state level (generally accomplished through state constitutional measures), Protestantism remained widely institutionalized–established, by today's standards–from the formative years of the republic through the 1940s.[63] States enforced laws recognizing Protestant norms, and even blasphemy statutes remained on the books.[64] In addition to blasphemy laws, Protestant Christianity was accorded special respect in the states' educational systems, which included formal, teacher-led prayers and readings from the [Protestant] King James Version of the Bible.[65]

Since, as Tocqueville observed, the states were of greater importance than the federal government in ordering and regulating the day-to-day lives of Americans during the nineteenth century,[66] state laws enforcing unofficial Protestant establishments played a major role in directing citizens to conform their behavior to Protestant norms. Under circumstances wherein the large majority of both the general population and the political elite were Protestants and the laws of the land enforced a Protestant worldview, it was only to be expected that the overarching normative framework of the country as a whole was Protestant.[67] Moreover, the Christian character of American culture in the eighteen and nineteenth centuries determined the character of American society more than Christianity's formal legal status during those years. Given the deep-rooted nature of cultural constructs, culture is ultimately more important than law in sustaining a religiously vibrant society as seen in the unusual juxtaposition in many European countries of widespread atheism and formal establishments of religion. Since the United States was *culturally* a Protestant nation during those years, therefore, it was possible for the government to enforce Protestant values despite the protections of the establishment clause without anyone outside of the occasional Ingersoll noticing the inconsistency.[68]

When "Americanizing" either immigrants or Native Americans in the nineteenth century, inculcation of Protestant norms was deemed essential. In President Ulysses S. Grant's "Peace Policy" for the Native Americans, for instance, Protestant missionaries had the task of acculturating the tribes to "American" society.[69] They were selected to represent the United States for two primary reasons. First, they were deemed proper emissaries of American culture. Second, they were often the only whites willing to speak on behalf of Native Americans.[70] The missionaries, in other words, gave the Native Americans as much protection from rapacious whites as they could hope to receive, even as they replaced their religious traditions with Christianity—something that almost all whites agreed constituted a civilizational advancement.[71]

Only Roman Catholics, who by the 1890s were immigrating and settling in sizable numbers in northern industrial regions, could have posed a realistic challenge to the cultural predominance of their reformed brethren, but they chose for the most part to keep to themselves, within protective ethnic enclaves. The minority of Catholics who did choose to join the mainstream during the 1890s tended to acclimate themselves to Protestant norms even as they maintained their theological orthodoxies, such as papal infallibility.[72] Non-Christians and a few Christian fringe groups, such as the Shakers, were sometimes persecuted, but more often they were ignored. Their theologies contributed little to the mainstream national religious culture during the nineteenth century.[73] According to Winthrop Hudson, "As a consequence of Protestant predominance, even non-Protestant groups tended to take on a somewhat Protestant coloration in the American environment."[74] Without question, American culture in 1898 embodied and projected the Protestant norms shared by most of its citizens.

When Darwin's evolutionary model first appeared, in 1859, it met with fierce resistance from Christians, who recognized instantly the epistemological threat that its materialism posed to their theistic worldview. By the 1890s, however, liberal American Protestants had learned to accommodate themselves to it, despite Darwin's insistent atheism, in part because the theory's structural progressivism paralleled their own theological-historical framework.[75] Evolutionary doctrines came to be seen as providing a scientific explanation for religious conceptions of progress, and liberal Protestants elaborated a philosophy in which science and religion were made consistent. By integrating evolutionism into their theological perspectives, religious leaders were able to unify their worldviews.

Theologians could square evolution with revelation in one of three ways. Their first option was to subscribe to the Lamarckian formula, consciously or unconsciously. By arguing that species evolved to fit their environment, Lamarck's theory of evolution was more amenable to the possibility of divine intervention than Darwin's because it could conceive of evolution as leading toward a predetermined, rather than environmentally selected, end. The most prominent Lamarckian theorist to advance this view was a University of California geologist, Joseph Le Conte, who defended a cyclical version of evolution. Although he was a scientist, not a theologian, Le Conte believed that evolutionary theory reconciled science with religion, and he was convinced that it explained the way that human societies, and not just the "natural order," adapt and change. His theory was that societies and civilizations all rise, "culminate," and decline, but that upon declension they leave a little germ of themselves behind. The subsequent civilization then gathers the germ left behind by the previous civilization and from it builds a phase higher than the last. This idea of residual accumulation applied to every kind of evolution: animal, individual, or group. Le Conte argued that men have a duty to strive to advance the best aspects of their civilizations in order to keep progress moving in the right direction, and he applied his model in particular to religion. While he argued that Protestantism represented the most advanced stage of religious evolution then in existence, he thought that there was a higher phase yet to come—an ideal that, when reached, would culminate the evolutionary process and signal the arrival of the kingdom of God on Earth. Presented in this way, evolution could easily be seen as following the dictates of a superintending intelligence.[76]

The second alternative was to adopt Calvinism, which had long advocated a sort of spiritual natural selection. A central tenet of Calvinism holds that God elected only a handful of people to join him in the city of God, the "visible saints." According to Calvinists, an individual cannot behave in any way that will affect God's decision; one's fate has been predetermined. However, by acting piously, a person can manifest his or her election, or at least the possibility that he or she has been chosen by God to join the saints. The Puritans brought this soteriology with them to America, which had been elaborated by the English conception of an elect nation.[77] When social and economic success came to be understood as being the fruits of Christian virtues like thrift, self-restraint, and hard work, the elite, simply by being elite, became identified with those virtues and deemed morally superior to the poor. (William Graham Sumner's social Darwinism was a secular variant of this argument.) Darwin's theory of natural selection appealed to some Calvinists because it seemed to describe in scientific terms God's way of selecting the spiritually superior—those who were to join him in the city of God. Given this framework for interpreting salvation and explaining human behavior, it is not difficult to see how Americans in general, and Calvinists in particular, found Darwin's natural selection thesis to be a compelling extension of the doctrine of divine election.[78]

Finally, theologians could square evolution with the apparently contradictory account of man's origins in Genesis by adopting the modernist approach to reading the Bible. This was the most popular solution to the Darwinian dilemma (although Calvinism's imputation of moral supremacy also resonated with non-Calvinist Americans). Modernists such as Kidd resented the notion that as theologians they should have to choose between science and religion.[79] They instead defended a theological perspective that explicitly embraced scientific developments, arguing that God's truths cannot be contrary to science. Radical modernist Gerald Birney Smith of the Chicago Divinity School, for example, advocated the institution of an "empirical theology" that would "draw its inspiration from the world in which we live."[80] Another modernist, Paul Carus, defined a core attribute of modernism when he said, "The nature of religious truth is the same as that of scientific truth. There is but one truth."[81] Inserting evolutionary ideas into theological frameworks was not without consequences for religion. In particular, it contributed to a transformation in how modernists explained the path to salvation, ranging from appealing to a transcendent judge of man to focusing on "the world itself as the prime locus of salvation."[82] Insofar as this theological approach contributed to the sacralization of the temporal world, it made possible the jingoistic deification of the state that characterized the age. The modernists' scientific approach to theology, as well as their growing commitment to hermeneutic theories of biblical interpretation,[83] would eventually prompt a fundamentalist backlash in the 1920s.[84] During the 1890s, though, modernism captured the mainstream of American thought.[85]

Liberal Protestantism developed an activist wing known as the Social Gospel movement. Social Gospel theologians emphasized the social dimension of Christian doctrine. Their concentration on the temporal status and "personhood" of individuals prompted them to engage in social programs such as prohibiting the use of tobacco and alcohol and helping to improve the conditions of the working poor.[86] (In a revealing pamphlet, a Social Gospel preacher complained about the behavior of American soldiers in the Philippines. His concern was not that they were committing atrocities against the Filipino nationalists—which they were—but that they were getting drunk too easily and frequently.)[87] The Social Gospel movement incorporated the era's normative and ideological commitment to evolutionary progress: social Darwinism's model of human endeavor underlying social progress was particularly attractive to theologians interested in helping individuals here and now.[88] The Social Gospel was only the most conspicuous feature of the changed American religious landscape at the end of the nineteenth century. American religious culture remained heavily dominated by Protestantism, and its mainstream by 1898 was heavily flavored by liberalism and evolutionism.[89]

Millennialism in 1890s Religious Culture

The impact on U.S. foreign policy of liberal Protestantism's cultural hegemony in American society in the 1890s was immediate and direct. First, since most of the population and practically all of the leaders accepted its norms without question, they naturally pursued political ends that they perceived to be consistent with those norms. More directly, since they believed in Providence and frequently in the historicity of the kingdom of God, many American leaders tried explicitly to position their nation's international actions within the normative-historical framework of postmillennialism. Based on the Revelation of Saint John, the kingdom-of-God historical framework posits a progressive view of history that culminates in "an earthly *utopia*, an age at the end of all history, in which, not Christ in person, but Christians and Christian principles would really be triumphant." Millennial thinking was a central theological tenet for Americans in the nineteenth century, and it is important to stress that many Americans did not treat the kingdom of God as a metaphor but as a real historical construct. Certainly, only a minority believed at any one time that the millennium was imminent and that they must therefore prepare for "the end of the world"–the United States was not one giant doomsday cult. But the kingdom-of-God paradigm was widely accepted by Protestants (and, ironically, by many Roman Catholics) as an accurate description of the structure and flow–the teleology–of history, and through the massive influence of periodic religious revivals it imparted to many Americans a sense of urgency that they keep their country focused on the world to come.[90]

Along with Americans' fastidious commitment to the idea that human history was progressing steadily toward the kingdom of God went the conviction that God–Providence–actively directed this movement within history. As chapter 1 discussed, the Puritans introduced this notion to American soil, and the colonists' amazing success in the Revolutionary War had confirmed its relevance to American identity.[91] By the 1890s, the belief that God had created the United States because he had a plan for the country as part of the unfolding of divine history was so entrenched in the American psyche that the only real disagreement about it related to the responsibilities of the Americans themselves in this cosmic drama.[92] Should Americans actively abet the plans of Providence by undertaking global actions that would take mankind one step closer to the fulfillment of divine history? Or should the country simply continue in its struggle to do right in God's eyes, hoping thereby to secure his favor? In other words, how much was the United States an active partner to a God who is not only interested in but involved in the world?

How one answered these questions depended on whether one was a "premillennialist" or a "postmillennialist," a distinction that emerged during this era out of the broader rift separating modernists from "traditional" (or, as they would be called in the twentieth century, "fundamentalist")

American Christians.[93] Premillennialists believe that Armageddon, with all its devastation and misery, still looms on the horizon and the best that anyone can do is to pray that one is among the elect. Those who are so blessed will ascend to heaven and avoid the punishment accompanying the transition to the final stage of history. Only after this moment of awful judgment will Christ return to Earth and initiate the kingdom of God. There is nothing that one can do–political or otherwise–that can affect in any way when or how Armageddon will come and what one's fate will be when it does. Premillennialists tend to be pessimistic about the value of human society, and they often regard democratic political involvement as essentially meaningless. For this reason, others have sometimes accused them of being unpatriotic.[94]

Postmillennialists, on the other hand, believe that the world is progressing *gradually* toward the millennium and that it is up to God's people to bring about the culmination of the grand historical plan–to usher in the utopia at the end of history.[95] As Michael Lienesch writes, "postmillennialists see themselves as taking an activist approach. Unlike premillennialists, who see the world as a sinking ship, they describe it more as a kind of construction site, a foundation and a set of blueprints from which believers are in the process of building a potential paradise. In place of pessimism, they preach a message of ethical reform, calling on Christians to build the kingdom from within the world, accepting responsibility and taking power through a process of conquest and dominion."[96] During the 1890s most Protestants were postmillennialists, including the liberal Protestants who built from this eschatology their Social Gospel doctrines. Postmillennialism was also popular among evangelicals in the nineteenth century, although it lost its appeal during the fundamentalist resurgence.[97] The kingdom-of-God historical model that influenced Americans to engage actively in reforming the world in partnership with God was postmillennial.

Postmillennial conceptions of the kingdom of God had become fairly painless by the 1890s.[98] The self-celebratory aspect that postmillennialism had acquired reveals that Americans had come with a fair degree of certainty to view themselves, collectively, as the elect, and they sensed that the kingdom of God was waiting for them just around the corner–but without the fire and brimstone. Indeed, this self-understanding lies at the heart of American nationalism. As Frank H.

Littell notes, "For most of the baptized around us, America *is* that new age, that changed world."[99] Americans in 1898 considered themselves to be the chosen nation in part because they also believed that theirs was the "universal" nation.[100] Since the kingdom of God was to be a time of utopian, universal peace, all of mankind is implicated in its cosmic history, making it only natural that the universal nation should take the lead in realizing the goals of Providence. The tension that grows out of Americans' conceiving themselves as the universal nation, on the one hand, and pursuing a particularistic national self-interest, on the other, has typically been resolved by Americans by presuming that their narrow self-interest is, in fact, the same as the world's interest.[101]

Religious leaders drew on the tripartite belief in Providence, the kingdom of God, and America as "chosen nation" to encourage a new interventionist approach to the world that would allow them, in a generous spirit of pseudo-ecumenism, to unite the world under America's universalist umbrella. The typical expression of American Protestant "ecumenism" was foreign missionary activity.[102] Churches in the United States had a rich history of missionary work;[103] for example, the American Board for Foreign Missions dated from 1810, while the General Convention of the Baptist Denomination for Foreign Missions began its operations in 1814.[104] These and other missionary societies eagerly urged global expansion in the 1890s, seeking a marriage of evangelism and nationalism. As one missionary of the time declared, "I believe in imperialism because I believe in foreign missions.... If the nation multiplies its sails, we must write on every one of them glad tidings of great joy. We have come into the kingdom for such a time as this. The imperialism of the Gospel is the emancipation of humanity."[105]

Not everyone agreed with these sentiments, however. For example, the president of Stanford University, David Starr Jordan, a prominent antiimperialist, insisted, "To Christianize our neighbors is no part of the business of our government. . . . Missionary work against Mohammedism, Catholicism, or even Heathenism our government cannot aid. It is our boast, and a righteous one, that all religion is equally respected by the States. . . . When the flag and the police are sent in advance of the Bible, missionaries fall to the level of ordinary politicians."[106] Others rejected the self-celebration of postmillennialism by adhering to the prophetic side of American civil religion, which holds that God will maintain his special tie to the United States only if the nation acts in accordance with his will.[107] This prophetic reading of providential history underlay the Puritans' covenant theology, including those constructions of America as "God's New Israel" that emphasize the Israelites' duty to honor God.[108] Thus, when contemplating whether the United States should keep the Philippine Islands, which seemed to fall into the country's lap at the conclusion of the Spanish-American War, one speaker warned, "God, the real God, is not indifferent to which of two courses we take; he does not take care of us in any case; only if we take the right are we safe, and if we take the other he conducts us to destruction."[109] With rare exception, in short, Americans in 1898 used the concept of "Providence" as a standard both for judging their own conduct and also for defining themselves in relation to others.

The word *Providence* therefore had powerful rhetorical value for inciting Americans to patriotic ebullition. President William McKinley, for instance, regularly described the United States as being "guided" by Providence or as having a sort of partnership with God. In one postwar speech, for example, he declared, "[T]his Nation has been greatly blessed, and [at] this hour we are a united, a prosperous, and a patriotic people. And may that Divine Providence who has guided us in all our undertakings from the beginning of the Government continue His gracious and assuring favor to us forevermore."[110] The same view was voiced by his opponents. In a speech before Congress that was typical of those heard in the weeks leading up to the declaration of war against Spain, Representative Jeremiah D. Botkin (Kans.), of the Fusionist Party, alerted his peers to what he saw as a national duty:

> The Prince of Peace has not yet established His kingdom in all human hearts. Nor will He, in my judgment, until this cruel nation [Spain] shall have been blotted off the map. I do not believe a government can commit the crimes that Spain has committed in Cuba and escape just and awful retribution. If it is God's order that retributive justice shall be meted out to her through the instrumentality of this Government, I voice the universal sentiment of Kansas and of the country when I say, All hail the task![111]

Underlying this more common view of Providence was the belief, as described by Stanford's Jordan, that Providence does not shape human history independently of human endeavor, but "acts only through men with strong brains and pure hearts. The hand of Providence is never at the helm when no hand of man is there."[112]

Applying these theological concepts to U.S. foreign policy, some Americans articulated fully developed conceptions of their nation's role in God's master plan. One pamphleteer, the Reverend L. B. Hartman, argued, for example, that the United States had been prophesied in various parts of the Bible as the nation destined to serve during the late nineteenth century as "the politico-religious handmaid of Providence in the aggressive civilization of the world."[113] While Hartman insisted that the United States was chosen to serve this role because it had a perfect government, he also claimed that it had that perfect government because God wanted the country to have it:

Our Republic is not an accidental or fortuitous aggregation of political elements, but rather God's own thought formulated and crystallized into a government according to His own Divine ideal, and in harmony with His own eternal purposes; and therefore, they who fought to maintain its integrity and uphold its institutions, fought for God and His cause. . . . *[T]he internal and external structure of our Republic is more fully allied with the principles of Christianity, and is better adapted to their true and progressive development in the building-up of the truest citizenship, the noblest manhood and the highest civilization than any other form of government in the world.*[114] (Emphasis in the original)

Hartman, perceiving every act of the United States as a mere expression of Providence, thus equated America with virtue and saw the nation's success in all endeavors ensured: "[H]istory demonstrates the fact that until our Republic shall have fulfilled its mission and accomplished the work to which Heaven ordained it, no civil power on earth can prevail against it."[115]

That mission, of course, was to further the designs of Providence in establishing the kingdom of God:

Speaking with all due regard for other nations, we cannot but believe that our own glorious Republic . . . is thus favored and elected. It bears superior affinities for the development of true manhood among all ranks and classes; and also a civil polity most favorable to the steady advancement of civilization and national righteousness. . . . Our Republic . . . has been created and ordained to do a specific work, to serve the cause of freedom, humanity and civilization, even in fields unsought which have been thrust upon her; and although her mission may involve the sacrifice of treasure and even life itself, yet the God of nations will hold her responsible for the discharge of her divinely appointed duty—a duty whose voice shall not be silenced until Anglo-Saxon institutions shall prevail in all lands and become the civil heritage of all nations and tribes and peoples.[116]

Another religious pamphleteer, the Reverend David Gregg, also posited a central role for the United States in divine history, and he specifically considered international relations to be crucial to God's plan for the United States and the world.[117] Like Hartman, Gregg argued that the United States enjoyed its position of preeminence because Providence put it in that position, and he insisted that the United States had been anointed by Providence to employ force to "perfect the human race through international intercourse":

When the leading nation of the world is true to God and His principles, knowing no compromise and no hesitation, when it lives these principles, incorporates them into its laws and institutions, builds them into the code by which it governs its international relations, makes them part of its foreign policy, and, so far as it has in its power, insists upon other nations honoring them and administering their affairs by them, it is always sure to win the day, and to rule as a mighty influence among all the nations of the world, and to lift them up towards the level of its own high civilization. But remember that it cannot do this by compromise or by a magnificent indifference or by a cowardly neutrality. . . . A nation with the truth of God, a nation in covenant with God, that is what the world needs for the true peace and progress and good of all nations. When a nation is such, then like Israel of old it blesses the whole circuit of the earth.[118]

Gregg typified religious writers of the era in his using the opportunity presented by international affairs to remind his countrymen of the prophetic dimension of their civil religion. Not only did these reminders serve to keep religious principles important in the minds of the nation, but they also reinforced belief in providential history.

CONSTITUTIONALISM, REPUBLICANISM, AND U.S. FOREIGN POLICY NORMS IN THE 1890S

Americans have most commonly chosen to define themselves by reference to the nation's political principles. As the preceding chapter discussed, political ideals lie at the heart of American national identity; all other attitudes, values, and behaviors must be made to appear to conform with those ideals if they are to be considered "American." For this reason above all others, almost all Americans in 1898 pursued the goal of attaining consistency between religious, racial, and interest-based arguments, on the one hand, and those based on American political principles, on the other.

Because this subject was discussed in chapter 1 and will be examined more systematically in chapter 9 in a review of the imperialism debates, the present treatment has been truncated, but brevity here should not give a wrong impression about the relative importance of the topic. In particular, liberty, equality, and self-determination–the core principles of American political thought, as embodied in the Constitution and the Declaration of Independence–helped to shape the dialogue about American national identity and foreign policy during the debates before and after the Spanish-American War. These principles were not merely latent in the arguments heard at the time but were appealed to explicitly, with reference to the founding documents, in order to dress policy preferences in the robes of legitimacy. Sometimes the principles were invoked to refute and other times to support the racial and religious assumptions that underlay the American ethos, but always they were employed to underline the justice of one's position.

This section will address itself in particular to the following questions: To what degree did Americans ground their arguments in appeals to the Constitution or the Declaration of Independence in order to lend their arguments legitimacy? How did those who supported the imperialist consequences of the war try to square their political goals with the principles elucidated in these documents? To what extent did opponents of expansion rely on arguments based explicitly on regime principles when refuting the racial and religious assumptions of the expansionists? By addressing these questions, one can glimpse the normative value of the Constitution and the Declaration of Independence in turn-of-the-century political discourse, especially in comparison with other cultural sources, and gain insight into how political principles are presumed to be a bedrock of American national identity.

Throughout the history of the United States, Americans have justly prided themselves on their commitment to liberty and republicanism. As William Lee Miller put it, republicanism has been in the United States "something like the ideological ground music that can be heard in any political culture: Everybody hears it, all sides appeal to it, it is taken for granted."[119] The Declaration of Independence–despite the cultural predominance of social Darwinism and millennial Protestantism's implicit favoritism toward elect souls, each of which seemed to undermine its message of basic human equality–still exerted a mighty influence on the 1890s American mind. The Constitution was also revered for putting the Declaration's principles into action, but the latter document was considered to be *the* official mission statement of the American ideology. It laid out in unambiguous language the philosophy of freedom and equality that Americans accepted as their birthright and that they regarded as their seminal contribution to human history. The language that Thomas Jefferson used to express the American political philosophy is now so familiar as to appear trite, but it could not be ignored by Americans debating their country's foreign policy in the 1890s: "We hold these truths to be self-evident: that all men are created equal; that they are endowed by their Creator with certain inalienable rights; that among these are life, liberty and the pursuit of happiness; that to secure these rights, governments are instituted among men, deriving their just powers from the consent of the governed."

The first "truth" explicated in the Declaration was especially troublesome for staunch adherents to the paradigm of racial hierarchy ("all men are created equal"), while the last phrase complicated the colonial ambitions of the expansionists ("governments . . . deriv[e] their just powers from the consent of the governed"). Needless to say, both phrases appeared in many pamphlets, books, and articles and were repeated countless times in the chambers of Congress. (As Senator Donelson Caffery [D-La.] declaimed at one point, "The immortal Declaration by Jefferson says that 'Governments derive their just powers from the consent of the governed.' This one sentence makes the name of Jefferson revered throughout the earth, wherever the eagles of freedom plume their flight. It is the keystone of the arch of republican institutions. It is the basic principle of our political life, and faith, and hope. It follows the American citizen wherever he goes. It is enshrined in his heart; it is a part of his being.")[120] If the Declaration's ideals were true, the thinking went, and they defined the soul of the American nation, then they must bear on the nation's relations with all the other peoples of the world. William Jennings Bryan, the perennial presidential candidate and leading antiimperialist, declared that the United States must honor those principles "for it was God himself who placed in *every* human heart the love of liberty" (emphasis added).[121] In other words, the American political order is only one particular manifestation of the precepts set forth in the Declaration of Independence, which should be understood to have universal applicability; however much the Declaration might be glorified as a sort of American nationalist manifesto, its message is internationalist in the sense that it was meant for humanity.[122]

Those opposing expansionism after the war most strenuously reminded their countrymen of the connection between America's founding principles and the issue before them. For the antiimperialists, as they were called, accepting the Philippines and Puerto Rico as part of the war's settlement would flatly contradict the core values of the regime. One pamphleteer noted, for example, "To rule the people so acquired as colonists without voice in the government, would be clearly contrary to the principles laid down by our forefathers in the Declaration of Independence, and to the views entertained by the framers of the Constitution and expressed in that instrument by them."[123] Antiimperialists argued with some force that since those principles and the documents that expressed them essentially defined the American republic, then ignoring them for the sake of territorial expansion would undermine the nation as a whole and essentially destroy its mission.

Supreme Court Justice David J. Brewer, for instance, objected to the treaty's colonial scheme

> because it antagonizes the principles upon which this Government was founded, which have controlled its life up to the present time, and the perfection of which has been the hope and aspiration of every true American. . . . We stand consecrated to the single political idea of government by the consent of the governed. To introduce into the life of the nation the other thought of government by force is, at the very outset, to precipitate a conflict which, sooner or later, must inevitably result in disaster.[124]

The eminent Carl Schurz similarly located the source of America's greatness in its defense of the democratic principle: "It was the noblest ambition of all true Americans to carry this democratic government to the highest degree of perfection and justice, in probity, in assured peace, in the security of human rights, in progressive civilization; to solve the problem of popular self-government on the grandest scale; and thus to make this republic the example and guiding star of mankind." Colonialism, argued Schurz, would undermine the country's capacity to serve this role for mankind: "If we turn that war which was so solemnly commended to the favor of mankind as a generous war of liberation and humanity into a victory for conquest and self-aggrandizement, we shall have thoroughly forfeited our moral credit with the world." Stanford's Jordan convincingly argued, meanwhile, that a colonial system of government would be not only philosophically but structurally incompatible with the American framework of government. If America chose to adopt imperialism at the conclusion of the war, he counseled, then it must prepare to refocus its vision almost exclusively on the external world and to adjust its governmental system accordingly. This policy would result in a redefinition of the nation, one that would run counter to the established creed of individualism.[125]

Racial constructs were central to many interpretations of the relationship between imperialism and American democracy. Given the prevailing conviction that held that one's capacity for participating in "elevated" forms of government depended on his or her race (and no form of government was more elevated than that of the United States), the prospect of adding several million nonwhites to the body politic was incomprehensible. As one antiexpansionist averred, "The nation with the greatest number of moral, intellectual, healthy Caucasians will come very near being the greatest nation on earth." That being the case, he wondered, "Can we enhance our power in this respect by annexing the dregs of the earth?"[126]

According to this line of thinking, the United States enjoyed a perfect form of government because it was designed by Anglo-Saxons, for Anglo-Saxons. Nonetheless, the documents wherein America's political principles were elucidated did not make this distinction, leading others to the conclusion that the United States had not yet learned how to properly apply those principles to its own society. As a result, the country had no business extending the "blessings of its civilization" to other peoples until it had gotten it right for itself. As one antiimperialist pamphlet explained:

> It appears to the writer that we have not yet arrived at that state of perfection as a self-governing people which justifies us in professing to be models worthy of imitation by the rest of the world, and still less in extending our dominion by force where it is not desired. After we shall have solved the race problem in our Southern States, abolished political corruption and the other evils which now infest both the Federal and State Governments of our Union, and secured to all our citizens the equal rights, privileges, and immunities to which they are justly entitled, we may properly consider the question of territorial expansion, but not until then.[127]

This position did not disagree with the notion that the United States had the most perfect form of government or that it had a mission to mankind. Rather, it insisted that the United States did not yet live up to its ideals and should therefore concentrate on realizing them in practice before attempting their universal promulgation.

Expansionists naturally had a different understanding of things. They agreed with their opponents that America's political principles were of universal value (even if, as some argued, they had to be administered to dependent inferior races from above), and they also agreed that there were some apparent inconsistencies between the way those principles were expressed in the Declaration of Independence and the way they had actually been embodied in American society up to that time; nevertheless, expansionists believed, those principles could attain the universal application that they deserved only through the agency of the United States. While the ideal of individual liberty that lay at the heart of American culture was presumed to rest on a universal human nature, in other words, its realization in the world relied on implementation by the United States. The political exercise of human freedom and equality had hitherto been truly manifested only in the United States, and so the United States was perceived in a literal way as embodying those values. The expansionists, in other words, transmuted the country's universalist philosophy into a nationalist one.[128]

The most obvious conceptual difficulty with this position that expansion's proponents had to overcome was the denial of Filippino self-government entailed in the proposed colonial policy. One dubious way of squaring that circle was to reject the notion that the Declaration's promise of government "by the consent of the governed" meant self-determination. As one pamphleteer wrote, "The unalienable [sic] right which [the founders] proclaimed was not the right of every *community* of men to national independence, but the right of every individual *man* to life, liberty, and the pursuit of happiness, that personal right which our government is trying to secure to the Filipinos, and which they cannot be sure of except under the American flag" (emphasis added).[129] Since the Declaration's promises were made to men as men, those guarantees could be respected by any government, regardless of whether or not the individual participated in electing it. If England had reformed itself in a suitable manner prior to the Revolutionary War, this argument held, then the Americans would have been unjustified in revolting. Despite its title, then, the Declaration of Independence did not demand independence, only individual freedom under a just regime. Because the United States embodied freedom more purely than any other society, therefore, it simply *could not* violate anyone else's liberty. As with Midas, whatever the United States touched became free.

Some faced the inconsistency more squarely, claiming that the Declaration of Independence guaranteed liberty only to those who were properly prepared to exercise it. This position did not exactly contradict the premise that "all men are created equal," but it did limit the nature of that shared equality in such a way that allowed individuals to enjoy different levels of political freedom. Just as children were their parents' equals in the eyes of God without having equivalent political stature, so "child" races and nations could have less political freedom without undermining the Declaration's fundamental premise.[130] This logic was clear to Americans in the 1890s; persistent discrepancies between the political treatment of racial, religious, and gender minorities, on the one hand, and their white, Anglo-Saxon, Protestant male counterparts, on the other, had long since acculturated Americans to the notion that political inequality could coexist with fundamental human "equality." Of course, this American conception of equality deprived the term of any meaning that could practically anchor a universal framework of justice.

The effect was that the meaning of the term *equality* as expressed in the nation's founding political documents was rigidly bracketed so that it could conform with the culture's other ideological norms. As one expansionist noted, "among the inalienable rights of man which the Declaration sets up, the right to political equality is not enumerated."[131] If it had been, then Americans would have "persistently departed from it in establishing various property and educational limitations on the suffrage, in denying political rights to the Indians, in governing the territories when first acquired (and some of them still) by Federal agents, in withholding the right of self-government from the inhabitants of the District of Columbia, in refusing to let the people of the Southern States set up an independent government of their own, and in many other particulars."[132] Among those "other particulars," of course, were the myriad ways that whites had deprived blacks of any semblance of liberty or equality.

The only conclusion that one could draw was that "political equality and self-government were regarded as ideals merely, to be realized as soon as the people should be capable of living up to them; that civil liberty, not political equality, was the immediate aim of the Fathers."[133] While all people were equal on some fundamental level, in other words, political freedom required capacities that were of a less universal variety. This argument also rests on the conviction that the United States simply cannot violate the tenets of the Declaration of Independence. In the eyes of those advocating this position, the United States was a symbolic embodiment of the Declaration's ideals, and so the nation's behavior dictated the meaning of those ideals, just as popes defined through their edicts the meaning of Western Christianity in the centuries before the Reformation. Thus, after acknowledging that in numerous instances the United States had seemingly delimited or contravened the Declaration's promise of self-government, expansionists then excused those apparent violations by stating simply that those slighted must not have been capable of living up to freedom's responsibilities.

The argument that the Declaration's guarantees were of limited applicability converted that document essentially into a nationalist tract. America was founded under circumstances that lent to the Declaration's principles a practical validity; the important thing for other peoples was that their governments treated them justly. As one of America's most respected leaders, Elihu Root, then secretary of war, declared:

> The doctrine that government derives its just powers from the consent of the governed was applicable to the conditions for which Jefferson wrote it, and to the people to whom he applied it. It is true wherever a people exists capable and willing to maintain just government, and to make free, intelligent and efficacious decisions as to who shall govern. But Jefferson did not apply it to Louisiana. He wrote to Gallatin that the people of Louisiana were as incapable of self-government as children, and he governed them without their consent. . . . Government does not depend upon consent. The immutable laws of justice and humanity require that people shall have government, that the weak shall be protected, that cruelty and lust shall be restrained, whether there be consent or not.[134]

Applying this logic to American expansion into the underdeveloped Philippines, he then came in one long sentence to the nationalist argument:

> When I consider the myriads of human beings who have lived in subjection to the rule of force, ignorant of any other lot, knowing life only as the beast of the field knows it, without the seeds of progress, without initiative or capacity to rise, submissive to injustice and cruelty and perpetual ignorance and brutishness, I cannot believe that, for the external forces of civilization, to replace brutal and oppressive government, with which such a people in ignorance are content,

by ordered liberty and individual freedom and a rule that shall start and lead them along the path of political and social progress, is a violation of the principle of Jefferson, or false to the highest dictates of liberty and humanity.[135]

The final, most honest way of defending colonial expansion despite the Declaration's exaltation of the principle of self-government came from Washington Gladden, who suggested that the language used to enunciate America's core principles be changed to accommodate their breach under colonialism:

> We shall need some carefully considered laws, some new forms of administration; I rather think that we shall be obliged to have some constitutional amendments. All this involves a considerable extension and some reconstruction of our political system. It involves the abandonment, in such populations, of universal suffrage, and the introduction of limited, tentative and progressive methods of enfranchisement. It involves the frank admission and enforcement of the truth that some men do not know as much and are not as good citizens as other men; and that there are those who do not know enough and are not good enough to take part in governing their fellow-men.[136]

Clearly, Americans in 1898 were aware that their foreign policy and the nation's political principles were at least facially inconsistent. The intellectual calisthenics that they practiced in an effort to overcome or deny this inconsistency reflected their respect for liberal norms—it would have been easy to say in a Darwinian spirit that liberalism had become passé and that the time had arrived to institute a new manner of political organization. The fact that they did not do so shows clearly that liberalism retained its central place in American national identity even if Americans still had not learned how to live up to its principles.

The four normative structures identified in this chapter—social Darwinism, racism, liberal Protestantism, and nationalist liberalism—were understood by most white Americans to be mutually reinforcing. Together, they formed the basis of American national identity, and as such they provided guidance to leaders as they groped forward in their efforts to chart a new course in the nation's foreign policy. In 1898, the

United States turned an important corner in its relations with the world. Its national identity reassured the people that they deserved to lead the world to a new and better future and, importantly, that in doing so they would be doing good to others, making it possible to justify intervening in Cuba and annexing territories after the war. Had these normative structures not patterned Americans' thinking in 1898, it is most unlikely that the nation would have confidently pursued either of these unprecedented policies.

CHAPTER THREE

Entering the War:
The General Background

IN ORDER TO interpret accurately Americans' motives for waging their war against Spain in 1898, it is important first to disentangle the imperialist outcome of the war from the conflict itself. The powerful sense that the United States ought to end Spanish rule in Cuba did not reflect a sublimated redirection of burgeoning imperialist sentiments. Rather, it expressed a complex mixture of emotions and rationales, of which basic humanitarianism was the most prominent. The American people were outraged by images circulating in the press of starving women and children—the civilian victims of Spain's vicious "reconcentration" policy—and they were galvanized by the Cuban rebels who fought, as Americans' own forbears had, for self-determination. To be sure, an important segment of American leadership—notably, Theodore Roosevelt and Senator Henry Cabot Lodge (R-Mass.)—eagerly welcomed the war as a chance to usher in a "large policy" of territorial expansion. But in the public demonstrations, pamphlets, and petitions to Congress that provided the primary impetus for war, the American people clamored not for territorial conquest but for the relief of a brutally oppressed people living at the nation's doorstep. The people's representatives in Congress translated this moral indignation into a call for armed intervention in Cuba, and President William McKinley ultimately heeded that call—but only after he set the terms by which the nation would fight. The result was a war through which the United States sought to define itself as a great power and protector of "civilized" values.

The rhetoric used to agitate for and justify the war built upon a contrast between the civilizations of Spain and the United States. Americans regarded Spanish civilization as irredeemably corrupt and criticized Spain for being cruel, backward, unenlightened, and monarchical; sometimes they faulted Spanish civilization for being Roman Catholic.

Americans considered their own civilization, by contrast, to be the pinnacle of human progress—advanced in its political values, religion, and racial composition. They characterized the horrible circumstances in Cuba as an inevitable consequence of Spanish rule and insisted that conditions on the island would be incomparably improved if Spain's civilization were replaced by America's. Americans became convinced that they would fail in their moral duty as God's chosen people if they continued to refuse to intervene on behalf of the Cuban people and thereby bring the blessings of American civilization to the island. The Spanish-American War would never have happened, in short, if the people of the United States and their leaders had not believed that theirs was an enlightened, Christian, and republican civilization of Anglo-Saxons with a mission to advance human history—in this case, by ending Spanish rule in Cuba.

Americans had other, less noble, motives for fighting Spain, of course, including, for some, expansion. Another common motive became revenge after the battleship *Maine* mysteriously exploded in Havana's harbor. When investigators determined (incorrectly) that the explosion was caused by an external source—probably a mine—Americans' thirst for vengeance made war inevitable. Before the ship went down, however, the groundswell for war was already huge; the *Maine*'s destruction was simply fuel on an already large fire. Historian Richard Hofstadter gave one underlying explanation for this agitation when he argued that a "psychic crisis" gripped the American people throughout the late 1890s. Hofstadter noted that the population was jittery with a sort of restless energy that had much to do with economic discontent, and Americans were eager, almost desperate, to find an outlet for it. The result was a public temper ready to believe yellow-press accounts of Spanish cruelty on Cuba, willing to blame Spain when the *Maine* exploded, and eager to take violent action in response.[1]

The Spanish-American War was a direct response to the Cuban insurrection of 1895, in which Cuban nationalists attempted forcibly to end Spanish colonial rule over the island. Spain's hold on Cuba had been shaky for some time. All through the nineteenth century, revolutions had periodically broken out on the island, and each had captured the attention of an American public divided between those supporting the island's independence and a segment that coveted Cuba as a potential new U.S. territory. The longest of these uprisings had lasted from 1868 until the signing of the Treaty of Zanjón in 1878. Called the Ten Years War, this conflict generated intense support from both the Cuban and the American people, and this support never really disappeared. The reemergence of the Cuban struggle for independence on February 24, 1895, thus found in the United States a receptive audience that was familiar with and sympathetic to its neighbor's plight.[2]

The 1895 conflict emerged directly from the Ten Years War; in fact, the insurrection itself never fully ended after 1878. The 1895 reemergence is better understood as the start of a marked increase in the uprising's scope and intensity than the initiation of a totally new conflict. Even the rebels' two military leaders in the later war, General Máximo Gomez and General Antonio Maceo, had exercised their initial battlefield leadership in the earlier conflict. This latest uprising was conceived and initiated by Jose Martí, a poet, philosopher, and nationalist who had spent several years organizing Cuban émigrés in other countries into a vast revolutionary movement while encouraging the two generals to enlist foot soldiers on the island.[3] Because the groups of supporters that Martí had organized operated in foreign countries, they could provide sustained logistical support for the rebels while avoiding direct Spanish interference. These pockets of Cuban expatriates and sympathizers outfitted filibustering expeditions that sent arms and other supplies to the rebels from various ports in Latin America, Great Britain, and, overwhelmingly, the United States.

The costs and headaches of intercepting these ships fell primarily on the U.S. government,[4] which quickly wearied of the task but nonetheless maintained an active presence in the Caribbean and along its Atlantic coast.[5] Although a substantial but never sufficient amount of supplies managed to elude the Revenue Cutter Service (forerunner of the Coast Guard) and reach the Cuban rebels, America's patrolling of its coastal waters did prevent many ships from arriving at their destinations.[6] Even so, Spain continually complained that the United States was not doing enough to curb the influx of contraband and accused the Cleveland and McKinley administrations of abetting the rebel cause through willful impotence.[7] Aside from delivering weapons and supplies to guerrillas, in other words, the filibustering missions had the effect of aggravating both Spain and the United States and inducing each to be suspicious and annoyed with the other.[8]

Still, in the early years of the conflict, despite the public's clear desire to act, President Grover Cleveland resisted all pressure to engage Spain in a war over Cuba.[9] Even with as pugnacious a secretary of state as Richard Olney, Cleveland refused to escalate the simmering tensions between the two countries. In his final annual message, however, Cleveland suggested that there was a limit to America's patience. Citing Americans' "large pecuniary stake in the fortunes of Cuba," as well as their concerns of a more "sentimental or philanthropic character," Cleveland warned that "it can not be reasonably assumed that the hitherto expectant attitude of the United States will be indefinitely maintained." Proposing that Spain grant autonomy to the Cubans, Cleveland added that if Spain refused and the situation continued to degenerate, then "a situation will be presented in which our obligations to the sovereignty of Spain will be superseded by higher obligations, which we can hardly hesitate to recognize or discharge."[10] The conditions that Cleveland feared did in fact come to pass, but not while he was in office. Instead, the election of 1896 put William McKinley in the White House, and the headache in Cuba was his to deal with.

The public mood was clearly anti-Spanish, and politicians were sitting up and taking notice. Of course, public officials generally shared their constituents' revulsion over the reports that were coming in from Cuba—even the verifiable accounts could be stunning in what they detailed—and the same religious, racial, and ideological prejudices that shaped the mainstream culture influenced them as well. But once the election of 1896 was over, widespread public attention transformed Cuba into a *political* issue, and Congress responded. (Strangely, however, it was not at all a factor in the 1896 presidential campaign, which was dominated by currency, labor, and trade issues.)

Petitions poured into Congress from around the country, many from religious groups and several from state governments, all of them demanding action on what was becoming the "Cuban issue." Typical of these petitions was one submitted on May 12, 1897, by the "government and legislature of Utah," which read: "A memorial to Congress representing the conditions existing in Cuba, and praying that honorable body to intervene to protect American citizens and to take immediate steps to stop the carnival of blood now being enacted on that island."[11] The colorful phrase *carnival of blood* that appeared in the petition also found its way into much of the other public correspondence that was read in Congress. The reason for that expression's popularity is that it was used in a reprinted article that had originally been written in 1620 by Bishop Las Casas to describe the cruelty demonstrated by the Spaniards in their conquest of the New World.[12] That a piece written in 1620 describing Spanish cruelty could gain such wide credibility suggests that Americans attributed Spanish maladministration in Cuba to a moral deficiency in the mother civilization itself. It also revealed the growing influence of the yellow press.

The pro-Cuban groups responsible for enlisting financial and moral support for the filibustering expeditions were led by a coordinating committee called the Junta, headquartered in New York City.[13] The Junta's greatest service to the Cuban cause came less in the form of war materiel than in the propaganda (such as the Bishop Las Casas piece) that it fed to America's newspapers, particularly the yellow press. The leader of the Junta, Tomás Estrada Palma, had been the head of the Cuban rebels in the Ten Years War, and he would later serve as Cuba's first president.[14] Under Palma's leadership, the Junta fed a steady stream of "news" to American journalists in New York, who tended to publish these reader-friendly dispatches without hesitating over authenticity. Naturally, the Junta's reports recounted only Spanish cruelty. The two largest consumers and broadcasters of the Junta's propaganda were William Randolph Hearst's *Journal* and Joseph Pulitzer's *World,* both in New York. Engaged in a fierce circulation war with each other, these two publishing giants each rushed to be the first to print the most sensational stories, under the most colorful headlines, to attract the largest number of undiscerning readers.[15]

Spain compounded its poor image with yellow journalists by barring press coverage of the Spanish-Cuban War. By instituting and strictly enforcing its press ban, Spain rankled American journalists and publishers, inclining them to bias their stories in favor of the rebels and to print "first-person" accounts of events that were provided by prorebel sympathizers on the island. The war correspondents themselves usually "reported" from Havana hotels and bars as a result of the ban, although a few enterprising journalists would daringly sneak past the Spanish authorities to gather incriminating information.[16] The sensationalist stories they produced were invariably anti-Spanish. One early article from the *World*, for example, described the Cuban situation as follows: "The horrors of a barbarous struggle for the extermination of the native population are witnessed in all parts of the country. Blood on the roadsides, blood in the fields, blood on the doorsteps, blood, blood, blood! The old, the young, the weak, the crippled–all are butchered without mercy. . . . Is there any barbarism known to the mind of man that will justify the intervention of a civilized power?"[17] Such stories were repeated in style and form on a daily basis, often on the front page under shocking headlines and accompanied by lurid artist "renditions" of Spain's crimes. Needless to say, the press's coverage of the Cuban insurrection did not endear Spain to the American public.

Pro-Cuban bias was reinforced by the belief that the rebel cause mirrored that of America's own Revolutionary heroes.[18] It was easy for citizens of the United States to sympathize with the Cubans since the rebels' cause was depicted as an effort to advance core American values and institutions and in so doing to help America in its mission to universalize democracy and the American way of life. As one pamphleteer reminded his countrymen, "The true American patriot is he whose sympathies are always with men everywhere who are struggling for freedom and self-government."[19] As time went on, Americans' sympathy for the rebels increased. As one contemporary historian wrote, "At once, as if by an electric flash, the sympathy of the American people was enlisted with the Insurgents who were (as the Americans believed) fighting Spain for their *liberty*. Public opinion was on the Insurgents' side and against Spain from the beginning." Humanitarian sentiments and a strong belief in the idea of American mission were the foundation of their support for the Cubans, and these were among the attributes of mainstream American culture that the yellow press exploited to sell their papers.[20]

The war in Cuba between Spain and the island's nationalists seemed intractable by 1897. Spain was as committed to retaining Cuba as the Cubans were to becoming independent. Not only was Spanish honor tied to holding the island but its political order also teetered precariously on the brink of total dissolution. Under the circumstances, it was impossible for any Spanish ministry to appear willing to besmirch the nation's proud history by abandoning the last remnants of its once glorious empire.[21] Antonio Cánovas del Castillo was Spain's Conservative prime minister at the outbreak of the Cuban insurrection of 1895, and his power was challenged both from within his own party and by the Liberals, headed by Práxedes Mateo Sagasta. Successfully squelching the Cuban revolution and preserving the national honor was essential if Cánovas was to remain in power.[22]

Cánovas initially sent General Martínez de Campos to put down the rebellion, but Campos was unwilling to undertake the extreme measures necessary to end the strife quickly. In his place in 1896 went General Valeriano Weyler, a veteran of the Ten Years War who had no qualms doing whatever was required to achieve victory. His brutal policy of "reconcentration," which entailed moving the entire rural population into small, fenced-in compounds, aggravated the American conscience and escalated popular discontent with affairs on the island. Inadequate provisions for the *reconcentrados* led to mass starvation, and diseases ran rampant through the camps, but anyone attempting to leave them would be shot. Since both sides in the conflict had made it an official policy to burn down all arable fields, destroy all crops, and kill all livestock, moreover, relief was not readily forthcoming.[23] A reasonable estimate of the number of civilian deaths caused by Weyler's reconcentration policy is between one hundred thousand and three hundred thousand.[24] More than anything else, even more than the mysterious explosion of the battleship *Maine*, Weyler's reconcentration policy was responsible for moving the United States to war. As Washington Gladden insisted, "The constant sight of unspeakable cruelties has become intolerable; we will bear it no longer. . . . The conduct of Spain in Cuba up to date is a crime against civilization."[25]

As a result of his reconcentration policy, Weyler was nicknamed "the butcher," and America's worst suspicions about Spanish civilization being cruel and morally primitive seemed to be confirmed. The text of a contemporary slide show designed for distribution to American schools, for example, said that "in her present condition, Spain is utterly unfit to govern either herself or any dependency whatever"; the American children who saw the presentation were told that Spain was "decadent."[26] In another popular narrative history of the country, the author drew this lesson for his readers: "The virulent, obstinate, even brutal ignorance of the masses cannot be penetrated by any sentiment of sympathy with high aspiration or disinterested devotion to principle.... The war with Cuba was but an episode; yet it was also the legitimate outgrowth of Spain's policies, which–as already explained–have been consistently cruel and unjust toward her colonists, from her earliest occupation of American territory."[27] In another example of Americans' opinion of Spain, a patriotic song written to rally the country to war included the following stanza:

> Down with the flag of Spanish reign.
> They stab their victims in the dark,
> Women, children, torn apart,
> Down with the bloody flag of Spain.
> Shout the cry of Freedom long,
> Freedom waits the starving throng,
> Down the cruel Spanish Don,
> Rally round the flag and hold her steady.[28]

This attitude about Spanish cruelty was widely expressed, and Weyler's reconcentration policy was perceived as consistent with, not aberrant from, the general character of Spanish civilization.

Spain became a symbol of the past–an earlier, less-enlightened age when darkness and superstition clouded men's minds. As one writer put it, "In the great march of civilization of Europe and America, Spain has sullenly and uniformly remained in the rear guard, advancing only under compulsion, and retarding, rather than helping, that onward march toward the goal of perfection which Christianity and civilization have ever before them, and which, though still in the far-off distance, is year by year less distant from those who strive honestly to reach it."[29] The eminent Charles Francis Adams offered the following estimation of Spain's progress:

> I want some one to point out a single good thing in law, or science, or art, or literature–material, moral, or intellectual,–which has resulted to the race of man upon earth from Spanish domination in America. I have tried to think of one in vain. It certainly has not yielded an immortality, an idea, or a discovery; it has, in fact, been one long record

of reaction and retrogression, than which few pages in the record of mankind have been more discouraging or less fruitful of good.

Adams added, "[F]rom the year 1492 down, the history of Spain and Spanish domination has undeniably been one long series of crimes and violations of natural law."[30]

There were often religious undertones to these unfavorable evaluations of Spanish civilization, since Spain was "still" Roman Catholic and had been home to the Inquisition. In the fall of 1895, for example, mass demonstrations protesting against Spanish rule in Cuba included participants from organized labor groups, patriotic organizations such as the Grand Army of the Republic (GAR), and Protestant evangelicals, some of whom were notably anti-Catholic. The featured speaker for New York City's rally, for instance, was Baptist minister Thomas Dixon,[31] who had once preached that the contemporary "fruits" of Catholicism were Italy and Spain, which he called "the two most hopelessly ignorant nations in the civilized world."[32] Another writer assessed Spain's development according to the millennial worldview that marked the Protestant Reformation as a turning point in divine history:

> On the continent the Anglo-Saxons, steadily advancing step by step, unsettling old opinions, reforming, lifting, improving, making more beneficent its aggressive and growing civilization. On the island [of Cuba] was the civilization of the 16th century. Spain has been asleep for three hundred years. The Reformation that stirred all Europe never disturbed the Peninsula.... (F)rom that turning point the face of all Europe, save Spain, slowly grew brighter, the people gradually opened their eyes to their own wretched condition, felt more sensibly the yoke of slavery pressing upon them, rested more uneasily under the intolerant superstition of the inmates of the cloister and the convent. ... But throughout all this revolt Spain has lain dormant and torpid. ... Her days have been centuries. ... Her history has been written in blood and in violence from the days of Alva and the inquisition to the days of Weyler and the reconcentrado.[33]

Although anti-Spanish and anti-Catholic sentiments were commonly fused prior to the war,[34] however, once the war began the loyalty and impressive jingoism of American Catholics helped to persuade American

Protestants that not all varieties of Catholicism were as inherently corrupt as the Spanish version, leading to a reduction in published attacks on that faith.

THE PROXIMATE CAUSES OF THE WAR

From late 1897 through early 1898, the calls for armed intervention to "rescue Cuba" became more urgent, more intense, and more insistent, and they clearly built upon the cultural constructions of American national identity—especially religious ones—described in previous chapters. "Compliance with evil is worse than war," argued one pamphleteer. "One thing, as Christian men, I hold we cannot do. We cannot, as Christian men, tolerate the statement that the unendurable woes of Cuba are no business of these United States. . . . The cause of freedom in Cuba is the cause of God and man."[35] Not only pamphleteers made these sorts of arguments; Congressmen did so, too. Senator John Morgan (D-Ala.), for instance, noted, "The . . . horrors of persecution, rapine, and extermination visited upon the people of Cuba . . . [are] so incredibly inhuman and so disgraceful to the civilization of this age that it stuns the mind into disbelief that such things can be true." The American people, he concluded from this observation, "are not content to suffer these wrongs, within earshot of their frontier," and they considered intervention to be "a duty that we owe to humanity, to Christian civilization, to the spirit and traditions of our own country and our people, and to the lives and liberties of our people in Cuba who are now held beneath the cruel power of Spanish jealousy and revenge."[36]

Not everyone agreed that the United States should get involved, however. In keeping with American tradition, one wing of the public objected to the war on the grounds of pacifism. Some argued that evolution was yielding a spirit "of Christian love" and "human progress" that would "render [war] an outlaw among civilized nations."[37] Other opponents of the war cringed at the way Christianity was enlisted in the service of nationalism and militarism. "It is the 'original savage' that we are asked to resuscitate within us in the name of Christ!" wrote one author. "I am driven reluctantly to a conclusion which I only express here under a grave sense of duty, and that is that the churches are the chief strongholds in Christendom of the spirit of warfare."[38] Another author argued that justifying war by appealing to Christianity was akin to creating a "new religion," a religion of the state. Insisting that "the Kingdom of Christ Our Lord" would only arrive when God judged it proper, he wrote that to argue that the kingdom would come through the agency of a political power is to introduce worldliness to the church, as Constantine did, which could only corrupt Christianity by falsely temporalizing its concerns and bringing it into history. The true duty of Christians, he held, was instead to work for peace. But most American Christians disagreed.[39]

Momentum toward war increased markedly on February 9, 1898, when a private letter written by the Spanish minister to Washington, Enrique Dupuy de Lôme, was published on the front page of Hearst's *New York Journal*. In the letter, the Spanish minister insulted the president and implied that Spain had been dealing dishonestly with the United States.[40] The *Journal*'s headline, "WORST INSULT TO THE UNITED STATES IN HISTORY," captured the public's response to the letter and turned an already hostile and excitable American public almost into a mob bent on vindicating their leader's honor. McKinley, however, despite being the object of de Lôme's insults, was more concerned with other parts of the letter. In late 1897, the president had brokered an agreement with Sagasta (who had replaced Canovas in August, after he was assassinated) in which Spain had promised to grant autonomy to its colony if the United States would avoid actions implying sympathy for the insurgents. Both the Cubans and their American sympathizers had hoped that autonomy would be the first step toward independence. De Lôme's letter, however, strongly implied that the agreement was a sham designed to buy time. McKinley and his allies in restraint began to get the feeling that they could not trust Spain, and that the Cuban issue would never go away.[41] The letter destroyed what little American confidence remained in Spain. Appropriately, the Spanish minister resigned and returned to Spain, and the American mood darkened.

Then, abruptly, the battleship *Maine* exploded in the Havana harbor. It was an ominous portent. The *Maine* had been sent to the Havana port to provide a tangible symbol of American power to Spanish dissidents who had been acting in a threatening manner toward Americans residing in Cuba. Leading up to the warship's arrival on January 25, the Spanish population had become as restive as its American counterpart, and the feeling had grown that at any moment the Spanish loyalists on the island would direct their hostility at the American presence there. The *peninsulares*–the white Spanish citizens living on Cuba–saw the autonomy agreement brokered by McKinley and Sagasta as a unilateral concession to the United States and an affront to Spanish pride. They believed that the United States had no business being in Cuba and that the Cuban rebellion was being almost wholly sustained by the Junta and their filibusters, whose activities the United States could curb if it chose. These festering feelings of resentment, bitterness, and general anti-American hostility finally burst out on January 12 in a wave of riots that swept through Havana. Although these riots, which were not especially destructive, subsided after a few days, their occurrence signaled that Americans on the island were vulnerable to further acts of violence unless the United States provided for them some form of protection. It was when, in late January, the possibility of further riots seemed to be growing that the *Maine* was sent to Havana.[42]

Although the battleship moored in Havana's harbor with the grudging approval of Spanish authorities, its presence embittered the peninsulares. While the *Maine* was not in Cuba actually to *do* anything, its mere presence indicated the level that tensions between Spain and the United States had reached. When it blew up on February 15, 1898, an important turning point in the relations between the two countries was reached. Two hundred and sixty-six Americans died in the explosion, which came as a complete shock to Cubans, Spaniards, and Americans alike. All sides implicitly recognized that if Spain were found culpable for the act, then war would result. The *Maine*'s captain, Charles D. Sigsbee, urged restraint in responding to the incident. McKinley agreed, and a court of inquiry was established to investigate the cause of the explosion.[43] As the president told Senator Charles Fairbanks (R-Iowa), "I don't propose to be swept off my feet by the catastrophe. My duty is plain. We must learn the truth and endeavor, if possible, to fix the responsibility. The country can afford to withhold its judgment and not strike an avenging blow until the truth is known. The Administration will go on preparing for war, but still hoping to avert it. It will not be plunged into war until it is ready for it."[44]

Still, "the national tragedy dominated American thinking."[45] After a brief period of admirable calm and ostensible patience to wait until it was clear how the battleship was sunk, the public reverted to its accustomed anti-Spanish stance. Many government officials, including the president, believed an internal explosion from the ship's coal bunkers had been responsible for the *Maine* catastrophe. Most Americans, however, were certain that Spanish authorities were somehow behind the event. As one prominent newsman of the time wrote in a contemporary history of the war: "Hence it was that the destruction of the *Maine,* following quickly upon the enforced exit of the Spanish minister, and the controversy which led up to that exit, not merely came to the people of the United States like a flash of lightning out of a clear sky, but fell upon a public opinion already sensitive to ill impressions from that particular quarter, and prepared to believe almost any evil of Spain and the Spaniards."[46] The yellow press fomented this belief with garish headlines, either suggesting or stating outright (sometimes falsely) that evidence pointed to Spanish responsibility.[47]

The mood in the country shifted palpably toward an immediate declaration of war. "Across the country, thousands gave themselves up to emotional excesses like those of tent-meeting revivals. Theater audiences cheered, stamped, and wept at the playing of the Star-Spangled Banner."[48] However, the president pointedly refused to rush to judgment. As Charles Dawes admiringly recorded in his journal on February 21, "The Spanish situation continues perplexing and ominous. [But the president] has withstood all efforts to stampede him. He will endeavor in every possible way consistent with honor to avoid war. . . . In the greatness of McKinley the safety of the situation lies."[49] The Congress reflected the popular attitude more directly, and almost unanimously its members held Spain accountable for the explosion. The Senate passed a resolution calling for a formal investigation of the conditions on Cuba that also asserted that Cuba's proximity to the United States obliged it to provide the island with humanitarian assistance. In a speech introducing the resolution, Senator William V. Allen (Pop-Neb.) referred to the recent massacres of Christians in Armenia and contrasted that situation with Cuba's:

> Sir, the farther from us atrocities take place the more some senators talk about them. But here, lying 90 miles from Florida, is an island that entered on a war for independence less than four years ago—three years ago last May. It was then an island with fifteen hundred thousand population. Five hundred thousand of them have been starved to death by the cruelties of the Spanish Government. It is about time

for us, Mr. President, to do something or to quit talking about being a big and powerful nation.[50]

The public remained agitated throughout March as it awaited confirmation that Spain had blown up the *Maine* (any other conclusion would have been met with skepticism). Business leaders, however, were considerably less eager than the general public to fight a war. Their opinion changed after Senator Redfield Proctor (R-Vt.) gave a speech to the Senate on March 17 that summarized the findings from his unofficial tour of the island. It was not long after this change occurred in the attitude of businessmen that McKinley took the final steps toward war. This fact has figured prominently in historians' conclusion that McKinley's foreign policy was dictated by the business community. The business leaders wanted to prevent the recognition of Cuban independence so that its markets would remain available to them, some argue, and McKinley dutifully obeyed their wishes and declined to do so. The argument of Philip S. Foner is illustrative of this position:

> With the support of a substantial section of, if not the entire, business community, McKinley moved to war. Thus it is clear that [historian Julius] Pratt's conclusion that most big businessmen opposed the declaration of war in 1898 requires a thorough re-evaluation. Likewise in need of re-evaluation is the concept in many historical works that the President moved hesitantly and fearfully under the impact of a public clamor too great for him to withstand. . . . As we have seen, McKinley moved resolutely to war, following a course mapped out months before, and in doing so, contemptuously ignored the overwhelming popular and Congressional demand for recognition of the independence of the Cuban Republic. . . . The war to liberate Cuba was thus a war to prevent its independence, eliminate Spain from Cuba and the Philippines, and open the door for the economic and political domination of both islands by the United States.[51]

Since Senator Proctor's speech was crucial in shifting the opinion of business leaders toward intervention, it is important to assessing this line of argument. Scrutiny of the speech and the reasons for its persuasiveness undermines seriously the claim that the business community (and through it, McKinley) had designs on the island for pecuniary reasons.

Proctor's fact-finding tour of Cuba was a subject of deep interest both to business leaders and the general public in large part because it was widely known that the conservative senator had always been skeptical of the usually hysterical accounts of Cuba's condition that were provided elsewhere. It was also widely believed that Proctor had traveled "as McKinley's observer and that his speech had been cleared with the President."[52] Still, Proctor's speech was influential because it was "above all, credible."[53] The speech persuaded most of the remaining opponents of Cuban intervention to join the march to war because it provided a seemingly objective confirmation that Spain was engaging in morally repugnant behavior in Cuba, as this contemporary account of it shows: "Senator Proctor was known to be one of the least imaginative and most just-minded of men, a hard-headed Yankee. . . . One of the best characterizations of the speech was made by Senator Frye, of Maine, a few minutes after its delivery. 'It is,' said he, 'just as if Proctor had held up his right hand and sworn to it.' That, indeed, was the impression it made upon the Senate. It constituted America's highest and best justification for going to war and had more influence in determining public opinion than any other single agency."[54]

In particular, Proctor's description of Weyler's reconcentration policy validated many of the worst stories that people had previously heard, whether from less reliable or disinterested sources:

Outside Habana [*sic*] all is changed. It is not peace nor is it war. It is desolation and distress, misery and starvation. . . . [The reconcentrados'] huts are about ten by fifteen feet in size, and for want of space are usually crowded together very closely. They have no floor but the ground, no furniture, and, after a year's wear, but little clothing except such stray substitutes as they can extemporize; and with large families, or more than one, in this little space, the commonest sanitary provisions are impossible. Conditions are unmentionable in this respect. Torn from their homes, with foul earth, foul air, foul water, and foul food or worse, what wonder that half have died and that one quarter of the living are so diseased that they cannot be saved? A form of dropsy is a common disorder resulting from these conditions. Little children are still walking about with arms and chest terribly emaciated, eyes swollen, and abdomen bloated to three times their natural size. . . . I went to Cuba with a strong conviction that the picture had been overdrawn; that a few cases of starvation and suffering had inspired and stimulated the press correspondents, and that they had given free play to a strong, natural, and highly cultivated imagination. . . . What I saw I cannot tell so that others can see it. It must be seen with one's own eyes to be realized.

No matter what influence Proctor had with the business community, these descriptions were not likely to have been calculated to appeal to their business sense.

Instead, Proctor spoke directly to the issue that had animated the American public with more or less intensity for the past three years: the humanitarian crisis in Cuba. His brief, qualified foray into position advocacy reflects this concern:

To me the strongest appeal [for intervention] is not the barbarity practiced by Weyler nor the loss of the *Maine*, if our worst fears should prove true, terrible as are both of those incidents, but the spectacle of a million and a half people, the entire native population of Cuba, struggling for freedom and deliverance from the worst misgovernment of which I ever had knowledge. . . . I am not in favor of annexation. . . . But it is not my purpose at this time, nor do I consider it my province, to suggest any plan. I merely speak of the symptoms as I saw them, but do not undertake to prescribe.[55]

Proctor's speech would not have had the effect on the United States that it did if the idea of American mission were not part of the nation's self-understanding. His speech appealed to norms prevalent in American culture that supported humanitarian assistance to horribly maltreated human beings. It did not posit facts, conditions, or strategies that would support an economic or geopolitical argument for intervention.

A week after Proctor moved the country with his dispassionate presentation of what had become familiar facts, other senators stepped forward to offer the findings from their own journeys to Cuba. These speeches were considerably more earnest than Proctor's and more willing to recommend solutions to the problems on the suffering island. Senator Jacob H. Gallinger (R-N.H.), for instance, declaring in his speech of March 23 that "[p]eople in want and suffering are everywhere seen and walking skeletons meet one on every hand," declared that the United States must replace Spain in Cuba. His arguments reveal that the anti-Spanish sentiments described earlier were held by public officials in addition to the pamphleteers:

> Mr. President, it is not accident or chance which had brought about the present situation. It is inexorable destiny, which decrees that Spain's ill-gotten possessions in this hemisphere will be lifted to freedom by the one Republic which represents everything that Spain has antagonized during her whole history. . . . Religion and humanity alike demand that this unholy war shall cease, and cease it should, even though the glitter and glamour of military rule shall end and a decaying and dissolute throne shall pass away never to return.

Gallinger admitted proudly that his speech would qualify him as a jingo. After noting that the "demands of advancing civilization" would "sooner or later . . . of necessity" require it, the senator declared himself to be in favor of annexing the island. As he reminded his peers (as well as those in the galleries who stood to applaud his jingoism), "For Cuba the present is dark and foreboding, but we must not forget that God reigns, and that the mighty sweep of human progress will not rest until oppression and cruelty are overcome."[56]

The following day, Senator John M. Thurston (R-Neb.) openly wept as he shared the report of his fact-finding mission. Thurston's wife had accompanied him to the island and she died during the trip. The senator claimed that the cause of her death was shock, bought on by her inability to process the magnitude of Cuba's misery; his passionate call to arms was therefore informed by personal sentiment. "We cannot refuse to accept this responsibility which the God of the universe has placed upon us as the one great power in the New World. We must act!" he thundered at one point, before accusing the "money changers" of alone obstructing the "holy cause" of intervention. If Thurston seemed sure of anything in the speech, it was that God would support the United States if it went to the rescue of the Cuban people:

> The lowly Nazarene on the shores of Galilee preached the divine doctrine of love, "Peace on earth, good will toward men." Not peace on earth at the expense of liberty and humanity. Not good will toward

men who despoil, enslave, degrade, and starve to death their fellow-men. I believe in the doctrine of Christ. I believe in the doctrine of peace; but Mr. President, men must have liberty before there can come an abiding peace. Intervention means force. Force means war. War means blood. But it will be God's force. The time for God's force has come again.

Flushed with a powerful anger toward Spain that was at once personal, religious, and patriotic, the distraught senator concluded his speech–to "long, continued applause in the galleries"–by averring, "Others may hesitate, others may procrastinate. . . . But for me, I am ready to act now, and for my action I am ready to answer to my conscience, my country, and my God. . . . My dearest wish, my most earnest prayer to God is this, that when death comes to end all, I may meet it calmly and fearlessly as did my beloved, in the cause of humanity, under the American flag."[57] Jingoism never had a better spokesperson than Senator Thurston that day.

The norms to which these speeches, like much of the pro-war rhetoric of the time, drew upon were strongly informed by the contemporary understanding of Christian responsibility. McKinley, for example, never failed to invoke concepts of "duty" or "obligation" in his speeches and messages, often in the context of discussing the country as a Christian civilization. Others related American duty to the theology of the kingdom of God, emphasizing that the role of the United States in providential history conferred upon it special responsibilities. On March 21, for example, Representative Joseph "Fighting Joe" Wheeler (D-Ala.), the old Confederate war hero, offered this justification for intervention:

It is the will of God that the atrocities which for three years Spanish officials have perpetrated in Cuba shall cease; it is God's will that humanity should prevail throughout the world, and when he created this great Christian Republic He imposed upon it the duty of obeying this admonition. We cannot neglect this duty any longer. If we do so, we will lose all of that great prestige which we now enjoy throughout the world, and I very much fear that some disaster may come to punish a people recreant to so sacred a duty.[58]

David J. Brewer, associate justice of the U.S. Supreme Court, described the nature of America's responsibility in this way: "A nation is, in my judgment, a great moral entity, expressing in its life the sum of all the moral obligations which rest upon its individual citizens, and so there are times in the history of every nation when humanity calls upon it to look beyond the mere matter of dollars and cents, and even at personal sacrifice to interfere in the affairs of other nations." He added, however, that such moral responsibility should not be construed as turning the nation into a knight-errant: "And yet, because this national duty may sometimes arise, and when it arises should always be bravely met, it does not follow therefrom that there is a continuous obligation to be looking into the affairs of other nations to see if there are not wrongs that ought to be righted, oppressed that should be delivered, and strug-gling people set free."[59] In Brewer's estimation, however, easing the suffering of the Cuban population was an obligation that had to be met, not a crusade that was actively sought.

The passionate drive toward war was not purely selfless, however, but was overlaid with a boastful pride that found "jingoes sitting in the House and Senate galleries wrapped in American flags, and ladies who urged on their favorite demagogues with roses and smiles."[60] The surge to war crested after the release of the report of the naval board of inquiry on March 24 concluded that an external explosion, and not an internal spontaneous combustion in the ship's coal bunkers, caused the *Maine* to sink. At that point, revenge became mixed in with the other motives for war, even though it was obvious that the Spanish government did not order the sinking the *Maine*. Spanish authorities were outraged and offended by suggestions that they were responsible: the last thing they wanted to do was provoke the United States into war. Few Americans in positions of responsibility seriously believed that Spain intentionally sabotaged the battleship, yet they still blamed Spain for its sinking because it was in Spanish waters at the time.

The president somberly passed the report on to Congress on March 29 with only a short message attached. He held Spain account-able for the sinking of the *Maine* because it was responsible for what-ever happened in the Havana port. The fact that someone was able to plant a mine in the harbor, McKinley reasoned, demonstrated the utter lack of control that Spanish authorities exercised in Cuba. But he did not call for war.[61] Still, wrote Watterson, "Within an hour after the find-ing of the report was known to the country, no one doubted that war was inevitable."[62] By mid-March, certainly after Senator Proctor's speech, the possibility of war was too great to ignore, and after the *Maine* report was released it was practically a foregone conclusion. Only one thing remained to be settled at that point: the terms on to which the United States would fight. The Cuban issue dominated not only America's churches, newspapers, and living rooms but also the halls of both Congress and the White House.

The public attended the debate that the war resolution engendered in great numbers, and they applauded particularly strenuous expressions of jingoism. Several times each day the vice president of the Senate or the Speaker of the House threatened to clear the galleries to restore order. Expansionism was in the air even if few government officials openly supported it. Hitherto, the Americans had accepted as a matter of course that the United States would transform the world through its example. With the proposed intervention in Cuba, against a European power, the people of the United States knew they were embarking on a new sort of enterprise, one that required a new way of conceiving of their world role.

For the United States to empower its ideals with the sword and take up a crusade on behalf those ideals was unprecedented. But the nation had been restless to achieve the greatness that it believed to be its birthright, and there before it was a chance to make the vision more concrete. The intervention would validate the highest ideals of the United States, if undertaken for the right reasons, and Americans were loathe to pass on an opportunity to expand the influence of ideas and norms that they believed to possess universal merit. The U.S. worldview in 1898 was pervaded with visions of national destiny, reinforced by a strong sense of Christian duty, and these norms motivated the nation to fight Spain on behalf of the Cubans.

CHAPTER FOUR

McKinley and Congress Frame U.S. Intervention in the War

OVERWHELMINGLY, THE POLITICAL leaders of the United States agreed that their country should invade Cuba, not primarily for material gain but to "fix" the island. While legislative momentum pushing for war had been building for years, it was in the debates that swirled in the final weeks before the war that national sentiment congealed into concrete policy. Although the speeches excerpted in this chapter were made in the course of defending actual policy proposals, the cultural norms discussed in chapters 2 and 3 very clearly shaped their form and content. Unambiguously, American policy makers defined American intervention in the Cuban crisis as an action pregnant with meaning for both American and global civilization.

Still, the debates that led up to the Spanish-American War were mostly structured along partisan lines, with Democrats and Populists favoring recognition of Cuban independence and Republicans supporting President William McKinley's call for unilateralism. As senators and representatives explained the nature of America's duty to the Cubans, however, they all spoke in the same language of progress, Christian responsibility, liberty, Spanish corruption, and American power—regardless of their party affiliation or the specific policy that they advocated. The same worldview informed all members' understandings of the nation's character and duty, which helps to explain why, despite the interminable partisan bickering,[1] everyone agreed substantially on what needed to be done. The United States would intervene in the Cuban insurrection as part of its national mission to the world. Such an action would allow America, the agent of divine justice, to empower the values and ideals for which it stood at the expense of their corrupt, obsolete Spanish equivalent.

Tellingly, the aspirations of the Cubans themselves were deemed less relevant to American actions than the cause of progress that the

United States was meant to serve. Although the minority parties insisted on the need for Cuban independence, their reasons for holding this position often stressed the costs and burdens a protectorate would entail for the United States. But concern for the fate of other peoples independent of any consideration of the national interest, whether defined materially or morally, has never been central to U.S. foreign policy–or the foreign policy of any other nation, for that matter. As a consequence, American humanitarianism in 1898 was very self-centered; the national self-definition in which American politicians engaged was more important than the aspirations of the Cubans themselves.

The impetus for war came from Congress, and the president followed only when he realized that his colleagues might declare war without him. Thus, the initial characterizations of American interest in the Spanish-Cuban War took place on the floors of the legislature. By far the most commonly heard rationales used to justify American intervention into Cuba were those that held the United States to be duty-bound to aid an oppressed people and to punish their wicked persecutors. For example, Senator William E. Mason (R-Ill.) gave a long, impassioned speech wherein he insisted that selflessness not expansionism was the motive of those urging war. In an interesting interlude whose evocation of Lincoln's second inaugural address earned him enough applause from the galleries to draw complaints from the senators on the floor, he drew a parallel between the situation in Cuba and that in the United States prior to the Civil War, where the injustices of slavery had to be atoned for with blood:

> Mr. President, I do not know what your religious faith may be. I, who have studied in a modest way the evolution of nations, am here to say to my colleagues in this Senate that there is no vicarious atonement for a nation's crime; no suffering on the Cross of Calvary will lift the shadow of the law of compensation. For a hundred years we set our flag in the sky, and said: "This is the land of the free and the home of the brave," at the same time selling women and children to the highest and best bidder for cash. . . . It was not the fault of the South; it was the fault of the country, but we committed a national crime and the law of compensation demanded settlement. To be sure, we tore down the slave pen and the whipping post, but we did not have material enough to make headboards for our graves.

It was time, Mason argued, for Spain to suffer the "law of compensation" as well, for its sins against the reconcentrados. Thus, "if it must be war, let it be a glorious war in defense of the weak against the strong, in defense of Christian civilization. If it must be war, let it be war in defense of the honor of our country, which is more precious than jewels, more sacred, more glorious than life."[2]

In the House, members also drew a sharp contrast between Spain's "corrupt" civilization and America's "enlightened" one. Rep. William C. Arnold (R-Pa.) insisted, for example, "In this emergency Providence points the way, duty bids us move on in the pathway of progressive civilization, humanity demands that we march resolutely forward, and justice insists that we punish deceit, perfidy, treachery, cruelty, tyranny, and savagery, which are the predominant traits of Spanish character."[3] Rep. Harry Skinner (Pop-N.C.) added,

> After all, it may be Divine design and retributive justice that has brought this proud, tyrannical, long-sinning nation [Spain] to judgment, to confront the Republic of liberty, equality, justice, and civilization, where the wage, the issue, is the triumph of justice, truth, liberty, humanity. With the God of these attributes and the Father of nations to direct our councils in peace and our armies and navies in war, we should not, we do not, fear the result. . . . [Our forefathers] were providentially guided to a home and refuge then beyond the sunset. Their first work was to dedicate this country to God and liberty. . . . The same Providence, in his own time and way, cares for the starving Cubans. He has given this country to them as their promised land, and these people as their guardians, defenders, and protectors.[4]

By choosing to employ this sort of rhetoric to frame U.S. intervention in Cuba, legislators characterized the proposed conflict as a pivotal moment in divine history, when the principles of American government, sanctioned by Providence, would be vindicated on the battlefield—when U.S. foreign policy could become a means for advancing human progress. Some speeches were explicit on this point, as when Rep. Mason S. Peters (D/Pop-Kans.) declared to the House:

> A war between the United States and Spain at this time would be fraught with deep significance. It would result not only in the freedom

of Cuba, but the exaltation of a principle which would be an object lesson to the world for all time. It would not be simply the United States pitted against Spain; it would be the opposing forces which have been at work shaping human destiny through all the ages. On the one hand, the shriveled and decrepit survival of a semi-barbarous system of oppression, cruelty, inhumanity, and violence; on the other, civil and religious liberty, equality, human rights, progress. On the one hand, the divine right of kings; on the other, the divine right of man. Why need we shrink from such a conflict? Such a war would be a blessing to the world.[5]

In the upper chamber, Senator William V. Allen (Pop-Neb.) further explained why the United States acted in the situation as the agent of progress:

Our ancestors declared to the world that all men are by nature free and equal and entitled to certain inalienable rights, among which are life, liberty, and the pursuit of happiness. They did not confine themselves to the inhabitants of the colonies; they did not limit the declaration to the people of the Western Hemisphere; but they held that all men, under whatever sun they might be born or whatever soil they might live, were created free and equal and entitled to life, liberty, and the pursuit of happiness. Sir, I hold human freedom and the right to self-government is God-given and inalienable, and whoever violates it flies in the face of Providence and wrests from the individual the most precious gift of all.[6]

His colleague Senator Clarence D. Clark (R-Wyo.) added, "God is on the side of the right, and in this coming contest we are in the right. We stand for freedom of peoples and for representative government, for free institutions and national honor."[7]

In addition to normative arguments such as these, America's legislators also argued that the United States should eliminate Spain from Cuba because, as a nascent great power, America needed to enforce its vision of justice within its sphere of influence. As Senator H. De Soto Money (D-Miss.) declared, "We do not ask the approval of the nations of the earth. . . . We have reached at last that stage in the development of nations when we can afford to stand singly before the earth upon our own responsibility and do the thing approved by our judgment."[8] In a speech to the House, Representative William Sulzer (D-N.Y.) added, "[The American people] will win if this great Republic, which should stand as a shining light, as a beacon, and as an example for all the other republics of the world, and for every people struggling for liberty and independence, will simply do its duty. . . . We are the greatest Republic the sun of noon ever looked down upon. We are invincible and invulnerable. . . . We must do our duty and fear nothing."[9] Senator George C. Perkins (R-Calif.) agreed: "I enroll my name among those who believe that our country is greater than any man or combination of men; that our country is next to our Creator."[10]

Representative Charles E. Pearce (R-Mo.) made the case most starkly that the United States needed to use the opportunity presented by the Cuban situation to transform itself into a military giant in his speech of April 1:

I have believed for twenty years that this Government can not maintain her standing among the nations of the earth or hold her own in the race of commercial enterprise and development or continue to exert her benevolent influence upon civilization, for which, in my judgment, God Almighty created this Republic, without keeping pace year by year and month by month with all her sister governments in all that appertains to power upon the sea as well as power upon land. . . . On and on have [Americans] swept with ever-increasing strength, and wherever they have gone they have set up . . . the banner of freedom and progress and industrial development; and, Mr. Chairman, wherever that banner floats in the breeze, there will abide the genius of liberty and the sovereignty of the United States. This, sir, and this alone, is the divine mission, the true glory of the Republic. . . . (T)he spirit of the present age is one of commercial aggression and conquest. Nearly all the nations of the earth, pagan as well as Christian, are moving along these lines. The American people are no exception. They could not divest themselves of this impelling spirit if they would. The organic principle of their existence is the principle of progress. I believe that if Congress had done ten years ago what it is doing today under the constraint of impending danger, Cuba would be a free republic, moving forward and upward in the peaceful race of life under the sheltering protection of the United States.[11]

Pearce's sentiments were those of a Republican expansionist, and he might have been expected to express such views. The speaker who took the podium after him, Rep. Jerry Simpson, on the other hand, was a Populist from Kansas who rejected Pearce's expansionism enough to argue that "the nation having no other aim than national aggrandizement is the nation whose decline is already written in the book of fate." Nevertheless, Simpson agreed substantially with his Republican colleague on other points, particularly the notion that the United States must become powerful in order to improve the world. He declared that "because of the operation of natural laws, the progress of human society must be evolutionary," and many nations remained in a state of barbarity. Thus, under the prevailing circumstances of international society, the use of military power remained a necessary evil, which meant among other things that a large navy was necessary if the United States were to accomplish anything good in the world.[12] Such visions of American greatness, inspired by the anticipated invasion of Cuba, swept across party lines. On the other hand, economic disagreements, which were flavored by regional interests, lurked just beneath the surface of the Cuba debate, and seething resentments about completely unrelated issues, such as bimetallism, often shattered the consensus. The resulting partisan rancor obscured the fundamental unity of purpose regarding Cuba that in fact existed in the country and its government at the time.

A good part of the blame for this partisanship lies with President William McKinley, whose inaction fueled suspicions rooted in his friendship with the nation's plutocrats. An in-depth analysis of his political and cultural identity, however, shows that his nationalism paralleled that of the jingoes and that his norms lay even more centrally in the mainstream of the national culture than did theirs.[13] Given the president's bland conformism, therefore, the complex reasons for his resistance to an exceedingly popular war movement merit scrutiny. Ultimately, the following analysis shows that McKinley's foot-dragging can best be explained by his insistence that the United States fight only when it was prepared to do so, and when its interests required it—in short, when it could fight in a manner that would allow it to shape foreign affairs in crucial and long lasting ways. To help clarify the institutional and partisan dynamics of the prewar debates, it is worthwhile now to review McKinley's character and leadership.

Previously the governor of Ohio and a representative of that state in Congress for fourteen years, McKinley was elected to the White House in 1896 by an American citizenry impressed with his economic policy positions and personal character. Shortly after his election, the candidate's ardent defense of high tariffs and the gold standard, the causes that defined his candidacy, quickly receded in importance in the public mind as "the Cuban issue" forcefully reasserted itself as the overriding issue of the day. But McKinley took some time getting his presidential feet under himself, and his initial inclination was to restrict his attention to domestic economic issues, where he felt comfortable. His conservative character prevented him from rushing into important decisions, and he hence tended to adopt positions that allowed him the greatest flexibility and discretion. When he was thrust into a foreign-policy crisis almost immediately upon taking office, he thus avoided committing himself to any course of action until he felt some degree of certainty that their outcomes would be consistent with his values and vision for the country. As his presidency wore on and he grew secure in his ability to direct the nation's foreign policy, however, his leadership grew firmer and his policies more decisive.

McKinley's election in 1896 helped to secure the historic partisan realignment that had begun in the congressional elections two years before. In the aftermath of a serious and prolonged depression, he was elected in large part because he projected a calming image to an unsettled nation seeking economic stability and growth above all else. This commitment to the nation's economic rebirth contributed to McKinley's initial reluctance to intervene in Cuba. Once he assented to the wisdom of war, however, his input into defining the purposes and parameters of the conflict became determinative of the course actually taken by the country.[14] The process by which McKinley ultimately arrived at this decision displayed his general philosophy of governance: by reference to his own values, which he would not transgress; by paying heed to the people's expressed views, which he felt compelled at least to take into account; by considering the nation's business interests;

and by carefully considering (his understanding of) the long-term interests and values of American civilization.

THE ELECTION OF 1896 AND MCKINLEY'S CHARACTER AND PUBLIC PHILOSOPHY

The presidential campaign between McKinley and William Jennings Bryan in 1896 had been surprisingly devoid of attention to the Cuban issue. The voters instead put aside their obsession with that situation for a few months and looked for a candidate to finish the job of pulling the country out of the Depression of 1893. The Democrats had been hammered in the 1894 congressional elections as a result of the depression, losing a whopping 113 seats and seeing their membership of the House drop from 61 percent to 29 percent.[15] In a resounding defeat they lost control of the Senate as well, showing that the electorate blamed the Democrats, who in 1893 had also controlled the White House, for the economic collapse. It had been a devastating defeat for the party.

The Democrats hoped that Bryan, a Populist from Nebraska, could secure the rural vote in the West and Midwest. The Democrats already controlled the South and hoped to make inroads into the Republican West, where silver miners sought to introduce the extensive coinage of silver as a means of shoring up the currency. Bryan led the Democrats to the silver platform—there was dissension in the party on this issue—with his captivating "Cross of Gold" speech during the party's nominating convention. In his speech, which is widely regarded as one of the masterpieces of American political oratory, Bryan portrayed the defenders of the gold standard as oppressors of the common people. The climax of the speech, from which derives its title, went as follows:

> If they dare to come out in the open field and defend the gold standard as a good thing, we will fight them to the uttermost. Having behind us the producing masses of this nation and the world, supported by the commercial interests, the laboring interests and the toilers everywhere, we will answer their demand for a gold standard by saying to them, *"You shall not press down upon the brow of labor this crown of thorns! You shall not crucify mankind upon a cross of gold!"* (Emphasis in the original)[16]

This famous oration established Bryan's reputation as the preeminent speaker of his day and led the Democrats to the Populists' position on the issue. The Republicans–though, like the Democrats, divided on the currency issue–leaned on the whole toward upholding the gold standard. When McKinley committed to the gold standard, Western free-silver delegates bolted the party to form the "Free-silver Republicans," who aligned in Congress with the Democrats, and the currency debate became, by far, the overriding issue in the electoral campaign.[17]

If Bryan's constituency lay in the South, where the party of Lincoln hardly existed in most places, and among the populists of the West and Midwest,[18] McKinley's stronghold was in the Northeast and among the industrialists, whose financial support was enlisted and organized by his masterful campaign manager and friend, Marcus Alonzo Hanna. Because conservatives and the holders of concentrated wealth–the "robber barons"–regarded the gold standard as practically the bulwark of civilization, they poured their money into McKinley's war chest after he committed to upholding it.[19] In addition to his defense of the gold standard, McKinley's other major campaign pledge was to support high tariffs. As he insisted in one campaign speech in New York, for example, "Protection, Reciprocity, and Sound Money must continue to be cardinal doctrines, a trinity of the patriotism, plenty and prosperity in the Republican faith."[20] In speech after speech, McKinley equated the maintenance of the gold standard with the national honor and insisted on protectionist tariffs. On one representative occasion, for instance, he averred in classic protectionist fashion that "the true policy in the United States is the one that causes American work to be done at home and not abroad; that employs American labor to make what we want, rather than have it done by the labor of another Nation that owes its allegiance to a foreign flag."[21]

On election day, the vote split along largely regional lines, although religion played a role in the outcome as well. Bryan succeeded in capturing the Western vote, and the Southern states, as expected, also voted the Democratic line. But the Democrats' decision to nominate the Populist firebrand ultimately backfired. First, as an outspoken evangelical preacher, Bryan drove many ordinarily reliable Roman Catholic voters to McKinley, who enjoyed a very public friendship with Archbishop John Ireland, one of the most prominent religious leaders in the country.[22] Second, Bryan unabashedly endorsed and symbolized radical reform, which frightened conservative voters, including mainline Protestants who might otherwise have been receptive to a preacher's candidacy. Finally, Bryan's explicit championing of rural voters, combined with McKinley's protectionism, served to bring urban and industrial voters into the Republican fold. Thus, the realignment begun in 1894 was strengthened in 1896. Moreover, McKinley's enormous postwar popularity earned his party further victories in 1898 and 1900, cementing a party realignment that would hold for the better part of the following three decades.[23]

The election was generally perceived as a choice between the radical, perhaps revolutionary, pursuit of economic justice, on the one hand, and stability, order, and calm on the other. The then-fantastic sums of money accumulated and spent on McKinley's campaign by Hanna did much to aid the Republicans' cause and also served notice as to whose interests the party served. But the election was won to a considerable degree on the strength of McKinley himself: he was very early the party's nominee because his personality and reputation embodied the virtues that the Republican organization hoped to project to the electorate. A genial, stable man, McKinley conveyed a calming image that reassured voters that he could be trusted to look after their best interests. The conservative Ohioan was patriotic and morally upright, he listened to those around him (and rarely spoke himself), and he was straightforward in his support of policies that benefited big business.[24] There was no mystery to the man, and little threat that he would rock any boats. Though of humble, working-class origins, moreover, the candidate's positions on economic matters were considered acceptable to business interests: his common touch and belief that he really was standing up for the best interests of the average American thus made him the perfect front man for the trusts.

McKinley's nationalism was to some degree rooted in his personality, which was marked by a desire for harmony.[25] Unlike his opponent, McKinley was not known to enjoy getting in the trenches or engaging in aggressive debates. Rather, he saw the presidency as a platform for achieving national consensus.[26] To be sure, McKinley espoused a traditionalist construction of American nationalism. He was concerned as president to uphold the nation's conservative traditions and ideals, and he worked to maintain consistency between what he considered to be the nation's defining values and the ephemeral interests of his contemporaries. Thus he defined America's political and religious heritage (particularly Protestant moralism and democratic individualism) both as forming the foundation of American national identity and as providing the touchstone for policy making. But McKinley was never really the "President of the whole people," as he once claimed.[27] African Americans and other racial minorities surely felt left out of his nation, and if the poor believed that he acted on their behalf, they were sadly mistaken. Government programs and regulations to improve the poor's abysmal working and living conditions were never seriously entertained during his administration. Still, McKinley truly believed that he spoke and acted for all the people–past, present, and future–and for the most part the people, in turn, believed him.

McKinley successfully represented himself as a symbol or embodiment of the nation in part because his political instinct, his ability to read and connect with men, both individually and in crowds, led him intuitively to say and do all the subtle things that would inspire their confidence. Representative Joe Cannon (R-Ill.) captured this quality well when he said, "The President's ear was so close to the ground it was full of grasshoppers."[28] McKinley's behavior during the war, and later in determining the conditions of its settlement, revealed a leadership style of assessing the public mood and then capturing it and directing it to his preferred outcome–of getting what he wanted, but giving the people what they thought they, too, wanted. The president, in other words, was a conformist who yet also knew how to manage people and bend them to his will. As a young Charles G. Dawes noted with admiration, "The President as always, remains the firm, cool, able leader of men."[29] Noting that McKinley believed that public opinion "was a proper yardstick of leadership," one biographer wrote that, "He had a splendid eye for a bandwagon and never mounted one until he was sure of its direction."[30] President McKinley was by all accounts an excellent orator, if not in the same league as Bryan, and he often used his speeches to sound out public opinion on issues. He would repeat the same themes over and over, tweaking them here and there, adding new phrases and dropping others depending on their applause value, until he discovered both what the public wanted and also how to frame his own policy preferences in the language most congenial to his audience—two goals that often seemed to meet halfway.

In the speeches that McKinley made as president, therefore, one can find a template of the 1890s American cultural lexicon. He regularly invoked the themes "duty" and "destiny," for example, in part because those words were easy on Americans' ears. They fit the image of the United States that Americans liked to maintain for themselves of being a noble and virtuous people, and they rendered intelligible the unprecedented issues, such as humanitarian crusades and colonial expansionism, that the country grappled with during his tenure. McKinley was able to reassure the American people that the nation's policies conformed to their most deeply held values because he mastered the language that bridged the nation's actions with its ideals.[31] Much of the imagery that McKinley evoked centered on the flag, and much of it was Christian, and as a spokesperson for either set of ideals, patriotic or religious, McKinley was especially persuasive because he spoke from conviction.

When elected in 1896, for example, McKinley declared in his inaugural address: "Our faith teaches that there is no safer reliance than upon the God of our fathers, who has so singularly favored the American people in every national trial, and who will not forsake us so long as we obey His commandments and walk humbly in His footsteps."[32] This civil-religious rhetoric, however, expressed not only the usual inaugural-address platitudinizing but also the president's sincere and earnest piety, which had earned him a national reputation for integrity and unimpeachable character.[33] McKinley's public religiosity reflected a lifetime of religious commitment that began in his early childhood. His mother had maintained the Methodist church in his hometown of Niles, Ohio, which in the 1840s and 1850s, when he was growing up, was sufficiently rural that it received ministration not from a regular parish clergyman but from circuit riders—itinerant preachers who roamed the countryside on horseback to reach isolated Americans too scattered to support an ordained ministry locally.[34] In effect, therefore, day-to-day, Nancy Allison McKinley *was* the Methodist church in Niles, and she imparted to her doting son her deep piety.[35] The president's religious scruples, like his nationalism and political instinct, informed his leadership style. Simply put, McKinley believed, both as a private individual and as the leader of the country, that America's was a Christian civilization, whose citizens should celebrate not only its religious freedom but also its enjoyment of providential favor.

A speech that he gave in 1898 on Washington's Birthday at the University of Pennsylvania is revealing of McKinley's civil-religious beliefs. In his speech commemorating the leadership of the first president, McKinley declared:

> At the very height of his success and reward . . . he did not forget that his first official act as President should be fervent supplication to the Almighty Being who rules the universe. It is He who presides in the councils of nations and whose providential aid can supply every human defect. It is His benediction which we most want and which can and will consecrate the liberties and happiness of the people of the United States.

McKinley went on to note how Washington, "assuming that he but voiced the sentiment of the young nation in thus making faith in Almighty God and reliance upon His favor and care one of the strong foundations of the Government," proceeded to lay out the nation's civil religion in his first inaugural address. McKinley then drew for his audience this lesson:

> Not alone upon days of thanksgiving or in times of trial should we as a people remember and follow the example thus set by the fathers, but never in our future as a nation should we forget the great moral and religious principles which they enunciated and defended as their most precious heritage. In an age of great activity, of industrial and commercial strife and of perplexing problems, we should never abandon the simple faith in Almighty God as recognized in the name of the American people by Washington and the First Congress. . . . With education and morality in their homes, loyalty to the underlying principles of free government in their hearts, and law and justice fostered and exemplified by those intrusted [sic] with public administration, we will continue to enjoy the respect of mankind and the gracious favor of Almighty God. The priceless opportunity is ours to demonstrate anew the enduring triumph of American civilization and to help in the progress and prosperity of the land we love.[36]

In his Washington's Day speech, McKinley laid bare his civil-religious beliefs. When he framed his policy proposals with language appealing to Providence and national destiny, therefore, he spoke from the common religio-cultural ground that he shared with the people who elected him.

Despite his appealing religiosity and nationalism, however, President McKinley rapidly squandered his political capital with the people over the course of his first year in office. He had underestimated both their desire to fight a war and their congressional representatives' willingness to force the issue. As bellicose as the national mood had become by the time he took office, however, McKinley was almost equally devoted to keep the nation out of a war, for four main reasons.

First, he had a strong, sincere aversion to the suffering and destruction caused by war, and a profound discomfort with the prospect of being responsible for war's evils being visited upon the American people during his stewardship of the country. As he confided to Leonard Wood, Theodore Roosevelt's commanding officer in Cuba and the military governor there after the war, "I shall not get into a war until I am sure that God and man approve. I have been through one war; I have seen the dead piled up; and I do not want to see another."[37] The "one war" to which McKinley referred was the Civil War, where the young volunteer had distinguished himself with bravery and risen through the ranks to that of major (Major McKinley became his informal sobriquet). He had fought in many of the war's bloodiest battles, including Antietam, and harbored no romantic illusions about what war meant to its participants.[38]

Second, McKinley resisted the pressure on him to declare war because the country's army was logistically unable to wage an effective campaign, and its navy needed more ships and equipment. The United States had no standing army to speak of: the regular troops who fought in the Indian Wars were minuscule in number and grossly inadequate to fight against even a weak state like Spain. While most Americans were confident that they would be able to defeat Spain if a war came, they mistakenly believed that Spanish forces, particularly the Spanish navy, were capable of inflicting great damage on the United States. The almost complete lack of any coastal defenses was therefore deeply troubling.[39] These were not auspicious conditions for hastily embarking on an armed crusade. The president's difficulties were compounded as it became apparent that the secretary of war, Russell A. Alger, whom McKinley had appointed for political reasons,[40] proved incapable of rising to the challenge of preparing the nation for war, and his name became a synonym for ineptitude: *Algerism.*[41]

The third reason for McKinley's resisting the hawks was the economy. McKinley's background was in domestic policy—his specialty had been economic policy—and he wanted to devote his time to restoring the nation's fragile economy.[42] A war would unsettle American life and undermine the president's quest to stabilize the economy. Many business leaders stood against the war movement to the bitter end and came to be seen by the jingoes as unpatriotic and worse. The stock market would drop whenever it seemed that war was inevitable; it would rise again after McKinley signaled otherwise.[43] There was good reason to believe that a war would undo all of the economic progress that the president accomplished during his first year in office.

Finally, McKinley's strategy of delay was based on his long-term vision for the country. He kept an eye on his historical legacy, and it was not immediately clear to him how a war with Spain would appear to future generations. The president did not want the war to emerge from and encompass only transient passions; he wanted to be sure that it conformed in meaning and purpose to the enduring values and interests of the country. As he told his private secretary and confidante, George B. Cortelyou, in exasperation over the public's rashness, "The country should understand that we are striving to make our course consistent not alone for today, but for all time."[44] Just as McKinley's pacifism reflected his personal religious values, and his economic worries demonstrated his basic agreement with the values and interests of the business community, this attitude was in keeping with his nationalism.

In his first year in office, McKinley thus resisted the rising public pressure to start a war against Spain on behalf of the Cubans. He wanted to keep his options open and find a peaceful solution to the Cuban crisis if possible. His initial actions thus reflect this conservatism, and the earliest one of significance was to propose a congressional appropriation of $50,000 in May 1897 to ameliorate the condition of American citizens on the island.[45] Congress immediately acquiesced unanimously, pleased that a president was taking concrete steps toward dealing with the situation.[46] McKinley also protested formally to Spain about the horrors of the reconcentration camps.[47] The real momentum toward war, however, remained in the legislature; the president's first year in office dealing with Cuban affairs was devoted primarily to pursuing, fruitlessly, a peaceful diplomatic solution with Spain.

McKinley's first State of the Union address, for instance, counseled peace. After offering thanks to Providence because "Peace and goodwill with all the nations of the earth remains unbroken," McKinley embarked in the address on an extended recitation of the Cuban situation, including the by-then-customary accusation that Spain had committed crimes against humanity and civilization in Cuba. Still, he urged caution on the legislature, because a new government was in power in Madrid. Prime Minister Cánovas had been assassinated by an Italian anarchist on August 8, 1897, and the Liberals, headed by Sagasta, were much more willing to compromise with both the Cubans and the Americans than their Conservative predecessors had been. McKinley did hint, however, as Cleveland had the year before, that American patience had its limits: "If it shall hereafter appear to be a duty imposed by our obligations to ourselves, to civilization and humanity to intervene with force, it shall be without fault on our part and only because the necessity for such action will be so clear as to command the support and approval of the civilized world."[48]

While Spain breathed a sigh of relief that the message was not more belligerent,[49] some members of Congress (mostly members of the opposition parties) immediately pressed ahead with their call to recognize the independence of Cuba, despite the president's explicit refusal to do so in his address. Populist Senator William V. Allen gave a speech two days after McKinley's that captured the sentiments of those pushing for war: "The American people believe in political and religious liberty, and they are anxious to accord to others what they esteem the birthright of all, and I am confident they will not be content with the course advised by [the president]." After suggesting that the Republican president's reserve in dealing the crisis was a result of "cold and merciless commercialism" (i.e., pressure from the business interests), the Nebraska senator laid out the principles animating his position on the subject: "I am a believer in human freedom. I do not believe God ever created one man to be the bondslave or victim of another. The right of freedom is as universal as the human race, and wherever the rays of the sun shine they should fall on freemen, regardless of color or condition."[50] The president, however, preferred to pursue avenues other than military action.

Among the more unusual schemes that were devised to prevent war was a plan to buy Cuba from Spain. Financier John J. McCook had organized a Wall Street syndicate that offered to pay a large chunk of Spain's 400 million peso national debt,[51] most of which grew out of the country's efforts to suppress the Cuban rebellion, in return for Cuban independence—with the syndicate receiving for its efforts $150 million worth of interest-bearing bonds secured by customs revenues from the island. In effect, the syndicate would control the international trade of an otherwise "independent" Cuba. The Cuban government-in-exile, the Junta (with whom McCook had close ties), endorsed the plan, and McKinley, too, privately gave his tacit approval. Spain, however, stoutly refused to sell off its honor, and the scheme fell apart.[52]

With the pressure to declare war growing, McKinley decided to explain some of his reasons for standing pat in an interview with the *Pittsburgh Dispatch* in March 1898. McKinley stressed that his patience with Spain was rapidly running out, but he would not, he said, lead the nation into a war that grew out of national emotionalism. At the time of the interview, the nation had seemed ready to explode with war fever, and the longer the president resisted, the deeper his popularity plummeted. The president was engaged in last-ditch diplomacy with Spain in a desperate effort to keep the peace, but he was also trying to hasten the massive mobilization already under way that would allow the country to fight the war if in fact it came. In the interview, McKinley called the United States "the arbiter of its own destiny" whose "march of progress has not been stayed," and he noted that "[i]t is the inherent duty of every people to maintain peace with others as long as reason, as judgment, as honor permit." He went on, however, "But if there comes a time when all these demand action . . . we must then answer the call of duty."[53]

While McKinley was struggling to maintain the peace, congressional rhetoric against his inaction continued to heat up. Senator Frank J. Cannon (R-Utah) charged, "In the rush and hurry of events . . . we are likely to lose sight of the one significant fact, which has existed from the beginning and which now exists, that the President of the United States can by a pen stroke stop the barbarities in Cuba, free the people there, and relieve the island from the burden which it sustains."[54] He then proposed a resolution demanding that Spain recognize Cuban independence. If Spain refused, then the United States (i.e., the U.S. Congress) would on that date recognize the belligerence of the rebels, and ninety days thereafter it would recognize Cuban independence. The resolution passed.

Recognizing that McKinley, in persistently refusing to take meaningful action regarding Cuba, was forcing many in his party to take a stand contrary to the manifest will of the people, Democrats and Populists in the legislature sought to convert the Cuban crisis into a referendum on the respective fiscal policies of the different parties. The clearest example showing that the members of the minority parties in the House sought to use the Cuban issue to malign the economic philosophy of the Republicans came on April 12, when Representative Charles S. Hartman (Silver Republican-Mont.) read a mock "platform of the Republican party in 1900." The "platform" focused almost exclusively on bimetallism, which had dominated the presidential campaign of 1896, but when it did touch briefly on Cuba its harsh tone was enough to earn admonishment even from some inveterate McKinley bashers. The platform's inflammatory section on Cuba showed clearly how the minority parties correlated the administration's fiscal and Cuban policies:

> While our great and good commander [McKinley] informs us that we were sorely shocked and grieved by the barbarities perpetrated by the Spanish soldiers against the Cuban patriots in their struggle for liberty, resulting in the butchery or starvation of hundreds of thousands of men, women, and children, yet he gives us the comforting assurance by way of complete exoneration of his Administration for permitting the long continuance of these atrocities, that the victims were nearly all from the poorer classes, and it is doubtful if this depletion of their ranks is seriously to be regretted.
>
> Our affectionate master further comforts us with the knowledge that by refraining from prohibiting the slaughter and starvation of these thousands of poverty-stricken wretches he preserved from severe shock the refined and tender sensibilities of the very best and noblest class of the citizens of the world—the holders of Spanish bonds. . . .

We therefore congratulate our greatly cherished commander upon the wise, generous, and humane policy applied to the Cuban troubles which found its warrant in the sacred motto of the party, "Money the master, everything else the servant."[55]

As this "platform" illustrates, differences between the parties' economic philosophies had attained the status of moral argument. Republicans, the minority parties argued, were capable of committing or countenancing any kind of evil action as long as the wealthy classes benefited financially from it. Certainly, they reasoned, the fiscal policies enacted by McKinley and the Republicans inflicted grievous injustices upon America's own poor, which was evidence enough of the Republicans' callous indifference to the underprivileged everywhere. According to the Populists' presentation of Republican beliefs, policies that contravened the economic interests of the wealthy were both invalid and immoral. Democrats and Populists insisted by contrast that all evil shared the same root—greed, and greed was headquartered on Wall Street. Republicans were ineffective in their efforts to counteract these arguments, in part because they knew that McKinley really did fear the effects that a war would have on the economy, but mostly because they shared the impatience of those on the other side of the aisle with the president's foot-dragging and were not always interested in defending it.

Nevertheless, McKinley was not totally alone; many Republicans did in fact defend their leader. Senator Stephen B. Elkins (R-W.Va.), for example, lauded the president's forbearance:

This is a time of serious concern—a supreme moment in the life and affairs of this nation. We are making history rapidly, but are we making [it] wisely? We are in danger not from foreign foes. These we can conquer. We are in danger from ourselves, from passion, from teaching a lesson, establishing a precedent, that may be used some day against us, and doing an act that will not have the approval of the national conscience nor the sanction of the civilized world. A great Republic can not afford to make such a record. Conscious of our great strength, we should be patient, temperate, just, and fair in all our dealings with the peoples and nations of the world.[56]

Elkins made his speech in support of the war, but he wanted to emphasize that McKinley's maligned behavior was a product of responsible statesmanship, not dubious, unpatriotic motives.

Occasionally a member also indirectly defended McKinley by advocating peace in what surely was the height of political courage. Representative John W. Maddox (D-Ga.), for example, presented an analysis of the Cuban situation that reflected the bitterness of a Southern Democrat still stinging from the memory of Reconstruction: "Sympathy for others will not justify us in hazarding the lives of thousands of American citizens and plunging this nation into war," he began. "Gentlemen who are crying aloud for war on account of the cruelties practiced by Spain on the peaceable citizens of Cuba would do well to read the history of their own country, and especially that of the late Civil War, and you will find out that other people as well as the Spaniards have resorted to methods to accomplish their purposes when their passions are aroused that were not at all creditable to a civilized nation."[57]

Senator George L. Wellington (R-Md.) also opposed the war, in part because he did not share his fellow countrymen's romantic perception of the rebels:

> The insurgents began a system of war as cannot be justified by the Christian civilization of this era. . . . They began, as would outlaws and bandits, a system of guerilla warfare, a series of bushwhacking attacks. . . . The insurgent bands, by their incursions upon neutral territory and cultivated zones of the island, began the burning of houses, the destruction of plantations, the plunder of villages, and murder of inhabitants. . . . Both parties in this contest have transgressed the laws of God and nations. . . . I have a solemn, firm and fixed conviction . . . that to precipitate the American people into war with Spain at this time would be a crime against Christian civilization, justice, and right.[58]

As a factual matter, Senator Wellington was correct to assess some blame to the rebels for the conditions on Cuba, as most members well knew, but he was almost alone in considering that information, since it did not add to the country's Manichean understanding of the conflict as one pitting evil Spaniards against noble Cubans.[59] A very few other lonely men did oppose the mad rush to war, but the rest of the legislators were itchingly restless to hear McKinley deliver a war message that would initiate the inevitable.

The president's reputation as a popular leader continued to slide as a result of his resistance to the jingoist forces. The vitriol directed at him from the Congress was mild in comparison to the public's expressions of impatience. As McKinley biographer H. Wayne Morgan wrote, "In Virginia a raging mob burned twin effigies of McKinley and Hanna. McKinley's picture was hissed in theaters and torn from walls in some cities."[60] Crowds chanted in the streets, "Remember the *Maine!* To Hell with Spain!"[61] For McKinley, a leader whose long public career had always been characterized by a natural affinity with those whom he represented, peace began to lose its appeal.

Ultimately, then, it was the politician in McKinley that dictated his decision to surrender to the pressure, and he finally delivered his war message on April 11, 1898. A common perception among historians is that the president gave in to the will of Congress, and this assessment is accurate. Nonetheless, McKinley had stood fast against a massive surge for war for two weeks (once the *Maine* report was issued on March 28, it was almost impossible to avoid war)—and he could have sent a war message to Congress at least two months sooner. While a handful of congressmen opposed the war to the end, the nation's war fever in 1898 would have swept away almost any leader in McKinley's position. Historian David Trask cites evidence that McKinley acted only when it appeared clear to him that the Senate would declare war without him and that he would thereby lose any power to shape the course of events.[62] In addition, the president risked losing control of his party, who in turn would become vulnerable to a Democratic takeover in that year's congressional elections.[63] The time for presidential leadership in this dramatic affair was at hand. Even with such powerful motivation, however, McKinley's war message was far more tepid than its public and congressional audiences had hoped for.

THE WAR MESSAGE

McKinley painstakingly detailed in the war address the conditions in Cuba that provoked the sympathy and indignation of the United States, the costs and consequences of those conditions for the United States, and the reasons why they were sufficient to justify war.[64] His purposes were to frame the country's actions in such a way that would compel later generations to agree that intervention was warranted and to establish that the United States should act unilaterally in the matter, with the president in charge. The president began his address cautiously, remarking that "the course which it is now incumbent upon the nation to adopt must . . . accord with the precepts laid down by the founders of the Republic." McKinley then assessed the costs to American business incurred by the Cuban revolution, including losses in trade and capital investment, before moving on to a lengthy description of the reconcentration camps—"a new and inhuman phase happily unprecedented in the modern history of civilized Christian peoples." He noted that the "present revolution has . . . by the exercise of cruel, barbarous, and uncivilized practices of warfare, shocked the sensibilities and offended the humane sympathies of our people"; continuance of the conflict was intolerable, but no possibility of the parties ending it themselves was in sight. It was therefore, he claimed, his "duty . . . to seek to bring about an immediate termination to the war."[65]

Two possible courses of action were available: recognition of the Cuban rebels, which would free up the United States to send to them material aid, and intervention by the United States itself to impose its own peace. McKinley preferred the latter course and explicitly rejected extending recognition to a Cuban republic, a controversial decision that generated significant congressional debate. Nonrecognition afforded the president flexibility for the future and kept the United States in control of the situation. McKinley was also skeptical of the Cubans' ability to maintain a stable regime. If the United States was going to intervene, in other words, it would do so unilaterally, for its own reasons.

McKinley offered four arguments to justify U.S. intervention. The first was the humanitarian reason: "In the cause of humanity and to put an end to the barbarities, bloodshed, starvation, and horrible miseries now existing there, and which the parties to the conflict are either unable or unwilling to stop or mitigate. It is no answer to say that this is all in another country, belonging to another nation, and is therefore none of our business. It is specially our duty, for it is right at our door." The other three reasons conformed more closely with traditional constructions of the national interest: to protect American citizens in Cuba, to protect American trade, and to put an end to "the present condition of affairs in Cuba [that] is a constant menace to our peace, and entails upon this government an enormous expense." McKinley then noted how the conditions to which he referred led to the sinking of the *Maine*. He did not accuse Spain of actually sinking the battleship ("That remains to be fixed") but noted simply that the event dramatically illustrated how Americans could not feel safe in their persons or property in or around Cuba. The situation was intolerable. "In the name of humanity, in the name of civilization, in behalf of endangered American interests which give us the right and duty to speak and to act, the war in Cuba must stop."[66]

McKinley concluded the address by asking the Congress "to authorize and empower" him "to take measures to secure a full and final termination of hostilities between the Government of Spain and the people of Cuba, to secure in the island the establishment of a stable government, capable of maintaining order and observing its international obligations, insuring peace and tranquility and the security of its citizens as well as our own, and to use the military and naval forces of the United States as may be necessary for these purposes."[67] In summary, the president's plan was for the United States to use its developing military might to invade Cuba and rebuild it in America's image ("secure in the island the establishment of a stable government"), and he asked his legislative cohorts to draft a resolution that would make this course effective and legal.

Senator Henry Cabot Lodge (R-Mass.) described the Senate's reception of the message: "The reading of the message was listened to with intense interest and in profound silence, broken only by a wave of applause when the sentence was read which said, 'In the name of humanity . . .'"[68] Lodge implied that that was the only well received line in the entire speech, an observation shared by others. As journalist Henry Watterson noted, "The war party in Congress was in an overwhelming majority, and to this majority the message of the President proved a disappointment."[69] Almost immediately after the text was read, Senator Marion Butler, the North Carolina Populist, stood to announce, "I am greatly disappointed, to say the least, at the message of the President which has just been read. . . . The message does not mean the independence of Cuba."[70]

If congressional speakers evaluated the message on the whole unfavorably, however, they were receptive to its invitation to action. For two days, the committees of both houses that dealt with foreign relations met to prepare their respective versions of the joint resolution that would put the president's directives into effect and to polish accompanying reports that outlined *their* understanding of the motivations and purposes of the expected war. In the meantime, a few members, such as Butler, fired the opening salvos of the partisan battle that was developing. The Democrats and Populists wanted independence for Cuba (as did many Republicans), and they argued that the president refused to extend it for much the same reason that he had delayed delivering the war message: he was listening to the business interests, who presumably wanted to annex the island. Butler was explicit on this point:

> If there is anyone who for political advantage could for a moment take pleasure in seeing the Administration take such a course that would bring humiliation upon our nation . . . then I have no more respect for that person than I have for the stock jobbers and bond shylocks who like vultures have been hovering around the White House and who are trying to put their fingers into this grave situation and make merchandise out of the bones of our murdered sailors and the tarnished honor of the nation. . . . Every civilized nation and all Christian people would be bound to uphold our hands and approve our conduct if we were to use our Army and Navy to drive every Spanish vessel from the sea and lay waste to her towns and cities to avenge that most foul crime [the sinking of the *Maine*]. We have a chance, however, to force atonement for that crime on a plane higher than justifiable revenge. We have an opportunity to avenge it in the interest of humanity and liberty.[71]

The way to raise the nation's actions to that "higher plane," Butler argued, was to recognize Cuban independence.

The goal of recognition had been supported in several resolutions passed in Congress over the preceding three years, often by substantial majorities. The president could easily have recognized the insurrectionists, and the Congress would immediately and overwhelmingly have joined him. But all of the important elements of McKinley's message showed that he wanted the war to be fought on *his* terms. First, he had been extremely careful to explain America's reasons for intervening not only by reference to humanitarianism but also by invoking arguments grounded in America's economic interests. Congressional speeches had clamored on vengefully about the sinking of the *Maine*, but otherwise the legislators seemed unconcerned about justifying their desire to fight Spain on any but moral grounds. McKinley, by contrast, provided only one moral argument for the war–the first and thus the most important one, to be sure–but had given three reasons that had nothing to do with the suffering Cuban people and everything to do with *America's* suffering (business) people. A president who was merely doing Congress's bidding would have come up with a different set of rationales for intervening in Cuba.

There is little doubt that the president shared the humanitarian sympathies of his congressional peers. The great majority of his message, after all, had been devoted to describing Spain's fantastic oppression of the Cuban population and the infamous consequences of Spanish misrule. Rather than concluding that the Cuban insurgents should be recognized as constituting an independent international entity, however, he argued that the situation in Cuba demonstrated only that Spanish sovereignty on the island must end. To truly "fix" the problems on the island would require Americans to institute a form of government that would ensure the stable implementation of justice; that is, a form of government like their own. The United States must remain free to act as it saw fit, in other words, and pursue *its* goals, not those of the Cubans. The independence of the revolutionaries was irrelevant to McKinley's purposes, a position that touched off a major debate over the wording of the joint resolution that would set the nation on the road to war.[72]

The Senate Committee on Foreign Relations initiated the formal debate about the terms that would define America's motives in the Spanish-American War on April 13, when it presented to the full Senate a joint resolution and an accompanying report detailing why the United States meant to force Spain's withdrawal from Cuba. The introduction to the resolution explained that the United States was preparing to intervene in Cuba because "the abhorrent conditions which have existed for more than three years in the island of Cuba, so near our own borders, have shocked the moral conscience of the people of the United States, have been a disgrace to Christian civilization, culminating, as they have, in the destruction of a United States battle ship . . . and can not longer be endured." The resolution proposed as a response to these conditions three directives: first, "That the people of the Island of Cuba are, and of right ought to be, free and independent"; second, that "it is the duty of the United States to demand" that Spain leave Cuba; and third, that the president "is directed and empowered" to use the nation's military force to carry into effect the terms of the resolution.[73]

A report clarifying the U.S. motives accompanied the resolution; it discussed the importance of recognizing the independence of the Cuban people—but not that of the rebel government—and it appealed to international law and to the norms regulating international relations for legitimation. According to the report's authors, Spain no longer possessed legitimate sovereignty over Cuba because it was both morally and administratively incapable of ruling. It described the sinking of the *Maine*, for example, as part of a "unity of events" in Cuba that stemmed from "the duplicity, perfidy, and cruelty of the Spanish character," which was ultimately responsible for all the evils that were then visiting the island.[74] Since sovereignty implies a moral fitness to rule, Spain had forfeited its right to that power as a result of its depraved treatment of the Cubans:

> When publicists and jurists speak of the right of sovereignty of a parent state over a people or a colony they mean that divinely delegated supremacy in the exercise of which man should show "likest God." They never mean that a usurpation of diabolism shall be sanctified upon the plea that it is sovereignty none the less than that of a well-ordered and humane government. Against such reasoning the—
> "Moral laws
> "Of nature and of nations speak aloud;"
> and declare that the State which thus perverts and abuses its power thereby forfeits its sovereignty.[75]

This construction of the legitimacy of colonial rule was meant to validate American intervention in Cuba on moral grounds. In other words, it allowed the United States to define its moral outrage as being a sufficient cause, under international law, to justify replacing Spanish sovereignty with a more morally acceptable sovereignty.[76]

Not wishing to rely exclusively on such novel and uncertain legal "authority," however, the report also provided a political basis for American intervention: the Monroe Doctrine, "which is based distinctly upon the assertion of an intention to intervene [in the internal affairs of America's neighbors] under certain circumstances." Comparing the doctrine to the European balance-of-power system, the report continued: "Each is a distinct and arbitrary policy of intervention, to be effected in certain contingencies in furtherance of national policies, and to justify which no canon of international law was ever invoked." Still, the report's authors deemed it prudent to soften the Monroe Doctrine's naked assertion of power with a moral argument:

> Justification for intervention is strengthened in such cases as the present, where the oppressions by a state of its subjects have been so inveterate, atrocious and sanguinary as to require intervention by other nations in the interests of humanity and the peace of the world, for the purpose of overthrowing that government and establishing or recognizing another in its place as the only means of extirpating an otherwise incurable and dangerous evil.[77]

The message of the committee report, in short, was that the United States was going to intervene in Cuba because Spain did not exercise its sovereignty over the island in a manner acceptable to the United States, which had the power and self-bestowed authority to adjudge what constituted proper governorship. Its assertion that the United States possessed such authority set the stage for Theodore Roosevelt's Corollary to the Monroe Doctrine, which he announced in 1904.[78] The report, however, was not simply a discussion of the principles of American foreign policy but a proposal for action.

Its underlying sentiment was a restless moralism seeking to end a nation's frustration with its formal impotence, and this adolescent nationalism found support during the speeches that followed. Senator William Lindsay (D-Ky.) declared, for example, "The duty of the United States, as the sovereign power on this side of the Atlantic, to interpose its fiat as the law of the occasion in favor of Cuban independence, is as clear to the minds of the peace-loving American people as the duty . . . to extend aid to any American colony struggling to free itself from European oppression."[79] Senator John L. Wilson (R-Wash.) added: "I am not versed in—nor do I care for—academic discussions of so-called international law. Divesting it of all subtleties and applying the principles of a sound common sense to this question, it must be acknowledged that the United States has some ground of complaint against Spain. . . . Mr. President, it is respect and honor for our flag and the principles it stands for that has made this country one of the great nations of the earth."[80] Wilson's point was clear to his colleagues: the United States could and should justify its actions by reference to its own traditions and values, not those of the international community.

But the committee report did not speak for a unanimous majority. Immediately after it was read, a minority report was presented to the Senate that urged "the immediate recognition of the Republic of Cuba, as organized in that island, as a free, independent, and sovereign power among the nations of the world." In addition to three Democrats—John W. Daniel (D-Va.), Roger Q. Mills (D-Tex.), and David Turpie (D-Ind.)—a Republican rival of McKinley's, Ohio's Joseph B. Foraker, signed onto the minority report. This splinter group recommended that the resolution under consideration include the phrase "And that the Government of the United States hereby recognizes the Republic of Cuba as the true and lawful government of that island."[81] Senator Foraker explained the minority's reason for disagreement: "If a people be free and independent, as we have in this first proposition declared that the people of Cuba are, they, and they alone, have the power to establish their government. Independence and sovereignty go hand in hand . . . and it is a denial of independence to . . . reserve the right and the power to establish for that independent people a government such as in our judgment and opinion may be stable."[82]

The battle lines were thus drawn in the Senate: who should create the sovereign government that would replace Spain's in Cuba (assuming Spain was ousted from Cuba, an outcome that was never questioned)—the people of Cuba or the United States? Embedded in this question were issues relating to the nature of self-government, which in turn implicated the nature of America's mission in the world. If, as the majority held, the United States needed to guarantee for Cuba a just form of government, then that implied as a general rule that the United States was a necessary agent by which other countries were to achieve self-government. If, on the other hand, the minority was correct, then no country could in principle serve as an intermediary for the act of achieving true independence. America's mission in the world, in the minority's analysis, was to serve only as an exemplar to the Cubans. Recognition of a Cuban Republic was a backdoor means of addressing this fundamental issue.

There were other, related reasons why complete unanimity was lacking. The deep mistrust that Democrats and Populists held for McKinley's economic motives in Cuba was central to their support of the minority report: if the goal of the Republicans was simply to conquer a foreign market, then the idea of American mission would not be served, and in fact would be undermined by the proposed intervention. Furthermore, some questioned whether the Cubans were racially fit to govern themselves, which rendered suspect the wisdom of the United States committing itself to the goal of Cuban democracy. It might therefore be best simply to remove Spain from Cuba and then leave the island's population to its own devices. Republicans argued, on the other hand, that the United States was intervening in Cuba in order to fix a broken system, and removing Spain from the situation would not go far enough to achieve the goal of justice. The exchanges were really about expansionism, not recognition. Anticipating the treaty debate that followed the war, many legislators were concerned to make clear that the United States would not annex of Cuba and thereby sully the nobility of a dramatic humanitarian mission.[83] But despite this dispute, there was a general consensus. After all, whether or not the United States recognized the existence of an independent Cuban Republic in April 1898, it was going to use military force in order to eliminate a morally repugnant and unjust regime. As Senator Redfield Proctor (R-Vt.) put it, "The resolutions differ in policy more than in principle."[84] Nevertheless, a robust exchange began between the supporters of the minority and majority resolutions.

Senator Foraker's speech defending the creation of a minority report, for example, detailed war aims that in their lofty vagueness were no different than those given by members of the majority. Successful U.S. intervention, he announced, would mean "a victory, Mr. President, for civilization over barbarism; a victory for the right and capacity of man to govern himself; a victory for the Western Hemisphere; a victory for Cuba; a victory for freedom and independence; a victory worthy of the heroic men who achieved our own independence, and worthy of the successors of those heroic men who have since preserved and perpetuated our priceless heritage."[85] A victory, in other words, for American values and for the idea of American mission.

The majority spokesman designated to rebut Senator Foraker and his cohorts was well chosen. Senator Henry Cabot Lodge was a man of broad (but racist) vision, and he was as impatient to get the war under way as were the Democrats and Populists. Lodge was pleased that war was coming because it gave the country an excuse, finally, to vastly augment its anemic military. The time for the United States to become a dominant world power was overripe, in Lodge's opinion, and if the United States took proper advantage of its opportunity in the present instance, it could at last establish its proper role of global leadership.[86] His view of the coming war with Spain was therefore expansive and deeply influenced by his Darwinian conception of international politics:

> Mr. President, we are not in this crisis by an accident. . . . We are face to face with Spain today in fulfillment of a great movement which has run through the centuries. . . . In our veins runs the blood of Holland and the blood of England. If after all the centuries it comes to us, much as we pray to avert it, to meet Spain face to face in war, it is because we are there in obedience to a greater movement than any man can hope to control. We are there because we represent the spirit of liberty and the spirit of the new time, and Spain is over against us because she is medieval, cruel, dying.[87]

As Lodge and Foraker, both Republicans, began the debate in the Senate over the wording of the joint resolution, a similar debate got under way in the House when Representative Hugh A. Dinsmore (D-Ark.) read a report prepared by the Democratic members of the House Committee on Foreign Relations. The minority report recommended the immediate recognition of a Republic of Cuba "because recognition is the plain, honest, courageous, manly course, and will remove from the minds of men any suspicion that we are preparing to wage a war of conquest and to annex the island from motives of sordid greed, or as the beginning of a policy of imperial aggrandizement."[88] Dinsmore was rebutted by Representative Robert Adams Jr. (R-Pa.), who explained that the majority's refusal to recognize a Cuban republic was based on Cuba's lacking the following: a stable government, power, capital, ships, and law-enforcement authority. Without these, there was no functioning government to recognize capable of performing its obligations under international law.[89]

The remainder of the officially recorded debate over the wording of the resolution took place in the Senate after House Speaker Thomas B. Reed (R-Maine) squelched floor discussion on the subject. The senators approached the wording of the joint resolution as providing them with a chance not only to argue about recognizing Cuba but also to record their broader views on the proposed intervention. Because they were convinced that they were crossing a new threshold in American history, the senators wanted to be sure that future generations understood the connection between their actions and American national identity. As Senator Julius C. Burrows (R-Mich.) solemnly declared, "At such an hour we owe it to ourselves, to posterity, and to mankind to make known the reasons which force us to this final arbitrament of the sword. For what we do at this hour will be finally tried not in the hot heat of the passions of today, but in the cooler judgment of tomorrow."[90] Senator Stephen M. White (D-Calif.) agreed: "We are here compelled to make history," he announced, "not vaingloriously to seek to transmit our names to posterity, but to write the record of a nation which we love beyond self, a record which we should so make that when we have passed away will shine bright and unchanging in the full radiance of the intellectuality and morality of enlightened men."[91] By demonstrating such earnestness, the senators revealed that they approached the issue much as McKinley had when he prepared his message—with a sense of history and a conviction that they were contributing significantly to the development of American national identity. As a result, the speeches read primarily as models of late-nineteenth-century American jingoism, replete with Darwinian assumptions and millennial aspirations.

The venerable Senator George F. Hoar (R-Mass.), for instance, in defending McKinley's course of action throughout the war agitation, noted approvingly that America's cause was supported by England, "that nation on earth which is alike the freest, the most powerful, and the most nearly allied to us by language, history, and blood." By contrast, Spain was "a fifth-rate, weak power, a relic of the Dark Ages." Since the conflict between the United States and Spain was seemingly fraught with larger historical meaning, therefore, it was necessary that it be fought in the proper spirit: "If in the providence of God this country is called upon to do a great act of international justice, let us do it in the spirit of justice, and not in the spirit of vengeance."[92] Hoar had opposed the war spirit, but he accommodated himself to the coming conflict by interpreting it as the culmination of broad historical forces that the president and the Senate should harness together.[93]

Others in the Senate agreed, and many expressed the certainty that God was on the side of the United States. Senator Turpie (D-Ind.), for instance, after declaring the moral necessity of recognizing Cuba (he was a signatory of the minority resolution), averred: "I shall have confidence that God in His providence will overrule these gigantic evils for the good of liberty and the welfare of mankind."[94] Senator George Gray (D-Del.) added, "We cannot forever keep our place and say we are not our brother's keeper. God Himself will hold us to responsibility if we continue to plead thus."[95] Senator Charles W. Fairbanks (R-Ind.), like Hoar an erstwhile opponent of the war, now regarded intervention to be "a duty divinely imposed." He argued that "we are morally bound to put an end to the wrongs, the outrages, the evils which flow from Spanish rule" because the Cubans, though "not of our race, it is true, [are] fellow-beings created in the image of our Maker" and Spain "has not fairly emerged from the night of the Middle Ages." The intervention in Fairbanks's view was reflective of American national identity: "It is instinctive with us to desire to see people who are oppressed freed from the oppressor and secured in the God-given, inalienable privileges of life, liberty, and the pursuit of happiness. . . . To the high and holy cause of humanity and the vindication of our national honor we dedicate the lives and fortune of the Republic."[96]

As the speeches continued, each speaker seemed determined to outdo the last in his characterization of the United States as a noble, divinely favored nation seeking to achieve a higher justice in Cuba. Senator Shelby M. Cullom (R-Ill.) called intervention "our duty to God and humanity, liberty and to ourselves" and "our plain duty as a Christian people."[97] Senator Edward O. Wolcott (R-Colo.) thundered to gallery-clearing applause:

> The war which is already upon us, whatever the phraseology of our resolutions, must be fought because it is the manifest destiny of this

Republic to stand forever upon the Western Hemisphere as a sentinel of liberty. It must come, because if we fail to listen to the voice of the suffering or the cry of the downtrodden upon this continent, we shall be untrue to those principles of liberty, humanity and Christianity upon which this country is founded as upon a rock.[98]

Providence was a recurring theme in the speeches, and references to the "God of Battles"[99] appeared frequently. Senator Joseph R. Hawley (R-Conn.) argued, for instance, "We claim to be at the head of the world in wisdom, freedom, law, the liberty of our Constitution, and our system in general. Evidently, Mr. President, we can not expect that we should drift through the world, being thus crowded along, you may say, by Divine Providence, to this magnificent position, without taking some of the responsibilities that naturally fall upon such a power and such a situation."[100] Senator Frank Cannon was particularly grandiloquent. After remarking that he favored "a holy peace" that could be reached only by passing through "the brazen gate of war," he offered the following assessment of America's situation:

> Mr. President, upon whose invitation are we entering Cuba now? . . . It is more than invitation; it is a command. It was uttered from the Mount, "Blessed are the peacemakers," and the United States, in obedience to that command, will enter Cuba against the protests of all the governments of the earth and make peace there forever. If we keep our motive pure and our purpose high, we will be sustained by Providence. We will vindicate ourselves to our consciences, to the wisdom and honor of the world, and to the day of judgment; and when the war shall have ended the United States will be able, I trust, to write a story of the deed in this one sentence: "The hand of God moved this country to destroy in Cuba the divine right of kings and establish there the diviner right of the people."[101]

The debate that provided the pretext for these speeches was still actively engaged, however. Senator James H. Berry (D-Ark.) wanted to recognize a Cuban republic immediately so that there would not "lurk in the minds of people both at home and abroad that we mean something more than we say"; that is, he wanted to make it clear that intervention would not take place "on account of any desire to acquire additional territory."[102] Senator Benjamin R. Tillman (D-S.C.), meanwhile, opposed the vindicationist version of the idea of American mission in no uncertain terms. He responded to McKinley's plan as follows:

> We propose to take Spain's place and become the policeman of the Western Continent and keep in order on that island the Latin races that have settled there. We cannot afford it. Duty demands that we expel the Spanish robbers and tyrants. There our duty ends. We cannot afford, Mr. President, to set up any government there. We cannot afford to do anything except to recognize the existing government and let them work out their own redemption, as the other Spanish Republics have had to do. They have had their revolutions and counter-revolutions. I do not believe the people of that race are capable of self-government.

He then made his position starkly unambiguous:

> I, for one, stand here and protest in the name of American freemen, in the name of decency, of Christianity, of fairness and justice and peace . . . against the adoption of any resolution, against the leaving out of any word which ought to go in to make it absolutely plain and clear and unmistakable that we do not intend to annex the island; and that we do not intend to interfere with their internal affairs, other than to expel Spain and enable the Cuban patriots to inaugurate, under their own auspices and under their own machinery, a government of the people, by the people, and for the people.[103]

The two issues conjoined in these speeches—the recognition of Cuban independence and the disavowal of any intent to annex the island—were disentangled at last by two crucial speeches. Senator John C. Spooner (R-Wisc.) made the first one, on the third wearying day of the resolution debate. Spooner had long opposed the war, was close to the president, and was an acknowledged expert in constitutional and international law. Senator Henry M. Teller (D-Colo.) made the second speech the following day, and his contribution came not in the form of expertise, but common sense.

Spooner noted that the power of recognition was a foreign policy responsibility delegated to the executive by the Constitution and that recognition by the United States would not in any event lead to Cuba's independence. His argument built on an analysis of the Declaration of Independence, which he characterized as "an enunciation of a high *purpose* by a people to be free. . . . That means that all men ought to be free and independent in fact, but it does not mean that all men are in fact free and independent." If that claim were true, he went on, then there would be no need for the United States to go into Cuba to help set the people free–they would be free and independent already. "Independence is a fact. It is not an expression of sympathy," he said. Coming to the crux of his argument, Spooner then reminded his colleagues that the Constitution gave to the executive branch the power to send and receive ministers and to negotiate treaties, acts constituting a form of recognition. Formal recognition of the existence of a foreign power was, in keeping with these powers and also with the president's role as commander-in-chief, an executive prerogative under settled constitutional doctrine.[104] Given the executive's exclusive power on this point, Spooner argued, the senators were essentially engaged in legislative navel-gazing since nothing could come of their debates either way. They should quit wasting their time and move on to subjects over which they had some power.

Teller, meanwhile, opened the door to compromise. In his speech he celebrated "American pluck" and "Anglo-Saxon vigor" and said that if any European power disagreed with U.S. supremacy in the Western Hemisphere, that was no matter, because the United States was too powerful to be swayed. For this he earned great applause. The main thrust of his speech, however, concerned the necessity of the United States not appearing to have any desire to annex Cuba.[105] Teller was far from alone in making this point, but he moved the discussion forward when he proposed an amendment to the resolution that held that the United States disclaimed "any disposition or intention to exercise jurisdiction or control over said island except for pacification thereof and a determination when that is accomplished to leave the government and control of the island to the people thereof."[106]

What Teller accomplished with this motion to amend the resolution was to allow the senators to debate annexation without having to deal with the sticky issue of recognition. His amendment was ignored when he introduced it, until Senator Cushman Davis (R-Minn.), the Republican chair of the Senate Foreign Relations Committee and a known expansionist, reintroduced it later that day in modified form. The joint resolution, now featuring the celebrated Teller Amendment, passed the Senate by a vote of 67 to 21. But forging a resolution that could enjoy bicameral as well as bipartisan support temporarily proved to be elusive. A joint "committee of conference on the disagreeing votes of the two Houses" issued a report on the progress of the deliberations between the House and Senate members that in its entirety read: "They have been unable to agree."

The committees then continued to haggle and argue, and tempers flared as the legislators acknowledged that they were tired and aggravated with each other. As fatigue overcame decorum, the debate even got nasty and explicitly partisan in the Senate. At last, after many negative votes on various versions of the resolution, the House approved, by a vote of 311–6, the exact language that had been accepted by the Senate many hours earlier.[107] The resolution passed, the president signed it, and Spain declared war. On April 25, 1898, the United States declared war in return, and the Spanish-American War was officially under way.

The president had seized control of the war movement with his message and subsequent backroom legislative maneuverings. McKinley's policy of nonrecognition demonstrated his belief that, if the United States was to rebuild the world in its own image, then it had to remain in control of the areas that it wanted to improve. His acceptance of the Teller Amendment to the joint resolution, which expressly disavowed any intent on the part of the United States to annex Cuba, showed that he did not regard explicit territorial expansion to be a necessary part of that mission. On the other hand, his refusal to countenance the independence of Cuba demonstrated clearly that he *did* consider the expansion of U.S. international power and influence to be a logical prerequisite to the realization of America's broader aims. The United States would no longer remain a mere exemplar of its values. Through the war resolution, with its distinctive combination of nonrecognition and nonannexationism, the president and legislature announced to the world that the United States was ready to start remaking the world in places that it thought it could and should, and in ways it deemed proper. Taking Spain out of Cuba would prove to be only the first of such actions.

CHAPTER FIVE

"American Greatness" in Popular Culture and Political Analysis

VICTORY IN THE Spanish-American War was swift and spectacular. No one had expected it to come as quickly or as easily as it did. Less than five hours after the shooting began on May 1, Spain's Pacific fleet was shattered. During that first day of fighting, the only U.S. casualties were eight wounded soldiers; no ships were lost. Spain, meanwhile, suffered 380 casualties and lost seven ships—its entire Asian fleet.[1] This auspicious inauguration of hostilities provided evidence to Americans that they had been correct to believe that Providence would favor their cause, and this conviction would only grow firmer after the war ended and the United States basked in victory.

Importantly, the war experience helped the North and South to overcome sectional prejudices that had lingered since the Civil War (or so it was believed in the brief spell of postwar euphoria),[2] and an inspired nation set about reinterpreting its mission. In fiction, plays, poems, and songs, Americans reveled in their excellence, because in the trials of war they found confirmation that theirs was the nation of progress—religiously, politically, and racially. America's thunderous triumph in 1898 validated the norms underlying this belief and added a new dimension: certitude that the nation had the power not only to protect its ideals within its sphere of influence but also to spread them around the world, if and when it saw fit to do so. Power, at last, was allied to progress.

Americans had entered the war with a smug assurance that God supported their cause and that victory would therefore be theirs. They often seemed to view the war more as a moral event than a violent one, with one author describing it, for instance, as "in itself an ennobling act."[3] To many Americans, in fact, the conflict barely registered as a war at all. For jingoes, it was easier to perceive it as a convergence of divine with American history, brimming with heroism and glory, than to recognize that like any war it was dirty and bloody, and in this case disease-ridden as well.[4] Many religious leaders had opposed the war during the early stages of the prewar agitation, but once it became clear that the nation was committed to fight, they took solace in the fact that the United States was, as they believed, the providential nation. For example, one New York Presbyterian preached:

> [W]e as a Nation lie close to His heart and His purposes, and those who love Him in reverent obedience, and who at the same time love their country in Christian patriotism, will become in His almighty hand, the instruments through which we shall be delivered from danger, led out from incertitude on to ground that is wide and clear, and conducted forward toward a future that shall make us to be more and more a joy unto ourselves and a light unto all the nations of the earth.[5]

Many Americans, following this reasoning, entered the war focusing on its symbolic aspects, and they seemed to believe that their nation's pure motives would guarantee its military success.

Had Americans been aware of the underdeveloped state of their military, they might have been less enthusiastic about their prospects. As of April 1, 1898, the army, counting both officers and enlisted men, consisted of 28,747 men.[6] When a $50 million bill for military development breezed through Congress on March 7, moreover, the secretary of war, Russell A. Alger, interpreted it as allowing only for the improvement of the nation's defensive, not offensive, capabilities.[7] In other words, he did hardly anything productive to prepare the army for meaningful engagement with Spain prior to the declaration of war on April 25. Fortunately, the navy took advantage of its allotment and purchased the ships and other resources that would prove crucial to American success.[8] Indeed, the navy, impressed both by Alfred T. Mahan's arguments regarding the importance of sea power and by its own obvious weakness, had begun building its muscle in 1890.[9] If the navy had taken the same conservative course pursued by the army, the war would likely have taken much longer to prosecute, and the early smashing victory by Commodore (soon to be Admiral) Dewey probably would not have taken place.

The army, on the other hand, needed some time to mobilize upon the war declaration, and when it did its efforts revealed more zeal and confusion than organization and foresight. The aggressively patriotic sentiments of young American men translated into a rush to serve as volunteers in the armed forces when war was declared, but the army could accept only a fraction of them—approximately six times as many men offered their services as were needed.[10] The volunteers who were accepted to serve were sent to army base camps along the East Coast. These camps were hastily cobbled together to organize and train the volunteers. From the largest and most important camp in Tampa, both the volunteer and regular units were to embark for Cuba, but fewer than one-sixth of the volunteer units ever left. Those who remained in camp suffered from the outbreak of several diseases, particularly typhoid and yellow fever, with preventable unsanitary conditions being the main culprit. An insufficient supply of disinfectants and other basic items greatly aggravated conditions. The shortage of tents, for example, resulted in men sleeping in closer quarters than was healthy, a lack of cooking utensils forced men to use roof shingles as plates and otherwise improvise how they ate, and shovels that were to be used to dig latrines and garbage pits arrived to units late or not at all. The trains carrying supplies to the camps were backed up the tracks for scores of miles, and they frequently lacked invoices describing their contents, which led to officers having to break into the train cars and rummage about to get what supplies they could. The situation was scandalous, and the volunteers complained bitterly. Disease claimed the lives of ten times more soldiers than were killed in combat, and a significant proportion of the cases were those of soldiers who never saw action in the field.[11]

One consequence of this experience, however, was the enlargement and reorganization of the army. Never again, vowed McKinley, would the nation find its military as undermanned, undersupplied, and disorganized when the time came to meet an exigency as it had been before the Spanish conflict.[12] The abhorrent conditions at Tampa and the other base camps, and the inability of the War Department to address them quickly and adequately, indicated to informed Americans how far their military was from being world class when the war began. If the United States was to become a dominant world power, it would need to maintain a larger and better-equipped fighting force. The most important step taken in this direction came when in 1899 McKinley replaced the inept and petulantly recalcitrant Alger with the gifted Elihu Root. Root thoroughly reorganized and modernized the army, accomplishing much of his most important work while serving in Theodore Roosevelt's administration after McKinley was assassinated in 1901.[13]

Some individuals, however, notably those opposed to expansion, argued against any permanent enlargement of the army and navy. They recognized that an increase in the military's capacity was likely to result in a corresponding enlargement of its role in the nation's foreign policy. Yale University's William Graham Sumner, among the most outspoken critics of the postwar imperialism, considered the militarizing of the United States to be an example of the country "submitting to be conquered by [Spain] on the field of ideas and policies."[14] To Sumner and others, such as Stanford University president David Starr Jordan, the military's enlargement was inextricably tied to America's nascent colonialism, and it indicated a transformation in the nature and purpose of the U.S. government.[15] Although arguments like Sumner's were prescient and on target, they were no match for the vivid images that Americans had of their soldiers dying of disease in their inadequate base camps. In combination with the continued presence of U.S. soldiers in the Philippine Islands, which required a vigilant maintenance of the U.S. military apparatus, the poor performance of the armed forces in the early stages of the war preparation ensured that the army and navy would be strengthened in the future.

During the conflict itself, fortunately for the United States, the strength of its navy and the decrepitude of the Spanish forces compensated for the sorry state of its army. Spain's army, after all, lacked both spirit and substance, so that by summer the United States boasted a more efficient military, despite being a slapdash operation. Indeed, Spain was so weak that the Cubans likely would have defeated Spain themselves, without American intervention. Had the enemy not been so weak, tired, underfunded, and dispirited, the unprepared state of the U.S. Army at the start of the war would have been a difficult liability to overcome, and Secretary of State John Hay's "splendid little war" would have been considerably less splendid.[16]

As it turned out, the navy was more than adequate to the task of maintaining the myth of American excellence. Dewey's dismemberment of Spain's Philippine squadron on the first day of fighting contributed much to the developing American belief that their moral preeminence would translate into martial success. According to the Philadelphia journalist Henry Watterson, "To the American people the victory at Manila was indisputable proof of the superiority of American training, discipline, intelligence, mechanical skill, and courage over the ignorant and undisciplined bravery of the Spaniard."[17] Another contemporary account added to the picture of Americans' reaction to Dewey's success: "From public buildings and private homes, in commercial centres and manufacturing districts, new flags were added to the wealth of bunting which had already been floating on the breezes; whistles were blown, bells were rung, men whistled the national airs, and children sang them as they paraded the streets. It was a time when the veterans grew more than usually reminiscent."[18] The president was hardly more circumspect in his speech to Congress commemorating the event: "Outweighing any material advantage is the moral effect of this initial success. At this unsurpassed achievement the great heart of our nation throbs; not with boasting or with greed, but with a deep gratitude that this triumph has come in a just cause and that by the grace of God an effective step has been taken toward the attainment of the wished-for end of peace."[19]

As the Battle of Manila was the first engagement of the war, it set the tone for how Americans viewed the conflict for its duration. More accurately, it allowed Americans to *continue* to view the conflict between the United States and Spain as the event that would signal the nation's long-awaited rise to global preeminence, as they had expectantly regarded Spanish-Cuban-American affairs since 1895. One Methodist minister offered a religious interpretation of the navy's accomplishment. "The sun of Heaven now greets the stars of hope in liberty's banner during every hour of every revolution of the round earth," he announced. "A blow from the strong right hand of this nation, designed to break the grasp of a cruel oppressor in an island just off our coast, has first paralyzed the same oppressor's hand, deprived her of her richest colony, and liberated millions of her victims on the other side of the world." And what was the significance of this victory and the larger war in which it was ensconced? "It is impossible to minify [sic] or narrow the scope and meaning of the contest. . . . It is a contest in which the character of civilization and the interpretation of the Decalogue and the Sermon on the Mount are involved."[20]

This assessment was typical of existing Protestant interpretations of the conflict as a whole, as the following excerpt from a Presbyterian minister's sermon of May 1 demonstrates:

> The forces that have led up to this conflict are far deeper than politics or commerce. They are, in fact, the primal forces of society; the elements that contend forever in mighty strife between light and darkness; the love of liberty against the pride of power; the passion of humanity against the interests of ancient oppression. Two great types of civilization—one anchored to the past and lying across the channel; the other moving towards the future on the full tide of progress—have come into collision.[21]

When news reached the United States recounting how the U.S. Navy defeated Spain at Manila on the day this sermon was given, popular opinion began to settle into a firm conviction that civilization was indeed progressing, with helpful nudges from the bayonet. As the battlefield victories accumulated and the scope of U.S. success became clear, all the pieces seemed to come together in the American mind: the nation's character *was* yielding military success, and global leadership was sure to follow. It was a heady time, during which the idea of American mission was regarded almost as received truth, and Americans were eager to grapple with the implications of their great triumph.

CONTEMPORARY DEPICTIONS OF THE U.S. VICTORY

When describing the significance of America's victory over Spain, contemporary historians, politicians, and commentators stressed three themes. The first was that the war allowed the United States to come together again as a nation and heal the wounds of the Civil War. The second insisted that the crushing of Spain marked the moment that the United States became a great power. The third held that the scope of the victory confirmed that the United States was the nation of progressive civilization, and that the divine favor enjoyed by the American people, sustained by their republican institutions, would ensure continued glory. Taken together, these three themes portrayed a nation standing self-consciously at a crucial historical juncture, to which destiny had led it and from which it could envision at last the achievement of its world-transforming mission. It was both a vision and a mood, and President McKinley articulated it perfectly when he announced to the people of Richmond, Virginia, after the war, "Standing near the close of the century, we can look backward with congratulation and pride, and forward into the new century with confidence and courage. . . . It is for us to guard the sacred trust transmitted by the fathers and pass on to those who follow, this government of the free, stronger in its principles and greater in its power for the execution of its beneficent mission."[22]

National Reunification

During the debates preceding the declaration of war against Spain, it became increasingly clear that Northerners and Southerners were coming together in patriotic unison against their common foe. Americans recognized this rather unexpected development and took great pride in their new sense of shared identity. As the war progressed to its satisfying conclusion, people from all over the country, but especially the South, were eager to describe how the war cathartically allowed them to wash away the psychological detritus left over from the Civil War and Reconstruction. While statements to the effect that the country had finally overcome its sectional animosity turned out to be somewhat premature, the implicit hope for national unity that they communicated indicated that a turning point, at least, was reached in relations between the North and the South. After generations of mistrust and overt mutual disdain, it was possible to admit fraternity with those living on the other side of the Mason-Dixon line and to conceive of a single nation comprised of one people, sharing norms, ideals, and traditions. Unfortunately, however, membership in this newly reconstituted union remained restricted to whites and, to a lesser degree, Protestants, but by agreeing that a single national culture was desirable, Americans took an important step toward attaining the unified yet pluralistic society that their forbears had mythically founded more than a century before.

During the prewar period, acknowledgment that the sectional breach was being healed found frequent expression in the speeches of the nation's legislators. Representative William C. Arnold (R-Pa.), for instance, had declared, "A new South has sprung up, and joining hands with their brethren of the North we are all moving onward and upward to attain to the highest possibilities of this our nation–one God, one flag, one country, one destiny."[23] In the upper chamber, Senator Donelson Caffery (D-La.) concurred: "If we, unhappily, must go to war with Spain, it will be waged on our part by a solid Union. There will be no North nor South nor East nor West."[24] Representative Peter J. Otey (D-Va.), in a lengthy speech on the subject, noted to "long and continued applause" that "the clouds of prejudice necessarily engendered by our civil strife have now happily given way to the bright sunshine of magnanimity and good feeling." Otey added:

> Posterity will be gladdened when they read that the sons of [Civil War] heroes joined together to sustain the honor and dignity of their great nation. And today we look at the flag of our common country, and as we recognize that the honor of the country is threatened, the sons of the boys who wore blue and those of the boys who wore gray will salute it and join us as we say to that flag, in the language of Ruth, "Whither thou goest we will go . . . thy people shall be our people, and thy God shall be our God."[25]

Sectional rapprochement was also evident when army units moved under the U.S. flag through the South en route to their base in Tampa. Colonel Leonard Wood and Lieutenant Theodore Roosevelt, the commanding officers of the First Volunteer Cavalry–more famously known as the Rough Riders–described their unit's reception as it passed through New Orleans. Wood related, "New Orleans was very enthusiastic; streets full of people and best of all an American flag in the hands of all. The cost of war is amply repaid by seeing the old flag as one sees it today in the South. We are indeed once more a unified country." Roosevelt added, "Everywhere we saw the Stars and Stripes, and everywhere we are told, half-laughing, by grizzled ex-Confederates that they never dreamed in bygone days of bitterness to greet the old flag as they were now greeting it, and to send their sons, as they were now sending them, to fight and die under it."[26]

Not all Southerners were prepared to join the patriotic groundswell, however. Before the war, a few Southern newspapers voiced opinions that reflected the entrenched differences between the rural, Democratic South and the industrial, Republican North. In their editorials they argued, for instance, that the North's munitions factories and shipyards would provide the region with economic benefits that the South would not enjoy. They also noted the war was likely to impose a heavier burden on the South than the North, since Cuba lay just off the shores of the South, making whatever offensives Spain might choose to mount directed in all probability at the South's coastal cities. Recruitment in some parts of the South was low—the timing of the war declaration on April 25 coincided with planting season—and the crowds that greeted the Rough Riders apparently stayed home when the time came to see off less-famous units. The atmosphere throughout much of the South, in other words, was clearly ambivalent. Nevertheless, Southerners took pride in the fact that, despite their reservations, they had responded to the call of duty, and they greatly appreciated gestures such as the appointments of Fitzhugh Lee and Joe Wheeler to important positions in the nation's effort. Ultimately, as time wore on, the South came to look back on the war with pride and the feeling that their sacrifices at last made them the national equals of their Northern neighbors. As the war was incorporated into the nation's collective memory, moreover, symbols such as the sunken *Maine* carried great meaning for all Americans, with the effect that, North and South, Americans believed that the victory over Spain had helped to heal old sectional wounds.[27]

Contemporary historians were eager to emphasize the war's contribution to national reconciliation. As one author wrote, "The effect of Joe Wheeler and Fitzhugh Lee laying aside their coats of gray to wear the Union blue cannot be overestimated. The spirit of patriotism was a solvent of hatreds and animosities. The Spanish War, as its first fruit, contributed to the solidarity of the Union and made it again a union, not of constraint, but of affection."[28] The journalist Henry Watterson agreed: "In 1861 the country had been divided. Now it was united. Then the sections stood in opposing battle. Now they stood shoulder to shoulder and heart to heart. . . . The swaddling clothes of National babyhood were gone. The giant stood forth in all the pride of his manhood, . . . arrayed on the side of humanity and liberty."[29] Henry Cabot Lodge added, "[T]he war came, and in the twinkling of an eye, in a flash of burning, living light, they saw that the long task was done, that the land was really one again without rent or seam, and men rejoiced mightily in their hearts with this knowledge which the new war had brought."[30]

No one embraced the nationalizing effects of the war more than President McKinley. Ever the nationalist, McKinley was eager to encourage his countrymen to bond together in common cause, before, during, but most of all after the war. During a speaking tour of the Midwest following the end of the conflict in the fall of 1898, the president invoked the theme of national unity repeatedly as he subtly gauged and manipulated public opinion regarding the looming expansionism that would become the war's enduring legacy. As he rode a train from small town to small town (with an occasional stop at a big city), speaking from a platform on the rear of the caboose to throngs of patriotic heartlanders, McKinley stoked the pride of an exulting people and placed it within the broader context of the nation's religious and political traditions. In Saint Louis, for example, his commemoration of sectional reconciliation had a distinctly Lincolnesque flavor: "Not since the beginning of the agitation of slavery have there been such a common bond of name and purpose; such genuine affection; such unity of the sections; such obliteration of party and geographical divisions. . . . North and South have mingled their best blood in a common cause and today rejoice in a common victory."[31]

Elsewhere on the tour, McKinley consistently reassured his audiences that in the crucible of war the people of the United States had become a single, unified people. "Never before has there been a more united people," he exclaimed in Denison, Iowa. "Never since the beginning of the government itself were the people of this country so united in aim and purpose as at the present hour."[32] The president's earlier, carefully considered decision to appoint prominent ex-Confederates to important leadership posts in the war effort, noted above, also showed that sectional reconciliation was a clear objective of his as he worked to endow the war with a meaning that transcended its immediate causes. In these gestures toward national reunification, McKinley hoped sincerely that the war that he oversaw as president would lay to rest the ghosts of the war in which he had served as a much younger man. And if they also helped to prepare the country to embark in a new direction—expansion—so much the better.[33]

In his important intellectual history *The Metaphysical Club,* Louis Menand shows how the years during which the United States fought Spain were part of a larger era in which Americans worked to develop a new approach to thinking about the world. The Civil War had destroyed many of the old frameworks by which Americans had defined themselves and the problems confronting them, leaving a void at the heart of American thought. From the 1870s through the Progressive Era, therefore, American intellectuals such as Charles Sanders Pierce, William James, and John Dewey articulated a new, pragmatic philosophy that held, among other things, that individuals and societies create and do not "discover" truth. The evolutionary doctrines discussed in chapter 2 were part of this effort to reconstruct from the Civil War's debris an intellectual edifice capable of accommodating Americans' encounter with a rapidly changing world. The effort to rechannel Americans' intellectual energies in constructive new directions helped to foster a renewed sense of common purpose and social activism in the country, as evidenced by the Social Gospel movement, for example. Seen in the light of Menand's analysis, the explicit nation building and sectional reunification that took place during the Spanish-American War was an important part of this broader effort to build a shared American identity capable of confronting the challenges of the modern era. Under these circumstances, Americans were particularly susceptible to interpretations of their identity and mission that instilled pride while emphasizing the moral agency of the American people.[34]

In this cresting spirit of national unity, sectionalism was the primary object of Americans' attention as Northerners and Southerners consciously strove to identify with each other as fellow co-nationalists. Less successful were attempts to think across religious and racial lines. While Americans took pride in the belief that their country ensured religious equality under the banner of religious freedom, they harbored no such illusions about race. In an era in which the dominant culture deemed Anglo-Saxons the pinnacle of human evolution, it was rather easy for whites to sacrifice the needs and interests of racial minorities, especially where they interfered with the goal of the sectional reunification. Religion was a trickier issue, however, and the results were mixed. In the era's spirit of lip-service ecumenism, Roman Catholics and other religious minorities were granted a more prominent seat at the national religious table, but they still were clearly guests.

If America's national religious culture remained Protestant, religious minorities were eager to take advantage of the atmosphere of national fellowship created by the war to try to join the mainstream on an equal footing. The best way for them to do so was to demonstrate their patriotism. America's Jewish population, for instance, eagerly joined the flag-waving masses by denouncing Spain in ways consistent with the period's civil-religious motifs. They repeated the prevailing opinion that Spanish society was medieval and an impediment to progress while insisting that the United States was the agency through which human civilization would advance. Jewish authors emphasized their agreement with the Protestant conception of a providential role for the United States and stressed that they, too, were a part of "this chosen people of free men."[35] There is no evidence to suggest that Jews were insincere in expressing these sentiments during the war. Rather, they appear, as Americans, to have been jolted by the same nationalistic fervor that electrified the rest of the country in 1898, in much the same manner that casual sports followers often become ardent fans of a team during its championship-winning season.

In order to align oneself with the patriotic mainstream of public opinion a religious minority needed to toe the civil-religious line drawn by the nation's Protestant majority. While McKinley asserted that "[o]ur patriotism is neither sectional nor sectarian,"[36] Catholic Americans in particular had reason to be skeptical. Some Protestant journals and preachers had been eager to point out before the war that America's foe was a Roman Catholic nation, with the mainstream (secular) press intimating that the Vatican and, possibly, American Catholics, sided with Spain as a result.[37] Tiring of defending the members of their faith from such baseless accusations, the Catholic archbishops of the United States finally issued a pastoral letter, which they all signed, defending the loyalty of American Catholics. "Whatever may have been the individual opinions of Americans prior to the declaration of war, there can now be no two opinions as to the duty of every loyal citizen," they wrote in the letter, released on May 14, 1898. "We, the members of the Catholic Church, are true Americans, and as such are loyal to our country and our flag and obedient to the highest decrees and supreme authority of the nation."[38]

Overt anti-Catholicism quickly abated after the war got under way, but the blithe assumption by Protestants that it was a responsibility of theirs to "Americanize" Spain's former colonies at war's end rankled both American Catholics and their Cuban and Filipino coreligionists. The islands were already Catholic. Protestant missionaries seeking to convert new souls (in some cases, they claimed to have a duty to "Christianize" them) were not alone, however, in upsetting American Catholics. The U.S. government also affronted them when it quickly moved to disestablish the Roman Catholic Church in all of Spain's former island possessions by taking such steps as replacing the islands' church-school system with the U.S. secular-Protestant counterpart. These measures upset Catholics, who feared that their religion would lose ground to its Protestant rivals, with help from the government. In part, Catholics' concerns were valid–some of the military appointees sent to create a new, "American," order on the islands had aggressively Protestant goals in mind as part of their Americanizing agenda. There was also an aspect to Catholics' concerns, however, that seemed to support one of the more commonly heard accusations made against American Catholics: the argument that Roman Catholicism was inherently a statist religion that was unable to survive in a milieu guaranteeing religious freedom and equality to all. After Theodore Roosevelt assumed the presidency, however, these issues largely abated. Roosevelt, a New York politician with experience in dealing with Catholics, actively took measures in the overseas possessions designed to assuage Catholic voters, such as sending Philippine governor William Howard Taft to the Vatican to help settle some of the problems stemming from disestablishment. By 1903, Roosevelt's actions helped to finish the job of legitimizing Catholics' patriotism that their own prewar jingoism had begun. While Roman Catholics were by no means on an equal footing with Protestants by 1903, they appear at last to have successfully staked their claim to rightful membership in American society.[39]

The odds that African Americans would be able successfully to integrate into a unified national culture, however, were much longer than they were for Catholics and other religious minorities. The severity of their challenge can be glimpsed in a pamphlet in which the author, who was writing on the subject of national reconciliation, took special pleasure in commenting on how the Spanish-American War had helped the American people to come together. When his paper turned to the subject of race, however, he had this to say about reunification: "You must know that as long as the brain of the Anglo-Saxon continues superior to the brain of those with whom he comes in contact, so long will the white man of the South remain the master of the situation. But whatever way the problem of the South be solved . . . it must be solved by keeping the races separate, because amalgamation means debasement."[40] Thus, in a tract celebrating the coming together of the nation, racial separation was explicitly advocated. The president, though he disagreed with racist policies and attitudes, did nothing to help blacks. On his speaking tour of the South, for example, he stopped at the Georgia Agricultural and Mechanical College, a black college, to praise "the splendid heroism of the black regiments which fought side by side with the white troops." His message to the students was hopelessly naive, however, and revealed his administration's plans for addressing their concerns: "You will solve your own problem. Be patient. Be progressive, be determined, be honest, be God-fearing, and you will win, for no effort fails that has a stout, honest, earnest heart behind it."[41]

Certainly, the African American soldiers whom McKinley praised acted with "stout, honest, earnest hearts." In the words of one author who struggled to salvage their quickly deteriorating reputations, they acted in the field of battle with "patriotism, heroism, bravery, and excellence." This evaluation was based on newspaper accounts of the ability of black soldiers in the field, but because many of these soldiers did the dirty work for the Rough Riders,[42] they received almost no credit for their deeds aside from next-day journalistic recountings of their actions.[43] Moreover, a few racist comments by white commanding officers (blacks were not allowed to be commissioned) overshadowed in the public mind any recognition of their achievements. It was almost impossible, it seemed, for white Americans to give honest, sustained praise and credit for the noteworthy military accomplishments of black soldiers.

African American experiences during the opening stages of the conflict gave an early indication of how their actions would be received by a nation devoted to "reunification." As one black regular recorded, "In Georgia . . . it mattered not if we were soldiers of the United States, and going to fight for the honor of our country and the freedom of an oppressed and starving people, we were 'niggers,' as they called us, and treated us with contempt. There was no enthusiasm nor Stars and Stripes in Georgia. That is the kind of 'united country' we saw in the South." The soldier noted that in the base camps, only whites could leave their units unsupervised, and that the ships transporting the troops to Cuba were segregated. Whites enjoyed preferential treatment in every respect: they received coffee and rations before blacks, for instance, and did not have guards detailed to their units to make sure they "kept their place," unlike their black fellow soldiers.[44]

In short, the celebrated "reunification" effected by the Spanish-American War was limited. Northerners and Southerners did engage in a significant rapprochement in 1898, but a racist construction of the American national character prevented blacks from joining the majority culture. Similarly, the Protestant character of America's dominant culture was reinforced. Insofar as Catholics and other religious minorities were able to improve their standing in society, it was because they conformed to Protestant-based norms of civil-religious patriotism. It is true that important steps were taken toward the tripartite religious culture identified by Will Herberg in the 1950s, in which Protestants, Catholics, and Jews each occupied a distinctive, productive role in the American mainstream, but insofar as political and cultural discourse had religious overtones in 1898, the language was still unmistakably Protestant. Still, the collective focusing of energies and attention outward led Americans to conceive of themselves and their nation in a more unitary fashion than they had in decades. Intense labor strife most recently, and of course slavery and abolitionism before that had habituated the American people to think in terms of "us" and "them," with both groups included *within* American society. In the brief glow surrounding the war, however, during which time they tried to believe that their entire society was included in the "us," the American people excitedly engaged in the task of defining the character of their newly homogenized nation. It was, unfortunately, a too-predictable travesty of American cultural construction that a significant portion of the U.S. citizenry was explicitly excluded from joining this newly evolving nation, leaving the job of building a truly inclusive democracy once again to future generations.[45]

America the Great Power

The quality that Americans pointed to first as a defining feature of their reborn nation was power. Beginning with Dewey's stirring victory, the

Spanish-American War was regarded by Americans as a great coming-out party for their nation as it entered the world stage. "The capture of Manila [on August 13] completed a series of military events of the most brilliant description [that is] destined to change the map of the world, placing America in the front rank of naval and military powers, a position which she had not held up to the time of our War with Spain, owing to the fact that it has never been necessary for us to take on the character of a military nation," concluded one historian-politician, breathlessly.[46] The implicit message of this comment was that the time *had* come for the United States "to take on the character of a military nation."

The United States had humiliated a European power, and this surely meant that the torch of world leadership was being passed across the Atlantic. "In these less than four months of war the United States has taken a new position before the world, a higher and nobler attitude," argued another historian. "Europe has discovered that we are more than a nation of shopkeepers; that we are a people who can strike shrewdly for the right, and one that is destined to be a leader in the van of human progress, an example to the world of the value of free institutions, peaceful industries, high aspirations, and moral energies."[47] Americans gushed with pride over their victory like proud parents, as if they knew all along that their nation was great and powerful, and finally had the evidence to show everyone. Jingoism scaled new heights:

From [Dewey's victory] forward the United States of America has been a world power. It has actually dominated every European nation in the China affair. It has leaped to a place where it towers above the Powers of older lands, and commands them. And they must obey. A nation with such a navy as Dewey exhibited, with such power as the fleet under [Admiral Winfield Scott] Schley demonstrated at Santiago, is a nation to make terms with. A nation which could in a month fling an army of 97,000 men across twelve thousand miles of ocean, and never miss them at home, is a nation to respect. A nation with such a navy and army and such boundless resources, which had also possessed itself of Hawaii, the half-way house in the wide Pacific; which also held the Philippines, garrisoned and guarded the very doors of Asia, and which made the islands of the Atlantic its out-posts against an advance from Europe—that nation is Master of the World.[48]

Although most sober commentators did not go quite so far in their estimations of American might, they would have agreed with the author who argued, less extravagantly, that "we are finally awake, and before many years will no doubt be able to cope with the most powerful nations on earth."[49]

By bringing such unprecedented power realistically within the reach of the United States, the Spanish-American War fired the imagination of the country. "The nation emerges from the late war with a new temper, a new national consciousness, a new apprehension of destiny," observed the Social Gospel leader Josiah Strong. Surely, Strong argued, it was not a coincidence that the United States found itself at the juncture at which it then stood: "How happens it that all these lands are found under Anglo-Saxon flags in the very generation when the Pacific becomes decisive of the world's destinies?" he asked. "Such facts are God's great alphabet with which he spells for man his providential purposes. For a hundred years now, blind men have been quarreling with our national destiny or with divine Providence." But the time for such "quarreling" was now over, Strong continued. "This race has been honored not for its own sake, but for the sake of the world. It has been made powerful, and rich, and free, and exalted—powerful, not to make subject, but to serve; rich, not to make greater gains, but to know greater blessedness; free, not simply to exult in freedom, but to make free; exalted, not to look down, but to lift up."[50] For Strong, the lesson of the war was clear: the United States had been ordained by Providence to win the war and, through it, to become the world's great power, so that it might fulfill its destiny and initiate the millennium. Victory was not a reward but an opportunity.

It was a heady time. Few seemed to disagree that "the beginning of the new life under the Stars and Stripes at the dawning of the new century will mark an epoch . . . in the history . . . of the whole world."[51] One of the war's few nationally celebrated heroes (Roosevelt and Dewey were probably the only ones more famous), Lieutenant Richmond P. Hobson, wrote and spoke of his experiences at the war's conclusion. He would conclude his speeches by declaring longwindedly:

> When I supplement this picture with another no less vivid, no less real, of our country sending its strong arm out over the earth preparing for the future to use its strength, to exert its enormous influence on behalf of what is high and right, of extending free institutions, our own freedom, our own type of manhood over the earth, my feelings and emotions are indescribable, and I can only say I have thanked heaven that it is vouchsafed me to devote my exertions–even, I trust, my whole life–to the service of my country.[52]

Hobson's was the pride of a soldier victorious, but it was also the pride of a nation eager to flex its muscle. With apparently little effort or sacrifice, the United States became in four short months a player on the world stage, a force that the so-called Great Powers would now have to reckon with.

The Purpose of American Power

Strong and Hobson had captured the essential meaning of the war in the minds of most Americans. To those like Strong–preachers, politicians, and educators–who were charged with endowing the event with meaning for the country as a whole, the war was a turning point in history. Through it, the United States had attained a higher level of power and glory than it had previously enjoyed, and this power, it was thought, had to have a purpose. The scale of America's victory seemed to confirm even the most extravagant interpretations of the nation's mission and role in human affairs. The United States had fought a war for noble, humanitarian reasons against a medieval, monarchical, Roman Catholic empire, and had crushed it. Good had triumphed over evil. The jingoes who had made grandiose claims about their nation, it seemed, were right.

"Let us believe that the untoward events of the war with Spain were brought about for some all-wise purpose by the Supreme Ruler of the men," wrote the journalist Watterson, concluding his history of the war, "and that the hand which has led American manhood through every emergency to the one goal of the American Union, has in store for that Union even greater uses and glory than irradiated the dreams and blessed the prayers of the God-fearing men who gave it life."[53]

The "uses" of the United States—its mission to the world—included, above all, spreading freedom and democracy. Andrew S. Draper, the president of the University of Illinois, wrote a history of the war "for young Americans" entitled *The Rescue of Cuba: An Episode in the Growth of Free Government* that stressed this point. The book's title and subtitle were revealing. As Draper stated in its preface, the work had two purposes: "first, to exhibit the war of 1898 as one more step, and an important step, in the steady progress of the world towards universal liberty"; second, "to offer such a faithful picture of the heroism and manly quality of the American soldiers who gave their lives for the rescue of their oppressed neighbors," that readers would be able "to realize what it costs to extend free institutions, and to appreciate what it means to be an American citizen." As Draper explained, America's victory "was only an episode in this worldwide contest for self-government." But it was a significant episode. "In the unselfish, neighborly, and resolute spirit which prompted it, in the magnificent heroisms which it revealed, and in the uplift which it gave to the good cause of popular liberty in all parts of the world, it was a remarkable part of the long, continuous, and not yet ended contest."[54] Indeed, as the developing war in the Philippine Islands showed, that contest was just beginning.

Religious interpretations of the conflict stressed the role of Providence in America's success. At a banquet in St. Louis, for instance, the postmaster-general, Charles Emory Smith, an evangelical Protestant occupying what was at the time an important cabinet post, gave a speech celebrating both the nation and the president in which he announced that "our present Chief Magistrate has been as distinctly called by Providence for a great work for this people and this world as either George Washington or Abraham Lincoln. In all the future years this year of 1898 will be looked back to as marking as distinct an epoch, as eventful an era in the history of this country as any epoch through which we have passed." Smith surmised that "the hand of Providence has been in this work as distinctly as the hand of Providence was in the war of the Revolution, or in that great war of 1861."[55] Other speakers who followed Smith spoke to similar themes, which was perhaps to be expected during a banquet that took place during a victory tour. Still, the recurrence of this theme in the books, pamphlets, and speeches that followed the war indicates that Americans truly regarded their country's victory as an immense accomplishment, a triumph for all times, and the belief that the United States was a nation selected by Providence to accomplish great works certainly contributed to this sentiment.

A sermon that was delivered on three separate occasions, to massive audiences, as part of McKinley's reelection campaign, took the theme of Providence to a ridiculous level. As an example of the period's religious jingoism, the sermon, delivered in the fall of 1900 by Bishop C. H. Fowler to packed auditoriums in New York, Cleveland, and Chicago, demonstrates how intoxicated some Americans were with their nation's victory. "Signs from heaven and blessings have been seen on every hand, and the people will surely cry, 'The Lord, He is God,' and will feel that McKinley is a true prophet," declared the bishop, who added: "As a believer in American history I am an expansionist." Fowler continued, "Three of the greatest missionary events since the tragedy on Mt. Calvary are, *First, the conversion of St. Paul. . . . Second, the firing on Fort Sumter.* That made the Anglo-Saxon race fit to be used in the world's evangelization. . . . *Third, the blowing up of the Maine. . . .* That explosion made this Anglo-Saxon race one and set us about our job, namely the deliverance and salvation of the nations" (emphasis in the original; a transcript of the sermon is included in McKinley's papers). Complaining that the antiimperialists were "fighting not merely McKinley and the Rough Riders and the American people, but . . . also the resistless force running through all the ages of nature, the force of natural selection, and . . . God's eternal purpose to elevate the races," Fowler then explained how Providence had led the United States to its victory:

> God said, "I will show you what to do," and he led our ships past all the forts, and around all the concealed mines in Manila Bay, saying, "Turn those Spanish ships into colanders, and I will give you a coaling station and an archipelago. You shall exile despotism; give to an oppressed people a free press, a free Bible, a free school, and a free government." We obeyed, and now the flag waves over the Philippines. . . . Expansion is in our blood, in our history, in our religion. It is our destiny. *President McKinley is a providential man.* Like the prophets of old, he is on an errand. He is the prophet of our times. (Emphasis in the original)[56]

While it would be unfair to characterize a sermon in which God was said to instruct the U.S. Navy to turn Spain's "ships into colanders" as representative of the religious viewpoint in 1898, its general message that the United States won the war as part of God's larger plans for both America and the world was indeed typical.[57] Moreover, the sermon was given before large audiences, indicating the speaker's popularity, and it was filed in McKinley's papers along with clippings of messages delivered by, for example, President Andrew Jackson, which McKinley consulted when writing his own speeches. While excessive, the sermon was not exceptional.[58]

McKinley, it should be noted, actively worked to reinforce this interpretation of the conflict on his speaking tour of the Midwest, in which he tried to persuade the people that keeping the Philippine Islands was part of the nation's grand destiny.[59] Whatever the sincerity of McKinley's oratory, it is clear that it resonated with the people. The motifs that he and other opinion leaders drew upon–Providence, national unity, power, and so on–trickled down to the lower reaches of American culture and were quickly incorporated into dime-store novels, sappy poems, and forgettable songs and dramas.

IMAGES OF AMERICA IN POEMS, PLAYS, AND FICTION

Popular culture is revealing of the lifestyles, folkways, and mores of the people who participate in it. At the turn of the century, the exciting Spanish-American War provided much fodder for writers and poets seeking an outlet for their muse, and the output of these writers reveals that Americans wanted their entertainment products to glorify their nation. In novels, plays, and poems generated for popular consumption, idealized images of American society and its presumed importance to global civilization suggest that the American people shared with their leaders the belief that the United States, due to its inherent greatness, had a mission to the world, and that the Spanish-American War was an example of that greatness. In particular, pop-culture writers and poets demonstrated in their works a racist and jingoistic mindset that differed from that revealed in the congressional debates only in its crudeness and simplicity.

Included in the Pamphlets of American History collection were thirteen novels whose plots, with one exception, were based on the Spanish-American War.[60] The tales were not riveting, and one story appears to have had no other purpose than to allow the author to mimic Peter Finley Dunne's skill in transcribing the accents of ethnic Americans.[61] The rest of the novels shared the same plot: A brave, noble, white, God-fearing American male overcomes the treachery of a Spaniard or the cunning of a Filipino to effect some terrific deed for the glory of the United States, usually winning the heart of a beautiful Cuban woman along the way. In every case, the story's details reveal the author's worldview (many of the stories were penned by a young Upton Sinclair).[62] One obvious example was the depiction of race. The stereotypical portrayal of the characters demonstrated how Americans corresponded moral and other personal qualities to the different races, with race and nationality presumed to have a natural affinity with each other. In every novel in which they were depicted, the Filipino characters, for example, all shared the same faults—deceitfulness, backwardness, and cunning—while blacks were invariably portrayed as stupid, ignorant, superstitious servants. Also pertinent is the way that (white) Americans were without exception depicted as embodiments of Roosevelt's "manly virtues," bringing liberty, morality, and uplift to backward races and peoples wherever they went.

The Spanish characters were uniformly evil, delusional, or both.[63] One author described the nature of the differences between Spaniards and Americans as follows: "The sanguine nature of the Spanish don of today, and his remarkable ignorance of the true position held by his decaying nation in the estimation of a progressive world, have been marked features in the close of the century. It has been reserved for America to awaken dreaming Spain with a rude shock, and point out the road to reform and modern ideas along which she must press if desirous of maintaining even a humble place in the procession of nations."[64] In another novel, set in the Philippines, the chivalrous American hero acted on his "abiding faith in the grandeur of the mission that lay before the Anglo-Saxon race."[65] Other stories commented on America's mission, invariably concluding that under the tutelage of the United States, both the Philippines and Cuba would improve and flourish.[66] In short, the novels, written as they were for an audience similar to that which read the yellow press, reinforced jingoistic views of a knight-errant United States that was superior in virtue and racial composition (they implicitly communicated that only Anglo-Saxons were "true" Americans) to all other peoples in the world and that was ably suited to expand its reach around the world.

More serious and established writers tended to oppose the expansionist movement. Historian Richard E. Welch writes that only the following authors supported American policy regarding expansion: Julia Ward Howe, Bliss Carman, Richard Hovey, Gertrude Atherton, Brooks Adams, and Julia Hawthorne. A much longer list of writers opposed it: George Adee, Thomas Bailey Aldrich, Ambrose Bierce, Gamaliel Bradford, George W. Cable, John Jay Chapman, Ernest Crosby, Peter Finley Dunne, Henry Blake Fuller, Hamlin Garland, Thomas Wentworth Higginson, William Dean Howell, Edgar Lee Masters, Joaquin Miller, William Vaughn Moody, Bliss Perry, Edwin Arlington Robinson, Lincoln Steffens, Mark Twain, and Charles Dudley Warner.[67] With notable exceptions, however, the authors did not express their views through their craft, as the dime-store novelists did, but more often wrote essays and editorials to express their views.

If possible, the images of jingoism and racism depicted in popular fiction were even more starkly drawn in plays. Included in the Pamphlets of American History series are dramas inspired by the Spanish-American War featuring stock characters, racist stereotypes, and unabashed jingoism. No play in the collection deviated from these themes. The plays included no notations indicating whether they ever made it to the stage or, if they did, how popular they were, but it is noteworthy that every play in the series made use of racial and national stereotypes and drew upon jingoistic sentiments.

In Frank Dumont's *The Scout of the Philippines: A Military Comedy Drama in Three Acts,* for instance, Filipinos were called "yellow niggers," and the play's Chinese character, presumably included for comic relief, spoke in rhymes. For example:

Me no sleepee, me no lazy
When workee for Mellican [probably a "Chinese" version of "American"] man
See in dark, like pussycat,
Bitee like snakee, all same quick![68]

The play, drawing on another stereotype, also insinuated that Spain was behind the Filipino uprising. Another play passed itself off as a comedy by imitating Irish accents; its characters referred to blacks as "darkeys."[69] As expected, Spain did not fare well in the dramas. Spanish characters were invariably characterized as congenitally amoral. In one play, for example, the American characters (and the token Irishwoman; every play seemed to have one) described their Spanish counterparts as "Spanish viper," "Spanish greaser," "scoundrel," "thief," "underhanded villain," "unscrupulous scoundrel," "rascal," "Spanish devils, scorpions, and lizards," "copper colored devil," "Spanish snakes," "demon in human form," "miserable viper," "despicable wretch," and "brutal and remorseless in your day of power, abject and pitiful in your hour of terror."[70]

Americans occupied the heroes' roles in the plays. In *Old Glory in Cuba*, for instance—the play that included the above references to Spanish people—a parallel between Americans and Spaniards was provided by having both the American hero and his Spanish foe, at different moments, face execution at the hands of the other. The American magnanimously spared the Spaniard's life, for which the latter had groveled and begged. By contrast, when the American was about to be shot, the following transpired: First, the American refused to be blindfolded ("No, I will die facing my foes as a true American should"); then his companion ("a representative of the U.S.") gave the following short speech: "Robert Adams is an American and the free born subject of a country whose proudest boast is that the poorest and humblest have, at least, liberty and protection beneath its flag—a country of which every true-born American is justly proud; and I warn you that if you persist in murdering one of her peaceful and unoffending subjects, she will exact for her outraged honor a bitter, terrible retribution." The plea was ineffective, as was the intercession of three American women who stepped in front of their compatriot. The evil Spaniard instead prepared to shoot them all. Then the "American representative" wrapped the condemned in an American flag and challenged the executioner, "Then fire upon this if you dare!" The ploy apparently worked because the scene ended and all of the characters returned in the next one.[71]

Other plays were also scripted with the intent of firing up the patriotic passions of American audiences. One book, for example, compiled several one-act plays, poems, and songs that were meant to be presented as a single evening's performance. Among the songs it included were, "The Star Spangled Banner," "The Battle Hymn of the Republic," "Once Again Sweet Peace," and "Columbia, the Gem of the Ocean." The poems were put to music, and everything was to be performed by children dressed either in red-white-and-blue or as Uncle Sam. Throughout the performance, everyone on stage was to wave a flag.[72] Many jingoistic plays included references to Rudyard Kipling's "Recessional." Included in the poem are the lines

> God of fathers, known of old–
> Lord of far-flung battle-line–
> Beneath Whose awful Hand we hold
> Domain over palm and pine–
> Lord God of Hosts, be with us yet,
> Lest we forget–lest we forget!

The repetition of the last line in particular was mimicked frequently in other poems and speeches after the war. For example, "Accessional, A Victorious Ode" copied the structure of Kipling's verse in order to mock its message. The poem reads, in part:

> Jehovah, Lord, beneath Whose smile
> Our fathers fought in Freedom's name
> And wrestled from the British Isle
> Our Country, loved and known to fame–
> Oh Gracious Lord, withhold Thy hand,
> While we expand–while we expand.
>
> Ye heathen hordes of Cuba's Isle
> And Aguinaldo's lesser breeds,
> Ye may not bask in Freedom's smile–
> Your Uncle Samuel knows your needs
> Throw down your arms and meekly stand,
> While we expand–while we expand!

The poem continued in this vein for four more verses, and its publication was accompanied by illustrations depicting racial stereotypes of the sort relied on by expansionists to support their arguments.[73]

Another play depicted "the truth" about the *Maine* (that is to say, Spanish authorities were behind the sinking because they deeply loathed Americans). The play closed with the entire cast singing "The Star Spangled Banner" onstage. For the convenience of the audience, a copy of the song was to be included in the playbill, along with a "supplemental verse" about Cuba that the author penned.[74] Clearly, these plays were calculated to capitalize on the jingoism that was in the air at the time, and their themes and language are suggestive of how Americans viewed their country and its conflict with Spain in the period immediately following the war's conclusion.

Unlike the novels and dramas that appeared after the war, poems and songs were evenly divided on the subject of American greatness: some were jingoistic, but others denounced the growing pride of American foreign policy. Racism, too, was less prominent in the poems and songs than in the plays and novels, while religious themes often occupied a place of central importance. Still, as the examples that follow will demonstrate, where race did appear in a poem, Anglo-Saxons were often presumed to occupy the highest tier of the racial hierarchy, and where religious themes were manifest, they embodied mainstream Protestant beliefs; in other words, even if poets and songwriters disagreed about whether American expansion and the greatness it supposedly entailed were to be celebrated or condemned, they all drew from the same pool of norms and cultural constructs to express their feelings.

Most of the songs that were written to mark America's victory in the war were created by taking familiar songs such as "Auld Lang Syne" or, most commonly, "The Battle Hymn of the Republic" and replacing the original lyrics with patriotic new verses. These "songs" were meant to inspire the listener to consider the events of the recent war in the spirit associated with the original song. Thus, one songstress set her poem "The God of Battles" to the tune of "The Battle Hymn of the Republic" in order to correspond the subject of her work—the war against Spain—with the battle hymn's spirit of holy crusade.[75] The following verse is typical of songs based on "The Battle Hymn":

Let us pray the God of Battles that the Cubans may be free,
Let us march with Cuba's hero-sons unto their victory,

Let us furl again Old Glory in the name of Liberty,
Our God is marching on![76]

Not every war-inspired song was derivative, however. A few that commemorated specific events, such as the sinking of the *Maine* or Dewey's victory at Manila, were given original melodies.[77]

Poems celebrating the U.S. victory and expansion ranged from simple expressions of pride to sprawling monuments of self-importance and myopia. The subjects these poems honored, as well as the language they used, reveal some of the ways that Americans drew lessons from the conflict. During the Atlanta Peace Jubilee, for example, celebrants could read a book of poems dedicated to commemorating the war and its dead that included peons to national reunification.[78] Such poems suggest that when the president cheered national reunification in Atlanta and throughout the country, he was not manufacturing the sentiment as much as he was capitalizing on and repackaging it.

Other poems celebrated America's victory more grandiloquently, such as this excerpted tribute to Dewey's accomplishments:

On the forward bridge the Chieftan stood
A hero and almost the nation's god
God grant the white-winged angel of peace
May proclaim freedom for every wild island race
And from border to border, and every inland sea
Beneath the eagle's wing all forever set free.[79]

Perhaps the most ambitious effort to extract epic significance from the war with Spain was the sixty-page poem *Armageddon,* a saga that explicitly interpreted America's victory as a major step toward the kingdom of God. As the poet explained in a preface to the published work, the poem's original goal was to indict Spain for its past sins, but that focus was simply insufficient to capture the magnitude of the conflict. Referring to himself in the third person, the composer of this epic wrote:

Inspired as he was with an ardent love of free institutions and being an enthusiastic admirer of the grand ideal handed down to us by the fathers of the republic, as the wisest, noblest and best system of human government ever instituted among men, he took an unusually deep interest in the persistent struggles of the Cuban patriots against the tyranny of Spain. . . .

The inspiring subject upon which he wrote soon deepened and broadened into grander conceptions. . . . [T]he signs of the times indicate with almost infallible accuracy the realization of the great ideal vision of the battle of "Armageddon."[80]

In the poem's final verse, the United States wins a looming global holy war that ushers in "that millennium and its promised rest," with "equal rights, just laws and noble aims."[81]

A final example of postwar jingoistic poetry is a book of poems written by a woman who described herself as "intensely patriotic," with "great love for the Army and Navy." She dedicated each poem to either an individual who fought in the war, to a regiment, or to all the soldiers and sailors who served. The poems touched on all facets of the war and had titles such as "Mother Dear My Country Calls Me," "The 71st Regiment," "On the Battleship Texas," "The Return of Our Heroes," and "Once upon a Time this Nation was a Baby." In a poem entitled "Oh Father Dear We Are the Nation," the poet imagined a dialogue between a father and his son that included this exchange:

"But, father, will we have the world
Then at our beck and call?
Will we live to see that right is might
And see the nation's fall,
And only those who fear our God
And live as we now do,
To heal the sick, and feed the hungry,
And be men strong and true?"
"Yes, yes, my boy, we'll conquer all the worlds in sight,
And keep on fighting, son,
Until there are no worlds left to fight,
Or they'll turn tail and run."[82]

The above collections of rhyming lines indicate that many Americans reacted to their nation's victory with an emotional pride very much in keeping with what Richard Hofstadter called the "aggressive irrationality" of the American people in the 1890s.[83]

The poems that criticized the temper of America's postwar foreign policy, on the other hand, show how opponents of imperialism who were poetically inclined could highlight both the hypocrisy of the religious arguments used to support expansion and the racism inherent in the policy. For example, one epic (the poem was 150 pages long) included these accusations:

> Ye say, "We are Anglo-Saxon!"
> And ye strut in the pride of birth,
> Ye are drunk on a lie, and waxen
> So mean that ye covet the earth.[84]

One poet, an evangelical Protestant, felt that his nation was betraying its Christian ideals. In one poem he expressed his fear that the United States was sacrificing its status as God's favorite nation for the sake of material gain:

> We boast of being a great Christian nation,
> And of teaching the heathens the truth of salvation,
> Then we fill them with bullets and liquid damnation,
> And really act pious, "like Hell."
>
> ....
>
> And oh, when I think that a just, righteous God
> Who created all nations on earth, of one blood,
> Is the one who shall mete out to each their reward,
> I shudder at what we have done.[85]

Another poet expressed a similar view:

> You carry into distant tropic lands
> The flag of progress, and the Christian cross–
> Alas! Your house is founded on the sands
> Your pride is baseless, and your glory, loss
>
> Though flights of angels hovered o'er our path
> The swift decay
> From day to day

Of high ideals, purpose great
And brave imaginings for the State–
The lust of empire, pushing to the wall
The weaker races–greed of trade that pays
No heed to aught but sordid gain–these all.[86]

In poems such as these, religious interpretations of America's mission to the world were transformed into criticisms of the nation's postwar expansion. It is important to emphasize, however, that the millennialism that inspired the jingoistic poets was not being rejected in these critical works. Rather, the poets who opposed American imperialism used millennial and other Christian motifs to argue against what they regarded as a base materialist policy of territorial conquest. In other words, the same Protestant worldview informed the poetry of both jingoes and their opponents.

Taken together, these poems, songs, plays, and novels reveal the patterns of thought, the cultural assumptions, and the basic normative frameworks according to which Americans interpreted the events of 1898. Given the nature of the works, moreover, it is reasonable to assume that they are representative of the mainstream of American public opinion: they were not written by or for Harvard scholars or cloistered monks but "average" Americans. With rare exception, the compositions reveal that Americans analyzed both themselves and others according to ethnic and racial stereotypes, that they took for granted that the United States was a Christian nation, and, excepting the poets who opposed the war, that they believed fervently that their nation was great and good and destined as a result to lead the world in the coming century.

It is difficult to imagine today that Americans in 1898 and 1899 could assign such enormous significance to a war that barely registers on the modern consciousness. Certainly, the Spanish-American War was important in transforming the United States from a continental power into a global one, but it was only a first step in that direction. Contrary to the apparent expectations of the jingoes, America's gunboats did not usher in the kingdom of God, and the European powers, though they regarded the United States with heightened respect after the war, did not suddenly renounce their claim to global leadership and pass the scepter to their transatlantic rivals.

The fact that many Americans believed that the Spanish-American War would yield such results is traceable to the war's combination of a quick victory of unforeseeable scope and vigor and a national ideology of religious, political, and racial progress. The dominant culture in the United States during the 1890s led Americans to believe that it was their destiny to rule the world. They entered the Spanish-American War expecting their providential favor, racial evolution, and political organization to yield a victory that would advance the moral development of humanity; an easy victory over a hapless opponent confirmed this expectation. Although the subsequent decrepitude of the Philippine War more than disabused many Americans of their more grandiose designs in just a few years, victory in the war planted the seeds in Americans' minds that the time had arrived when their nation could transform the world so that it would be molded in the disinfected, shining image of their own civilization.

CHAPTER SIX

Power and Expansion

THE PEACE PROTOCOL ending hostilities was signed in Washington on August 12, 1898–barely three months after Dewey's victory. With the shooting over, the United States stepped back and apprised its situation. Its military was in command of Cuba, Puerto Rico, Guam, and, with an uneasy alliance with nationalist insurgents, the Philippine Islands. The question facing the country was, What to do with these territories? The Teller Amendment settled the issue with regard to Cuba (there would be no annexation), but the other islands had no such restrictions attached. The only certainty was that the islands were not to be returned to Spain, especially after it came to light that Spanish misrule and cruelty had, if anything, been worse in the Philippines than on Cuba. Racism clouded Americans' judgment against the granting of immediate independence to any of the island peoples. While self-rule was considered by most to be the best option for the future, there was considerable disagreement as to when (and for racial essentialists, whether) it would be possible. Thus, Americans asked themselves, should the United States annex the islands, becoming thereby an imperial power, and undertake to "civilize" these foreign lands in its own way? This became the central postwar question, and the way that Americans grappled with it produced one of the most fascinating and important debates in the nation's history. This debate and the policy with which it was concerned will be the subject of the next four chapters.

The burgeoning fashionability of the imperial norm reflected a mixture of old and new influences. Of recent vintage was the attraction of some Americans to the European model of foreign policy, which stemmed from their recognition that European states set the standards of international relations due to their preponderant power. The "martial spirit"–a romantic belief in the inherent value of military virtues, which the Europeans possessed—contributed as well to the attraction of European-style imperialism. The belief that the United States needed to acquire foreign markets in order to sustain its economy was another spur to expansion. This theory had been influential for about twenty years, but it received apparent empirical verification during the Depression of 1893 and fed the expansionist urge. The oldest influence on Americans' attraction to expansionism, however, was the ideology of Manifest Destiny, whose popularity had originally peaked during the 1840s and 1850s. This imperialist philosophy reemerged in American thought partly because the nation's attention was trained on Cuba, long an object of expansionists' fancy, and partly because the frontier was believed to have closed during the 1880s.

These vague tendencies in American thought allowed the people to accept expansionism as a national policy, and their dissatisfaction with domestic conditions led them to embrace it. Expansionist theories were not peripheral but central to the thinking of some governmental and opinion leaders, moreover, and these men consciously tried to implement or encourage a "Large Policy" of territorial annexation. The Large Policy group, whose members were strategically placed in both the government and the organs of public opinion, sought to shore up America's defensive capability by increasing its sea power. They knew that European states controlled both the oceanic trade routes and overseas markets and that these powers were more capable of threatening American security than ever before. The Large Policy group thus endeavored to increase American power by acquiring territory that could be used as coaling stations along trade routes and as military and commercial bases. Although this group did not create America's foreign policy, they encouraged all policies that supported their ends and helped to create the intellectual and political contexts in which U.S. expansion ultimately took place. And while their importance has frequently been overstated, this group was influential in the government and they coalesced the above-mentioned arguments into a persuasive rationale for imperialism.

President McKinley, who was *not* a member of the Large Policy group, pressed his own imperialist program upon the country. McKinley was committed to upholding a moralistic conception of American national identity that presupposed the right, duty, and destiny of the

United States to assume control of the Philippine Islands and its under-civilized population. It was his vision that shaped American policy, not that of the Large Policy group (we will have more on this later). A size-able and influential segment of the American public steadfastly op-posed expansion, however, and they became outspoken against both McKinley and his foreign policy after it became clear that the treaty set-tlement would include provisions annexing some of Spain's former colonies.

Arrogance had underlain America's humanitarian interest in the prewar Cuban crisis. Since Americans defined themselves as the champions of civilized humanity, they felt that sitting idly by as the Cubans suffered reflected poorly on *them* and implied that their country was too weak to alter events. This thought rankled them. In terms of military strength, however, this impression of American im-potence was not entirely inaccurate. The U.S. Navy was ranked twelfth in the world, beneath those of Turkey, China (a partitioned victim of other countries), and land-locked Austria-Hungary. Even Chile, a na-tion that no one at the time would have confused with being a great power, paid no respect to the U.S. military. A well-publicized episode that brought the two countries to the brink of war in 1891 had made this fact clear when a barroom brawl in Santiago resulted in the deaths of two American sailors and injuries to seventeen more. Although the episode ultimately passed without further hostilities, Chile's defiance, backed by its superior navy, gave the United States a wake-up call regarding the limits of its power.[1]

An even more bitter and pertinent, if somewhat distant, memory was the *Virginius* affair, a filibustering incident from the Ten Years War (the first Cuban insurrection of 1868–78). In 1873, a ship flying the U.S. flag was captured by Spanish authorities near Cuba. When munitions headed for the rebels were discovered on board, the Spanish authori-ties summarily executed fifty-three American crew members and pas-sengers. Public outrage was intense, but the official response was more muted after it was shown that the ship's U.S. flag had been flown ille-gally, the ship's documents had been forged, and the contraband aboard violated U.S. law. Great Britain mediated the affair and elicited from Spain an apology and an indemnity for some of the families of the executed.[2] Pamphleteers who recounted the affair at the turn of the century, however, ignored the fact that Spain was well within its rights in its handling of the matter, characterized Spanish behavior as treacherous and unjust, and suggested that closure of the issue had not been achieved.[3] As one contemporary historian wrote, "The diplomatists smoothed matters out so as to avoid war, but twenty-five years were by no means long enough to cause the outrage to be forgotten."[4] Indeed, memory of the *Virginius* incident fueled American animosity toward Spain in the 1890s and pricked the pride of a country that believed itself to be too powerful to be pushed around as it thought it had been in 1873.[5]

Americans in 1898 wanted their military to match their economic strength. Although the United States by the late 1890s had not yet recovered fully from the Depression of 1893, it was still an economic powerhouse that had achieved enormous growth during the second industrial revolution. In 1860, the U.S. trade balance was negative $38 million. By 1897, it was plus $264 million, and the overall volume of its trade had increased from $670 million in 1860 to $1.795 billion in 1897.[6] The challenge before the country was to translate this economic might into international clout so that episodes such as the *Virginius* incident might have more satisfactory outcomes. As a speaker before the Union League Club (a patriotic organization comprised of prominent Republicans and a breeding ground for Large Policy theorists) put it in 1895, "The fact is, while we are rich in resources, rich in skill, rich in energy, we are poor in the matter of accumulated wealth, poor in the science of political economy and finance, poor as regards statesmen fitted by education and training for the difficult tasks of the day." He concluded, "It is time for us to change, and one of the most desirable changes would be an increase in our commercial relations with other countries, and an extension of the dominion of the United States in the right direction."[7] Statements such as this reflected the sense that the United States was part of a larger society of nations in which America's place should become more prominent–through expansion.[8]

Others made the case for increased involvement in world affairs more forcefully. Most influential by far was Alfred T. Mahan, the respected naval strategist and expositor of a moralistic martial spirit. Mahan had made his name in 1890 with the publication of *The Influence of Sea Power upon History*. The book, which linked the power of nations to their ability to control the sea, became an immediate classic. The book's timing helped make Mahan one of the more important figures of the age since it was precisely in the years that his books gained wide circulation that transformations in naval technology shrank the oceans and leveled the playing field between traditional naval powers, most notably Great Britain, and ambitious up-and-comers, such as Germany. No one before Mahan, however, had explicitly made the link between naval strategy, military strategy, and national greatness. The German kaiser was so impressed with the American's ideas that he required every German ship to carry a copy of the *Influence of Sea Power* text.[9]

Most excited by Mahan's ideas was Theodore Roosevelt, who invited Mahan to join him and Senator Henry Cabot Lodge as they charted naval strategies that would help the United States to take its rightful place among the world's Great Powers. These three men formed the core of the Large Policy group, and, of the three, Mahan was the earliest advocate of expansion.[10] Some scholars have argued that the ideas of this group had a greater impact on the events of 1898–99 than those of anyone else, an argument that has led them to the conclusion that the Spanish-American War was "a decisive step taken by [the United States] on its way to the hegemony of the imperialist world."[11] These scholars point, for example, to the telegram that Roosevelt sent to Commodore Dewey in Hong Kong ordering him to keep his ships full of coal in anticipation of "defensive operations in the Philippines" as evidence that the war itself was fought in pursuit of expansionist ends. Roosevelt sent the telegram when his superior, Secretary of the Navy John D. Long, was taking a day off to rest, and he was not fired for the action. This series of events prompted the argument that the McKinley administration must have agreed to his action—and with his motives.[12] Whereas it is likely that the basic preparations ordered by Roosevelt, commonsensical as they were, were not inconsistent with the general war plans prepared by the administration, the presumption that their acceptance indicates official approval of Roosevelt's preference for a Large Policy is less supported by the evidence.

It is clear that Roosevelt did chafe at what he regarded as a foreign policy insufficiently ambitious for American greatness. In his glowing review of Alfred T. Mahan's study of sea power, for instance, he exclaimed that "we need to have the lesson taught again and again, and yet again, that we must have a great fighting navy in order to hold our proper position among the nations of the earth and to do the work to which our destiny points."[13] His sentiments were echoed by Henry Cabot Lodge, his close friend and fellow historian, who wrote in his history of the Spanish-American War:

> For thirty years the people of the United States had been absorbed in the development of their great heritage. They had been finishing the conquest of their continent, and binding all parts of it together with the tracks and highways of commerce. Once this work was complete, it was certain that the virile, ambitious, enterprising race which had done it would look abroad beyond their boundaries and seek to guard and extend their interests in other parts of the world.[14]

Clearly, Lodge meant to imply that the United States went to war against Spain for reasons in addition to, or perhaps other than, humanitarianism, and his satisfaction with the war's outcome—which provided the United States with an aura of Great Power legitimacy—was, as we have seen, widely shared. In the words of one pamphleteer, "By the admission of all nations the United States is now, for the first time, conceded to be a 'Power' of the same rank as Great Britain, Germany, or Russia."[15]

It was Mahan, however, who recognized that it was now essential to expand national power because the era of "free security" had come to an end. Mahan was less interested in winning for the United States a glorious empire than in enhancing its national security. He reasoned that if the United States did not protect and enhance its interests by gaining control of the seas, then it would remain at the mercy of other powers. Germany, for instance, was seeking to establish a presence everywhere, it seemed, from the Far East, where it sought to secure its trade interests in China, to the Dominican Republic, where it tested the United States's commitment to the Monroe Doctrine. Mahan's concern with American power was thus not inherently imperialistic but reflected his understanding that the goal of extending American ideals was utopian unless the country acquired commensurate power. Mahan wrote:

> Protected from any serious attempt at invasion by our isolated position, and by our vast intrinsic strength, we are nevertheless vulnerable in an extensive seaboard, greater, relatively to our population

and wealth–great as they are–than that of any other state. . . . We are also committed, inevitably and irrevocably, to an overseas policy, to the successful maintenance of which will be needed, not only lofty political conceptions of right and of honor, but also the power to support, and if need be to enforce, the course of action which such conceptions shall from time to time demand.[16]

Mahan did favor–and he earnestly encouraged–acquiring territory that could be used for coaling stations and communications, but these goals did not require the acquisition of entire colonies. The occasional odd island would do.

Mahan and his Large Policy compatriots argued that the morality defended by great powers had objective validity and was consistent with "higher law," not only because they subscribed to social Darwinism but also because the great power they had in mind was the United States. Mahan did not insist that the justice upheld by the United States, when it chose to assert itself, stemmed merely from the preponderance of its power; instead, Mahan believed, the power and the virtue of the United States went hand in hand, in conformity to the general paradigm of civilizational evolutionism popular at the time. Certain that the United States stood for the most "advanced" morality in the world, Mahan therefore insisted that it acquire a complement of power suitable to its moral stature and that it use force to defend its ideals. In the international struggle for survival, held Mahan and his fellow Large Policy enthusiasts, it was a moral imperative that the United States stand up to its retrograde competitors.[17]

These arguments resonated in a society in which, as Richard Hofstadter described it, "[t]he persistence of jingoism . . . [was] too suggestive to be ignored."[18] One prominent Bostonian, for instance, put these options before his listeners: "We can either take part in the movements of the twentieth century that our position, abilities, necessities and the inherited aspirations of the people call for, or we can stand aloof in selfish, timid, unenlightened isolation, and let the march of civilization roll around the globe without us."[19] For President Cleveland's last secretary of state, Richard Olney, the choice was clear:

[The United States ought] to recognize the changed conditions and to realize its great place among the powers of the earth. It behooves it to accept the commanding position belonging to it, with all its advantages on the one hand and all its burdens on the other. It is not enough for it to vaunt its greatness and superiority and to call upon the rest of the world to admire and be duly impressed. The mission of this country . . . is not merely to pose but to act—and, while always governing itself by the rules of prudence and common sense and making its own special interests the first and paramount objects of its care, to forego no fitting opportunity to further the progress of civilization.[20]

Olney had persuaded President Cleveland, a staunch antiimperialist, to pursue an assertive foreign policy. For example, a noteworthy event during his tenure as secretary of state was an aggressive defense of—and reinterpretation of—the Monroe Doctrine against Britain during the Venezuelan crisis of 1895. Britain (on behalf of British Guiana) and Venezuela were engaged in a border dispute after some gold was found in a region that both British Guiana and Venezuela claimed. The United States took Venezuela's side by demanding to arbitrate the issue, and Olney issued a daring note in which he proclaimed to Britain, at the time the most powerful country in the world:

Today the United States is practically sovereign on this continent, and its fiat is law upon the subjects to which it confines its interposition. Why? . . . It is not simply by reason of its high character as a civilized state, nor because wisdom and justice and equity are the invariable characteristics of the dealings of the United States. It is because, in addition to all other grounds, its infinite resources combined with its isolated position render it master of its situation and practically invulnerable as against any or all other powers.[21]

Great Britain indignantly refused the American offer of arbitration and stated flatly that the Monroe Doctrine had no bearing on the issue. Cleveland then delivered a message to Congress on December 17, 1895, that threateningly declared the Western Hemisphere to be the United States's sphere of interest. It was a not-so-subtle warning to Britain, which promptly accepted arbitration rather than risk an increasingly likely war.[22] The United States in this affair had announced to the world that it was becoming an important force in international affairs. By 1895, in order to avoid future embarrassments such as the Chilean episode, it had already embarked on a massive shipbuilding campaign, and now the country was even daring to go toe-to-toe with Great Britain.

Cleveland's example in particular demonstrates, however, that the desire to enhance American power was not inherently imperialistic. Although many Americans seemed to have felt that their nation deserved a larger stake in the control of the world, this does not mean that they concluded that their nation should expand its borders. Not everyone who wished to see the United States become more powerful, in other words, subscribed to the Large Policy. But the desire to see the nation's power expand, in whatever form, was practically universal. Hofstadter described the American mood best: "[T]he civic frustrations of the era created also a restless aggressiveness, a desire to be assured that the power and vitality of the nation were not waning."[23] The striking disparity between American industrial might, on the one hand, and domestic malaise and lack of traditional international power, on the other, fed this restlessness.[24] Thus, Robert Dallek argued that, "[v]ictims of a terrible depression at home for which they had no cure, Americans identified with and found considerable appeal in rescuing other victims abroad."[25] Expansionism, in particular, was for many the best cure for the nation's domestic malaise.[26] Foreign policy was a means by which Americans could assure themselves that they were a great and worthy people. Given the temper of the times and the machinations of Large Policy theorists, the nation was fully prepared to expand.

JOINING THE AGE OF IMPERIALISM

A noteworthy factor underlying Americans' postwar expansionist spirit was that the Spanish-American War was fought at the height of the so-called age of imperialism, when all of the Great Powers competed against each other for colonial possessions and trade advantage. These international norms were significant to U.S. policy makers, in part because the Americans simply had to take greater account of them than before. Remaining an entity apart from the European international system no longer seemed possible, even had Americans so desired. During the 1890s, the United States sought to be regarded as equivalent to the great European powers and to define itself according to standards of international power that by default had been established by the Europeans, and this aspiration inevitably translated into a tacit acceptance of their norms. The foreign-policy standard, "no entangling alliances," that was born with the nation had hitherto governed America's approach to foreign relations. Balancing the continued appeal of unilateralism with the growing attractiveness of European standards of power and glory—which now seemed to be perfectly within the grasp of the United States—quickly became a major challenge to American statesmen. After all, the United States had always prided itself on being *not* European, and this insistence on standing apart had helped to safeguard its isolated development by keeping it free of the convulsions that so frequently disrupted the Continent. What Hans Kohn called "the illusion that the United States was fundamentally different and remote from Europe," in fact, was a central part of American national identity. The United States therefore had to find a way to overcome its anti-European bias.[27]

It did so by combining expansionist values with the idea of U.S. mission. McKinley and the proponents of the Large Policy thus cooperated to institute policies that unmistakably resembled European imperial practices but that supposedly differed because the United States would develop the occupied lands according to a different model. Simeon E. Baldwin, a Yale constitutional authority, thus prepared a study for the U.S. Congress during the treaty debate in which he argued that annexing the Philippines would not require the adoption of a European-style colonial system. Baldwin insisted that because the United States is exceptional, it will extend such rights to the Filipinos as they can handle, unlike the Europeans, who engage in foreign conquest only to advance their own commercial interests. He also noted favorably America's long history of annexing foreign territories (i.e., Mexico, Texas, Louisiana, etc.) and governing them in a distinctly American way.[28]

Ironically, then, given the rootedness of American national identity in the belief in American exceptionalism, the norms to which the United States appealed for international legitimacy at the end of the nineteenth century were defined by *other* civilized powers. The reason for this was simple: Europe controlled and hence defined the international system. Over a period of centuries, the states of Europe had globalized this system by conquering and colonizing the rest of the world. With the global order partitioned by the 1890s between the different European powers, a fierce competition for supremacy among them developed, particularly after Germany united and began to flex its considerable muscle. It was not until the decolonization era, which peaked in the 1950s and 1960s, that the international order became global in a more than geographic sense. In 1898–99, therefore, the norms dictating international behavior were still defined in London, Paris, and Berlin, and the United States perhaps unconsciously began to incorporate them into its identity.

Part of the reason for the shift toward European-style internationalism can also be explained by the Europhilia of the group described by Ernest May as the "foreign policy public." Influential in shaping public opinion concerning foreign affairs, this educated and cosmopolitan group by the 1890s "regarded European experience as a no less valid guide for the United States than, for example, the country's own historic tradition." Furthermore, Europeans justified imperialism by claiming that it advanced the progress of civilization. This argument resonated deeply among an American public that defined itself as *the* nation of progress and helped to erase the stigma attaching to an Old World practice. Expansionism according to the European model thus came increasingly to be regarded as an acceptable course of action. An increasingly influential view emerged: The time was ripe for the United States to join the society of Great Powers. This opinion was buttressed by the ascendance of what was called "the martial spirit," a philosophy of morality and politics that esteemed values not inconsistent with the norms of Europe's colonial systems.[29]

The martial spirit mixed devotion to a life of excitement with a celebration of the militarism that seemed best to encourage it. Its truest representative and most ardent defender was Theodore Roosevelt. Celebration of the martial spirit was part of what George Cotkin calls a "reorientation of American culture" toward "a cultural system based on the powers of desire, excitement, and self-expression."[30] This cultural system valued attributes called the "manly virtues"–toughness, courage, bravado–and it often led to a perverse glorification of war itself. As one proponent argued, "It is not only necessary to have good laws but the power also to enforce their obedience. . . . Strength cannot harm justice, but by reason of weakness virtue is often overcome. . . . No decisive war has ever been detrimental to humanity as a whole. Public questions and theories must be settled and put at rest."[31] This author went on to argue that peace brings corruption and decay and that war has a salutary effect on the character of both individuals and nations. Roosevelt agreed, as his attitude about the Spanish-American War suggests. "This is going to be a short war. . . . I am going to get everything I can out of it,"[32] he declared before quitting his "desk job," hopping on a horse and leading his Rough Riders on a cavalry charge up San Juan Hill. Roosevelt was a national hero even before this daring and inspiring act, but his leadership of the Rough Riders cemented his reputation as a literal embodiment of the manly virtues.

Roosevelt was not the only distinguished leader to celebrate the martial spirit. A different defense of the sentiment came from the unlikely pen of William James. Although, unlike Roosevelt, he did not dedicate himself to a life of excitement–Roosevelt for example hunted big game in Africa and traveled to the West to suffer the hardships of a *real* cowboy–James did defend martial ideals, declaring:

> So far as the central essence of the feeling goes, no healthy minded person, it seems to me, can help to some degree partaking of it. Militarism is the great preserver of our ideals of hardihood, and human life without hardihood would be contemptible. . . . The duty is incumbent on mankind, of keeping military characteristics in stock . . . so that Roosevelt's weaklings and mollycoddles may not end by making everything else disappear from the face of nature.[33]

James, of course, was not celebrating war itself. He abhorred the wastefulness, the bloodshed, and the wanton destruction of war enough to put himself "squarely into the anti-militarist party."[34] He proposed instead a plan that would encourage the ennobling and service-oriented military spirit but that would channel it to productive ends:

> [S]ome of us have nothing but campaigning, and others nothing but unmanly ease. If now–and this is my idea–there were, instead of military conscription a conscription of the whole youthful population to form for a certain number of years a part of the army enlisted against *Nature,* the injustice would tend to be evened out, and numerous other goods to the commonwealth would follow. The military ideals

of hardihood and discipline would be wrought into the growing fibre of the people; no one would remain blind as the luxurious classes now are blind, to man's relations to the globe he lives on, and to the permanently sour and hard foundations of his higher life. To coal and iron mines, to freight trains, to fishing fleets in December, to dish-washing, clothes-washing, and window-washing, to road-building and tunnel-making, to foundries and stock-holes, and to the frames of skyscrapers, would our gilded youths be drafted off, according to their choice, to get the childishness knocked out of them, and to come back to society with healthier sympathies and soberer ideas. (Emphasis in the original)[35]

James considered the martial spirit to be productive of virtues such as discipline, humility, service, and teamwork. And, since he doubted it could be abolished, James thought it best to harness the martial spirit and spread it evenly throughout society, rather than limiting its burdens (and blessings) to those too poor to have a choice about it.

If James characteristically identified the positive lessons latent in the martial spirit, others were more suspicious of it and associated it with Europe's reactionary spirit. They pointed out its aggrandizing nature and inconsistency with American ideals. "Well, I can assure you that if we fall in with the new militarism we shall have more of it, whether we want it or not," argued one commentator. While acknowledging that it "will take us right into the circle of the great warlike powers of the world," this author nevertheless insisted that the military spirit would erode the American ideal "to live and let live; to be free and let other people be free; to abhor conquest and force save against those who in some sense belonged to us, or whom we expected to make a part of us."[36] One professor's economic analysis of militarism also warned that, since as a political ideology militarism would require a larger government and higher taxes than Americans were accustomed to, it would reallocate national values to prioritize those with its aggrandizing spirit. Conceding that "[n]o imperial power can economize, or should think of doing so," he accepted that the United States would be required "to learn to play the war game as others play it; and must not be guilty of such gaucherie as talking about economy, which is a homely luxury which only unheroic republics can afford to indulge."[37]

The president of Stanford University, David Starr Jordan, and the Yale University sociologist and public intellectual William Graham Sumner offered the most trenchant critiques of the new militarism and its conso-ciated romanticism of European international norms. An important part of Jordan's opposition to the expansionism that followed the war explic-itly rested on his identification of it with the European style of govern-ment. "A movement toward the British system would require changes in the Constitution, a movement toward further centralization and toward greater party responsibility," he argued. "The strength of empire, how-ever disguised, lies in brute force and that alone . . . [but] it has been the mission of the United States to teach respect for manhood," he added.[38] To celebrate the martial spirit and mimic the norms of the great Euro-pean powers, in other words, would be to transgress the individualism that is the true heart of American national identity. "The primal duty of Americans is never to forget that men are more than nations; that wis-dom is more than glory, and virtue more than dominion of the sea. The Kingdom of God is within us. The nation exists for its men, never the men for the nation."[39] If the United States were to move too far in the di-rection of militarism and imperialism, he warned, it would be abandon-ing the values that made it an exceptional nation.

Yale's Sumner pointedly entitled his criticism of the Spanish-American War and its consequent expansionism: "The Conquest of the United States by Spain." Sumner wished to highlight how the imperial-ism of the war's settlement constituted a triumph of Spanish political values over America's. "We have beaten Spain in a military conflict," he plainly stated, "but we are submitting to be conquered by her on the field of ideas and policies. . . . If we Americans believe in self-government, why do we let it slip away from us? Why do we barter it away for mili-tary glory as Spain did?" Sumner condemned the martial spirit as Jordan did, but he located its source not in an emulation of Europe per se but in the nation's overzealous pursuit of its mission:

> There is not a civilized nation which does not talk about its civiliz-ing mission just as grandly as we do. . . . We assume that what we like and practise [sic], and what we think better, must come as a welcome blessing to Spanish-Americans and Filipinos. This is grossly and obviously untrue. They hate our ways. They are hostile

to our ideas. Our religion, language, institutions, and manners offend them. . . . If the United States takes out of the hands of Spain her mission on the ground that Spain is not executing it well, and if this nation, in its turn, attempts to be schoolmistress to others, it will shrivel up in the same vanity and self-conceit of which Spain now presents an example.[40]

Sumner's social philosophy held that government intervention in the social order is inherently wrong. A social Darwinist, he held that individuals should stake out their own place in the hierarchy of men and that government, whenever it strays from its narrow administrative purposes, does nothing but sustain an unnatural order of men that is both unjust and, because subversive of nature's rule–"survival of the fittest"–destructive to society itself. The militarism and imperialism of the European powers, he held, require large governments, which inevitably must impose unjust taxes on the people and play an excessive role in the lives of their people. For the United States to copy their political practices, it would have to adopt their form of government, and in so doing it would corrupt its deepest values, offend the natural order of society, and introduce into the body politic a leprous virus that would slowly eat away at its vitality. "[W]e cannot govern dependencies consistently with our political system," he concluded, "and if we try it, the state which our fathers founded will suffer a reaction which will transform it into another empire just after the fashion of all the old ones."[41] In making these arguments, Sumner and Jordan thus articulated a prominent theme of the antiimperialists–that overseas expansionism would take the United States far afield from its best and defining traditions and bring it closer to the European style of governance, rejection of which had hitherto been a staple of national pride. Militarism and imperialism might make the United States more like one of the era's great powers than like the nation of the founding fathers, but it was far from obvious that doing so was a worthy goal to pursue.

"GLUT THEORY" AND OVERSEAS MARKETS

Another proximate cause of American imperialism was that the United States was in search of new markets at the turn of the century. The latter years of the nineteenth century witnessed the consolidation of many of the most important U.S. industries–oil, steel, and the railroads, for example–into large, monopolistic trusts. Their influence over the Republican Party and the national government was powerful but widely resented. Since these trusts possessed more influence over the nation's foreign economy policy than did any other sector of the national economy, and because the prevailing economic theory of the time–the "glut" theory of economic growth–insisted that the marketplace must constantly expand to match increasing production, many scholars have concluded that the McKinley administration engaged in an imperialistic foreign policy in support of the trusts' economic interests. Walter LaFeber, for instance, argues that "[t]he president's role, one that McKinley and Roosevelt played brilliantly, was to provide an overarching foreign policy that benefited as many of these interests as possible."[42]

The glut theory of economic growth, however, broadened the economic basis for expansion beyond the narrow interests of the business community to encompass the well-being of the country as a whole. As a contemporary scholar, Carman Randolph, succinctly explained the theory as expansionists were applying it to the United States, "1. Our ability to produce so greatly exceeds our capacity to consume that wider markets are necessary. 2. Other nations are overrunning vast fields of present and prospective commercial value in order to monopolize their trade. 3. The United States must, therefore, seize compensating fields, or at least acquire such strongholds as will tend to check the advance of their rivals."[43] David Healy notes that this reasoning became "one of the standard explanations of the disastrous depression which began in 1893."[44]

The prevailing sense in the United States was that the nation's productive capacity had *permanently* outstripped its consumptive ability and that depressions were therefore bound to recur, with business booms reliably being followed by sustained periods of stagnation and depression–unless the country found external outlets for its goods. As one expansionist urged, "Foreign markets, foreign commerce, foreign investments have thus become a necessity to the United States if the present scale of wages and the present standards of life are to be maintained."[45] The glut theory, in other words, described economic forces that greatly impacted the lives not only of business owners seeking profits but also of wage earners and everyone else who had been affected by the Depression of 1893.

The glut theory understandably earned the keen interest of the business community, particularly in the South, where the textile industry was growing rapidly.[46] But it would also prove influential to the thinking of national politicians such as McKinley, who were likely to pay heed to a theory that most economists agreed affected the well-being of the entire nation. Many pamphleteers, however, insisted that colonial acquisitions were unnecessary to satisfy the demand for new markets. One such writer noted, for instance, that "[w]e may gain our world's trade without annexing an acre of land over sea [sic]."

When colonialism became a live political issue during the treaty debate and the presidential election of 1900, Democrats issued many broadsides against the argument that colonies had to be acquired in order to support economic expansion. In one of the most thorough critiques of that position, a writer argued:

> That a country should own the markets wherein it sells is an absurdity, yet nothing is more popularly believed. . . . Expansionists point to England as an example of colonial empire; but England, with all her colonies, does not exceed the exports of this country. She sells no more to her colonies to-day than she did fifty years ago, notwithstanding the fact that millions of acres and inhabitants have been added to her domain. . . . Expansionists say we are a nation of producers hindered by overproduction. Overproduction, while one thousand people starve to death in the city of New York every year. . . . Let us hunt up markets in our own starved and stricken country.[47]

On the other hand, the argument that the European powers were consuming the last available markets by acquiring them as colonies made rejecting expansion seem to be something of a gamble. One expansionist captured the sense of urgency that grew out of this belief when he wrote, "The industrial battle-ground of the twentieth century will be in Eastern Asia, and in fifty years the commerce of the Pacific Ocean will rival that of the Atlantic. Are we, situated in the middle of this contest, to take no part in it, and have no share in its results? Are we, though nearer to the ports of China than any European power, and having at least an equal capacity for sea power and industrial production, to ignominiously allow the commerce of the world to pass us by?"[48] In short, few people at the time had any doubt that the United States needed new markets, and if there was even a chance that those markets had to be under the dominion of the producer nation in order to flourish, then the well-being of the United States seemed to dictate territorial expansion.

MANIFEST DESTINY'S RESURGENCE IN THE 1890S

The sense that the United States lacked its fair share of international prestige resurrected the spirit of Manifest Destiny, a term evocative of past glories in the fin de siècle mind. The expression *manifest destiny* had made its first appearance in 1845, when John L. O'Sullivan, an influential editor, used it to designate the national mood of expansion that was then seizing the country.[49] O'Sullivan had for some years been helping to create an ideological rationale for the United States's history of territorial growth, writing in 1839, for instance:

> We are the nation of human progress, and who will, what can, set limits to our onward march? Providence is with us, and no earthly power can [stop us]. . . . Yes, we are the nation of progress, of individual freedom, of universal enfranchisement. . . . We must [proceed] onward to the fulfillment of our mission—to the entire development of the principle of our organization—freedom of conscience, freedom of person, freedom of trade and business pursuits, universality of freedom and equality. This is our high destiny, and in nature's eternal, inevitable decree of cause and effect we must accomplish it. . . . For this blessed mission to the nations of the world, which are shut out from the life-giving light of truth, has America been chosen.[50]

O'Sullivan wrote most of his articles during the 1840s, when the United States was not only involved in a disagreement with Great Britain over the border of Oregon Territory but was also fighting a war against Mexico over "disputed" territory. The themes of mission and providential destiny that he and others refined were used to defend the U.S. cause in these territorial battles. Narrowly, they were designed to assert the position of the United States in these contests as being morally, if not legally, superior to that of its rivals, but on a deeper level they reflected and systematized the widespread belief that the growth of the United States involved the expansion of not just a sovereign nation but of the superior values and ideals that it embodied. Therefore, while O'Sullivan might have coined the term *manifest destiny*, the notion that the United States was morally or philosophically justified in expanding its borders was by his time already a staple of American thought. Thomas Jefferson, for instance, had argued in a letter to his friend Dr. Mitchell that America's "geographical peculiarities may call for a different code of natural law to govern relations with other nations from that which the conditions of Europe have given rise to there."[51]

During the 1890s, Americans' belief in their nation's manifest destiny once again became prominent.[52] In addition to the public's dissatisfaction with domestic affairs, identified by Richard Hofstadter, Robert Dallek, and others, two factors explain why Manifest Destiny reacquired its popularity during the 1890s. First, Americans' outward attention at the time was directed toward Cuba, and that island had for generations been contemplated fondly by expansionists, particularly those in the South. The more Americans paid attention to the awful state of affairs in Cuba, the stronger grew the conviction that the whole mess would never have arisen had the island been a part of American, rather than Spanish, civilization.[53] Second, Frederick Jackson Turner published his classic essay "The Significance of the Frontier in American History" in 1893, which depicted the supposed closing of the American frontier in 1890 in terms that alarmed his countrymen and motivated them to seek new avenues for their traditional restless energies.

The geographical proximity of Cuba to continental North America had long made that island appear to American statesmen as a "natural appendage to the North American continent,"[54] a fact that expansionist writers during the 1890s emphasized.[55] As early as 1850, an article had appeared in *DeBow's Review* asserting that "the possession of Cuba is indispensable to the development and security of the country."[56] Historically, this view was most popular in the South, not only because of Cuba's proximity to that section of the country but also because both were slaveholding territories. Of course, it was precisely that attribute that prevented a national consensus from developing in favor of annexation during the tense antebellum years. Nevertheless, Secretary of War Jefferson Davis had persuaded President Franklin Pierce in 1854 to issue the Ostend Manifesto.

This manifesto was the result of events that had transpired earlier that year, when Spanish authorities had improperly boarded an American steamer, prompting the United States to demand three hundred thousand dollars as compensation. When Spain delayed, the manifesto was issued. Much of its language and terms demonstrate how at least a segment of official opinion in the United States had come to link Cuba with the ideology of Manifest Destiny:

> We firmly believe that, in the progress of human events, the time has arrived when the vital interests of Spain are as seriously involved in the sale, as those of the United States in the purchase, of the island and that the transaction will prove equally honorable to both nations. . . . It must be clear to every reflecting mind that, from the peculiarity of its geographical position, and the considerations attendant on it, Cuba is as necessary to the North American republic as any of its present members, and that it belongs naturally to that great family of States of which the Union is the providential nursery. . . . Indeed, the Union can never enjoy repose, nor possess reliable security, as long as Cuba is not embraced within its boundaries.[57]

In a passage that would prove prophetic, the manifesto also noted that "should the Cubans themselves rise in revolt against the oppression which they suffer, no human power could prevent citizens of the United States and liberal minded men of other countries from rushing to their assistance."[58]

The Ostend Manifesto was often cited in the 1890s in support of arguments urging once again that the United States annex Cuba in order to solve the problems there and fulfill America's manifest destiny. One expansionist referred to the document as being "perhaps by far the most open, candid, diplomatic declaration in all the literature of diplomacy." The same author went on to argue that "[b]etween the date of the messages of John Quincy Adams and William McKinley there is a consensus of expression, all looking to the same direction, to-wit: Cuba is an integral portion of the territory of the United States. The sovereignty of Spain over the island is strained and unnatural. The commercial, industrial, and political interests of the United States demand that the unnatural relation should be broken and the natural relation should be assumed." The historical point was mostly accurate: many U.S. statesmen since the 1820s had expressed interest in annexing Cuba, although most did so only vaguely, by asserting, for instance, that the island should at some unspecified time in the future join the United States, and few even hinted that the merger should proceed forcibly. In the last decade of the nineteenth century, as the United States once again found itself paying particularly close attention to Cuban affairs, these sentiments began to be expressed with a new-found stridency.[59]

In one article condemning the expansionist spirit, for instance, Hermann E. Von Holst, a University of Chicago historian (one of Ernest May's aforementioned foreign-policy opinion leaders), cited several published statements that had been made by political leaders in support of Cuban annexation. Senator Lodge, for instance, wrote in 1895 in the *Forum* that Cuba "would soon become a necessity to us," and Senator Shelby Cullom, of Illinois, was quoted in the *New York Tribune* as asserting that Cuba was "the natural property of the United States" and that "it is time that some one woke up and realized the necessity of annexing property." Most striking, however, was the statement by Senator William P. Frye (R-Maine) in the *Nation's* issue of March 28, 1895: "I had hoped that . . . Spain would assume such an arrogant and belligerent tone that it would be necessary for the United States to go over and take possession of Cuba. We certainly ought to have that island in order to round out our possessions as they ought to be, and if we cannot buy it, I for one should like to have an opportunity to acquire it by conquest."[60] Von Holst considered these sentiments to be dangerous but typical, since, "[f]or generations [the American people] have been systematically worked upon by the charm of the 'manifest destiny'-doctrine."[61]

People in the United States felt newly flush with the spirit of Manifest Destiny not only because their attention was centered on an island that had always seemed to many to be a prodigal territory of their country but also because Frederick Jackson Turner had gotten them to thinking that the "spirit of America," that nebulous something that the country was trying to recapture, depended for its vitality on continued expansion. Turner's essay on the closing of the American frontier initially received almost no attention, but as the decade progressed, it loomed larger and larger in the public mind.[62] Turner's thesis reflected his philosophy of material and cultural evolution, which was best demonstrated in his 1891 essay "The Significance of History." There he argued that the task of the historian is not merely to provide a chronology of events but to describe the "stages of growth" of human civilization. Turner insisted that a proper analysis of American society must include the study of European history, since the men living in America "have come to us historical products" who "have brought with them deeply inrooted customs and ideas." The United States, Turner insisted, thus represented in some ways merely a divergent path in the evolution of European civilization.[63]

But the influence of America's European heritage on its culture was not controlling, argued Turner in his celebrated essay on the closing of the U.S. frontier, because Americans were constantly reinventing themselves along their frontier line. Turner called the frontier "the outer edge of the wave [of civilization's advance]—the meeting point between savagery and civilization." Along the Atlantic coast, civilization evolved in the usual fashion, making that coast in a very real sense Europe's frontier. Along America's western frontier line, however, settlers were forced to "accept the conditions which [the environment] furnish[ed], or perish." Gradually, Turner observed, these hardy frontiersmen had to develop from scratch new social organizations that suited their peculiar needs and that were adapted for their uniquely challenging environment: "Little by little he transforms the wilderness, but the outcome is not the old Europe. . . . The fact is, that here is a new product that is American." The qualities that were required to tame the frontier wilderness, moreover—fortitude, independence, energy—reinforced the democratic features distinctive to American society. "Thus the advance of the frontier has meant steady movement away from the influence of Europe, a steady growth of independence on American lines." In addition, "[t]he isolation of the region increased its peculiarly American tendencies," so that "[i]n the crucible of the frontier the immigrants were Americanized, liberated and fused into a mixed race, English in neither nationality or characteristics." The end result was a new kind of man—an American. A crucial lesson that Americans learned from Turner's argument was thus that the act of expanding American civilization was itself critical to American national identity. However derivative in its origins from European practices, in other words, American expansionism in practice reinforced American exceptionalism.[64]

Turner's thesis had a profound effect on the American public once it processed the essay's message. If the United States acquired its identity and developed all of its redeeming characteristics as a result of the frontier, then what was to become of the nation now that the frontier was gone? Moreover, if the steady progress across the North American continent was expressive of a preexisting tendency or restlessness, as Darwin and others suggested, then where could those energies be directed? One answer that satisfied both concerns began to seem obvious to some Americans. The United States could enlist its natural energies in service of the conquest of *new* frontiers, overseas frontiers. By civilizing these new places, America could share its blessings with their inhabitants while fulfilling its national mandate. In this way, Americans could remain, as it were, American.

Each of the factors described above are useful to a point in explaining American expansionism after the Spanish-American War. The United States *did* wish to indicate its emergence as a great power on the world stage in 1898, and the imperial norm was attractive to this end. Economic considerations, especially regarding the acquisition of foreign markets, *were* influential in shaping the foreign-policy decisions of the country's leaders.[65] And, for the reasons described above, the old ideology of Manifest Destiny enjoyed a resurgence in its popularity and respectability during the 1890s. These facts, however, do not support the conclusion that the United States went to war against Spain in order to initiate a new phase of American expansionism; nor do they mean that U.S. expansion reflected a simple application of the Large Policy advocated by the country's more ardent expansionists. Colonial expansionism only became a seriously entertained goal following the war, and as a policy its substance was shaped by prewar attitudes, not vice versa.

Least defensible is the conclusion drawn by some scholars that the United States entered the war expressly to expand and thereby become a Great Power. As the evidence in chapters 3 and 4 demonstrates, at a minimum, American motives were far more complex than that. Being a Great Power, moreover, meant to most Americans not so much acquiring a global empire as maintaining the capacity to act unilaterally in matters relevant to both the national interest and the nation's mission. While some leaders sought to advance the nation's power on the world stage through expansion, just as many equally prominent individuals opposed such expansion. It was, furthermore, not self-evident that the new markets coveted by economic expansionists had to come in the form of colonial vassals, a point widely argued by the anti-imperialists. Finally, the most important and purely "colonial" overseas acquisition from the war was the Philippine archipelago, and practically no one in the entire country had expressed any interest in those islands at all until after the war was already under way. Few Americans had an idea that they even existed until their military conquered them in 1898. Still, it remains true that economic expansionism and the desire to become a Great Power contributed significantly to U.S. foreign policy in the 1890s and made imperialism an attractive course for the nation to pursue.

Commitment to the idea of American mission, however, also figured significantly, even decisively, into U.S. foreign policy in 1898. Only by presuming that American rhetoric during the war period was baldly two-faced and insincere can one conclude that these sentiments were inconsequential. Moreover, by carefully examining *why* American leaders pursued greatness, were persuaded by the glut theory, and rediscovered their nation's Manifest Destiny in the 1890s, one discerns that base selfishness was not entirely the root of expansionist sentiments. Even if their logic could be myopic, most American expansionists considered their goals to be necessary for national security. Furthermore, given the simultaneous imperialism of the (in their eyes) more morally primitive and dangerous European powers, expansionism was deemed ethically superior to the isolationist alternative. Lands that the United States did not colonize would not become independent but would become, instead, the colonies of some other power–*that* was the reality facing American policy makers in 1898–99.[66] Given the genuinely humanitarian spirit by which at least some in the United States initially pledged to fight the Spanish-American War, its expansionist outcome must be apprised accordingly. Furthermore, the American quest for greater international power had acquired a certain urgency during those years due to a palpable sense that, by standing still, the United States was actually falling behind other nations. Without commensurate power to effectuate its vision, the American ideology of progress would become a meaningless program, and might even be threatened by states that had a superior capacity to act internationally.

The elements of America's imperial mindset discussed above only explain the context in which the country's expansionist policy was formulated—that and the motives of some of its supporters. They explain, in other words, how expansionism lost its stigma and became a politically feasible foreign policy to pursue in a country that had for a hundred years defined itself as politically isolationist. Even taken together, however, they do not provide a full explanation of why the country annexed the Philippine Islands—the focus of the nation's great debate on imperialism. To gain a proper understanding of why the United States expanded in 1898, therefore, one must investigate the logic and motives of expansion's chief architect, President McKinley, since it was his decision—not Roosevelt's—to annex the Spanish islands after the Spanish-American War.

CHAPTER SEVEN

McKinley and the Decision to Expand

TO PRESIDENT MCKINLEY, expansion was an act of national self-definition. Understanding the nature of his role in and contribution to U.S. imperialism, however, has been difficult due to the relative paucity of materials he left behind. As a result, two unlikely interpretations have been able to gain wide currency. The first is that McKinley was a devious Machiavellian who had always intended fully to implement the Large Policy and only feigned resistance to the war movement.[1] In the words of one representative of this group, "As we have seen, McKinley moved resolutely to war, following a course mapped out months before,"[2] the goal of which course was imperialism. The other position holds that McKinley was actually an innocent dupe who was manipulated by the *real* masterminds of American expansionism in 1898, the Large Policy group.[3] On this interpretation, the president essentially implemented a policy formulated by others, either because he was weak or because he lacked strong convictions on the matter. A middle ground of ascending popularity has emerged between these two positions, however, which holds that McKinley was a "reluctant expansionist" who directed the nation's foreign policy (after recovering the leadership he had abdicated during the prewar period) and who only gradually made up his mind that expansion was the proper course for the nation.[4]

The available evidence best supports the middle ground. In particular, the cultural analysis used in this book allows us to recognize how McKinley's decision is best understood as a compromise with unexpected and possibly distasteful realities that were leavened by a belief that imperialism at least could be made to serve not only U.S. security interests but the idea of American mission as well. In other words, McKinley committed to keep the nation on the imperialistic course on which the war with Spain had unexpectedly led it only after persuading himself that imperialism could be made to square with and support the highest values and purposes of the nation as he understood them—and that the public was behind him.

As Julius Pratt observed, it is possible that President McKinley was influenced to some degree by the arguments of Protestant missionaries, who wanted the United States to acquire new territories that they could "Christianize."[5] In a famous anecdote, McKinley decided to follow the imperialist track after praying all night and heeding the divine guidance that he received thereby. As his biographer Charles S. Olcott recounts the episode, the president revealed this fact to a group visiting him at the White House who represented the General Missionary Committee of the Methodist Episcopal Church. After telling the delegation about his dilemma ("I didn't want the Philippines, and when they came to us, as a gift from the gods, I did not know what to do with them"), he noted that he "sought counsel from all sides," but still could not decide. McKinley continued:

I walked the floor of the White House night after night until midnight; and I am not ashamed to tell you gentlemen, that I went down on my knees and prayed Almighty God for light and guidance more than one night. And one night it came to me this way—I don't know how it was, but it came: (1) That we could not give them back to Spain—that would be cowardly and dishonorable, (2) that we could not turn them over to France or Germany—our commercial rivals in the Orient—that would be bad business and discreditable, (3) that we could not leave them to themselves—they were unfit for self-government—and they would soon have anarchy and misrule over there worse than Spain's was; and (4) that there was nothing left for us to do but to take them all, and to educate the Filipinos, and uplift and civilize and Christianize them, and by God's grace do the very best we could by them, as our fellow-men for whom Christ also died. And then I went to bed, and went to sleep, and slept soundly, and the next morning I sent for the chief engineer of the War Department (our mapmaker), and I told him to put the Philippines on the map of the United States, and there they are, and there they will stay while I am President![6]

Scholars have struggled to evaluate the significance of this revelation. Lewis L. Gould, for instance, questions the interviewer's reliability, while Margaret Leetch, perhaps McKinley's most sympathetic biographer, wrote that the president "betrayed his intellectual limitations . . . by an explanation which belittled a great quandary of statesmanship to resolve a dilemma of conscience."[7]

It seems likely, however, that McKinley was both being sincere and simply speaking to his audience. He was a religious man, and it is certain that religious claims figured prominently in his grappling with a decision as laden with moral implications as the acquisition of colonial populations. The explanation he purportedly gave to the Methodist delegation revealed his awareness of geopolitical constraints and of the economic implications of the different policy choices before him, yet it clearly stressed the benefits to American Christianity that could accrue to a colonial policy. McKinley knew that he had a sympathetic audience for this argument. The missionary impulse had been strengthening among various denominations throughout the period, and many sects zealously advocated expansionism under the impression that spreading the Protestant faith was the same as sharing American values.

It was during this era that, in Robert N. Bellah's words, "faith, nation, and empire seemed to flow together in a new synthesis. . . . Protestants and Catholics alike seemed to be prepared to believe that America 'can not conquer but to save.'"[8] Religious imperialists believed that the idea of America's mission meant "the emancipation of humanity," irregardless of whether the emancipated welcomed their converters.[9] The United States, thought the missionaries, must take advantage of the opportunity provided by its victory over Spain to realize the promise of its divine election. "The times are ripe for us to extend the blessings of free government to all those portions of the earth which God and the fortunes of war render it reasonably obligatory for us to extend them to," announced the Christian and Missionary Alliance.[10] To thus do God's work, the nation would also be engaging in self-purification and directly advancing the kingdom of God. For some, therefore, expansion was not simply an opportunity but a moral imperative. Thus, the author of a history of Christian missions insisted, "To save America, America must save the world."[11]

Two historians who independently reviewed the journals of various Protestant sects concluded that only the Unitarians, Universalists, and

Friends (Quakers) opposed expansion.[12] The rest viewed it as an opportunity to proselytize overseas—and the Methodists, whom McKinley was hosting when he revealed his desire to "Christianize" the Catholic Filipinos, were particularly vocal in making this point.[13] As the Central Illinois Conference of the Methodist Episcopal Church declared, "Never was the image of the angel flying in the midst of heaven cleaving the air with its might wings, bearing the everlasting gospel to every kindred, tongue and people, more clearly defined than now."[14] The *Christian Advocate*, a Methodist journal, added that the United States should "break the clutch which Rome has put upon these people, and give them a chance for a civilization which is something more than Christianized paganism."[15] The missionaries hoped to institute a global ecumenical movement under U.S. auspices and welcomed the chance to do their work under the protection of the flag. "With . . . 'the American flag floating over the Ladrones,' our missionaries may work unterrified by papal interference and Spanish treachery. . . . This is the Lord's doing, and it is marvelous in our eyes," announced the American Board of Commissioners for Foreign Missions. Elsewhere the board exclaimed, "American civilization and American ideals and institutions, with American power to uphold and extend them, have moved on, in the providence of God, to the islands of the Pacific; aye! Onward to the kingdoms and peoples of the far East, and soon we shall have no more talk of *foreign* missions, for every Christian man, in every land, will realize that humanity is one, as Christ is one."[16]

Their equating of America's expansionist purposes with their own goals made the missionaries particularly concerned to ensure the purity of the government's behavior overseas. The YMCA thus undertook actively to convert America's military personnel and to keep them on the straight and narrow. "When it is remembered that the soldiers and sailors in these faraway lands are, in a certain sense, our missionaries, an idea of the Christian work among them will be somewhat appreciated," the Women's Auxiliary of the YMCA reminded the group's supporters in a fund-raising newsletter, continuing:

> Natives receive their first impressions of our country—its civilization and its religion—from those in military service among them. If, then, it be true that "the world is upon the thresh hold of a deep spiritual

awakening" [thresh hold: *(sic)*] the men who as soldiers or sailors represent civilized nations among the peoples of half-civilized and heathen lands have a tremendous responsibility, which they should be helped to meet by the united effort of the church in the homeland.[17]

The behaviors that concerned the missionaries, of course, had less to do with their atrocious treatment of the "heathen" than with the more familiar vices of drinking, smoking, and prostitution. (These concerns, though misplaced given Americans' horrible mistreatment of the Filipinos, seem to have been warranted. Ferdinand Blumentritt, a German expert on the Philippines, in evaluating the effects of U.S. occupation, wrote: "To-day, wherever the American flag has been raised, the use of whisky has followed, and this seems to have been the only result which the Americans have as yet achieved.")[18] The YMCA and other organizations therefore thought it important to provide healthy, suitable diversions for the soldiers during their free time, "[f]or on the true thinking and right living of this class largely depend the power and stability of nations, as well as the rapid progress of Christianity."[19]

The YMCA and the other proselytizing organizations clearly felt perfectly at ease correlating the United States with Christianity, directly and explicitly. National and religious goals, they believed, were one and the same. The missionaries added urgency and intensity to the expansionist cause, and their denominational affiliations—which were large, institutionalized, and commanded the loyalty of huge swaths of the population—enabled them to become powerful political lobbies and mobilizers of public opinion. At the very least, politicians had to take heed of their existence and interests.[20] Even more, many government officials shared fully in their vision. The first American superintendent of the Philippine schools, Dr. Fred Atkinson, for example, crudely removed Roman Catholicism from the curriculum (the Americans took over an educational system that had been run by the church), removed crucifixes from the walls, and appointed only Protestants to teaching positions.[21] While some of these measures (but obviously not the last one) were consistent with the U.S. model of religious freedom, in other respects Dr. Atkinson conveyed unmistakably to the Philippines' Catholic population that the American occupying force was not religiously neutral, but Protestant.

President McKinley was generally supportive of the missionaries' goals. He appeared, for instance, before an ecumenical conference in New York in 1900 and showered the audience with effusive praise. "I am glad of the opportunity to offer without stint my tribute of praise and respect to the missionary effort which has wrought such wonderful triumphs for civilization," he told them.

> The missionary, of whatever church or ecclesiastical body, who devotes his life to the service of the Master and of man, carrying the torch of truth and enlightenment, deserves the gratitude and homage of mankind. The noble, self-effacing, willing ministers of peace and goodwill should be classed with the world's heroes. Wielding the sword of the spirit, they have conquered ignorance and prejudice. They have been among the pioneers of civilization. They have illumined the darkness of idolatry and superstition with the light of intelligence and truth. . . . Their contribution to the onward and upward march of humanity is beyond all calculation.[22]

Because the president considered civilization and Christianity to be mutually reinforcing, he readily accepted that Christianity was directly supportive of the American mission.[23]

It is possible to overstate the influence of the missionary movement on the government, however, including on McKinley and other sympathetic figures. The United States did not expand to serve religious imperialists, any more than it annexed foreign lands at the behest of the business community. The influence of the missionary opinion, rather, rested on the congruity of its goals with the idea of American mission. A speech about the American position in the Philippines given by Senator Cushman K. Davis (R-Minn.), a member of the treaty delegation and chair of the Senate Committee on Foreign Relations, reveals how the idea of American mission was understood by expansionists to include Protestant imperialism:

> We cannot escape the responsibilities which events, evolutionary or providential, have imposed upon us. . . . I believe there is a profound perception in the minds of the American people that part of all this force which has pushed and established us [in the Philippines] is an impetus which tells for civilization, for a better Christianity, and

that the United States, as the great evangelist of nations, is destined to play a leading part in the regeneration of the Asiatic Orient. . . . I would rear [the Filipinos] with the hand of paternal affection whenever possible, and by the hand of paternal chastisement whenever necessary. And when the time shall come in the development of that people [that] . . . they can be admitted to local autonomy, I would grant it to the fullest extent possible; . . . But, until that time shall come, the interest, the honor, the security of the American people demand that we shall hold the Philippine islands, not only under our protection but under our rule.[24]

Davis had always been an expansionist; the president had appointed him to the treaty delegation for precisely that reason. His interpretation of the idea of American mission was therefore an aggressive one. But how closely did it conform with McKinley's? One way to answer that question is to review the diplomatic correspondence between McKinley and the delegates on the peace commission who were negotiating the treaty.

SETTLING ON THE TERMS OF THE PEACE TREATY

McKinley, typically, did not wish to commit himself immediately to any policy. He agreed only that immediate self-rule for the islanders and renewed Spanish sovereignty were out of the question, and he favored taking any territory that might enhance the strategic position of the United States. The Monroe Doctrine disposed him to hold Puerto Rico, and concern with the ambitions of the European powers and of Japan inclined him to take at least some of the Philippine Islands. In his instructions to the peace commission in Paris, McKinley therefore used his control of the nation's diplomacy to set treaty terms that included expansionist provisions, and he was careful in selecting the members of the commission to include a majority of members who agreed with his position. Members of the peace commission in addition to Senator Davis were Senator William O. Frye (R-Maine), another expansionist; Senator George Gray (D-Del.), who opposed expansion; William R. Day, the outgoing secretary of state who was to serve as McKinley's direct spokesman in the process; and the editor of the *New York Tribune*,

Whitelaw Reid. Reid was a powerful player in the Republican Party, and his paper touted the party line. He was a committed expansionist.[25] While the president obviously favored expansion, his initial instructions to the commission show that he did not immediately seek to annex the entire Philippine archipelago, only enough to be used for naval bases and coaling stations.

Significantly, the president devoted a major portion of his instructions to defining the spirit in which the commissioners were to conduct negotiations and to explaining the national interests and values that they were to support in the negotiations. His comments in this regard—they were not public statements but secret instructions to a delegation on a crucial diplomatic mission—are thus revealing of how McKinley wanted future generations to regard his motives. Clearly, McKinley was convinced of his country's innate moral supremacy, and he hoped to use that stature as leverage in the negotiations with the Spaniards. Thus he reminded the commissioners:

> We took up arms only in obedience to the dictates of humanity and in fulfillment of high public and moral obligations. We had no design of aggrandizement and no ambition of conquest. Through the long course of repeated representations which preceded and aimed to avert the struggle and in the final arbitrament of force this country was impelled solely by the purpose of relieving grievous wrongs and removing long-existing conditions which disturbed its tranquility, which shocked the moral sense of mankind, and which could no longer be endured.

In the same spirit, he continued:

> It is my earnest wish that the United States in making peace should follow the same high rule of conduct which guided it in facing war. . . . Our aim in the adjustment of peace should be directed to lasting results and to the achievement of the common good under the demands of civilization, rather than to ambitious designs. . . . The presence and success of our arms at Manila imposes upon us obligations which we cannot disregard. The march of events rules and overrules human action. Avowing unreservedly the purpose which has animated all our effort, and still solicitous to adhere to it,

we cannot be unmindful that without any desire or design on our part the war has brought us new duties and responsibilities which we must meet and discharge as becomes a great nation on whose growth and career from the beginning the Ruler of Nations has plainly written the high command and pledge of civilization. . . . In view of what has been stated, the United States cannot accept less than the cession in full right and sovereignty of the Island of Luzon.[26]

These comments show not only that by mid-September the president had *not* fully committed to annexing all of the Philippines. Rather, as of mid-August he had decided to retain only the island of Luzon. His instructions to those superintending the Spanish evacuation of Puerto Rico reveal, however, that he also meant at that time to retain all of the Spanish islands occupied by U.S. forces in the Caribbean, except for Cuba.[27] His thinking on the rest of the Philippines, and on expansion in general, developed over the course of his correspondence with his negotiators in Paris, where the treaty was being hammered out. As demonstrated by the following review of the exchanges between McKinley and the peace commissioners, excerpted to focus on their attention to the disposition of the Philippines, McKinley's views were shaped in part by a misunderstanding of the nature of the Filipino nationalist movement, which he regarded as aberrational, and partly by the feedback he received on an October speaking tour he took through the Midwest.

A significant obstacle to U.S. control over the islands was the Filipino nationalist movement led by Don Emilio Aguinaldo, whose opposition to American occupation became, by the winter, a war of resistance against the United States. Even during the summer months, when Aguinaldo's and U.S. forces were cooperating, it was clear that this armed segment of the Philippine population desired independence—from the United States as well as Spain. Many crucial aspects of this resistance were unclear to McKinley. How widespread was its support—was it indicative of a universal antipathy to potential American rule, or limited to a small handful of rabble rousers? What were the reasons for the resistance? How costly, in dollars and blood, would the effort be to suppress the insurgency, if it became violent? What were the final goals of the resistance group? Were they capable of self-rule? What sort of society did they seek to achieve? As a preliminary to deciding on whether or not to retain the entire archipelago, therefore, McKinley endeavored to discover the character of the resistance.

Aguinaldo was a nationalist who patterned the independence movement that he led on the example of the United States. His group, called the Katipunan, was begun by Dr. José Rizal in 1892, and its dedication to overthrowing Spanish rule was a response to the unusually cruel and brutal character of Spanish governance, especially that of the Catholic friars who constituted the local government on the islands. The Katipunan was defeated in 1897, when Spanish authorities signed an agreement with the overmatched Aguinaldo, which required him to leave the islands in exchange for a sizeable cash payment and the institution of some minor political reforms. The reforms were never implemented, but Aguinaldo left for Hong Kong, biding his time and awaiting the next chance to renew the Filipino revolution.[28]

Aguinaldo believed that his opportunity arrived when the United States declared war against Spain. Some low-level American military and diplomatic authorities in Singapore had promised sympathy for the Filipino independence movement in exchange for Filipino assistance of the United States against Spain. The details of these meetings, however, were later disputed: the Americans recollected neither promises nor the invitation to form any kind of formal alliance—only expressions of sympathy—while Aguinaldo recalled the United States offering the Filipinos independence under a U.S. protectorate in exchange for a formal military alliance.[29] McKinley, in any event, was entirely unaware of the existence of Aguinaldo, let alone any deals that might have been brokered with him. Still, Aguinaldo viewed the U.S. assault on the Spanish position in the Philippines as the first step in the islands' liberation, as he announced in a proclamation issued in advance of Dewey's squadron:

Compatriots: Divine providence is about to place independence within our reach, and in a way the most free and independent nation could hardly wish for. The Americans, not from mercenary motives, but for the sake of humanity and the lamentations of so many persecuted people, have considered it opportune to extend their protection [sic] mantle to our beloved country, now that they have been obliged to sever relations with Spain, owing to the tyranny this nation is exercising in Cuba, causing enormous injury to the Americans, who have such large commercial and other interests there.[30]

In defiance of orders issued by the Spanish governor-general, the proclamation then instructed the Filipinos not to fire on the American ships: "Your natural enemies, your executioners, the authors of your misery and unhappiness, are the Spaniards who govern you. Against these you must raise your weapons and odium; understand well, against the Spaniards and never against the Americans."[31]

Shortly after issuing this document, Aguinaldo returned to his homeland to begin what he thought would be the final revolution for Filipino independence. Rightly or wrongly, he thought that his forces, which he mobilized immediately and efficiently upon returning, were allied with the United States. As the Americans overwhelmed the Spanish in the seas, Aguinaldo's forces defeated them on land. By the time the first U.S. land troops arrived on Luzon in June, Aguinaldo had already declared himself the president of the Filipinos and commenced setting up the institutional rudiments of an independent Filipino government. But the insurgents had not conquered Manila, the islands' political, cultural, and commercial center. By this point, McKinley was not only aware of Aguinaldo but deeply concerned about the nature of his involvement in the conflict. As the U.S. president sent troops to effect the overthrow of Manila, the Filipino forces also moved into position to accomplish the same end. A situation thus developed in which the Spanish, inside Manila, were arrayed against both the Americans and the Filipinos, who seemed to operate within the framework of a loose, informal alliance, but who clearly worked independently of each other, toward ends that were mutually inconsistent, and with increasing mistrust of one another. A three-way standoff had emerged.

After Spain capitulated–there never was any battle of real significance–the tensions between the U.S. troops and the Filipino nationalists rose to the surface. The Americans took charge of the situation, and Filipino resentment ratcheted dangerously upward. As McKinley, through his commissioners, negotiated with Spain over the Philippines as part of the final peace settlement, the need to ascertain the nature of the wider Philippine situation and of Aguinaldo's role became critical. In early October, therefore, the president gathered information from American officials who had experience in the Philippines. He met in the White House, for instance, with Maj. Gen. Francis V. Greene, USV, on three occasions in the days leading up to his speaking tour. Greene advised McKinley to retain the entire island group. Returning them to Spain, Greene argued, would lead to civil war; entrusting them to the Filipinos would result in anarchy; transferring them to Germany or Japan would be "cowardly"; and establishing a joint protectorate with the Filipinos would be difficult to achieve in practice. Greene recorded in his diaries that McKinley was not terribly receptive to his proposal and that the president favored only the maintenance of a coaling station and such islands as would be necessary for naval purposes. But, Greene also recorded, the president told him at the end of their third and final session, "Perhaps when I come back [from my speaking tour] I may think differently from what I now think."[52]

The president heard other opinions agreeing with Greene's recommendations from the commissioners in Paris. At the same time that McKinley was meeting with Greene, he had sent instructions directing the committee members to conduct a broader inquiry into the Philippine situation, and the results of that inquiry reached the White House on October 7, just days before the president left on his speaking tour. Most important of the opinions gleaned by the committee was that of Maj. Gen. Wesley Merritt, who had taken command of the situation at Manila on July 25. He insisted that "if a few ambitious insurgent chieftains [i.e., Aguinaldo and some other minor leaders] could be disposed of, [then the] masses of natives could be managed by the United States." He considered, moreover, the "natives incapable of self-government because [of a] lack of good examples, lack of union in Luzon and throughout [the] archipelago, and [the] existence of race, tribal, and religious differences." Merritt said of Aguinaldo that he was "the most popular leader, but [he] maintains control with difficulty. Some of his leading men [are] dishonest and many wealthy natives [are] opposed to him. Natives of Manila [are] generally opposed to [the] insurrection."[53]

The commission also solicited the opinions of Admiral Dewey, who added no insights of value, and of Colonel Jewett, who declared that the "natives would submit to any just, firm government, but [were] unfit for self-government." The Belgian consul at Manila, Edouard André, who managed the negotiations between Dewey and the Spanish at Manila, advised that the "United States take all or nothing." He called the "native character insincere" and regarded the Filipinos as "inferior and unfitted to rule. Their only examples [were] the monks and Spaniards." He added that Aguinaldo's "rebellion represents only half of one percentum [sic] of inhabitants. Only 30,000 rebels." All of these government officials agreed that the monastic orders were horribly oppressive, although the Jesuits were popular, and they suggested that "it would be unwise to let Protestant missionaries go there except as educators, and that not immediately." There was also a consensus among those testifying that a divided sovereignty of the islands, between the United States on Luzon and any other power on the other islands, would be untenable and provocative of conflicts, rivalry, and instability. The United States, in short, should take all or none of the islands.[34]

An interesting argument was made by Commander R. B. Bradford, but his testimony was not included in the telegraphed correspondence between the president and his commissioners. Bradford's position, however, would have appealed most strongly to the president:

> I would like to add something with your permission in connection with the Philippines which I think you have omitted. It is the moral aspect of the case. If we take a portion of the islands only, are we not open to the accusation of taking the best and leaving the poorest? Have we a moral right to make a selection? We have driven the Spanish government out of the Philippines; there is no Spanish authority there, or practically none. Are we going to take what we want and leave the remainder in a state of anarchy? I believe we have incurred a moral obligation to take all the islands, govern them, civilize the natives, and do the best we can with them.[35]

These comments were published by a Republican printing house as part of a longer pamphlet that served as an extended apologia of McKinley's policy. They were not communicated to McKinley during the negotiations. Nevertheless, Bradford's opinion, mirroring McKinley's as closely as it did, is indicative of the moralism that was embedded in the annexationist position.

The conclusions offered in the testimony that he did receive were reinforced by the final evidence regarding the state of affairs in the

Philippine Islands that McKinley acquired prior to embarking on his speaking tour. A businessman, John Foreman, had also shared his observations with the commission, and these reached the president on October 9. Foreman had lived in the Philippine Islands and had written what commissioner Reid called "the best book" on the subject.[36] Foreman provided detailed information about the outrages committed by the friars and explained how the Spanish authorities were "merely servants" of them, evidenced, for example, by their having General Rámon Blanco removed as governor-general because he was "not bloodthirsty." The insurrection was thus "caused by" and directed at the "oppressions of monks." The friars were sent by and accountable to Spain and the Vatican, but the "Native priests would not oppose the United States or resent [the] coming of Protestant missionaries."[37] The first task needed to restore a just order under American auspices, therefore, was the removal of the friars from power.

It was with this information and understanding of the Philippine situation that McKinley set off on his traveling inquiry of the American public's position on annexation. From the facts and arguments that were unanimously presented in the testimonies—that the insurrection represented only a tiny fraction of the population, that the main source of problems in the islands came from the friars, and that it would be politically unwise and militarily unsafe to divide the islands—it is easy to see how the president began to modify his views on annexation. Taking only Luzon, it seemed, was impractical, but the navy needed *some* sort of foothold in the Far East. Furthermore, Aguinaldo's insurrection did not appear to represent much of a threat, either to the ability of the Americans to secure their power in the islands or to the justice of their cause. Yet the president did not indicate whether he had moved from his initial inclination, communicated in his initial instructions to the commission, to retain only Luzon. The near debacle of his resistance to the war movement had taught him that any undertaking as significant as expansion required the people's approval. In the fall, therefore, after August's peace protocol had stopped the fighting, but before the peace treaty had settled the terms of that peace, McKinley embarked on an extended speaking tour through the Midwest, engaging in a dialogue with the American people about the nation's as-yet undecided course.

The president had two broad goals when he rode a train through the nation's heartland giving speeches to countless small-town crowds. First, he wanted to celebrate the fact that the United States had come together again as a nation as a result of the war. Second, he wanted to determine the public's sentiments about expansion even as he subtly tried to guide them to accept the wisdom of that course. McKinley had other purposes on the speaking tour, including exulting in the victory and stumping for local Republican candidates in the November elections. But his primary ambition was to determine the feasibility of annexing all of the Philippine Islands as he contextualized that act within the deeper traditions of U.S. civilization. The president had his aides take careful note of the crowds' reactions to his speeches,[38] and gradually he was able to settle his comments into an oratorical pattern that included hardly anything but proven applause lines, which invariably referred to some facet of the idea of American mission.

In this way, McKinley, while rarely saying explicitly that he was thinking about annexation of the Philippines, was able to soften the population toward such a policy. When the news became more public that annexation was in fact the policy that the administration intended to pursue, the president had already framed the matter in the public mind in a way that appealed to the people's highest ideals and deepest values. The themes that he relied on most often to accomplish this goal were humanity, civilization, destiny, and duty. His technique was to use these motifs to characterize American identity and to spell out the idea of U.S. mission in such a way that the American people would view territorial expansion according to the ideological framework that these motifs provided. As consistently favorable responses to his code phrases gave him increasing confidence that the public would support expansion, he became at times more direct in his references to the policy. By the time the tour was over, McKinley was certain that he and the public were once again on the same page and that he could count on their support as he led the nation on its new imperialist course.

One of McKinley's rhetorical strategies was to relate the war's outcome with its noble beginnings and thereby weave expansion into the fabric of humanitarianism. "We commenced the war not for gain or greed or new possessions," he announced for example at Kokomo, Indiana. "We commenced it for freedom and to relieve our neighbors of oppression. And having accomplished that we must assume all the responsibilities that justly belong to that war, whatever they may be."[39] In Belle Plain, Iowa, he was only slightly more explicit: "This war has taught us a great many lessons and one of the most priceless connected with the conflict has been the triumph of humanity. . . . What we want, my fellow citizens, is that the conclusion of this war, as written in a public treaty, shall be a triumph for humanity."[40] Since the war was fought for humanity, he deduced for the public, its outcome must logically serve humanity as well.

When McKinley insisted that the United States acted for the cause of humanity, he meant to convey not only that the decision to intervene was noble but that it reflected the essential character of American civilization. "I am sure it is the universal prayer of American citizens that justice and humanity and civilization shall characterize the final settlement of peace as they have distinguished the progress of the war," he told an audience in Chicago. "My countrymen, the currents of destiny flow through the hearts of the people. Who will check them, who will divert them, who will stop them? And the movements of men, planned and designed by the Master of men will never be interrupted by the American people."[41] At Cedar Rapids, Iowa, he declared, "We accepted war for humanity. We can accept no terms of peace which shall not be in the interest of humanity. . . . No achievements are worth having which do not advance civilization and benefit mankind. While our victories in battle have added new honors to American valor, the real honor is the substantial progress it has reached for civilization and humanity."[42]

If these speeches only insinuated that "humanity and civilization" required that the United States expand in the war's aftermath, another speech he gave in Chicago, at the end of the tour, was more explicit:

The war with Spain was not of our seeking, and some of its consequences may not be to our liking. . . . The progress of a nation can alone prevent degeneration. There must be new life and purpose or there will be weakness and decay. There must be broadening of thought as well as broadening of trade. Territorial expansion is not alone and always necessary to national advancement. There must be a constant movement to a higher and nobler civilization. In our present situation, duty alone should prescribe the boundary of our responsibilities and the scope of our undertakings. . . . We all hope and pray that the confirmation of peace will be as just and humane as the consummation of the war. . . . The Army and Navy have nobly performed their part. May God give the Executive and Congress wisdom to perform theirs.[43]

McKinley's favorite way to characterize America's overseas activities was by reference to Providence and the nation's destiny. As he intoned in Carroll, Iowa, "Providence has been extremely kind to the American people–kind, not only in the recent conflict of arms, but in every step and stage of our history from its very beginning until now. We have been singularly blessed and favored. The past of our country is all secured and it is glorious. It is the future with which we have to deal and if we shall be as wise as our fathers than this fabric of government will be carried on successfully by their sons."[44] Subtly, McKinley was characterizing expansion ("the future") as a policy in keeping with America's most exalted traditions. It was just another step to be taken on the path of destiny, the path that the founding fathers had charted out.

At the Trans-Mississippi Exposition in Omaha, Nebraska, McKinley's invocation of Providence was used more explicitly to cast the United States as a Christian nation, probably because the "Liberal Congress of Religion" was holding its fifth session there. Among the participants of the congress were many important religious and social leaders, including Hiram W. Thomas, Dr. Paul Carus, David Starr Jordan, Dr. Nathaniel Schmidt, W. M. Backus, Thomas Dixon, and E. G. Hirsch. As noted in chapter 2, liberal Protestants in America in 1898 believed that people needed to form a partnership with God in order to help achieve the kingdom of God. They believed that the here-and-now was relevant in God's grand scheme and that progress depended upon human initiative in addition to providential intent; they held, furthermore, that nations as well as individuals were implicated in millennial history. McKinley's comments seemed calculated to appeal to this logic:

The faith of a Christian nation recognizes the hand of Almighty God in the ordeal through which we have passed. Divine favor seemed manifest everywhere. In fighting for humanity's sake we have been signally blessed. . . . Right action follows right purposes. We may not at all times be able to divine the future, the way may not always seem clear, but if our aims are high and unselfish, somehow and in some way the right end will be reached. The genius of the nation, its freedom, its wisdom, its humanity, its courage, its justice, favored by Divine Providence, will make it equal to every task and the master of every emergency.[45]

McKinley's invocation of America's partnership with and reliance on God was even more direct in a speech he gave in St. Louis: "We must gather the just fruits of victory. We must pursue duty step by step. We must follow the light as God has given us to see the light, and He has singularly guided us not only from the beginning of our great government, but down through every crisis to the present hour, and I am sure it is a universal prayer of every American that He shall still guide and direct us."[46] What McKinley left unsaid was the end to which God was directing the United States, but this silence allowed Americans to interpret *any* policy as the one the God was leading them to. McKinley thereby glossed his foreign policy with the veneer of the great American destiny that no one dared to doubt.

The most effective and frequently declared theme in McKinley's speeches, however, was "duty": "We cannot shirk the obligations of the victory if we would, and we would not if we could," as he told the people of Indianapolis.[47] The concept of duty was useful in two crucial respects. First, it gave an appearance of Christian nobility and responsibility to an action—imperialism—that more typically was characterized as the ultimate act of national selfishness. Second, it prepared the nation more directly for expansion than any of the other themes that he used in his speeches. Destiny and humanity, for instance, could as easily have been invoked to gird the country for retreating back into its own borders, its noble crusade to end Spanish abroad completed, as it was to prepare the country for expansion. Duty, however, only made rhetorical sense if McKinley meant to brace the American people for continued overseas actions.

The president most explicitly discussed expansion as a national duty in his speech in Chicago. On that occasion McKinley strove earnestly to convince his audience that holding on to the Philippines was the solemn duty of the United States—and he did so without ever mentioning the Philippines or expansion directly. "The war," he began,

> has put on the nation grave responsibilities. Their extent was not anticipated and could not have been well foreseen. We cannot escape the obligations of victory. We cannot avoid the serious questions which have been brought home to us by the achievements of our arms on land and sea. We are bound in conscience to keep and perform the covenants which the war has sacredly sealed with mankind. Accepting the war for humanity's sake, we must accept all obligations which the war in duty and honor has imposed upon us. The splendid victories we have achieved would be our eternal shame and not our everlasting glory if they led to the weakening of our original lofty purpose or to the desertion of the immortal principles on which the National Government was founded and in accordance with whose ennobling spirit it has ever since been faithfully administered.

Then, tying America's duty to its destiny and invoking more sacred imagery, he added:

> Duty determines destiny. Destiny which results from duty performed may bring anxiety and perils, but never failure and dishonor. . . . It is not within the power of man to foretell the future and to solve unerringly its mighty problems. Almighty God has His plans and methods for human progress, and not infrequently they are shrouded for the time being in impenetrable mystery.[48]

In this way, McKinley told the American people indirectly—but, for the attentive, unmistakably—that the country was going to expand in accordance with its most deeply held traditions.

Confident that the American people would support his expansionist program, McKinley resolved at the conclusion of the speaking tour to retain the entire Philippine archipelago. The decision would create his administration's most important legacy. Although the United States had not entered the Spanish-American War due to the president's initiative, the country's refusal to extend recognition to a Cuban republic showed that it would fight on its own terms and for its own purposes, and this stance reflected McKinley's influence. As McKinley became more assertive in the formulation of U.S. foreign policy, the nation became correspondingly more committed to vindicationism. Unilaterally, the United States would refashion the regimes and societies of other countries, beginning with Cuba and the Philippines. This was McKinley's vision, and it was one that he soon shared with his peace commissioners in Paris.

The commissioners were themselves divided on the issue, however, and they communicated their differences in a lengthy dispatch to McKinley on October 25. They needed formal guidance from the president as to what goals they should pursue in their negotiations with the Spanish commissioners over the treaty. Senators Davis and Frye and Reid, the newspaper editor, presented the full-annexationist position. Day, the chairman of the U.S. commission, took a middle position that stuck to the terms laid out by McKinley in his initial instructions. "[B]earing in mind the often declared disinterestedness of purpose and freedom from designs of conquest with which the war was undertaken," he argued, "we should be consistent in our demands in making peace." Maintaining a base on Luzon for naval and commercial purposes would satisfy U.S. needs without creating the need for a colonial policy, with all of its attendant headaches and expenses.[49]

Democratic Senator Gray, on the other hand, made the case against annexing any territory starkly and unambiguously. Gray argued that to take the islands "would be to reverse [the] accepted continental policy of the country, declared and acted upon throughout our history." He argued that Cuba and Puerto Rico's "propinquity" to the United States put their disposition on different grounds than that of the Philippines and that the "Policy proposed introduces us into European politics and the entangling alliances against which Washington and all American Statesmen have protested." He continued, "It will make necessary a navy equal to [the] largest of powers; a greatly increased military establishment; immense sums for fortifications and harbors; multiply occasions for dangerous complications with foreign nations, and increase burdens of taxation." He saw little benefit that would outweigh these costs. But Gray's most vigorous and impassioned argument against annexation was moral:

[E]ven conceding all benefits claimed for annexation, we thereby abandon the infinitely greater benefit to accrue from acting the part of a great, powerful, and Christian nation; we exchange the moral grandeur and strength to be gained by keeping our word to nations of the world and by exhibiting a magnanimity and moderation in the hour of victory that becomes the advanced civilization we claim, for doubtful material advantages and [the] shameful stepping down from [the] high moral position boastfully assumed. We should set [an] example in these respects, not follow the selfish and vulgar greed for territory which Europe inherited from medieval times. Our declaration of war upon Spain was accompanied by a solemn and deliberate definition of our purpose. Now that we have achieved all and more than our object, let us simply keep our word. . . . Above all let us not make a mockery of the injunction contained in [the] instructions, where, after stating that we took up arms only in the dictates of humanity and in the fulfillment of high public and moral obligations, and that we had no design of aggrandizement and no ambition of conquest, the President among other things eloquently says: "It is my earnest wish that the United States in making peace should follow the same high rule of conduct which guided it in making war."[50]

Many in the United States shared Gray's opposition to annexation, and for the same reasons that he provided. McKinley, however, having weighed the opinions offered by the commissioners he appointed, the evidence contained in the testimony they gathered, and the feelings of the nation as he imperfectly measured them on his speaking tour, resolved to annex the entire Philippine archipelago.

He responded to the commissioners' telegram by arguing that annexing all of the islands "will entail less trouble than any other and besides will best subserve the interests of the people involved, for whose welfare we can not escape responsibility."[51] These instructions, sent on October 26, 1898, provide McKinley's first unambiguous statement that he intended to annex the entire Philippine archipelago. Everything he had said or written prior to that date indicated cautious indecision–a characteristic that McKinley had amply displayed in the months leading up to the war. There is no reasonable cause for believing that McKinley had settled on full annexation any earlier than late October, given the clear evidence that in fact his thinking had changed since mid-August as a result of the feedback he had received during the intervening weeks. In other words, the argument that McKinley intended all along (especially before the war) to annex the Philippines does not hold up under scrutiny.

In addition, the correspondence between McKinley and the commissioners was top secret, which meant that the president could change his mind without repercussion. In early November, he was certainly invited to do so, when Spain threatened to break off negotiations over what it regarded as usurious conditions that violated the terms of the protocol. Assumption of the enormous Cuban debt was a particular sticking point, and Spain wanted to bundle that issue up with the Philippine question. For a time it seemed to be a very real possibility that hostilities might resume. The commissioners thus sent the president another telegram stating their individuated recommendations on how to proceed and inviting further guidance. Once again, Day suggested holding only a portion of the islands—a naval and commercial base. "More than this we should not seek." Frye favored "taking the entire group and paying ten million dollars in gold." He also suggested limiting America's acquisition to a handful of islands "if [that course would be] necessary to secure [the] treaty, and I believe it is." Reid noted that the commissioners were then "at the end of six weeks of fruitless negotiation," which "suggests to me now the desirableness . . . [of] giving notice that we must either make some progress or close the protocol." Not wishing to renew hostilities, however, he thought it might be prudent to relinquish U.S. claims on several of the islands.[52] Three out of five commissioners, in other words, suggested that McKinley compromise on his position and demand only a partial annexation of the Philippines.

Only Davis remained staunchly in favor of full annexation. He suggested "that the United States present without much delay an ultimatum insisting upon the signature of a treaty for the cession by Spain of the entire Philippine Islands archipelago, Puerto Rico, and Guam." Senator Gray, meanwhile, suggested that it might be best to annex some of the Philippines after all, if only to preserve the peace and get a treaty signed. Gray knew that if hostilities were to resume, the United States would simply seize the entire archipelago, with Spain offering no resistance (since it lacked any capacity to fight another war against the United States). "It would . . . be most unfortunate if the United States should feel compelled to abandon the high position taken at the beginning of the war and, instead of crowning their triumphs by setting an example of moderation, restraint, and reason in victory, act the part of ruthless conqueror." Territorial cessions made during treaty negotiations, however distasteful, were at least morally preferable to the outright conquest of land that would surely take place if negotiations were to break down. Reluctantly, therefore, Gray sided with Day, Frye, and Reid in recommending only the partial acquisition of the Philippines, which the Spanish seemed willing to accept.[53]

McKinley's response to these suggestions was interesting and revealing. Four out of five of his treaty negotiators had declared that a compromise was necessary and that full annexation not worth the bother, but McKinley's thinking appears to have set into a mold contoured by the idea of American mission that was unyielding. The president first expressed that he "would regret deeply the resumption of hostilities against a prostrate foe" and that he deemed the United States entitled to an indemnity that could only be paid in the form of land (since Spain was broke). The main part of his response, however, reflected less concern with material interests–which could in any event be satisfied by the securing of the coaling and commercial base that Spain seemed willing to cede–than with the idea of American mission:

From the standpoint of indemnity both the archipelagoes [the Philippines and Carolines] are insufficient to pay our war expenses, but aside from this do we not owe an obligation to the people of the Philippines which will not permit us to return them to the sovereignty of Spain? . . . Willing or not, we have the responsibility of duty which we can not escape. You are therefore instructed to insist upon the cession of the whole of the Philippines, and, if necessary, pay to Spain ten to twenty millions of dollars, and if you can get cession of a naval and telegraph station in the Carolines, and the several concessions and privileges and guaranties, so far as applicable, enumerated in the views of Commissioners Frye and Reid, you can offer more [money]. The President can not believe any division of the archipelago can bring us anything but embarrassment in the future. The trade and commercial side, as well as the indemnity for the cost of war, are questions we might yield. They may be waived or compromised, but the questions of duty and humanity appeal to the President so strongly that he can find no appropriate answer but the one here marked out.[54]

It is possible that McKinley's appeals to duty and humanity, which were unnecessary given the U.S. leverage in the negotiations, were included in his instructions to salvage his nation's image in the event that negotiations broke down and hostilities resumed. Spain, after all, had been publishing a series of derogatory articles about America's "greedy" demands in the European press, and Day had asked Hay's permission to publish articles in response–if the talks broke off–that delineated the positions that the United States had staked out over the course of the peace talks. (The president approved of this suggestion.) Still, paying twenty million dollars for territorial acquisitions and offering additional funds for further concessions that were not in any event demanded, hardly qualifies as taking land as indemnity, especially given the unwelcome hardships that the American team by then knew would accompany the islands.

Especially given his consistent invocation of similar explanations of U.S. motives up to that point, the sincerity of McKinley's instructions should not be dismissed out of hand. Furthermore, in light of America's intensive restructuring of the Philippines' infrastructure, government, and social order subsequent to the treaty's passage, it seems likely that McKinley did feel a real obligation to "civilize" the Filipinos–however culturally insensitive or ignorant his thinking might have been. Throughout the course of negotiations, McKinley regularly received alarming telegrams from Dewey that detailed instability and chaos in the islands, and these were frequently accompanied by requests "from the inhabitants of" whatever particular locale was erupting for the establishment of a U.S. protectorate over them. Given the mindset by which McKinley had led the United States into its war with Spain, as a leader dedicated to rebuilding (and dominating) Cuba rather than recognizing its independence, there is no reason to doubt that he also saw the merit of rebuilding the Philippines, in addition to Cuba and Puerto Rico, in America's image. Spain inevitably agreed to the U.S. terms: it had no realistic option to do otherwise (although it consistently and with absolutely no success sought to enlist other European countries as military allies if the talks ever broke down), and McKinley signed the treaty on December 10, 1898. His next challenge was to sell the agreement to the nation—including to a skeptical and divided Senate. The amazing debate that transpired in that body—whether or not to ratify the treaty and its fantastic imperial adventurism, containing many profound but many base arguments about the nature of American civilization and the purpose of American power—is the subject of the next chapter.

CHAPTER EIGHT

Debating the Treaty and Expansion

MCKINLEY'S IMPERIAL PROGRAM met with stiff resistance. The most important discussion of the issue took place in the Senate, which was responsible for ratifying the peace treaty. Since the formal treaty debate took place in closed executive session meetings, antiimperialist senators seeking to provide a political focus for the public's debate on the subject introduced resolutions opposing the annexation of the Philippines on both constitutional or prudential grounds. They were unable to carry the day, however, and the Treaty of Paris was ratified in early February 1899. Undeterred, opponents of expansion then focused on the presidential election of 1900, which they sought to transform into a referendum on expansion. They lost this round, too, but continued vocally to oppose U.S. expansionism for at least two more decades. McKinley's reelection settled the issue, however, both as a matter of policy and in terms of redefining the United States as an international power committed to a vindicationist interpretation of the idea of American mission.

The debate began almost immediately after the initial convening of the third session of the Fifty-fifth Congress on December 6, 1898, when Senator George G. Vest (D-Mo.) introduced without comment Senate Resolution 191, which held that under the Constitution "no power is given to the Federal Government to acquire territory to be held and governed permanently as colonies. The colonial system of European nations can not be established under our present Constitution." The resolution allowed for the acquisition of lands "for coaling stations, correction of boundaries, and similar governmental purposes," but in all other cases there had to be an intention ultimately to organize "such territory into States suitable for admission into the Union." Since the treaty would not yet be signed for four days nor sent to the Senate for ratification until January 4, 1899, Vest clearly intended to preempt McKinley's expansionist ambitions.[1] By December, however, it was no secret that the treaty would include expansionist provisions, and Vest's resolution allowed the Senate to deal with the peace settlement's controversial elements in public and, at first, without addressing the treaty itself.

Vest explained his purposes in introducing the resolution a week later. He argued then that the principles for which the United States stood were diametrically opposed to colonization because Americans had fought the Revolutionary War "exclusively against the colonial system of Europe." Providence had rescued the United States from that system, and the Declaration of Independence, which was "codified in the Constitution," declared that the United States exists as a living refutation of colonialism. "The colonial system . . . is an appendage of monarchy," he argued. "It can exist in no free country, because it uproots and eliminates the basis of all republican institutions, that governments derive their just powers from the consent of the governed." Vest therefore declared himself unalterably opposed to expansionism in all forms. "I would rather quit public life and would be willing to risk life itself," he announced at the conclusion of his speech, "rather than give my consent to this fantastic and wicked attempt to revolutionize our Government and substitute the principles of our hereditary enemies for the teachings of Washington and his associates."[2]

Senator Orville H. Platt (R-Conn.) stood immediately to rebut Vest's speech by declaring that "the right to acquire territory is an inherent right in the nation . . . and it has no limitations either in the Constitution or elsewhere."[3] He subsequently elaborated upon this claim in a long speech that summarized most of the central arguments of the expansionists. Platt began the speech with a broad statement of purpose: "It is time to be heroic in our faith and to assert all the power that belongs to the nation as a nation." In Platt's opinion, the United States, as an equal to other world powers, should not feel restrained in its international relations from acting like any other state, and he argued that the Constitution placed no limitations on the exercise of inherent sovereign powers such as expansion.[4] Platt's argument was that the Constitution might regulate the manner by which the United States government reaches its decisions—that it structured the *procedures* of governance—but that the document was irrelevant to determining the *purposes* to which the government should address itself.

Platt's more controversial claim was that Congress could govern colonies as it saw fit, without constitutional restraint. Suffrage, he observed, the mechanism by which individuals give the "consent" celebrated in the Declaration, was neither a constitutional right nor regulated by the federal government. As he put it, "[c]itizenship confers no right of voting." Platt did admit that where the Congress possessed primary jurisdiction, it *should* govern justly and in keeping with "American" norms, but he steadfastly insisted that while the Congress might be "under moral obligations and constraints," those constraints were neither legally nor constitutionally defined. Thus, when he argued that "we must provide for the people of any territory that we may acquire the most liberal, just, and beneficent government which they may be capable of enjoying, always with reference to their development and welfare and in the hope that they may be finally fitted for independent self-government," he was not declaring that colonial populations had any *right* to such a government, but that Congress should nevertheless assume a paternalistic role over them.[5]

Platt's articulation of the administration's vindicationist position was strongly and unambiguously stated. It not only described Congress's role in carrying out America's mission to the Philippines as McKinley conceived it but it addressed constitutional issues and the arguments that had been percolating among the antiimperialists. The main point that he wished to drive home was that territorial acquisitions were perfectly acceptable under the Constitution. The Connecticut Republican closed his oration by asking how anyone could doubt the good intentions of a government that upheld the principles of the Declaration that the antiimperialists were trying to turn against it. "Why should any man . . . wish to detract from, to diminish or belittle the power of this Government? . . . Rather we should bid it godspeed in its mission to relieve the oppressed, to right every wrong, and to extend the institutions of free government." It was simply illogical to Platt that the United States could violate the tenets of freedom and justice, because as a nation it embodied those virtues as perfectly as had ever been accomplished. "For this is the people's Government; the Government of a great people, a liberty-loving people, a people that can be trusted to do right, and to guarantee to all men who shall come under its beneficent sway and be subject to its jurisdiction the largest measure of liberty consistent with good order and their general well-being."[6]

Senator Platt was the administration's mouthpiece, and he expounded as fully and earnestly as President McKinley could have hoped the vindicationist vision of the idea of American mission that he sought to realize. At a later point in the debate, Platt launched into a lengthy exposition of the idea of American mission's underlying assumptions. "I believe in Providence. I believe the hand of Providence brought about the conditions [i.e., the Philippines acquisition] which we must either accept or be recreant to duty," he averred:

> I believe the same force was behind our army at Santiago and our ships in Manila Bay that was behind the landing of the Pilgrims on Plymouth Rock. I believe that we have been chosen to carry on and to carry forward this great work of uplifting humanity on earth. From the time of the landing on Plymouth Rock in the spirit of the Declaration of Independence, in the spirit of the Constitution, believing that all men are equal and endowed by their Creator with inalienable rights, believing that governments derive their just powers from the consent of the governed, we have spread that civilization across the continent until it stood at the Pacific Ocean looking ever westward.
>
> The English-speaking people, the agents of civilization, the agency through which humanity is to be uplifted, through which despotism is to go down, through which the rights of man are to prevail, is charged with this great mission. Providence has put it upon us. We propose to execute it. We propose to proclaim liberty in the Philippine Islands, if they are ours. We propose to proclaim liberty and justice and the protection of life and human rights wherever the flag of the United States is planted. Who denies that? Who will haul down those principles?[7]

Clearly, Platt believed at the very least that Americans would support an imperialist policy if it comported with the wishes of Providence and with the goals of the founding fathers. According to the vindicationist interpretation of the idea of American mission, which Platt here expounded as directly as anyone in American history ever has, those goals and purposes were readily compatible. Others disagreed.

Opposition to the provision of the treaty annexing the Philippine Islands rested on a number of grounds, including (but not limited to) the race of the islands' population, the threat to U.S. labor interests posed by the large and impoverished Filipino workforce, the unnecessary violation of Washington's pronouncement against entanglement in European affairs, and the clear violation it would entail of America's moral and political values. Tying these positions together in a manner demonstrative of the era's cultural construction of U.S. regime principles was the central, overriding conviction that it would be impossible to annex the islands consistently with the Declaration of Independence, which was widely described as providing the philosophical basis and interpretive framework of the Constitution. Acquiring overseas colonies was for many both legally and morally offensive.

The image of nonwhite Filipinos from a barbarous, tropical culture merging with the Anglo-Saxon United States horrified the antiimperialists, but for the country to rule them as subjects and not as equal citizens would be to violate the central philosophy of U.S. government. It was an impossible dilemma to solve consistently with America's core values, but the most galling aspect of the situation was that the United States had little to gain from the policy; in other words, imperialism would entail extreme costs and dangers for Americans, would lead to the undermining of the nation's fundamental values, and would provide nothing in return of any value—moral or material. The best course for the nation to pursue was exemplarism. Thus, antiimperialists regularly and strenuously urged that the nation honor its mission to the world in the same way that it always had—by setting itself up as a model for the rest of the mankind to emulate.

Senator Augustus O. Bacon (D-Ga.), for instance, introduced a resolution about the Philippines, S.R. 211, that addressed not the constitutionality but the wisdom of expansionism. It quickly became the primary focus, along with the Vest resolution, of the treaty debate.[8] Bacon's resolution attached conditions to the Senate's ratification of the treaty in four parts. The first part reiterated that the United States had fought Spain for the reasons set forth in the joint resolution passed in April, and not for the "conquest of foreign territory." The second part declared that "in demanding and receiving the cession of the Philippine Islands" from Spain, the United States did not intend either to admit the territory as a State or to rule over the population "as vassals or subjects." Third, Spain was required to leave the Philippines because all governments "derive 'their just powers from the consent of the governed,'" and the Filipinos had evinced a desire to be independent. Finally, the resolution declared that the United States had no intention to exercise sovereignty over the islands and meant instead to help the Filipinos attain self-government, at which point it would leave the islands.[9] By means of this resolution, Bacon hoped to shift attention away from whether the United States *could* annex territory, a point on which the expansionists enjoyed a clear advantage, to the very different issue of whether it *should* do so.

A substantial portion of Bacon's address explaining his resolution described the nature and limits of America's mission to the world, which he interpreted in much narrower terms than Platt. "We went to war with Spain not for the purpose of correcting all the evils with which her people were afflicted," he explained. "We went to war with Spain not to break the chains of tyranny with which she might be binding her different colonies; we did not undertake to be the great universal benefactor and to right all the wrongs that Spain might be inflicting upon any of her people. . . . We were not charged with the duty of preserving order in Asia" or "seeing that they had a stable and orderly government in any part of the hemisphere." Rather, the United States went to war to correct an intolerable situation in Cuba, not only because it had a duty to do so but because "the disorders of that Government affected the peace of our community and were injurious to our material interest."[10] The war with Spain, in other words, was undertaken for limited purposes based as much in America's material interest as in its sense of mission, and neither America's interests nor its mission encompassed the well-being of the Philippines.[11]

The antiimperialists were particularly impatient with the expansionists' desire to emulate the European powers. As Senator Horace Chilton (D-Tex.) asked, "Why should England, Germany, and France be held up to the United States as objects of our imitation?"[12] Chilton's question reflected a commitment to American exceptionalism—the belief that the United States was qualitatively different from other nations—and it carried great weight among the antiimperialists. As Senator John W. Daniels (D-Va.) declared, "The American Republic set itself upon a different plan from the anterior nations. . . . We founded a government upon the recognition of human rights–that is our distinction–the right of men to be free, the right of men to govern themselves."[13] Senator Stephen M. White (D-Calif.) added, "If we have formed a nationality of which we are proud, a system concerning which we make no apology, a Republic which we claim to be peerless, it is our duty, solemnly and positively, to see that the organization which we have created remains pure."[14]

To mimic others was therefore to prefer the banality of the Old World to America's unique role in the world as the exemplar of liberty. As White said, "We will, indeed, hold a proud position if we prove that we differ from other nations whose accumulated powers were used for evil, whose rulers, in the midst of the splendors of transitory triumph, assailed the liberties of their fellows."[15] Emulating Europe in this definitive enterprise would, in other words, reverse the proper trend of history by placing Europe's institutions in the forefront of man's progress and reverse the gains that U.S. democracy had already yielded. Senator William E. Mason (R-Ill.), for example, noted how various revolutionaries and leaders around the world, such as Bolívar, Kosciusko, Lafayette, and Garibaldi, had been inspired by the almost biblical principles of the Declaration, which had been "a pillar of fire by night and a cloud by day to the downtrodden and oppressed all over the world." Addressing his expansionist opponents, he said:

> You ask for expansion. See how we have expanded in the time since [the Declaration] was written. Not only have republics started up in place of monarchies, but monarchies have themselves gradually broadened into constitutional governments, getting nearer and nearer to the voice of the people. Our own was the first great republic, and in the better and broader sense our flag floats from the dome of every republic.[16]

Senator Donelson Caffery (D-La.) added: "We have been the exemplars of liberty, and we have taught the world that the best Government upon the earth was the freest Government upon the earth." Europe, he observed, was rapidly progressing away from monarchical, despotic forms of governance toward wider suffrage and broader protections of individual liberties. "This is largely the fruit of our example."[17] Why, he asked, retreat from this success?

The United States was meant to be an *example,* not a purveyor, of liberty, according to the antiimperialists. The power to act need not translate into a duty to do so. "It is well enough to hug the pleasing thought that we are a great people and that there is no responsibility that can be thrust on us which we can not meet and face and accept with safety," said Senator George Turner (Fusionist-Wash.). "But it is the height of quixotism and is the reverse of the teachings of the fathers to go around in the world hunting responsibilities and courting dangers because we are able to meet them."[18]

The antiimperialists were particularly unimpressed with religiously grounded constructions of American vindicationism. Caffery, for instance, attacked vindicationism's crusading messianism by echoing the arguments against religious persecution that Roger Williams had first laid out in his *Bloudy Tenet Concerning Persecution,* to which James Madison and Thomas Jefferson hearkened when formulating the U.S. doctrine of religious liberty: "We are told, and sometimes from the pulpit, that we have a holy mission to perform; that we must evangelize the heathen; that we must spread the blessed precepts of Christianity, the doctrines of Christ, over the dark places of the earth, and we must do it by the sword. Mr. President, have we gone backward in civilization? . . . Sir, Christianity can not be advanced by force, and the twin sister of Christianity, the free government of a great people, can not be advanced by force."[19] Senator Mason likewise chastised the imperialists for seeking "to give civilization and Christian liberty hypodermically with 13-inch guns,"[20] while Senator John L. McLaurin (D-S.C.) added:

> The hand of God may have been in the war with Spain, but I do not feel that it is in obedience to the Divine will that we are pursuing a career of conquest in the Philippines. Conquest has never been the handmaiden of our civilization or the Christian religion; their triumphs rest upon a foundation of peace. The sword established the religion of Mohammed, but it will never spread and maintain the religion of Jesus Christ. I am in favor the United States continuing as a peaceful Republic, not a conquering empire.[21]

The United States, in other words, was not designed to be comprised of galloping crusaders.

Senator H. De Soto Money (D-Miss.) argued that U.S. national identity would fundamentally change for the worse should imperialists carry the day:

> Are we to be the great exemplars of human liberty, or are we to join the ranks of the monarchs of the world in the lust for territory, the greed for conquest, for aggrandizement, and depart from that simplicity of liberty, of freedom, of the rights of man as set forth in our Declaration of Independence, as guaranteed by our Constitution? The fate of millions of people in the Philippines, of untold millions in America, rests upon the decision of the Senate.[22]

This was the crux of the matter. If exemplarism lay at the heart of American national identity, then abandoning it would mean changing the nature and purpose of the United States from being a paragon of universal significance into just another nation. It seems clear, therefore, that the senators who opposed U.S. expansionism acted, at least in part, upon the conviction that nothing less than America's national identity was at stake in their deliberations about the treaty.

It would be facile to dismiss these arguments as "mere rhetoric"; they were voiced too consistently and frequently for that. If the senators spoke insincerely, then they obviously thought at least that exemplarist arguments would impress the voters who filled the galleries during their debates and who read assiduously the newspaper accounts of their historic deliberations. Since their statements were embedded in a larger national dialogue about expansionism, however, we need not guess about their rhetorical value. Private citizens opposing expansion were as likely to employ exemplarist arguments as public officials. Charles Francis Adams, for instance, urged: "Let us be true to our own traditions, and follow our own precedents. . . . Our fundamental principles, those of the Declaration, the Constitution, and the Monroe Doctrine, have not yet been shown to be unsound—why should we be in such a hurry to abandon them?"[23] Carl Schurz also endorsed exemplarism. If the United States were to embark on its imperialist course, he insisted, "then the great American republic will soon cease to be an encouragement to the progress of political liberty and become a warning example to all the world."[24] Elsewhere he argued, "We can exercise the most beneficent influences upon mankind, not by forcing our rule or our goods upon others that are weak at the point of the bayonet, but through the moral power of our example."[25]

The distinguished professor and opinion leader Herman E. Von Holst argued in pamphlets that the temptation to stray from exemplarism was rooted not in America's virtue, but its power. "The unparalleled, bewildering rate at which our power has grown and the proud consciousness that the future development of our boundless resources baffles imagination itself have taught us to deem feasible whatever we choose to will."[26] This was a dangerous mindset to settle into, however, he warned, because it would encourage an imprudent foreign policy. "The further we travel on this road the nearer we come to a fatal goal, the delusion that ours is the mission to right what is wrong and to give higher civilization according to our conception of it, a generous lift wherever we deem meet and whenever we think our power adequate to the task. . . . Providence has laid this tremendous charge no more on our shoulders than on those of any other nation."[27] Von Holst and other antiimperialists agreed with the expansionists that American exceptionalism meant that the success of the American experiment had paramount significance for not just the United States but for mankind. They disagreed, however, that the means by which the United States would succeed in its mission entailed vindicating its norms in foreign lands. The antiimperialists believed, in short, not only that expansionism was inconsistent with the nation's core values but that in both form and spirit it was destructive of them.

Racist Arguments against Expansionism

Arguments mustered against territorial expansion were not always noble, however, but often rested on shabby ethnic conceptions of America's national identity. Many antiimperialists argued that the political system of the United States presupposed a homogeneous culture defined by Anglo-Saxonism and Protestantism. Other races and religious cultures would be unable to conform to the rigors of America's political culture, and they would only corrupt American government and society if admitted. Racist arguments against expansionism were of four varieties. The first held that non–Anglo Saxons were incapable of adopting American institutions. The second was that the United States was never intended to incorporate broad racial diversity, especially since nonwhites could only degrade the excellence of Anglo-Saxon institutions and culture. Third, the Filipinos, like all racial minorities, were believed capable of subsisting on such meager sustenance that they would pose an overwhelming threat to American laborers. Finally, antiimperialists feared the morally degrading effect that a large new minority population would have on white Americans, who had not yet shown themselves capable of treating justly the nonwhites over whom they enjoyed essentially absolute power. These arguments were interconnected, and they reveal an American worldview that was still far from confronting the massive contradiction between the ascriptive bases of its national identity and the color-blind universalism of its regime principles.

The speeches of Louisiana's Senator Caffery are particularly effective in demonstrating how it was possible in 1899 for a subtle mind to hold simultaneously a commitment to freedom and self-government and a steadfast belief that some people deserved neither. He argued that it would be impossible for the United States to establish a constitutional, democratic government in the Philippines due to the race of its inhabitants. "Our power can go there; our flag can float there; but the genius of American liberty will remain upon our shores. It can not be implanted there. The material is not there for it to flourish and grow." He added:

> The proposition now before us is whether it is constitutional to incorporate [into the United States] 10,000,000 people no whit superior to the Africans in many respects, people who have been used to despotism all their lives, utterly unacquainted with republican institutions, and who never will be acquainted or familiarized with republican institutions. It is not their nature; they can not understand them; they have not that requisite degree of enlightenment and self-restraint that are absolutely requisite for a people to govern themselves.

It therefore was simply impossible for the United States to incorporate the Philippines unless it did so as a despotic overlord. Caffery also cited

Benjamin Kidd as an authority proving that whites could not thrive in the tropics. Different climates yielded different races of people with different qualities, characters, and capacities, and Anglo-Saxons were not constituted to live in the tropics. "You can extend your power, but if you want to extend your nationality, extend your institutions, extend your liberty, you must do it with people of your own kind." And as Kidd and other scholars had demonstrated, Anglo-Saxons could not flourish in the Philippines.[28]

South Carolina's Senator McLaurin explained that the United States would be forced to rule the Philippines in a way contrary to and debasing of American principles of governance, because of "the divine right of the Caucasian to govern the inferior races."[29] Following this principle, California's White thus declared, "Mr. President, especially in the Tropics, there is no occasion for civilization or capacity as we understand it, and there control is always by the sword."[30] Von Holst provided academic support for this position when he held that the "Anglo-Saxon" race had developed democratic government because it had the "racial faculties, instincts, and tendencies" to do so. The Filipino population that the United States hoped to annex, by contrast, was "of such a variety of hues and utterly destitute of the qualities" necessary for self-governance.[31] Mississippi's Senator Money elaborated:

> Others have the form of a republic, but not the genius and spirit. They are good enough republics on paper, but in practice they fall short of the principles which they declare. The Asiatic mind, in my opinion, never will conceive the idea of self-government as we understand and as we practice it. . . . Whatever form of government any people have is exactly the government which they need. It is the result, and has been everywhere, of an outgrowth and development; it is the evolution of the moral, spiritual, and intellectual nature of man, and it can not be anything else. If he wanted or needed anything to make him better or happier, he would have it by the very law which gave him that which he has; and it is useless for you to attempt to fit this Government upon them.[32]

Since the Filipinos were by nature unable to absorb Anglo-Saxon government, therefore, they must either devise some other form of governance by and for themselves or they must be ruled from above by

Americans following a colonial system fitted to their capacities. The simple transfer of U.S. institutions to the Philippines was impossible, which meant that Americans would have to govern the islands in a way contrary to their own principles.

Other senators presumed that the United States was designed by and for Anglo-Saxons alone. White, for instance, described the Filipinos as "a very peculiar mass, a heterogeneous compound of inefficient oriental humanity." In his opinion, "the vast mass of the inhabitants are, and will for many years remain, in a condition far below that which every well-informed American believes to be essential to citizenship within our borders."[33] Senator Daniel, from Virginia, a proponent of racial essentialism, spoke most alarmingly about the race of the Filipinos. "Mr. President, there is one thing that neither time nor education can change. You may change the leopard's spots, but you will never change the different qualities of the races which God has created in order that they may fulfill separate and distinct missions in the cultivation and civilization of the world."[34] From this premise, he contrasted in startling language the race of the Filipinos and the presumed racial identity of the United States:

> We are asked to annex to the United States a witch's cauldron—
> Black spirits and white, red spirits and gray,
> Mingle, mingle, mingle, you that mingle may
>
> We are not only asked to annex the cauldron and make it a part of our great, broad, Christian, Anglo-Saxon, American land, but we are asked to annex the contents of this brew—mixed races, Chinese, Japanese, Malay Negritos—anybody who has come along in three hundred years, in all of their concatenations and colors; and the travelers who have been there tell us and have written in books that they are not only of all hues and colors, but there are spotted people there, and, what I have never heard of in any other country, there are striped people there with zebra signs upon them.[35]

To modern ears, Daniel's weird rant about striped and spotted people might suggest an unrefined, back-woodsy intellect, but the Virginia senator's speech was, like Caffery's, replete with copious, refined references to history, literature, and U.S. political tradition, with citations from the Federalist Papers and Abraham Lincoln, among other venerated figures. Although he joked about zebra people, his were the fears of a sophisticated gentleman in 1899.

The most serious consequence of admitting the Filipinos into the Union on an equal footing as whites was that doing so would absolutely destroy the United States as it was then defined. Clearly, many senators regarded American national identity to rest on an ethnically and culturally defined construction of America's political principles. Senator Turner, the Washington Fusionist, for instance, railed against annexation because he thought it would yield "a universal miscegenation of blood, of religion, and of government with the yellow Buddhists, Mohammedans, and Confucians." While that policy would be consistent with "the principle of liberty on which our Government is founded," he continued, "it would do such violence to our blood, to the history and traditions of our race, and would leave such frightful results in mongrelizing our citizenship, that the advocates of the new movement in favor of a greater America prefer the alternative risk of debauching our institutions rather than do that."[36] In the event that the Filipinos were admitted to the Union, according to Turner, the choice for Americans was clear: either keep pure the nation's character or its institutions—one or the other, but not both. That would be impossible. As the Stanford University president David Starr Jordan explained, "Democracy demands likeness of aims and purposes among its inhabitants. . . . The Anglo-Saxon will not mix with the lower races."[37] These arguments presupposed that the United States was an Anglo-Saxon nation and that the challenge of expansion was to force the new populations into the Anglo-Saxon mold. No one ever considered accommodating cultural diversity as a worthwhile, possible goal, and certainly no one believed it to be required under "American" norms.

The third type of race-based argument was calculated more basically to appeal to the self-interest of American workers. Senator Chilton, of Texas, stated the issue most plainly: "There are two distinct dangers which it is hardly possible to avert. Those dangers are, first, the competition of the pauper laborers of the Philippine Islands who may come to our shores. The second is the danger of the competition of the pauper-made products sent out from the Philippine Islands to flood and disparage American markets."[38] Opposition of this variety reflected the influence of the Populist wing of the antiimperialist movement, but nonetheless reinforced the other kinds of racial arguments. "In annexing these islands we annex labor which, thank God, is yet unknown in America," warned one pamphleteer. "We annex labor trained for centuries to subsist on nothing. It is an acknowledged fact that the Filipinos can live and become fat on what would starve the average American."[39] Imperialism might therefore aid the captains of industry in increasing their profit margins, went this line of argument, but it would devastate the labor market and harm American workers. "The annexation of those islands to the United States, in whatever form it may come, whether as States or as colonies, means free and full competition by the American laborer, of every trade and condition, with the underpaid and half-clad workers of the tropics."[40]

Senator McLaurin merged the labor-theory argument with the fourth race-based position, which held that mixing the races would tend to corrupt the white population: "To permit cheap Asiatic labor to come into competition with our intelligent, well-paid labor will be to degrade and lower our civilization. Already in Illinois Negroes from Alabama have been shot and driven from the State, and such actions defended by the governor."[41] McLaurin's observation that black workers had been "shot and driven from the State" was not meant to serve as a warning to Filipinos that whites might treat them unjustly, but to inform his colleagues of the righteous indignation that white Americans would feel when challenged by nonwhite competitors in the labor market. As Senator White reminded his colleagues, a similar problem to that which would be created by an influx of Filipinos had only recently been settled on the West Coast—that of the Chinese. "We excluded Chinese laborers from our shores," he noted proudly. "We kept them out, although they sought to come in occasional shiploads only. Here it is proposed to bring in an entire population, possessing to a large degree the same competitive character, containing millions and millions of people."[42] Where, he asked, was the logic in that policy?

Those who opposed expansionism on the streets rather than in the Senate chamber were most likely to argue that contact with "lower" races tended morally to corrupt whites. "The relation of our people to the lower races of men of whatever kind has been one which degrades and exasperates," Jordan complained.[43] Thus, it was unwise to annex more racial minorities, since the white majority would almost certainly debase itself by acting with unfettered and capricious cruelty toward its new charges. As Schurz wrote, "a good many of our people have very little regard for the rights and interests of so-called inferior races, and consider cheating and robbing such races a privilege of the superior being. . . . The idea that our colonial service will become a seminary of political virtue is, therefore, a highly grotesque one."[44] Another antiimperialist added, "We have a race problem here at home in our 'parochial politics' so vast that we should not be greedy of another in the Philippines. The latter will inevitably distract us from the former, which demands all the intellectual and moral energy we can command." He continued, "We do not have to go to Luzon for American barbarities. We have them nearer home. We have them in North Carolina, in South Carolina, in Ohio, in Texas, in Georgia. The recent lynching in Georgia cannot be overmatched for cruelty in any authentic report of savage cruelty that has come down to us. We have heard nothing of the Filipinos that approaches its infernal wickedness. I spare you the horrible particulars, the mutilation of the victim before he was set on fire, the evisceration of his charred and helpless corpse."[45]

For antiimperialists of this strain, the debate became an opportunity to rail against the racial barbarities then existing in American society. Moorfield Storey, one of the antiimperialist movement's leaders, put the issue graphically. "Our first claim is that we are a superior race, and so entitled to govern our inferiors," he noted, before asking pointedly: "How have we shown our superiority in dealing with such problems?" To answer his own question, he presented a litany of monstrosities committed by whites against nonwhites:

Look at home in the Southern States, in Kansas, in Ohio, in Delaware, and see men burned at the stake. A year ago a woman, innocent of any crime except accompanying her husband in his flight, was tied to a stake, her fingers chopped off piece by piece, her features mutilated, other tortures inflicted upon her which I will not describe, and then she was burned alive, while a crowd of spectators carried off souvenirs of the affair. This year two men are tied to a stake, smeared with kerosene, and then, before they are burned, the crowd separated that a photographer might perpetuate the scene. Men would not deal so with a horse or a dog. For these and like atrocities no one is punished. The public sentiment of the community does not condemn the perpetrators.

Explaining his purpose in recounting such horrors, Storey evoked Paine's characterization of the inherent decrepitude of monarchical governance and applied it to the unchecked power of white Americans over blacks: "The race hatred which permits [these acts], after slavery has been abolished for forty years, shows how men of our own flesh and blood are degraded by power over men whom they think inferior. The race problem . . . has dragged white men like our selves down to the level of savages."[46] Far from seeing the annexation of the Philippines as providing Anglo-Saxons with an opportunity to "uplift" other races, antiimperialists of Storey's ilk were convinced of precisely the opposite: that it would bring whites down.

Principled Reasons for Opposing Annexation

George Frisbee Hoar (R-Mass.), the distinguished elder senator, had a difficult time opposing the treaty. He was a lifelong, devoted partisan, and it pained him to contest the most significant policy that his party had championed in a generation. But the very importance of the policy and the profound values that were entwined in it forced him to take a stand against his fellow Republicans and on the side of principle and tradition.[47] Hoar's opposition to the treaty was based on his unwavering conviction that the Declaration of Independence lay squarely at the Constitution's interpretive center, and this belief caused him to reject in the strongest terms Platt's arguments concerning both expansionism's constitutionality and Congress's supposed sovereign prerogatives in annexed territories. The Declaration spelled out the nation's defining principles, according to Hoar, and the Constitution applied them in practice. "Over every clause, syllable, and letter of the Constitution the Declaration of Independence pours its blazing torchlight." Any government action contrary to the spirit of the Declaration of Independence was, therefore, ipso facto unconstitutional and destructive of America's soul. Although Hoar admitted that the United States had not honored the Declaration's pledge until it abolished slavery, he insisted that, having crossed that bridge, the nation was positioned at last to achieve the founders' vision of a just government—unless it sank into "this modern swamp and cesspool of imperialism."[48]

Hoar was therefore adamant that if the United States were to adopt colonies, it would violate the most fundamental norms defining the nation and destroy its sacred, universal mission.

> [These principles] were not . . . for a single generation. They were not glittering generalities. They were blazing ubiquities. They were eternal verities. They were like the Golden Rule and the Ten Commandments and the Moral Law, or rather they were the Golden Rule and the Ten Commandments and The Moral Law translated for the government of their States. . . . When the delegates of the Old Thirteen set their hands to that Declaration, the people of the United States stepped forth armed in its invincible panoply, like Minerva from the head of Jove, the greatest power the world had ever seen. . . . Whenever we depart from it the world power of the great Republic is at an end.

Hoar's grandiloquence reflected his sense of the importance of America's mission to the world: "It was not only the independence of America which was then declared—it was the dignity of human nature itself." It was therefore inconceivable to Hoar that a policy that violated the core tenets of the American nation could be constitutional. No exercise of a "sovereign power" could, in his mind, contravene the purpose of the sovereignty itself. "Mr. President, if the United States forsake this doctrine of the fathers, who shall take it up? Is there to be no place on the face of the earth hereafter where a man can stand up by virtue of his manhood and say, 'I am a man?'" He concluded his lengthy attack on the vindicationists by arguing, "You have no right at the cannon's mouth to impose on an unwilling people your Declaration of Independence and your Constitution and your notions of freedom and notions of what is good."[49]

Other antiimperialists also invoked the Declaration of Independence as a guiding principle of U.S. government that rendered expansionism both morally and constitutionally illegitimate. Asserting that the "inalienable rights of man" were "made sacred in a sacred instrument," for instance, Louisiana's Caffery proclaimed that their protection by the U.S. government was what made the nation what it was:

> We have held up this example of a free Government as one to be copied by all the nations of the earth. We have by that act estopped ourselves from setting up any kind of government anywhere, under any circumstances, other than a free government based upon the consent of the governed. . . . Every single step in our progress heretofore has been founded upon the glorious principle, the immutable principle, of the power of man to govern himself.[50]

Republican William E. Mason sarcastically jabbed as well at the jingoes who, having "outgrown" the Declaration, "will have to pardon me that I have not mentally, morally, and loyally kept pace with them in their wonderful growth."[51] On the other side of the debate, Senator Joseph B. Foraker (R-Ohio) argued that the Declaration of Independence contained no "complaint against the colonial system of government,"[52] but only catalogued specific, time-bound grievances against England. But this was a uniquely dubious and unpopular argument. Not only did no one else second its sentiment, but it was attacked in almost every subsequent antiimperialist speech.[53] At the least, in short, the speeches in the Senate debate demonstrated a widespread conviction that the Declaration of Independence provided a significant obstacle to the creation of an imperialist form of government.

Antiimperialists also argued that expansionism required such an extensive increase in the U.S. military apparatus that it would force a radical shift away from the traditional goals and values of American foreign policy.[54] They believed, furthermore, that the transformation of the United States into a European-style imperial power would generate of necessity a similar evolution in the structure and purpose of American government—away, significantly, from the values of the Declaration. William Graham Sumner, the sociologist, spoke most trenchantly to this issue. "Imperialism is a philosophy," he explained. "It is a way of looking at things which is congenial to people who are ruling others without constitutional restraints, and it is the temper in which they act." Militarism, he added, the "method for carrying out" imperialism, puts concern with military strength and preparedness at the forefront of all political decision making and "colors everything else." He continued: "Militarism

. . . consists in aggression and domination instead of conciliation and concession. It is militarism to 'jam things through' without consideration for the feelings and interests of other people, except so far as they can strike back." If the United States persisted in its infatuation with imperialism, therefore, it should prepare as well to alter its governing philosophy from democratic compromise to militarism's "fighting methods."[55]

In the Senate, Georgia's Senator Bacon also contended that annexation of the Philippines would entail the transformation of the United States into a European-style imperial power in contradiction to the nation's deepest principles. "The acquisition of the Philippines will commit this Government to the colonial or imperial policy. . . . It means vast armies . . . ready on a day's notice to cope in bloody conflict with the great military powers of the earth." To secure America's authority there against the predatory Europeans, it would need to create not only a large standing army but a vastly enlarged navy to protect the troops as they traveled across the Pacific Ocean to defend the country's new outpost. But the Europeans were not the only reason why a larger military would be needed: "If we are to maintain dominion over this foreign, alien people, these Mohammedans, these people accustomed to revolution, and to blood, and to disorder, if you please, we will be compelled to do it with an iron hand, regardless of the shedding of blood. . . . Only with the sword and gun can millions of the semi-civilized be kept in subjection." The imperial system forced a country to adopt means fitted to the ends of subjugation; the United States would have no choice but to stray from its established model of governance and descend into moral depravity if it wished to succeed in its imperial venture.[56]

Other senators agreed. "If we embark in a colonial system, it means the inauguration of a despotic power in Washington," argued Senator McLaurin. "It means a large standing army that will not only be used to rule outlying territories with an iron hand, but that sooner or later will be used at home to overawe and override the popular will. An imperialistic democracy, like an atheistic religion, is an impossible hybrid."[57] Fusionist Senator Turner added: "Democratic simplicity as taught by the immortal Jefferson, and which has been exemplified by honesty and economy in the administration of the Government and by unyielding jealousy of large standing armies, is to give way to imperial splendor, dazzling the imagination and corrupting the integrity of our people by its lavish expenditure, its loose and venal rule, and the pomp and circumstance of war, by which alone it could be supported."[58] As Virginia's Daniels summarized:

> I know also, Mr. President, if the history of the world has left any lessons for our guidance, that when you raise great standing armies, when you have vast commerce, when you appoint governors-general, when you make profitable employments for men whom you set as taskmaster over others, in the nature of things, by the inevitable tendencies and inclinations of human nature, you set up a great establishment in which there is every incitement of ambition and wealth for its perpetuity, and that those who share in its honors, in its emoluments, in its profits, however honorably, will be disposed to a continuance of a condition of things which is to their profit. It may be that we will do better than any other nation has ever done; I know we will do better than Spain; but at its best it is a most perilous relation; it is a most injurious relation; it is a relation that all should pray against who have felt the power of that prayer, "Lead us not into temptation."[59]

The money and energy that would be required build and maintain a sufficient fighting force, moreover, would have to be diverted away from more constructive endeavors. Senator Alexander Clay (D-Ga.) compared the sizes of America's military with those of some European powers. He noted that while the United States had only 77 naval ships (and it only had that many due to the naval expansion begun under President Benjamin Harrison), Great Britain possessed 621; France, 420; Germany, 227; and Russia, 371. The disparity in the size of each nation's standing army was even more startling: Great Britain maintained 211,532 troops; France, 561,848; Germany, 591,715; and Russia 761,400. The United States, by contrast, had maintained a standing army of 27,632 men at the outbreak of the Spanish-American War. "No wonder the growth of this nation has challenged the admiration of the world," Clay concluded. "Under our system of government we have maintained the friendship of all nations, and our citizens have been permitted to engage in industrial pursuits instead of wasting our energies and resources in unprofitable wars."[60]

The antiimperialists further insisted that the militaristic mindset had clouded the moral clarity of the vindicationists. Power, not virtue, was the currency of the imperialist program. As Senator Mason compellingly argued, "If you want the land, there is Canada; that is nearer. Take Canada. They talk our language. But when I say that to my expansionist friend, he says, 'That is different.' Oh, yes; it is different, and I will tell you the difference. It is the difference between the fleet of a Victoria and the fleet of Aguinaldo. That is all the difference."[61]

Of those participating in the broader public debates, Sumner in particular was impatient with the moral posturing of the imperialists, who claimed that the United States should civilize the Filipinos because it was able and worthy to undertake the task. "We propose to sit in judgment on the fitness of other people for self government. What are the criteria of this fitness? Who knows whether we possess it ourselves?" he asked, pointedly. "Is lynching, or race-rioting, or negro-burning, or a row in the legislature, or a strike with paralyzed industry, or a disputed election, or a legislative deadlock, or the murder of a claimant-official, or counting-in unelected officers, or factiousness, or financial corruption and jobbery, proof of unfitness for self-government?" The question was an indictment: "If so, any state which was stronger than we might take away our self-government on the ground that we were unfit for it. It is, therefore, simply a question of *power*, like all the other alleged grounds of interference of one political body with another, such as humanity, sympathy, neighborhood, internal anarchy, etc., etc." (emphasis in the original).[62] Sumner wanted his readers to be aware of one overriding fact–that the United States could impose its civilization on the Filipinos not because that civilization was superior to or more advanced than that of the Filipinos, but because it had the power to back up its claims. And there was no moral pride to be gained from that truth.

Antiimperialists feared that the corrupting influence of unchecked power over the Filipinos, a natural byproduct of imperial, militaristic rule, would combine with white Americans' racism to yield a debasing rather than uplifting colonial policy. As U.S. occupation of the islands increased in duration, these fears were confirmed with disturbing evidence of American atrocities that the antiimperialists broadcast to a distressingly uninterested country. A notorious practice among military interrogators of Filipino prisoners, for instance, was the so-called water cure, in which prisoners had their heads placed in buckets of water as they "stood" upside-down.[63] Other examples of torture, inhumanity, and cruelty were faithfully reported by antiimperialists.[64] Most unsettling, however, were the establishment of concentration "centers" into which the rural population was herded; these bore an extremely close and uncomfortable resemblance to the infamous reconcentration policy of the Spanish general Valeriano Weyler. For example, American troops were ordered to burn all crops and slaughter any cattle that might conceivably be used as sustenance by the guerrillas. They were also instructed to shoot on sight any able-bodied male who left his compound after sundown without permission. Any time an American was murdered or assassinated by the guerrillas, a prisoner was to be executed in return. Conditions on the whole were to be made "insupportable" for the disloyal population (however identified). Reasonable estimates placed the resulting death toll of nonbelligerent Filipinos at two hundred thousand people.[65]

Most exasperating to the antiimperialists was the fact that expansion was unnecessary to attain the international stature desired by the imperialists. If the United States wanted to become a great power, then the last thing it needed to do was to become an imperial nation. "We are becoming great. No little area is ours. Our domain is mighty. This is not a nation to be held in the hollow of even the imperialistic hand," observed Senator White.[66] In Professor Von Holst's estimation, "The world has long since ceased to consider us a 'negligible quantity.' . . . Thus we have been all the while in exactly the same position as all other powers, great or small, with this difference only: that it rested wholly and exclusively with ourselves to take a hand in international problems or not, while the leading powers of Europe have often, if not as a rule, had practically no choice in the matter."[67] By acquiring colonies in the maelstrom that East Asia was quickly becoming (the Boxer Rebellion erupted while America was still fighting in the Philippines), the United States was foregoing this advantage and entangling itself–probably irreversibly–in the chess match of European international politics. As Senator Chilton argued, "whenever we take the Philippine Islands we have furnished to the world a place to strike us. It will be our one weak point. . . . [W]e will be obliged to go across the sea and fight our future battles with the powers of the Old World at a place which they and not we will select."[68] Senator Money added that the Philippines, if America chose to abandon them, might in fact become the site of a European conflagration, as the expansionists warned, but "[i]f such a war comes, we will not be a party to it."[69] Only by annexing the islands would the United States tie its interests to those of the archipelago. Imperialism, in short, meant aping inferior European nations. It was both useless and dangerous. And when overlaid with racial considerations and the violation of the core principles of American government, it became positively offensive and indefensible. These considerations convinced the antiimperialists that the great and glorious mission of the United States could be achieved only through exemplarism.

THE IMPERIALISTS RESPOND

Those supporting expansion obviously disagreed, but they spent less energy than the antiimperialists in defending their position, which Senator Platt had staked out at the outset in his December speech. For the majority of Republicans, there was no need to add to that statement. Also, since the Senate debate regarded resolutions concerning the terms of a peace treaty, few senators felt obligated to defend the treaty publicly with anything other than their votes. Opposing a peace settlement, as the antiimperialists were doing, required some justification, both to the American public and to the administration, since a new treaty would have to be negotiated if the current one were defeated or amended. Endorsing the peace needed no such explanation. The few speeches made in support of the treaty stressed the permissibility of expansion and of Congress's ability to rule territory without the residents' consent, and they also emphasized that the character of the American people was the surest guarantee of just and reasonable governance in the Philippines. In addition, expansionists reminded their opponents that the debate was not being conducted in the abstract, but would determine whether the war against Spain could finally be concluded. Finally, expansionists articulated strong defenses of the vindicationist interpretation of the idea of American mission.

The most basic argument that expansionists made in response to the antiimperialists was that the United States had the power to annex the Philippines, which Congress could rule as it saw fit. After Platt had made this observation, several antiimperialists—for example, Hoar— had stood to deny that Congress possessed such authority, and many of these senators cited various Supreme Court rulings, most notably *Dred Scott,* to defend their position. Constitutional lawyers and historians among the expansionist ranks rebutted these claims, however, with convincing arguments and citations that essentially settled the issue. Senator Knute Nelson (R-Minn.), for example, cited three constitutional bases of Congress's "full and plenary power to govern, control, and regulate all our Territories, no matter how acquired." The first was the "inherent power of the Government to acquire territory"; the second was Article IV, Sec. 3 of the Constitution ("The Congress shall have Power to dispose of and make all needful Rules and Regulations respecting the Territory or other Property belonging to the United States"); and the third was the necessary and proper clause. Nelson also cited excerpts from the constitutional convention and from the congressional debates surrounding previous territorial acquisitions to indicate that a consensus of previous statesmen supported the expansionists' position.[70] In addition, even as the senators debated each other about the Philippines, he noted, the United States exercised sovereignty over the territories of Arizona and New Mexico as it had "for over fifty years," neither of which had consented to become U.S. territories, and also over Alaska and Hawaii, whose odds of ever becoming states he deemed to be long indeed. Clearly, Congress ruling territories without the full consent of the native inhabitants was not unusual.

Senators Henry M. Teller (D-Colo.) and John C. Spooner (R-Wisc.), however, provided the most thorough and authoritative evidentiary refutations of the antiimperialist claim that Congress could not govern the territories without the populations' consent. Teller, whose amendment to the war resolution had disclaimed annexationism, reviewed every territorial acquisition in American history to that point and cited the congressional acts that defined the methods by which the various territories would be governed—in most cases by governors appointed by Congress—commenting, "It does not appear that there was very much 'consent of the governed' in any of these early transactions."[71] And he dwelt in particular on the case of the Mexican acquisitions, which the United States had won through conquest. After taking all of these precedents into account, Teller argued, one had to conclude that there was absolutely no basis for maintaining either that the United States could not acquire territory or that Congress was bound by prior restraint to enforce fully the Constitution in administering territories.[72]

Spooner's detailed recounting of Supreme Court precedents and constitutional commentators reinforced Teller's review of government policy. For example, the Wisconsin Republican cited one opinion in which Chief Justice John Marshall had written that "[t]he Constitution confers *absolutely* on the Government of the Union the powers of making war and of making treaties; consequently that Government possesses that power of acquiring territory, either by conquest or by treaty" (emphasis in the original).[73] Spooner's testimony carried added weight with the antiimperialists because he disagreed with Platt and Teller by acknowledging that the Congress would have to recognize the individual liberties of the Filipinos. To defend this claim, Spooner again cited Chief Justice Marshall: "The personal and civil rights of the inhabitants of the Territories are secured to them, as to other citizens, by the principles of constitutional liberty which restrain all the agencies of government, State and national."[74] This concession was important because it acknowledged the right of the Filipinos to travel to the United States— the right underlying the antiimperialists' concerns about the Filipinos' race.[75] It also admitted that the Bill of Rights restricted absolutely the power of Congress to legislate in certain aspects, thereby guaranteeing that the noble character of American governance could at least be somewhat safeguarded. Spooner's concession did not extend as far as the right to self-government, however, which he called a political and not a civil right.

Spooner also added an important dimension to the discussion about governance according to the consent of the governed. After noting that the expression "All men are born equal" was true, "philosophically and in a subtle and abstract sense," he added, "In the world, in the practical life of the world, it is not true, and it never has been true." Quoting one of his colleagues who had said that the Declaration of Independence was "a high political declaration," Spooner explained, "But, Mr. President, it happens that 'in the corrupted currents of this world' it is impossible for men or for nations in all their conduct to be governed by strict abstract right." He then declared of the doctrine "consent of the governed" that "as a matter of practical affairs that abstraction could not be regarded." In Niebuhrian fashion, Spooner continued, "It never can be until the millennium comes. It never can be while government is intrusted to men and holds sway over men. It never can be until perfection comes into life, and until the weaknesses, the passions, the violence, the faults, and the foibles of our common humanity are eliminated."[76] The words of the Declaration of Independence, in other words, defined an ideal, not a practical directive for the nation's political affairs. Americans might work to fulfill their ideals and rely on them as guiding principles for ordering their affairs, but as a practical and legal matter, the institutions of United States were built upon the stern recognition that life, especially political life, is messy because people are flawed.

Beginning from this premise, Spooner then went where no one else dared to tread: he stated that the United States should ignore the Declaration of Independence in the case before them because it was inconvenient. "And so, not looking at it from the philosophical standpoint, not dealing with it as a mere abstraction, dealing with it as practical men, the servants of a practical people, with a momentous duty imposed upon us, I say that in this case the doctrine invoked from the Declaration of Independence has no place." He then explained why it should not apply: "Nations are selfish. They must be selfish or they can not live. I do not mean grasping and overweening of necessity, but they must look to their own interests and the interests of their own people." To illustrate how his peers on both sides of the aisle subscribed in practice to this position, he reminded them that the United States was annexing in the treaty Puerto Rico as well as the Philippines. No one except Senator Hoar had condemned that action, he noted, because the Monroe Doctrine, natural proximity, and so forth supposedly entitled the United States to occupy the island, with or without its people's consent. He thus challenged the antiimperialists:

> Does the constitutional power depend upon the number of marine leagues a territory may be from the mainland? Does the declaration that "governments derive their consent of the governed" not apply to a million people as well as to ten million? . . . The right asserted in the Declaration of Independence can not be suspended in the West Indies and potential in the Philippines. If it is a right which in

the sight of God must always be respected by nations, no nation can honorably disregard it for any selfish purpose, whether it be for safety or something else.[77]

Spooner's argument that statesmen properly behave realistically and not idealistically was unusual, but its logic was inherent in the imperialist position and representative of the true nature of the idea of American mission as carried out in practice. The idea of American mission was to him a nice goal that Americans perhaps should pursue, but only after taking proper account of their own self-interest. Believing with the founders that human nature was everywhere equally corrupt, Spooner considered the United States to be fundamentally *un*exceptional in that regard, and in the realm of international relations it was therefore obligated to defend above all else its own interests. Insofar as his position placed the American people on the same moral footing as the rest of the world, Spooner stood alone. Most treaty supporters in fact argued the opposite.

In addition to insisting that annexing and governing the Philippines was legitimately within the purview of the U.S. government, senators who supported the treaty's ratification also argued repeatedly that the fears of the antiimperialists were misplaced because they failed to take due account of the character of the American people. Senator Henry Cabot Lodge (R-Mass.) pressed this point most forcefully, accusing the antiimperialists of expressing "distrust in the character, ability, honesty, and wisdom of the American people."[78] The argument that the success of the U.S. Philippine policy rested with the judgment and character of the American people relied on two supporting propositions. The first was that the Constitution and the Declaration of Independence, on their own, were meaningless. Their living spirit came from the people who put them into practice. As Lodge declared, "Constitutions do not make people; people make constitutions. . . . If the American people were disposed to tyranny, injustice, and oppression, a constitution would offer but a temporary barrier to their ambitions." He continued by arguing that as long as "the American people believe in freedom and humanity, in equal justice to all men, and in equal rights before the law, . . . the great doctrines of the Declaration of Independence and of the Constitution will never be in peril."[79] Senator Thomas H.

Carter (R-Mont.) added that if the American people ever acquired a spirit in defiance of their traditions, "written constitutions will not long restrain it, and resolutions of Congress or of either branch will be but as ropes of sand to stay the mighty tide."[80]

The second foundation for the proposition that the American people could be trusted to administer fairly the Philippine Islands and other annexed territories was that Americans were Anglo-Saxons and therefore inclined by both nature and tradition to govern themselves and others justly. Senator Teller forwarded this argument most fully; his personal background as the resident of what was for some time a territory (Colorado) led him to believe that his race naturally formed fair governments when left to its own devices. As he recalled, "We organized government in the mountains of Colorado, and exercised legislative powers in the old democratic way of calling the neighborhood together and enacting laws." Coloradans, he recalled, also elected judges and empaneled juries that they empowered to execute men—and they did these things without laboring under the burden of constitutional necessity. And of all these governing institutions, he added, there was not a one "that did not understand that it was governed by the great fundamental principles that are necessary for the maintenance of free institutions." The reason for this proclivity for just government, he explained, was "our ancestors."[81] Clearly, Teller reasoned, Americans would govern the Philippines fairly and in accordance with the principles of their founding documents because it was in their nature to do so.

This confidence in the ability of the American people to govern the Philippines justly—the confidence so manifestly absent from the pamphlets and proclamations of the antiimperialists—contributed to the Republicans' support for an activist interpretation of the idea of American mission. As President McKinley's speeches launching the imperialist crusade indicated, expansionists considered the United States not only to have a mission to set an example for the rest of the world but also a duty to uplift those who happened to come into the nation's ambit. Senator Spooner presented this perspective by way of analogy:

If walking along the city street at night one comes across a sturdy brute beating a woman or a child into insensibility, a man would attack him, drag him away, disable him. Having done this, a man would not walk away and leave the woman or the child bleeding and helpless upon the street in the midnight to die, to freeze in the cold of winter, to starve, or perhaps again to be the subject of maltreatment. The same impulse which led one to defend would command one to further protect. Situations, Mr. President, create duties. This is as true of nations as it is of men.[82]

The United States, Spooner insisted, was in relation to the Philippines precisely as the man in the street was in regard to the beaten woman. It had a moral obligation to help the people of the archipelago get back on their feet, secure from the European ruffians, and only then could it leave. Although it was only a circumstantial duty, it was a duty nonetheless, and it presupposed that the American people had collective moral obligations to other societies.

Other senators agreed. Lodge, for instance, recounted that in "conversations" with his constituents he had maintained "we had by the fortunes of war assumed a great responsibility in the Philippines; that we ought to meet it, and that we ought to give to those people an opportunity for freedom, for peace, and for self-government; that we ought to protect them from the rapacity of other nations and seek to uplift those whom we had freed." And the people of Massachusetts, he observed, had agreed with him.[83] Senator Nelson also agreed with him: "We came there as liberators of the Philippine Islanders, and we are there as liberators today. . . . And now it is our duty under the providence of God and under the Constitution and laws of our country, and under all that pertains to true liberty on the face of the earth, to protect the Philippine Islanders against anarchy, chaos, and confusion, and the despotism that results form it."[84]

Senator Edward O. Wolcott (R-Colo.) had an even more expansive understanding of America's responsibilities, one that reflected the vindicationist conception of the idea of American mission in its full spread-eagle glory. "I am not unwilling to face the responsibilities of this treaty with all that its terms imply. We shall not put our hands upon that people except to bless them. American institutions mean liberty and not despotism, and our dealings with those islanders, be they brief or be they for all time, can only serve to lift them up nearer to the light of civilization and of Christianity." Wolcott then borrowed language from the antiimperialists and defined McKinley's expansionist program as the true expression of American exceptionalism:

> This Republic represents the first and only experiment in absolute self-government by the Anglo-Saxon race, intermingled and reinforced by the industrious of all the countries of the Old World. . . . Who is to say that in the evolution of such a Republic as this the time has not come when the immense development of our internal resources and the marvelous growth of our domestic and foreign commerce and a realization of our virile strength have not stimulated that Anglo-Saxon restlessness which beats with the blood of the race into an activity which will not be quenched until we have finally planted our standard in that far-off archipelago which inevitable destiny has intrusted to our hands?[85]

An important implication of the expansionists' arguments was that the antiimperialists overlooked the centrality of progress to American national identity. By stressing perhaps too greatly the legacy of the founders, in other words, the antiimperialists were overlooking the dynamism of the American character, which, when combined with the founders' principles, yielded the accomplishments for which the nation was most proud.

Senator Teller argued, finally, that the spirit that had impelled the United States to intervene in Cuba required Americans to remain in the Spanish islands until the people residing therein were capable of self-government: "We commenced this great work of humanity, and we are bound to carry it on until we have accomplished the great object for which we began." That "great object," Teller argued, was "that some day these people are to become self-reliant and self-governing, as we are, or they are to become a part and parcel of this Republic, entitled to all the rights and subject to all the duties of citizenship of states." But there was a catch in Teller's position. "There is a fundamental truth recognized in representative government, that a people are entitled only to such self-government as they can maintain. . . . The people who live in the Tropics are not qualified, and, I fear, never will be qualified to maintain such a government as is maintained by Anglo-Saxon people. A torrid climate does not develop high mental or moral qualities."

Moreover, "the Asiatic people will *never* maintain such a government as the Anglo-Saxon. He is not capable of it" (emphasis added).[86]

Thus, the United States would need to remain in the islands "for a time, with kindness and justice," and "for many years to come at least" the United States would also have to "speak to the world" for them in "all their international relations." Given the race of their inhabitants, however, it was clearly out of the question that the islands would ever qualify for statehood. Still, as Teller saw it, the United States could enjoy "no greater glory" than to "take eight or ten million men, bound down by the power of a wicked government, and lift them up and put them on the plane of citizenship in a great republic."[87] The logic was convoluted–the United States was to place "on the plane of citizenship in a great republic" a race of individuals who were "not capable" of maintaining such a government–but compelling to jingoes who imagined their nation capable of transforming the world. Teller's argument also demonstrated how racism structured liberal theory in American thought, such that Americans could act as conquerors while believing themselves to be liberators. When the treaty passed, this vindicationist position received its firmest endorsement.

It was not necessary for senators to support full-blown vindicationism, however, in order to vote in favor of the treaty. Several senators who had made antiexpansionist speeches, for instance, ended up casting their vote for it. The reason was basic: the debate over imperialism was structured around the ratification of a peace treaty and did not take place in the abstract. Thus, expansion and setting the terms of peace were interconnected in the McKinley-brokered treaty so that imperialism had become encumbered not only with practical considerations regarding the very real American interest in ending the war but also with the moral aspects that had pervaded the war from its outset.

Lodge explained the situation. To "reject the treaty or strike out the clause relating to the Philippines" would "hand the islands back to Spain." Rejecting the treaty, he continued, would also mean continuing the war against Spain and repudiating the president before the world. That would mean "the humiliation of the United States in the eyes of civilized mankind and brands us as a people incapable of great affairs or of taking rank where we belong, as one of the greatest of the great world powers."[88] It was necessary that the United States act as a unit rather than bicker internally, Lodge said, if it wished to secure for itself the Great Power status to which it felt entitled. Carter made this point forcefully:

> Mr. President, it must be borne in mind, in another point of view, that this Government has recently, by the common consent of mankind, become one of the great world powers, a recognized if not a dominating force on the globe, and whatsoever is done by the Congress of the country should be done with some regard for this universally recognized fact. In the light of such a fact, it seems to me that acting upon a theater or stage in the presence of the whole civilized world we belittle the dignity, we seriously invade the good name of the United States Government everywhere by undertaking upon the floor of the open Senate to make a dicker with the future as a price for present action in giving a vote upon a treaty of peace.[89]

The idea of acting like a great power, as noted previously, did not impress many of the antiimperialists, but the notion of showing solidarity for U.S. soldiers did carry great weight with them. This became an important consideration after the telegram arrived in Washington on February 4, 1899, stating that hostilities had broken out in the Philippines between Aguinaldo's and the American troops.

William Jennings Bryan, the head of the Democrats and their standard-bearer (again) in the upcoming presidential election, pressured the party to ratify the treaty, arguing that the policy of imperialism would be reversed when Democrats assumed control of the White House the following year. During the waning days of the debate, therefore, a handful of antiimperialists solemnly declared that they would in fact vote in favor of the treaty's ratification, but that they still did not endorse its expansionist provisions.[90] Senator William V. Allen (Pop-Neb.) declared, for instance, "Now, Mr. President, because I shall vote for the treaty it does not follow that I am in favor of annexation. I do it for the simple reason that in my judgment the Government of the United States can not afford to open up negotiations with the Spanish dynasty again."[91] Rather than expend their political energies on defeating a peace treaty, then, many antiimperialists ultimately resolved instead to use the elections of 1900 as the platform on which they would mobilize public opinion behind their position, and they turned those elections into a referendum on expansionism. The treaty debate, in their minds, was only one battle in a much larger war for America's soul. In the end, on February 6, 1899, the Senate ratified McKinley's treaty, barely mustering the required two-thirds majority with a vote of fifty-seven to twenty-seven. The Philippines, for the moment, was a U.S. territory.

The treaty clause annexing the Philippine Islands was an action fraught with profound significance for American national identity, and the debate about whether or not to ratify the treaty was phrased in cultural language that lay bare Americans' assumptions about the nature and sources of their civilization. This debate yielded some frank arguments that would otherwise have been unlikely to be voiced on the floor of the legislature. For instance, the Declaration of Independence was in the final analysis found to be a statement perhaps of noble ideals but not of actual political directives—a decidedly unjingoistic position to stake in 1899. The conception that the United States was an Anglo-Saxon nation that happened to house but not include as equals (even by the ideals of the Declaration) nonwhites was reinforced insofar as that position was consistently raised but never challenged. Christian values were presupposed as being determinative, where feasible, of American actions; the sense of duty that underlay Americans' pursuit of their national mission was understood as reflecting Christian imperatives. Darwinian competition with the European powers underlay the expansionists' concerns with prestige and power, but was resented by those favoring narrower conceptions of American exceptionalism. In short, this was a debate that could not be settled by mere reference to interest; it relied for its resolution as well upon elaborations of a national identity with which Americans could feel comfortable. Standing consciously at a turning point in their nation's development, Americans struggled to reconcile the sources of their heritage that made them proud with visions of what they hoped they might become.

CHAPTER NINE

Selling Imperialism

RATIFICATION OF THE treaty did not end the debate on expansionism. Public opinion remained sharply divided on the issue, and the treaty vote had been close. It was still possible that the country's imperial course would be reversed, and if so the election of 1900 would provide the most logical opportunity to achieve that end. The Philippine acquisition, after all, was embedded, albeit prominently, in a peace treaty. With the peace now secure, it was possible that the country would regard imperialism differently since the issue was no longer tied up with formally ending a war. President McKinley thus needed to reassure the country that the expansionist course on which it was embarking, which felt so new and unfamiliar, was right and good. His task was to convince the people that U.S. foreign policy was not only consistent with the nation's highest values and most honored traditions, but that it advanced the national mission. The leitmotif of the United States was progress, and McKinley sought to persuade the people, as he had already persuaded himself, that this new policy of imperialism served its cause.

McKinley's first public statement after the treaty's ratification was a speech he gave to the Home Market Club in Boston, on February 16. The themes that he had tested on his October speaking tour, when he still had some doubts about expansion, found forceful reassertion in this speech, as they would in later speeches he would make to the country. "The Philippines, like Cuba and Puerto Rico, were intrusted [sic] to our hands by the war, and to that great trust, under the Providence of God and in the name of human progress and civilization, we are committed. It is a trust we have not sought; it is a trust from which we will not flinch."

McKinley then reminded his audience how the United States had gotten possession of the islands in the first place:

Could we, after freeing the Filipinos from the domination of Spain, have left them without government and without power to protect life or property or to perform the international obligations essential to an independent State? Could we have left them in a state of anarchy and justified ourselves in our own consciences or before the tribunal of mankind? Could we have done that in the sight of God or man? Our concern was not for territory or trade or empire, but for the people whose interests and destiny, without our willing it, had been put in our hands. . . . Did we ask their consent to liberate them from Spanish sovereignty or to enter Manila Bay and destroy the Spanish sea power there? We did not ask these; we were obeying a higher moral obligation which rested on us and which did not require anybody's consent.

Now that the islands were in America's hands, furthermore, the United States had a duty to uplift, transform, and redeem their inhabitants:

I do not prophesy. The present is all absorbing to me, but I cannot bound my vision . . . but by the broad range of future years, when that group of islands, under the impulse of the year just past shall have become the gems and glories of these tropical seas; a land of plenty and of increasing possibilities; a people redeemed from savage indolence and habits, devoted to the arts of peace, in touch with the commerce and trade of all nations, enjoying the blessings of freedom, of civil and religious liberty, of education and of homes, and whose children and children's children shall for ages hence bless the American Republic because it emancipated and redeemed their fatherland and set them in the pathway of the world's best civilization.[1]

American imperialism was not the same as European imperialism, McKinley implied, because the European powers paid no heed to the interests and needs of the colonized populations and instead cared only about themselves. The United States, by contrast, expanded primarily to liberate others from the corruption of the past and to invite them to join in the unmatched progress of the greatest civilization in history. McKinley did not argue in his Boston speech that the United States would benefit materially from its possession of the Philippines, but that the Filipinos would be the real winners. McKinley repeated this claim with dull consistency in both public and private when referring to either the Cubans or the Filipinos. He also believed that by increasing American power, expansion would benefit the United States as well as its charges, but that belief existed alongside of and not in contradiction to his certainty that U.S. imperialism was a blessing for the host societies.[2]

There was clear evidence, however, that the Filipinos did not share McKinley's confidence in American beneficence. On February 4, simmering tensions between Aguinaldo's forces and the U.S. occupying troops turned violent. Aguinaldo immediately declared war, and armed Filipino resistance to American designs on their land became official. The outbreak of armed hostilities between the Filipinos and Americans occurred only two days before the treaty vote was scheduled to take place and may have helped to get the agreement ratified (with a vote of only fifty-seven to twenty-seven, only two switched votes would have defeated the treaty). McKinley's interpretation of the hostilities, however, was shaped by his belief, acquired from the October testimony of the peace commission, that Aguinaldo was merely the head of a small, unrepresentative group of malcontents.[3] His ignorance compounded by self-righteousness, McKinley never did see the insurrection for what it was: a nationalist movement fighting for self-determination.

In a speech he gave in August 1899 to soldiers returning from the Philippine campaign, his tone was indignant and even defensive as he described the situation: "A body of insurgents, in no sense representing the sentiment of the people of the islands, disputed our lawful authority, and even before ratification of the treaty by the American Senate were attacking the very forces who fought for and secured their freedom." Perplexed by the insurgents' inability to recognize that the United States and freedom were coterminous and could in no ways work at crosspurposes, he continued: "Our kindness was reciprocated with cruelty, our mercy with a Mauser. . . . Our humanity was interpreted as weakness, our forbearance as cowardice. The misguided followers in rebellion have only our charity and pity. As to the cruel leaders who have needlessly sacrificed the lives of thousands of their people . . . I will leave to others the ungracious task of justice and eulogy."[4] Throughout his speech, McKinley's attitude toward the insurgents resembled an angry schoolteacher complaining about the ungrateful insolence of his students more than that of the leader of a nation denigrating an enemy in war.

The president remained convinced of American innocence, and in the fall of 1899 he decided to go on another speaking tour, as he had done the previous year, to remind his countrymen of their nation's mission. Unlike his 1898 tour, in this one he knew where he stood on expansion, and he determined to convince the people that that policy was best for their nation and that their soldiers were not dying needlessly for it. He invoked familiar themes to comfort the people in the face of a war that was quickly becoming uglier and more costly than the Spanish-American War had been: "From Plymouth Rock to the Philippines the grand triumphant march of human liberty has never paused. . . . May we not feel assured that if we do our duty, the Providence which favored the undertakings of the fathers and every step of our progress since, will continue His watchful care and guidance over us, and that 'the hand that led us to our present place will not relax His grip till we have reached the glorious goal He has fixed for us in the achievement of His end'?"[5]

McKinley was reassuring the people that they remained an exceptional people and that their covenant with God remained potent. "Unhappy will be the day for our glorious country when the people become indifferent of its principles and its mission; unfortunate indeed if the people should lose their interest or relax their vigilance," he told the crowd at Watseka, Illinois, in an effort to bolster their commitment to the war effort. "Providence has blessed us. We have opportunities that come to no other peoples in the world. Let us keep sacred this great fabric of government that dispenses its blessings equally over all."[6] In Minneapolis, he invoked the theme of progress. "The century now drawing to a close has been most memorable in the world's progress and history. The march of mankind in moral and intellectual advancement has been onward and upward. . . . Civilization has achieved great victories and to the gospel of goodwill there are now few dissenters."[7]

In other speeches McKinley spoke more directly to the Philippine situation. "We are in the Philippines. Our flag is there, and our flag is never raised anywhere for oppression. It floats for liberty wherever it is raised," he said in rebuke to antiimperialists who denounced the policy as contrary to the nation's principles.[8] At Fargo, North Dakota, he described the injustice of the insurgents' actions: "We never dreamed that the little body of insurgents whom we had just emancipated from oppression—we never for a moment believed that they would turn upon the flag that had sheltered them against Spain."[9] In Redfield, South Dakota, he explained in greater detail how and why the United States was in the Philippines:

> We have not only been adding territory to the United States, but we have been adding character and prestige to the American name. . . . There has never been a moment of time, my countrymen, when we could have left Manila Bay or Manila Harbor or the Archipelago of the Philippines without dishonor to our name. We did not go there to conquer the Philippines. We went there to destroy the Spanish fleet that we might end the war, but in the Providence of God, who works in mysterious ways, this great archipelago was put into our lap, and the American people never shirk duty. And the flag there now is not the flag of tyranny, it is the flag of liberty, and wherever the flag goes, character, education, American intelligence, American civilization and American liberty go.[10]

Since Providence put the islands "in our lap," McKinley argued, we had a duty to improve them. "It is given the strong to bear the burdens of the weak; and our prayer should be, not that the burdens should be rolled away, but that God should give us the strength to bear them."[11]

Familiar exculpatory themes recurred throughout McKinley's speeches—duty, Providence, and the unforeseen manner of America's initial involvement in the islands. In Sioux Falls, he declared: "God proposes and man disposes. . . . So, my fellow citizens, when the war with Spain commenced—commenced in the interests of humanity, commenced to relieve the Cuban people of that oppression under which they had suffered for long years—nobody at that moment had any thought of Puerto Rico or the Philippines."[12] At Iowa Falls, he announced, "I believe, my fellow citizens, that this territory came to us in the Providence of God. We did not seek it. It is ours, with all the responsibilities that belong to it; and as a great, strong, brave Nation we mean to carry our education and civilization there."[13] His message in Manchester, Iowa, was broader: "The ship of state has sailed uninterruptedly on its mission of liberty; one thing that cannot be said of this Nation for which should all give thanksgiving and praise, it never raised its arm against humanity, never struck a blow except for civilization and mankind. . . . I do not think we have lost our vigor, our virtue, our courage, our high purpose, or our patriotism."[14]

Symbolically connecting the Philippines with the United States and its values was the flag, which waved in almost every speech McKinley gave on the tour, but never as proudly as in an oration to the people of Warren, Ohio:

> Our flag is there–*rightfully* there–as rightfully there as the flag that floats above me is here; and it is there not as a flag of tyranny or as a symbol of slavery, not for exploitation, but it is there for what it is here, and for what is everywhere–justice and liberty and right and civilization. And wherever the American nation plants that flag, there go with it the hearts and consciences and humane purposes of the American people. (Emphasis in the original)[15]

In all of these speeches, McKinley was not only justifying U.S. foreign policy but using foreign policy to define the nation. He infused the national identity with a content drawn from traditional cultural constructs, particularly those concerning religious and political values, and he made those constructs meaningful and relevant by embedding them into the events and circumstances in the Philippines. Likewise, he rendered U.S. foreign policy intelligible by the same stroke. Ideology and policy were fused. Thus, the United States was not deviating from its traditions but following the same Providence that had always led the nation–and always to good and just ends. Nor was the United States conquering the Filipinos, but liberating them, by bringing them under the same canopy of freedom that shaded the whole nation.

In this way, McKinley incorporated overseas expansionism into American national identity. He led the United States into its first vindicationist venture and rendered that action both sensible and morally legitimate by characterizing it in the language of American exceptionalism and American progress. McKinley declared that he believed that "the century of free government which the American people have enjoyed . . . has fitted them for the great task of lifting up and assisting to better conditions and larger liberty these distant peoples who have through the issue of battle become our wards."[16] This meant that he believed the country to be not only morally but materially capable to be a civilizing agency, that it had matured to the fullness of its powers.

Americans were secure enough in their status and power, in other words, to turn their attention to others. Moreover, not only were they capable of sharing with others their virtue and excellence but their newfound stature made that task a duty.

McKinley made his most complete statement of American purposes in the Philippines during his State of the Union address of 1899. In the address, McKinley spoke consciously to both a national audience and posterity, and he used the moment to explain fully how the United States was fulfilling its national mission through expansion.

He began by discussing Cuban affairs. After quoting the Teller Amendment's pledge to leave the "government and control of the island to its people," McKinley described how the United States was preparing the Cubans to assume that role. He continued, "Our mission, to accomplish which we took up the wages of battle, is not to be fulfilled by turning adrift any loosely formed commonwealth to face the vicissitudes which too often attend weaker states." The responsibility of the United States was rather to shore up Cuban society by strengthening its economy, "which will give employment to idle men and re-establish the pursuits of peace."[17] Given the clear desire of Cubans for independence, the fact that McKinley refused to entertain that possibility—the only outcome that would fully conform with American principles—reveals that McKinley regarded Cuban interests as secondary to America's. More specifically, McKinley's insistence that the United States establish a protectorate over a people who clearly desired democratic independence shows how racism and U.S. interests were logically prior in his conception of the American mission to the liberal norms that defined its spirit.

McKinley devoted the bulk of his address to the Philippine situation, where the insurgents' resistance had taken the form of guerrilla warfare. After nearly a year of armed hostilities, the president still did not appreciate the nature and scope of Filipino nationalism. "Everything indicates that with the speedy suppression of the Tagalog rebellion life in the archipelago will soon resume its ordinary course under the protection of our sovereignty, and the people of those favored islands will enjoy a prosperity and freedom which they have never before known," he cheerily predicted. In his mind, of course, the rebellion was limited

to just a single tribe (the Tagalogs), while "the great mass of [the Filipinos believe] that peace and safety and prosperity and stable government can only be found in a loyal acceptance of the authority of the
United States."[18] The self-deception was breathtaking, but it was made
possible by McKinley's pious conviction that U.S. rule was, simply, so
self-evidently superior to any alternative that any reasonable person
could recognize the fact.

Other than reassuring the American people that the embarrassing
and morally dubious hostilities were nothing to worry about, McKinley wanted to use the address to remind the nation that U.S. Philippine
policy was a test of America's commitment to its mission—the sort of
test that would make the country stronger.

> Few graver responsibilities have ever been confided to us. If we ac-
> cept them in a spirit worthy of our race and our traditions, a great
> opportunity comes with them. The islands lie under the shelter of
> our flag. . . . They cannot be abandoned. If we desert them we leave
> them at once to anarchy and finally to barbarism. We fling them, a
> golden apple of discord, among the rival powers. . . . We shall con-
> tinue . . . in every way in our power to make these people whom
> Providence has brought within our jurisdiction feel that it is their
> liberty and not our gain we are seeking to enhance. Our flag has
> never waved over any community but in blessing. I believe the Fil-
> ipinos will soon recognize the fact that it has not lost its gift of bene-
> diction in its worldwide journey to their shores.[19]

By characterizing the bestowal of American civilization upon other
peoples as a "blessing" and a "gift of benediction," McKinley overlaid
U.S. foreign policy with civil-religious imagery and import. When he
called the islands both a "responsibility" and an "opportunity," he revealed his dedication to the notion that the United States has the task of
redeeming the world, bit by bit, and that doing so fulfills the promise of
American mission.

In a way, it does not matter if McKinley was sincere in his remarks.
He framed the issues in a way that made sense to the American people
and thereby reaffirmed, at the very least, that the norms to which he
hearkened were the proper touchstone for evaluating American behavior. There is evidence, moreover, that his arguments took hold

among those supporting expansion. "The disposition of these islands as a consequence of war, is a duty devolved upon us alone, and a duty that cannot be shirked," wrote one pamphleteer,[20] and in the introduction to his book about the treaty, Charles Henry Butler averred:

> The "Destiny of the United States" is not a mere phrase or a mere fancy—it cannot be dismissed with a sneer. . . . Surely our great advance has not been all by chance—surely thus far the Lord hath led us on, and surely he will not forsake us now. . . . Let us freely assume our new responsibilities as we have assumed those that came to us in the past, remembering that nothing brings its own reward so surely, and so completely, as the prompt recognition, and faithful performance of duty.[21]

These comments show that the president's arguments resonated with those who favored expansion. In an age before public opinion polls, it is difficult to tell if McKinley's arguments persuaded the people or were simply tailored to fit what they already believed. The truth is probably a combination of the two. In any event, the themes on which McKinley relied to sell imperialism to an isolationist but jingoistic nation reflected the norms of a national culture of which he was both a member and a figurehead. In his ignorant geniality and ethnocentrism, McKinley personified the cultural constructs that informed how Americans in 1898 interpreted and interacted with their world. But, then as now, Americans were divided on how they should be defined, and McKinley's vision for the United States, which everyone by 1899 agreed was understood by reference to U.S. foreign policy, did not go unchallenged.

IMPERIALISM AND THE PRESIDENTIAL ELECTION OF 1900

As promised, the antiimperialists determined to overturn the Republicans' expansionist program by removing them from office (except those who, like Hoar, opposed expansion). The Anti-Imperialist League in particular was supportive of William Jennings Bryan's candidacy, as its platform declared: "We propose to contribute to the defeat of any person or party that stands for the forcible subjugation of any people. We shall oppose for re-election all who in the white house or in congress betray American liberty in pursuit of un-American ends."[22]

The Anti-Imperialist League boasted deep pockets (thanks to Andrew Carnegie and others), pedigreed and influential leaders, and a broad constituency. It hoped to mobilize these assets in particular toward defeating McKinley in the election of 1900. As one author wrote, "One of the country's two parties has . . . retrograded one or two centuries and proposes to lead the grandest medium of true democracy and of a future full civilization back to the barbarous and monarchical times of the fifteenth century. Can they do it? is a question to be settled in November."[23]

The organization's diverse membership, while a boon for mustering support from all quarters of society, proved ultimately to be a liability, however. No matter how important antiimperialists believed their mission to be, it was in many cases the only thing uniting them. Union leader Samuel Gompers and Andrew Carnegie were as unlikely a pair of allies as the conservative Senator Hoar and Bryan, the populist Democratic Party candidate. Sharp differences in domestic political philosophy often made it difficult for antiimperialists to work together, particularly since the election of 1896 had been so divisive. Still, the fact that these individuals did join forces in an effort to defeat a foreign policy—and the fact that they pledged themselves to focus their political energies accordingly—attests poignantly to the mostly principled basis of their collective opposition.[24] The rallies and pamphlets that the Anti-Imperialist League regularly sponsored, moreover, contributed immensely to the scope and quality of public discourse.

The visions and personalities of the presidential contenders were pressed into service of the debate over expansion. Bryan was an evangelical preacher, and he discerned biblical importance in the policy's outcome, while McKinley stuck to his finely honed themes of duty and destiny as mandating a continuing American occupation of the Pacific outpost. Each candidate kept the level of the debate at a lofty and somewhat metaphorical level: America's expansion into the Philippines was not just a foreign policy, both men insisted, but an expression of national morality; it was either a debasement or a fulfillment of America's mission to human history. Neither candidate doubted that the identity of the United States would be determined by the voters' decision.

Bryan had supported ratifying the treaty. He did so because he wished to disentangle what he had regarded as two distinct policies: ending the war and recognizing the independence of the Philippines.[25] He explained in early January, while the Senate was actively debating the treaty's ratification, that if the American people were committed to expansionism, then they would engage in it whether or not it was included in the treaty. He also believed that if it were defeated, then "the opponents of the treaty would be compelled to assume responsibility for the continuance of war conditions and for the risks that always attend negotiations with a hostile nation."[26] On the other hand, once the Senate ratified the treaty, Bryan argued, their action, "instead of closing the door to independence, really makes easier the establishment of such a government in the Philippine Islands."[27] Bryan's condemnation of imperialism covered familiar themes, but bore the imprint of his considerable rhetorical gifts. One of his strategies was to define imperialism as the policy of the trusts. "Avarice paints destiny with a dollar mark before it, militarism equips it with a sword," he declared in one speech.[28] Elsewhere he argued, "Monopoly can thrive in security so long as the inquiry, 'Who will haul down the flag,' on distant islands turns public attention away from the question, who will uproot the trusts at home?"[29]

Bryan's religious credentials made him impatient with some of the imperialists' own religious arguments. In his speech accepting the Democratic Party's nomination to represent them in the presidential contest, for instance, he expressed resentment at the Republicans' merging of America's national goals with those of religious missionaries:

> If true Christianity consists in carrying out in our daily lives the teachings of Christ, who will say that we are commanded to civilize with dynamite and proselytize with the sword? He who would declare the divine will must prove his authority either by Holy Writ or by evidence of a special dispensation. Imperialism finds no warrant in the Bible. . . . Love, not force, was the weapon of the Nazarene; sacrifice for others, not the exploitation of them, was His method of reaching the human heart.[30]

Bryan's religious perspective also caused him to bristle at McKinley's suggestions that it was the nation's destiny to expand. "Destiny," he explained, "is not a matter of chance, it is a matter of choice; it is not a thing to be waited for, it is a thing to be achieved." Moreover, he insisted that the nation's destiny derived from the American people's sense of national mission. Expansionism, he argued, required Americans to reevaluate their understanding of the nation's purpose and discard how it had hitherto been defined.[31]

Although Bryan admitted that Americans in 1900 did not necessarily have to share the founders' purpose, he did think that the nation's destiny would be permanently altered if it strayed so significantly from their mission.[32] Bryan was certain, however, that America's purpose and mission, from which flowed its destiny, should not include imperialism. He often equated Europe with retrogression,[33] and he urged that by imitating those powers, the United States would be denying its distinct and valuable status as "a republic gradually but surely becoming a supreme moral factor in the world's progress and the accepted arbiter of the world's disputes–a republic whose history, like the path of the just, 'is as the shining light that shineth more and more unto the perfect day.'"[34] But Bryan's eloquence was in vain. As in 1896, the cause he championed in the election of 1900 was unsuccessful.

McKinley's quest for reelection was considerably easier than Bryan's goal of taking the White House from him. For starters, he was the incumbent during an immensely popular war, and like the imperialism that grew out of it, he was still bathed in victory's warm glow. Popular discontent with what had become (but which was not yet officially recognized as) the Philippine-American War was mounting, but a combination of factors muted the opposition's effectiveness and sometimes led to charges that the antiimperialists were unpatriotic cranks. (The most important one was a pervasive public ignorance about the true nature of a conflict that was taking place on the other side of the world in the age before television.) While Bryan received assistance from the Anti-Imperialist League, which held rallies and distributed pamphlets on his behalf, McKinley also was aided by a pamphlet campaign run by his party.[35] In his fall 1899 speaking tour, McKinley had very effectively defined U.S. foreign policy according to the normative constructs by which Americans interpreted their world, and his supporters drove home the image that he had created of a noble and benevolent great power civilizing benighted races in accordance with God's will and the nation's heritage. As Cushman Davis described America's imperial policy, "This is manifest destiny; it is written by an auspicious astrologer in the sky of a visible future."[36]

Mostly, however, McKinley's supporters attacked Bryan and tried to shift the focus of the election away from imperialism and back to the domestic and economic issues that had led to McKinley's 1896 decisive victory. As Senator Charles W. Fairbanks (R-Ind.), a member of the Republican nominating committee, announced at the convention, "Our Democratic friends assembled in convention in Kansas City declared that Imperialism was the great, the overshadowing issue of 1900. Not so, my countrymen, for the great and overshadowing issue is . . . whether we shall have Republican prosperity or Democratic adversity."[37] Also in this spirit, Republican pamphleteers often stressed the economic merits of the Philippine acquisition, arguing that McKinley's foreign policy was not only noble but that it reinforced the economic recovery from the Depression of 1893 that he had begun.[38] In addition, they noted, some of America's most significant previous territorial acquisitions, notably the Louisiana Purchase, had been Democratic initiatives, which made the party's current opposition to expansion appear quixotic at best.[39]

Because popular opposition to America's increasingly messy involvement in the Philippines had not yet reached a critical mass by 1900, the Democrats moved away from it as the campaign's "Paramount Issue" in the final weeks before the election.[40] As Republican pamphleteer George E. Adams observed, "The young men rather like what Bryan calls imperialism. A sense of new and larger responsibility which makes an old man anxious only stirs the blood of the young man. The young men of this country are glad and proud of the glory we have won, the influence we have gained, the splendid responsibility we have taken upon ourselves of spreading American institutions and American liberty over the far-off islands of the sea."[41] Adams's reference to characteristics that were commonly associated with Anglo-Saxonism was transparently meant to reinforce to Americans that imperialism accorded with the national ethos.

McKinley did not actively campaign on his own behalf, but, following Washington's example, waited ostensibly for the country to come to him. He counted on his speaking tour of 1899 to have framed imperialism congenially in the public's mind and otherwise allowed others to speak on his behalf. In his acceptance speech and inaugural address, McKinley kept his references to imperialism on the same high plane of friendly vagueness whereon he had already found success with his audiences. As before, he stressed the themes of duty and destiny. During his speech accepting the Republican Party's nomination, for example, he declared:

> The flag of the Republic now floats over those islands as an emblem of rightful sovereignty. Will the Republic stay and dispense to their inhabitants the blessings of liberty, education and free institutions, or steal away, leaving them to anarchy or imperialism? The American question is between duty and desertion—the American verdict will be for duty against desertion, for the Republic against both anarchy and imperialism.[42]

Rather than dwell on the economic and other benefits that might accrue to the U.S. annexation of the archipelago, in other words, McKinley continued to emphasize the moral accomplishment that the policy entailed.

After he was safely reelected—in a landslide—McKinley sought to heal the rifts that he recognized to be opening around his imperial policy. He used his inaugural address, therefore, as an opportunity actively to enforce the clear mandate given him by the electorate by reinforcing in the public's mind the fact that the U.S. annexation of the Philippine Islands was not only consistent with but also strengthening of the nation's most fundamental norms. Although he did spend a few moments reassuring the country that he would continue to implement the economic program that had hitherto been so successful and duly celebrating the national reunification achieved by the war ("We are reunited. Sectionalism has disappeared. Division on public questions can no longer be traced to the war maps of 1861"), he spent the majority of the address discussing U.S. Philippine policy. In the address, McKinley condemned the antiimperialists as "obstructionists who despair, and who would destroy confidence in the ability of our people to solve wisely and for civilization the mighty problems resting upon them." And he described the insurgents as unrepresentative of the Filipinos' attitudes toward the United States: "Our countrymen should not be deceived. We are not waging war against the inhabitants of the Philippine Islands. A portion of them are making war against the United States. By far the greater part of them recognize American sovereignty and welcome it."

Mostly, however, McKinley discussed the policy as an extension of American national identity and emblematic of America's noble character:

> The American people, intrenched in freedom at home, take their love for it with them wherever they go, and they reject as mistaken and unworthy the doctrine that we lose our own liberties by securing the enduring foundations of liberty to others. Our institutions will not deteriorate by extension, and our sense of justice will not abate under tropic suns in distant seas. As heretofore, so hereafter will the nation demonstrate its fitness to administer any new estate which events devolve upon it, and in the fear of God will "take occasion by the hand and make the bounds of freedom wider yet."

McKinley stressed how progress was the defining characteristic of the American nation, and that it was incumbent upon the American people to accept the burdens that it placed upon them. They were the heirs of the founders' purposes, he reminded them, and it was up to them to keep relevant the nation's defining norms, particularly progress, whose path "is seldom smooth." But, he added, "are we not made better for the effort and sacrifice, and are not those we serve lifted up and blessed? . . . The Republic has marched on and on, and its step has exalted freedom and humanity." Finally, he insisted that the nation's inexorable progress had at last led it to a position of full equality with the other Great Powers. The United States was in the Philippines, McKinley declared, as a great power like other great powers, except it was more noble, free, and equal than they, and due to these qualities it was not imperialist in the ordinary meaning of the term, but engaged in a "mission of emancipation."[43]

During his second term, McKinley continued to stress these themes, even as the antiimperialists waged their most effective publicity campaigns against the Philippine–American War by publicizing America's atrocities upon the Filipinos. In San Jose, California, for instance, McKinley emphasized the capaciousness of the Constitution's principles, clearly insinuating that they could readily encompass the Filipinos without inconsistency or corrosion:

> We live, my fellow citizens, under a constitution that was made for 4 millions of people, and yet it has proved quite adequate for 75 millions of people. It has embraced within it every national duty and

purpose and has never stood in the way of our development and expansion. That instrument seems almost to have been inspired to carry forward the holy mission of liberty. It seems not to have been made alone for those who framed it and their successors, but for all ages and for mankind.[44]

Embedded in this comment was the essence of the message lying at the heart of the idea of American mission: that America's values are good for and applicable to all of humanity. Thus McKinley could claim without blushing that "[t]he American people never extend their territory that they do not extend liberty."[45] It was an assertion typical not only of McKinley's foreign policy but of subsequent American leaders seeking to justify the position of global leadership to which they had led the nation throughout the twentieth century and beyond.

Conclusion

THE UNITED STATES did not enter the Spanish-American War in order to acquire European-style colonies. While many government leaders had anticipated and desired the possible imperialistic consequences of the war prior to the onset of hostilities, there was no widespread agreement that the war should yield any results beyond Spain's removal from Cuba. In addition, before the war, neither politicians nor opinion leaders gave any attention at all to the Philippine Islands, which became the focus of the postwar debate about imperialism. Nor was there a consensus that territorial expansion was desirable when the war's outcome made that policy an obvious option for the nation. But for President McKinley and others, imperialism was a policy that could fulfill the vindicationist model of the idea of American mission while also addressing some pressing security and economic concerns. Thus, after the dust had settled from the intense debates about the war resolution and peace treaty, Americans found themselves pursuing policies defined by an aggressive new spirit that blended humanitarian moralism, aggrandizing triumphalism, and crusading ethnocentrism.

The debates reviewed in this book represent a process of national self-definition. Americans, through their struggle to articulate the proper role their country should play in the world—as manifested first through intervention in the Spanish-Cuban War and later through colonialism—found themselves forced to confront the basic assumptions by which they organized themselves as a people and justified their national project. The culture that shaped Americans' thinking about these issues predisposed them to choose some policies over others. Like any cultural constructs, however, the dominant assumptions regarding the mission of the United States were sufficiently open to interpretation and contested within society to the point that both the policy outcomes and accruing identities could have been different. Yet the missionary dimension of American identity was never challenged, even if Americans quibbled over its requirements, and this framework intensively structured the form and substance of the debates. When applied by a culture believing itself ready to assume the mantle of world leadership, the vindicationist interpretation was ultimately more persuasive than exemplarism, and a precedent for global activism was thereby established. Both the United States and the world had changed since George Washington had advised his country to remain aloof from European affairs in 1796. By 1898, Americans thought it necessary that the United States adjust itself to the more immediately menacing international realities created by new naval and military technologies; crusading abroad to civilize (i.e., Americanize) "backward" peoples in the Caribbean and Far East could thus expand U.S. power while advancing the national mission.

The arguments that McKinley and others used to define the nation and its foreign policy conformed to each of the era's norms of progressive civilization. Unlike the antiimperialists, advocates of crusading expansionism rarely referred to race explicitly, but the arguments they made about the Filipinos' lack of fitness to govern themselves obviously implied acceptance of the era's prevailing racial paradigms. The testimonies on which McKinley relied to form his opinion on annexation made implicitly racial arguments, and McKinley saw no reason to question them, even after the antiimperialists had produced evidence that the Filipinos enjoyed a remarkable degree of literacy and had already begun to practice, in highly unfavorable conditions, a limited form of self-government. The Cubans' desire and capacity for self-rule should have been even more apparent to McKinley, but he obviously deemed their desire for national independence premature, at best. Clearly, racism trumped democracy in America's reconstituted identity, as it had throughout its history.

Americans' thinking was also strongly and obviously shaped by their Protestant worldview. McKinley's cautious sympathy for the missionaries' program, for example, was accompanied by a religious sense of duty regarding the disposition of the Filipinos. The sense of duty with which the United States approached the plight of both the Cubans before the war and the Filipinos afterward may have been myopic, paternalistic, and unwelcome, but it was sincere and grounded in Christian conviction. Religion was conceived in the abstract to be a universalizing, ecumenical source by which Americans could recognize the common ground between themselves and others in the world. In practice, though, it was wedded to American nationalism, which meant that the foreign peoples whom Americans conquered needed to be converted if they were to be truly Americanized. It was beyond the American imagination that one could be trenchantly American while simultaneously holding devoutly to Hindu or Muslim or Confucian beliefs. More ambitiously, some Americans felt that through foreign policy their country was taking another long step closer to the kingdom of God, when the saints would rule in postapocalyptic glory. Since Americans had no doubt that they were God's chosen people, the universal rule of the United States over the world's peoples was believed to constitute either a necessary stage preceding the end of history (much as state socialism was to precede Communism's utopia) or possibly even the end of history itself.

Self-evident as well to much of the country was the value of America's political institutions to others. Since the United States was believed quite literally to embody its political values, rejection of American imperialism implied resistance to the political norms and practices that came with it. Only nonenlightened peoples could reject those values, in McKinley's and others' minds, which led them to presume that those who resisted American rule were by definition uncivilized. Unquestionably, American rule in its new colonies was far superior in every respect to Spain's—a fact that seems to have been forgotten both by scholarly critics of American imperialism and by the conquered peoples themselves. But it was not benign, and it was not consistent with American ideals. In order to justify to themselves that democracy and colonialism were compatible, Americans therefore had to twist the meaning of the words they used to define themselves as a people and allow Anglo-Saxonism, for example, to become logically prior to liberty in their globalizing ontology. In this way, the culturally rooted manifestation of America's ideology, catalyzed by the exigencies of foreign policy, became newly fixed for later generations.

Finally, Americans adhered closely to social Darwinism's essential premises, which neatly fit into the realist streak of American identity.

McKinley repeatedly indicated that some other power would annex the Philippines if America refused; and since the United States was becoming involved in an international competition with those other powers, it was important to U.S. interests that it prevent that transfer of power from occurring. This was a very real and legitimate concern, although it would have been less important if the United States had no ambitions beyond its existing borders. Contemporary critics tend to ignore that America's conquered territories almost certainly would not have become independent had the United States set them free; the Europeans were in the midst of their own aggressive colonial campaigns, and it was a distinct possibility that the Philippines in particular would have been ruled by another power that was even less committed than the United States to democratic liberty. American self-interest, normatively constructed according to the logic of social Darwinism, made clear that it was better to plant U.S., rather than European, civilization in the territories. For McKinley and other American imperialists, it was practically unthinkable to reject the opportunity to begin Americanizing the international system during a time when the constitutive norms of Great Power status were prevalent and vindicationist goals suddenly seemed within reach.

According to the American worldview that won the debates of 1898–99, a Filipino society governed by American norms would be superior in every way to any possible alternative. It would be good for the Filipinos, good for Americans, and good for the continued progress of human civilization. For this reason, President McKinley led the country to imperialism. The American people were on the whole willing to accept his decision, and a group of more pragmatically motivated thinkers were happy to help him implement it. In this way, the president, with the help of the Large Policy group and a restless population, fused power and progress in a new way and thereby helped to bring the country one step closer to its ultimate goal: world leadership.

Today, world leadership is not a dream but a reality for the United States, and Americans regard this position as morally legitimate for many of the same reasons that were popular in 1898–99. Certainly, ethnographic constructions of social Darwinism are no longer accepted, and millennial aspirations only resonate with a small segment of the population. But a sense of global entitlement that has only been magnified since the end of the cold war remains deeply rooted in the national consciousness. In addition, the international system has in fact been Americanized to a considerable degree. On the one hand, the global acceptance of democracy and human rights as universal norms of governance (at least in theory), the strengthening of a system of international law clearly premised on assumptions consistent with American values, and the creation of international organizations that try to implement these norms, all represent the triumph of the missionary ambitions that Americans trumpeted as the nineteenth century turned into the twentieth. On the other hand, though, the tremendous growth of U.S. power that occurred in the new century allowed the nation's ethnocentrism to flourish unchecked by the humility and wisdom that accompany failure. Americans are overdue for another period of critical self-evaluation. They need to readjust their inherited identity to new conditions, as they did in 1898. This is not to say that the idea of American mission should be discarded, even if many of its cultural sources are obsolete. But it does need to be redefined to reflect the values of a society that is truly pluralistic in a world that has become irreversibly integrated.

Notes

INTRODUCTION

1. "Text: In Bush's Words: Iraqi Democracy Will Succeed," online, *New York Times*, November 6, 2003, www.nytimes.com/2003/11/06/politics/06TEXT-BUSH.

2. Woodrow Wilson, "The Ideals of America," *Atlantic Monthly*, December 1902, in Tony Smith, *America's Mission: The United States and the Worldwide Struggle for Democracy in the Twentieth Century* (Princeton: Princeton University Press, 1994), 38.

3. Robert L. Beisner, *Twelve against Empire: The Anti-Imperialists, 1898–1900* (New York: McGraw-Hill, 1968), xiv–xv.

4. Akira Iriye, *The Cambridge History of American Foreign Relations*, vol. 3, *The Globalizing of America, 1913–1945* (New York: Cambridge University Press, 1993), 13.

5. For an excellent, extremely thorough overview of the literature, consult Ephraim K. Smith, "William McKinley's Enduring Legacy: The Historiographical Debate on the Taking of the Philippine Islands," in James C. Bradford, ed., *Crucible of Empire: The Spanish-American War and Its Aftermath* (Annapolis: Naval Institute Press, 1993), 205–49. The bibliography following my endnotes also contains a more thorough listing of the relevant literature.

6. See, for example, Philip S. Foner, *The Spanish-Cuban-American War and the Birth of American Imperialism, 1895–1902* (New York: Monthly Review Press, 1972); Louis A. Pérez Jr., "Derailing Cuban Nationalism and Asserting U.S. Hegemony," in Thomas G. Paterson and Dennis Merrill, eds., *Major Problems in American Foreign Relations*, vol. 1, *To 1920*, 4th ed. (Lexington, Mass: D. C. Heath, 1995), 412–17; I. Dmentyev, *USA: Imperialists and Anti-Imperialists (The Great Foreign Policy Debate at the Turn of the Century)* (Moscow: Progress, 1979).

7. Walter LaFeber, *The Cambridge History of American Foreign Relations*, vol. 2, *The American Search for Opportunity, 1865–1913* (New York: Cambridge University Press, 1993), esp. 139–45. See also Daniel B. Schirmer, *Republic or Empire: American Resistance to the Philippine War* (Cambridge, Mass.: Schenkman, 1972), and Walter LaFeber, *The New Empire: An Interpretation of American Expansion, 1860–1898* (Ithaca, N.Y.: Cornell University Press, 1963).

8. William Appleman Williams, "Imperial Anti-colonialism," originally published in *The Tragedy of American Diplomacy* (Cleveland, Ohio: World, 1959); reprinted in *A William Appleman Williams Reader: Selections from His Major Historical Writings*, ed. with introduction by Henry W. Bergson (Chicago: Ivan R. Dee, 1992), 116–32.

9. Richard Hofstadter, "Cuba, the Philippines, and Manifest Destiny," in *The Paranoid Style in American Politics and Other Essays* (Cambridge: Harvard University Press, 1965), 145–87. See also Robert Dallek, *The American Style of Foreign Policy* (New York: Alfred A. Knopf, 1982).

10. Matthew Frye Jacobson, *Barbarian Virtues: The United States Encounters Foreign Peoples at Home and Abroad, 1876–1917* (New York: Hill & Wang, 2000).

11. Louis A. Pèrez Jr., *The War of 1898: The United States and Cuba in History and Historiography* (Chapel Hill: University of North Carolina Press, 1998).

12. See Walter Millis, *The Martial Spirit: A Study of Our War with Spain* (New York: Viking Press, 1931).

13. Walter Zimmerman, *First Great Triumph: How Five Americans Made Their Country a World Power* (New York: Farrar, Straus, Giroux, 2002). A more sophisticated version of this analysis can be found in Edward Rhodes, "Sea Change: Interest-Based vs. Cultural-Cognitive Accounts of Strategic Choice in the 1890s," *Security Studies* 5 (Summer 1996): 73–124.

14. Fareed Zakaria, *From Wealth to Power: The Unusual Origins of America's World Role* (Princeton: Princeton University Press, 1998).

15. Lewis Gould, *The Spanish-American War and President McKinley* (Lawrence: University Press of Kansas, 1982), and idem, *The Presidency of William McKinley* (Lawrence: Regents Press of Kansas, 1980). See also Kevin Phillips, *William McKinley* (New York: Henry Holt, 2003).

16. Zakaria does not seek to explain U.S. foreign policy processes; rather, he presents a theory of international relations that operates on a different, system level of analysis, although it does impressively incorporate domestic-level variables as well.

17. The standard work of the historical-inevitability school is David F. Trask, *The War with Spain in 1898* (New York: Macmillan, 1981).

18. Ivan Musicant, *Empire by Default: The Spanish-American War and the Dawn of the American Century* (New York: Henry Holt, 1998); Ernest May, *Imperial Democracy: The Emergence of America as a Great Power* (New York: Harcourt, Brace & World, 1961); and John L. Offner, *An Unwanted War: The Diplomacy of the United States and Spain over Cuba, 1895–1898* (Chapel Hill: University of North Carolina Press, 1992).

19. For the studies that come closest to this one in this regard, see David Healy, *US Expansionism: The Imperialist Urge in the 1890s* (Madison: University of Wisconsin Press, 1970), and Beisner, *Twelve against Empire*.

20. The terms *exemplarist* and *vindicationist* are borrowed from H. W. Brands, *What America Owes the World: The Struggle for the Soul of Foreign Policy* (New York: Cambridge University Press, 1998).

21. On the idea of American mission, see Brands, ibid.; Edward McNall Burns, *The American Idea of Mission: Concepts of National Purpose and Destiny* (New Brunswick, N.J.: Rutgers University Press, 1957); William W. Cobb Jr. *The American Foundation Myth in Vietnam: Reigning Paradigms and Raining Bombs* (New York: University Press of America, 1998); Brian Klunk, *Consensus and the American Mission* (Lanham, Md.: University Press of America, 1986); Walter A. McDougall, *Promised Land, Crusader State: The American Encounter with the World since 1776* (New York: Houghton Mifflin, 1997); Frederick Merk, *Manifest Destiny and Mission in American History: A Reinterpretation* (New York: Vintage Books, 1966); Tony Smith, *America's Mission: The United States and the Worldwide Struggle for Democracy in the Twentieth Century* (Princeton: Princeton University Press, 1994); Anders Stephanson, *Manifest Destiny: American Exceptionalism and the Empire of Right* (New York: Hill & Wang, 1995); Christopher Thorne, "American Political Culture at the End of the Cold War," *Journal of American Studies* 26 (1993): 303–30; Albert K. Weinberg, *Manifest Destiny: A Study of Nationalist Expansionism in American History* (Baltimore: Johns Hopkins University Press, 1935).

22. The Pamphlets of American History (PAH) series (Ann Arbor, Mich.: University Microfilms Int., 1989) is a microfiche source.

23. As Rhys H. Williams and Susan M. Alexander argue, "Rhetoric used by social and political movements is more than mere bricolage; political language is *constitutive* of a movement's self-understanding as well as reflective." Williams and Alexander, "Religious Rhetoric in American Populism: Civil Religion as Movement Ideology," *Journal for the Scientific Study of Religion* 33 (March 1994): 1–15, 1. For other accounts of the constitutive nature of rhetoric, as applied to the United States, see Roderick P. Hart's analysis of civil religion from the rhetorician's perspective, *The Political Pulpit* (West Lafayette, Iowa: Purdue University Press, 1977), and Dante Germino, *The Inaugural Addresses of the Presidents: The Public Philosophy and Rhetoric*, with a preface and introduction by Kenneth W. Thompson (Lanham, Md.: University Press of America, 1984).

24. Michael H. Hunt, *Ideology and U.S. Foreign Policy* (New Haven: Yale University Press, 1987), 13.

ONE. CULTURE, NATIONAL IDENTITY, AND THE IDEA
OF AMERICAN MISSION

1. See John Gerard Ruggie, "What Makes the World Hang Together? Neo-utilitarianism and the Social Constructivist Challenge," in *Essential Readings in World Politics*, eds. Karen Mingst and Jack Snyder (New York: Norton, 2001), 91–119; Alexander Wendt, "Anarchy Is What States Make of It," *International Organization*, 46 (Spring 1992): 391–425; and Paul Kowert and Jeffrey Legro, "Norms, Identity, and Their Limits: A Theoretical Reprise," in *The Culture of National Security*, Peter Katzenstein, ed. (New York: Columbia University Press, 1996), 451–97.

2. See Martha Finnemore, "Constructing Norms of Humanitarian Interventionism," in Katzenstein, *Culture of National Security*, 153–85.

3. Judith Goldstein and Robert O. Keohane, "Ideas and Foreign Policy: An Analytic Framework," in Judith Goldstein and Robert O. Keohane, eds., *Ideas and Foreign Policy: Beliefs, Institutions, and Political Change* (Ithaca, N.Y.: Cornell University Press, 1993), 3–31, 16.

4. Alastair Iain Johnston, *Cultural Realism: Strategic Culture and Grand Strategy in Chinese History* (Princeton: Princeton University Press, 1995); and Alexander Wendt, *Social Theory of International Politics* (Cambridge: Cambridge University Press, 1999). It bears comment, however, that Wendt's and other leading volumes are concerned primarily with explaining how the norms of the international *system* shape and constrain state behavior, whereas this study focuses on norms that are *internal* to the United States. For a counterargument based on the material interests of domestic coalitions, see Jack Snyder, *Myths of Empire: Domestic Politics and International Ambition* (Ithaca, N.Y.: Cornell University Press, 1991); and Peter Trubowitz *Defending the National Interest: Conflict and Change in American Foreign Policy* (Chicago: University of Chicago Press, 1998).

5. Hans J. Morgenthau, *Politics among Nations: The Struggle for Power and Peace*, brief edition, revised by Kenneth W. Thompson (New York: McGraw-Hill, 1948, 1985), 11; Hans J. Morgenthau, "The Mainsprings of American Foreign Policy," *American Political Science Review* 44 (December 1950): 833–54, 834; and Kenneth Waltz, *Theory of International Politics* (Reading, Mass.: Addison-Wesley, 1979). For an important exception to the strictly structuralist consensus of contemporary realism that retains Morgenthau's acknowledgement of nuance, culture, and human nature in the conduct of international relations, see the work of Kenneth W. Thompson, most notably *Traditions and Values in Politics and Diplomacy: Theory and Practice* (Baton Rouge: Louisiana State University Press, 1992). Henry Nau, *At Home Abroad: Identity and Power in American Foreign Policy* (Ithaca, N.Y.: Cornell University Press, 2002), also offers an important synthesis of constructivist and realist thought.

6. Peter Berger, *The Sacred Canopy: Elements of a Sociological Theory of Religion* (New York: Doubleday, 1967).

7. The inflexibility embedded in ideological as opposed to cultural analysis is the only significant difference in the approach taken by this study and Michael Hunt's useful and informative history of U.S. foreign policy, *Ideology and U.S. Foreign Policy* (New Haven: Yale University Press, 1987).

8. Thus Hans-Georg Gadamer refers to learning new languages and ways of thinking as "fusing horizons," rather than "changing" horizons. Hans Georg-Gadamer, *Truth and Method*, 2nd ed. (New York: Continuum, 1993), 300–307.

9. Louis J. Halle, *Men and Nations* (Princeton: Princeton University Press, 1962), 69.

10. Andrew Greeley, "American Exceptionalism: The Religious Phenomenon," in *Is America Different? A New Look at American Exceptionalism*, ed. Byron E. Shafer (Oxford: Clarendon Press, 1991), 94–115, 100.

11. For the influence of individual perceptions on international relations, see Robert Jervis, *Perception and Misperception in International Politics* (Princeton: Princeton University Press, 1976); on the existence of the society of actors conducting international politics, see Hedley Bull, *The Anarchic Society*, 2nd ed. (New York: Columbia University Press, 1982).

12. Wendt, *Social Theory of International Politics*, 170.

13. Peter Katzenstein, "Coping with Terrorism: Norms and Internal Security in Germany and Japan," in *Ideas and Foreign Policy: Beliefs, Institutions, and Political Change*, ed. Judith Goldstein and Robert O. Keohane (Ithaca, N.Y.: Cornell University Press, 1993), 265–95, 267.

14. See Katherine Verdery, "Whither 'Nation' and 'Nationalism'?" *Daedalus* 122 (Summer 1993), 37–46.

15. Benedict Anderson, *Imagined Communities: Reflections on the Origin and Spread of Nationalism* (Norfolk: Thetford Press, 1986), 15; John Breuilly, *Nationalism and the State*, 2nd ed. (Chicago: University of Chicago Press, 1994); and Anthony Giddens, "The Nation as Power-Container," in *Nationalism*, ed. John Hutchison and Anthony D. Smith (New York: Oxford University Press, 1994), 34–35, 34.

16. Liah Greenfeld, "Transcending the Nation's Worth," *Daedalus*, 122 (Summer 1993): 47–62. Benedict Anderson, *Imagined Communities*, places the birth of nationalism around the nineteenth century, as do, for example, John Breuilly, *Nationalism and the State;* Walker Connor, *Ethnonationalism: The Quest for Understanding* (Princeton: Princeton University Press, 1994); William Pfaff, *The Wrath of Nations: Civilization and the Furies of Nationalism* (New York: Simon & Schuster, 1993); and Barbara Ward, *Nationalism and Ideology* (New York: W. W. Norton, 1966). Studies that place nationalism's origins only slightly earlier (generally during the Age of Reason) include Greenfeld, *Nationalism: Five Roads to Modernity*, and Elie Kedourie, *Nationalism*, 4th ed. (Cambridge, Eng.: Blackwell, 1993). Adrian Hastings, *The Construction of Nationhood: Ethnicity, Religion, and Nationalism* (New York: Cambridge University Press, 1997). For an important qualification of Hastings' position, see Ernest Gellner, "Nations and Nationalism," in *Nationalism*, ed. Hutchison and Smith, 63; and Susanne Hoeber Rudolph and Lloyd I. Rudolph, "Modern Hate," *New Republic*, March 22, 1993: 24–29.

17. All quotes from Tony Smith, *America's Mission: The United States and the Worldwide Struggle for Democracy in the Twentieth Century* (Princeton: Princeton University Press, 1994), xiii, 147, 199, 241, 318. See also G. John Ikenberry, *After Victory: Institutions, Strategic Restraint, and the Rebuilding of Order after Major Wars* (Princeton: Princeton University Press, 2001); Michael Mandelbaum, *The Ideas That Conquered the World: Peace, Democracy, and Free Markets in the Twenty-first Century* (New York: Public Affairs, 2002); and Robert S. McNamara and James G. Blight, *Wilson's Ghost: Reducing the Risk of Conflict, Killing, and Catastrophe in the 21st Century* (New York: Public Affairs, 2001).

18. Morgenthau, "Mainsprings"; Henry Kissinger, *Diplomacy* (New York: Simon & Schuster, 1994); and John J. Mearshimer, "The False Promise of International Institutions," *International Security*, 19 (Winter 1994/95): 5–49.

19. Edward McNall Burns, *The American Idea of Mission: Concepts of National Destiny and Purpose* (New Brunswick, N.J.: Rutgers University Press, 1957), vii.

20. Seymour Martin Lipset, *American Exceptionalism: A Double-Edged Sword* (New York: W. W. Norton, 1996), 31; Connor, *Ethnonationalism;* Daniel Bell, "The 'Hegelian Secret': Civil Society and American Exceptionalism," in *Is America Different?* ed. Byron E. Shafer, 46–70, 50–51; and Michael Kammen, "The Problem of American Exceptionalism: A Reconsideration," *American Quarterly,* 45 (March 1993): 1–43.

21. See J. Victor Koschmann, "Review Essay: The Nationalism of Cultural Uniqueness," *American Historical Review,* 102 (June 1997): 758–68; Ian Tyrrell, "American Exceptionalism in an Age of International History," *American History Review* 96 (October 1991): 1031–55; and Reinhold Niebhur, *The Irony of American History* (New York: Charles Scribner's Sons, 1954).

22. Wilbur Zelinsky, *Nation into State: The Shifting Symbolic Foundations of American Nationalism* (Chapel Hill: University of North Carolina Press, 1988) 16–17; Brian Klunk, *Consensus and the American Mission* (Lanham, Md.: University Press of America, 1986); and Pfaff, *Wrath of Nations.*

23. Thomas Paine, "Common Sense," in *Common Sense and Other Writings,* ed. with introduction by Nelson F. Adkins (New York: Macmillan, 1953), 51; Walter A. McDougall, *Promised Land, Crusader State: America's Encounter with the World since 1776* (New York: Houghton Mifflin, 1997), 16.

24. Weinberg, *Manifest Destiny: A Study of Nationalist Expansionism in American History* (Baltimore: Johns Hopkins University Press, 1935), 17.

25. Theodore Roosevelt, "Inaugural Address," in *The Presidents Speak: The Inaugural Addresses of the American Presidents, from Washington To Clinton,* ed. Davis Newton Lott (New York: Henry Holt, 1994).

26. Winthrop Hudson, *Nationalism and Religion in America: Concepts of American Identity and Mission* (New York: Harper & Row, 1970); Ernest Lee Tuveson, *Redeemer Nation: The Idea of America's Millennial Role* (Chicago: University of Chicago Press, 1968); and Conrad Cherry, *God's New Israel: Religious Interpretations of American Destiny* (Chapel Hill: University of North Carolina Press, 1998).

27. *Providence* is the religious way of expressing *luck* or *fortuna.* While American exceptionalists have tended in the main to support religious interpretations of the quirky good luck that seems always to have arrived during crucial moments in American history, from discovering the Americas to improbably winning the Revolution onward, secular constructions of the notion have also been forwarded. Whether put in religious or secular terms, a recurring theme in discussions of American exceptionalism is that the United States has been on the receiving end of an astonishing number of lucky breaks, with the effect of reinforcing the sense of destiny that defines American nationalism.

28. Kammen, "Problem of American Exceptionalism," 8.

29. William W. Cobb Jr., *The American Foundation Myth in Vietnam: Reigning Paradigms and Raining Bombs* (New York: University Press of America, 1998), 7.

30. Quoted in Tuveson, *Redeemer Nation*, 119.

31. Lawrence J. Friedman, *Inventors of the Promised Land* (New York: Alfred A. Knopf, 1975).

32. Judith N. Shklar, "The Boundaries of Democracy," in *Redeeming American Political Thought*, edited by Stanley Hoffman and Dennis F. Thompson, with a foreword by Dennis F. Thompson (Chicago: University of Chicago Press, 1998), 127–45, 129–30; and Robert N. Bellah, "Civil Religion in America," in Russell E. Richey and Donald G. Jones, *American Civil Religion* (New York: Harper & Row, 1974), 21–44, 29.

33. Alexis de Tocqueville, *Democracy in America*, ed. J. P. Mayer (New York: Harper & Row, 1969), 35–39.

34. In a suspect but revealing passage, Jay continued: "With equal pleasure I have as often taken notice that Providence has been pleased to give this one connected country to one united people—a people descended from the same ancestors, speaking the same language, professing the same religion, attached to the same principles of government, very similar in their manners and customs, and who, by their joint counsels, arms, and efforts, fighting side by side throughout a long and bloody war, have nobly established their general liberty and independence." This illusion of ethnic unity underscores the deep-seatedness of American racism, which informs a parallel tradition of American nationalism that is also significant for U.S. foreign policy. John Jay, "Federalist No. 2," in Alexander Hamilton, James Madison, and John Jay, *The Federalist Papers*, ed. with introduction by Clinton Rossiter (New York: Mentor Books, 1961), 38.

35. See C. Vann Woodward, "The Age of Reinterpretation," in Thomas G. Paterson and Dennis Merrill, eds., *Major Problems in American Foreign Relations*, vol., 1, *To 1920*, 4th ed. (Toronto: D. C. Heath, 1995), 2–7.

36. Seymour Martin Lipset notes that studies indicate that geographic mobility, the sense that one can improve one's lot by moving to a better place, has worked against the formation of class consciousness in the United States. Lipset, *American Exceptionalism*, 85.

37. William Graham Sumner, "Sociology," in *Social Darwinism: Selected Essays of William Graham Sumner*, ed. with introduction by Stow Persons (Englewood Cliffs, N.J.: Prentice-Hall, 1963), 9–29. See also Burns, *American Idea of Mission*, 65–71, and Walter LaFeber, *The New Empire: An Interpretation of American Expansion, 1860–1898* (Ithaca, N.Y.: Cornell University Press, 1963).

38. John Adams, for instance, viewed the settlement of America "with reverence and wonder, as the opening of a grand scheme and design in Providence for the illumination of the ignorant, and the emancipation of the slavish part of mankind all over the earth." John Adams, *Works of John Adams*, ed. C. F. Adams (Boston, Mass., 1850–56), 1:66; quoted in Ekirch, *Ideas, Ideals, and American Diplomacy*, 23.

39. Cherry, *God's New Israel*, 61.

40. It should be remembered that Winthrop's sermon was not designed to make his fellow travelers feel especially virtuous or superior to those they had left behind.

Rather, the sermon laid out the covenant that his group was consecrating with God, and it emphasized the duties that ensued from the covenant far more than the rewards. The sentence following the often-quoted one above, for example, reads: "So that if we shall deal falsely with our God in this work we have undertaken, and so cause Him to withdraw His present help from us, we shall be made a story and a byword through the world: we shall open the mouths of enemies to speak evil of the ways of God and all professors of God's sake; we shall shame the faces of many of God's worthy servants, and cause their prayers to be turned into curses upon us, till we shall be consumed out of the good land whither we are going." John Winthrop, "A Model of Christian Charity," in *The American Puritans: Their Prose and Poetry*, ed. Perry Miller (New York: Columbia University Press, 1956), 83.

41. Tuveson, *Redeemer Nation*, 17–19.

42. Francis J. Bremer, *The Puritan Experiment: New England Society from Bradford to Edwards* (Hanover, N.H.: University Press of New England, 1995).

43. Greenfeld, *Nationalism*, 29–87.

44. Hudson, *Nationalism and Religion in America*, xx–xxxii.

45. Edmund S. Morgan *The Puritan Dilemma: The Story of John Winthrop* (Boston, Mass.: Little, Brown, 1958), 185–205.

46. Tuveson, *Redeemer Nation*, 97–99.

47. In Hudson, *Nationalism and Religion in America*, 16–17.

48. Abiel Abbot, "Traits of Resemblance in the People of the United States of America to Ancient Israel: In a Sermon Delivered at Haverhill, on the Twenty-Eighth of November, 1799, the Day of Anniversary Thanksgiving," in *The American Republic and Ancient Israel*, ed. Joseph Cellini [1799] (New York: Arno Press, 1977), 6.

49. See Hudson, *Nationalism and Religion in America*, 1–5.

50. Sidney Mead, "The Nation with the Soul of a Church," in Richey and Jones, *American Civil Religion*, 45–75, 52.

51. See Richard Carwardine, "The Know-Nothing Party, the Protestant Evangelical Community, and American National Identity," in *Religion and National Identity*, ed. Stewart Mews (Oxford: Basil Blackwell, 1982), 449–63.

52. Cherry, *God's New Israel*, 11.

53. David Ramsey, "An Oration on the Advantages of American Independence" (Charleston, S.C., 1778), in Hudson, *Nationalism and Religion in America*, 63; Cherry, *God's New Israel*, 11–12; Bellah, "Civil Religion in America," 30–32; and Tuveson, *Redeemer Nation*, 195–96. Catherine Albanese suggests that the Constitution "has functioned in American history as *itself* a religious object and center for a system of politics and government. We might see it as a powerful symbolic expression of the public religion that articulates the transcendent meaning we place on the nation." Catherine Albanese, "Response to Miller," in *Religion and the Public Good: A Bicentennial Forum*, ed. William Lee Miller et al. (Macon, Ga.: Mercer University Press, 1988), 23–31, 26–27.

54. Bellah, "Civil Religion in America," 24.

55. Dante Germino, *The Inaugural Addresses of American Presidents: The Public Philosophy and Rhetoric*, with a preface and introduction by Kenneth W. Thompson (New York: University Press of America, 1984).

56. Jayadeva Uyangoda, "Understanding Ethnicity and Nationalism," *Ecumenical Review* 47 (April 1995): 190–94.

57. Cherry, *God's New Israel*, 14.

58. W. Lloyd Warner, "An American Sacred Ceremony," in Richey and Jones, *American Civil Religion*, 89–111; Martin E. Marty, "Two Kinds of Two Kinds of Civil Religion," in Richey and Jones, ibid., 139–57, 146–47. All quotes of inaugural addresses are from *The Presidents Speak*.

59. Isaac Kramnick, introduction to *The Portable Enlightenment Reader*, ed. with introduction by Isaac Kramnick (New York: Penguin Books, 1995), ix–xxiii.

60. Baron d'Holbach, "No Need of Theology, Only of Reason," in *The Portable Enlightenment Reader*, 140–50, 143–44.

61. John Locke, *Two Treatises of Government*, ed. with introduction and notes by Peter Laslett (New York: Cambridge University Press, 1992), 265–428.

62. Marquis de Condorcet, "The Future Progress of the Human Mind," in *The Portable Enlightenment Reader*, 26–38, 28, 32, 37.

63. Anne-Robert-Jacques Turgot, "On Progress," in *The Portable Enlightenment Reader*, 361–65, 362.

64. But see Louis Hartz, *The Liberal Tradition in America* [1955], with a new introduction by Tom Wicker (New York: Harcourt, Brace 1991), 36.

65. Wilson Carey McWilliams, *The Idea of Fraternity in America* (Berkeley: University of California Press, 1973), 173.

66. See Hartz, *Liberal Tradition in America*, esp. 3–32.

67. McWilliams, *Idea of Fraternity in America*, 182.

68. Rogers M. Smith, *Civic Ideals: Conflicting Visions of Citizenship in U.S. History* (New Haven: Yale University Press, 1997), 1–39.

69. See Hans Kohn, *American Nationalism: An Interpretive Essay* (New York: Macmillan, 1957), 1–37.

70. Alexander Hamilton, "Federalist Paper No. 1," in *The Federalist Papers*, 33.

71. James H. Moorhead, "The American Israel: Protestant Tribalism and Universal Mission," in *Many Are Chosen: Divine Elections and Western Nationalism*, ed. William R. Hutchison and Hartmut Lehman (Minneapolis, Minn.: Fortress Press, 1994), 145–66, 146.

72. Adrienne Koch, *Power, Morals, and the Founding Fathers: Essays in the Interpretation of the American Enlightenment* (Ithaca, N.Y.: Cornell University Press, 1961), 5.

73. Schlesinger, "America: Experiment or Destiny," 512; Madison, "Federalist No. 51," in *The Federalist Papers*, 322.

74. See John G. West Jr., *The Politics of Revelation and Reason: Religion and Civic Life in the New Nation* (Lawrence: University Press of Kansas, 1996), esp. 1–78, 207–14.

75. Thompson, *Traditions and Values*, 19; Alexander Hamilton, "The Stand," in *Hamilton's Works*, 650–55, 651–52; and Hunt, *Ideology and U.S. Foreign Policy*, 97–100.

76. Madison, "Federalist 10," in *The Federalist Papers*, 77–84. For the best explanation of Madison's "balancing" solution, see Samul H. Beer, *To Make a Nation: The Rediscovery of American Federalism* (Cambridge: Harvard University Press, 1993), 244–307.

77. Matthew Frye Jacobson, *Barbarian Virtues: The United States Encounters Foreign Peoples at Home and Abroad, 1876–1917* (New York: Hill & Wang, 2000).

78. See G. John Ikenberry, "America's Liberal Grand Strategy: Democracy and National Security in the Post-War Era," in *American Democracy Promotion: Impulses, Strategies, Impacts* (New York: Oxford University Press, 2000).

79. Alden March, *The History and Conquest of the Philippines and Our Other Island Possessions* [1899] (New York: Arno, 1970), 147.

80. See Akira Iriye, "Exceptionalism Revisited," *Reviews in American History* 16 (June 1988): 291–97. Iriye rejects the notion that U.S. foreign policy has been exceptional, arguing that "in pursuing an exceptionalist policy, the United States may have become less exceptional," 297. His comment refers to the need of any active foreign policy, whatever its goals, to take proper account of the international environment, including geostrategic variables.

81. See Samuel P. Huntington, "American Ideals versus American Institutions," *Political Science Quarterly* 97 (Spring 1982).

TWO. AMERICAN CULTURAL CONTRUCTS IN THE 1890S

1. These ideas were most popular in England, home of Charles Darwin and Herbert Spencer. They filtered across the Atlantic to graft onto an existing American ideology of progress recently colored by the collectivist ideas of the romantic period. For the best discussion of social Darwinism in American thought, see Richard Hofstadter, *Social Darwinism in American Thought, 1860–1915* (Philadelphia: University of Pennsylvania Press, 1944).

2. Julius W. Pratt, *Expansionists of 1898: The Acquisition of Hawaii and the Spanish Islands* (Baltimore: Johns Hopkins University Press, 1936), 3.

3. Louis Menand, *The Metaphysical Club* (New York: Farrar, Straus, Giroux, 2001); Mike Hawkins, *Social Darwinism in European and American Thought, 1860–1945: Nature as Model and Nature as Threat* (New York: Cambridge University Press, 1997); and Hofstadter, *Social Darwinism.*

4. Charles Darwin, *The Descent of Man in Relation to Sex* [1871], with introduction by John Tyler Bonner and Robert M. May (Princeton: Princeton University Press 1981), 179–81.

5. Lewis G. James, *Our Nation's Peril: Social Ideals and Social Progress* (Boston, Mass., 1899), 11.

6. Jean Baptiste Lamarck's evolutionary theory, displaced by Darwin's, posited the inheritability of acquired characteristics. Darwinian evolution also admits, if uncomfortably,

that acquired characteristics can be inherited. The difference is that Lamarckians would argue that "inferior" members of a species can acquire "superior" characteristics that would allow them to catch up with their more advanced counterparts, while Darwinism would hold that they die off. As Hawkins writes, "[W]here Darwin saw animals and plants competing for survival, Lamarck saw a more harmonious process of mutual adaptation. Lamarckism, then, cannot be reduced to a belief in the inheritance of acquired characteristics as a mechanism of evolution. Rather, it must be seen as a world view in its own right in which change takes place from below as inferior organisms strive to adapt, improve and progress." Hawkins, *Social Darwinism in European and American Thought, 1860–1945*, 42–44.

7. George Cotkin, *Reluctant Modernism: American Thought and Culture, 1880–1900* (New York: Twayne, 1992); David Healy, *US Expansionism: The Imperialist Urge in the 1890s* (Madison: University of Wisconsin Press, 1970); Menand, *Metaphysical Club*.

8. Benjamin Kidd, *Social Evolution* (New York: Macmillan, 1894), 34–35.

9. As one writer of the period put it, "Jingoism . . . may perhaps be said to have partly had its source in a philosophy of materialism; Darwin's doctrine of Survival of the Fittest being misconstrued, as if the strongest were the fittest, which though true in the case of brutes, is untrue in the case of the moral and intellectual being, Man." Goldwin Smith, *Commonwealth or Empire: A Bystander's View of the Question* (New York: Macmillan, 1902), 37.

10. Richard Hofstadter, *Social Darwinism*, 37–52; and Stow Persons, introduction to Sumner, *Social Darwinism: Selected Essays of William Graham Sumner*, ed. Stow Persons (Englewood Cliffs, N.J.: Prentice-Hall, 1963), 1–8.

11. William Graham Sumner, "Sociology," in Sumner, *Social Darwinism*, 18.

12. Sumner, "The Forgotten Man," in Sumner, *Social Darwinism*, 113.

13. Sumner, "Socialism," in Sumner, *Social Darwinism*, 85.

14. William Graham Sumner, *What Social Classes Owe to Each Other* (Caldwell, Idaho: Caxton Printers, 1961), 88.

15. Sumner, "Socialism," in Sumner, *Social Darwinism*, 17.

16. See Sumner, *Social Classes*, 132–45. Distinguishing private, voluntary welfare from state-coerced public support for the poor, Sumner wrote, "I have relegated all charitable work to the domain of private relations, where personal acquaintance and personal estimates may furnish the proper limitations and guarantees. A man who had no sympathies and no sentiments would be a very poor creature; but the public charities, more especially the legislative charities, nourish no man's sympathies and sentiments. . . . What I choose to do by way of exercising my own sympathies under my own reason and conscience is one thing; what another man forces me to do of a sympathetic character, because his reason and conscience approve of it, is quite another thing." *Social Classes*, 135–36.

17. Brooks Adams, *The Law of Civilization and Decay* (New York: Macmillan, 1896).

18. Roosevelt wrote of Adams's work: "This is not a pleasant theory. It is in many respects an entirely false theory; but nevertheless there is in it a very ugly element of

truth." Quoted in H. W. Brands, *The Reckless Decade: America in the 1890s* (New York: St. Martin's Press, 1995), 38.

19. Adams, *Law of Civilization and Decay*, ix–x.

20. Ibid., x, xi.

21. Ibid., 383.

22. Brooks Adams, *The New Empire* (New York: Macmillan, 1902), xi, xv.

23. Charles Hirschfeld, "Brooks Adams and American Nationalism," *American Historical Review* 69 (January 1964): 371–92, 372.

24. James A. Field Jr., "American Imperialism: The Worst Chapter in Almost Any Book," *American Historical Review* 83 (June 1978): 644–68, 647.

25. Ibid., 651.

26. Walter LaFeber, "Comments [on Field, "American Imperialism: The Worst Chapter in Almost Any Book"]," *American Historical Review* 83 (June 1978): 669–72, 669.

27. Robert L. Beisner, "Comments [on Field, "American Imperialism: The Worst Chapter in Almost Any Book"]," *American Historical Review* 83 (June 1978): 672–78, 674.

28. As Benjamin Kidd explained in the preface to his influential *Social Evolution*, "One of the most remarkable epochs in the history of human thought is that through which we have passed in the last half of the nineteenth century. The revolution which began with the application of the doctrines of evolutionary science, and which received its first great impetus with the publication of Darwin's *Origin of Species*, has gradually extended in scope until it has affected the entire intellectual life of our Western civilization. One after the other we have seen the lower sciences revivified, reconstructed, transformed by the new knowledge. The sciences dealing with man in society have naturally been the last to be affected, but now that the movement has reached them the changes therein promise to be even more startling in character. History, economics, the science of politics, and, last but not least important, the attitude of science to the religious life and religious phenomena of mankind, promise to be profoundly influenced. The whole plan of life is, in short, being slowly revealed to us in a new light, and we are beginning to perceive that it presents a single majestic unity, throughout every part of which the conditions of law and orderly progress reign supreme. . . . That the moral law is the unchanging law of progress in human society is the lesson to be written over all things." Kidd, *Social Evolution*, vii–ix.

29. Michael H. Hunt, *Ideology and U.S. Foreign Policy* (New Haven: Yale University Press, 1987).

30. Cotkin, *Reluctant Modernism*, 57; and Hunt, *Ideology and U.S. Foreign Policy*, 78–79.

31. Cotkin, *Reluctant Modernism*, 51–73, and Hoftsadter, *Social Darwinism in American Thought*.

32. Matthew Frye Jacobson, *Barbarian Virtues: The United States Encounters Foreign Peoples at Home and Abroad, 1876–1917* (New York: Hill & Wang, 2000), 139–72; and Rogers Smith, *Civic Ideals: Conflicting Visions of Citizenship in U.S. History* (New Haven: Yale University Press, 1997), 508n5.

33. Smith, *Civic Ideals*, 348, 350.

34. California held a referendum on allowing continued Chinese immigration in 1879, with 883 in favor and 154,638 against; in 1880, Nevada voted 183 in favor and 17,259 against. Racial justifications for immigration laws were openly provided by legislators, citizens, and presidents. Jacobson, *Barbarian Virtues*, 179–219; and Smith, *Civic Ideals*, 357–71.

35. Opposed to philanthropic efforts by higher races to uplift lower races and peoples, Le Bon believed that "it was the lower race that succumbed and was annihilated in the case of prolonged contact between the two. To Le Bon, nature was aristocratic, and mercilessly punished impure blood." Hawkins, *Social Darwinism*, 186–89.

36. Smith, *Civic Ideals*, 364–65. Lodge's comments are from the *Congressional Record*, hereafter, *CR*, 54th Cong., 1st Sess., 2817–20.

37. Lodge was not an innovator of racial restrictions on immigration or of the idea that the United States was, fundamentally, an Anglo-Saxon nation. These concepts and practices began at the founding, as the racialist theories of Thomas Jefferson show, for example, and crested at various points throughout U.S. history, notably during the nativist movement of the 1840s. Lodge exemplifies, however, the 1890s version of American racism, which synthesized basic racism with "scientific" principles. See Martin E. Marty, *The One and the Many: America's Struggle for the Common Good* (Cambridge: Harvard University Press, 1997), 47–61, and Smith, *Civic Ideals*.

38. Cotkin, *Reluctant Modernism*, 67.

39. *CR*, 55th Cong., 3d Sess., 342.

40. C. Vann Woodward notes that between 1895 and 1910, the following states amended their constitutions using these and other strategies in an effort to prevent blacks from voting: South Carolina, Louisiana, North Carolina, Alabama, Virginia, Georgia, Oklahoma, Florida, Tennessee, Arkansas, Texas, Kentucky, and Mississippi. C. Vann Woodward, *The Strange Career of Jim Crow*, 2nd ed. (New York: Oxford University Press, 1957), 67–68.

41. Smith, *Civic Ideals*, 383.

42. 163 U.S. 537 (1896).

43. Woodward, *Jim Crow*, 19–22.

44. Quoted in Brands, *Reckless Decade*, 226; the background of the case is given on 219–32.

45. Daniel B. Schirmer, *Republic or Empire: American Resistance to the Philippine War* (Cambridge, Mass: Schenkman, 1972), 101.

46. Smith, *Commonwealth or Empire*, 43–44.

47. Edward A. Johnson, *History of Negro Soldiers in the Spanish-American War* (Raleigh, N.C.: Capitol Printing, 1899; reprint., New York: Johnson Reprint, 1970), 141.

48. Maxwell Bloomfield, "Dixon's 'The Leopard's Spots': A Study in Popular Racism," *American Quarterly*, 16 (Autumn 1964): 387–401, 389. (Dixon retired from preaching in 1902 and wrote *The Leopard's Spots*, a novel that became the basis of D. W. Griffith's infamous movie *Birth of a Nation*.)

49. Thomas Dixon Jr., "A Friendly Warning to the Negro," *Freelance* 1, no. 5, 112–20.

50. John W. Burgess, *Political Science and Comparative Constitutional Law*, vol. 1, 45–46; quoted in Pratt, *Expansionists of 1898*, 9.

51. *CR*, 55th Cong., 3rd Sess., 342.

52. Healy, *US Expansionism*, 134.

53. Washington Gladden, *Our Nation and Her Neighbors* (Columbus, Ohio: Quinius & Ridenour, 1898), 25. The cited passages are direct quotes from Kidd's *The Control of the Tropics*.

54. Gladden, *Our Nation*, 25.

55. James Marcus King, *The Situation and Justification of the Nation at War with Spain*, pamphlet (New York: Society of the Union Methodist Episcopal Church, 1898), 9.

56. The United States was exceptional in its explicit acknowledgment of this principle, even if it failed in practice to honor it in some ways. *Watson v. Jones*, 13 Wall (80 U.S.) 679, 728 (1871).

57. Winthrop Hudson, *Religion in America*, 4th ed. (New York: Macmillan, 1987), 108.

58. A study of religion in the United States published by H. K. Carroll in 1893 stated that, of a total population of 62,622,250 Americans, 49,630,000 (or 80 percent) were Protestants. Carroll's study, based in part on data from the 1890s census, said 7,362,000 Americans were Roman Catholics and approximately 5,000,000 were skeptics or disbelievers. H. K. Carroll, *The Religious Forces of the United States Enumerated, Classified, and Described on the Basis of the Government Census of 1890* (New York, 1893), xxxv–xxxvi; quoted in R. Laurence Moore, *Religious Outsiders and the Making of Americans* (New York: Oxford University Press, 1986), 12. The percentages in 1990, by contrast, were: Protestant, 60 percent, Catholic, 26.2 percent, "Other," 3.3 percent, and "None," 8.2 percent (2.3 percent refused to answer). Barry A. Kosmin and Seymour P. Lachman, *One Nation under God: Religion in Contemporary American Society* (New York: Harmony, 1993), 2–3. Carroll's statistics, however, do not correspond remotely with formal church membership rolls. According to Franklin H. Littell, the "best available" statistics on church membership show that only 35.7 percent of Americans in 1900 belonged to a church, which is still a notable increase over previous eras: 5 percent in 1776, 6.9 percent in 1800, and 15.5 percent in 1850. Franklin H. Littell, *From State Church to Pluralism: A Protestant Interpretation of Religion in American History* (Chicago: Aldine, 1962), 32. Church membership, however, has meant different things in different times, and rarely corresponds to actual levels of *belief*.

59. Joseph Story, *Commentaries on the Constitution*, vol. 3 (Boston, Mass.: Hilliard, Gray, 1833), 722; quoted in Richard E. Morgan, *The Supreme Court and Religion* (New York: Free Press, 1972), 38.

60. 133 U.S. 333, 33 L.Ed. 637, 640 (1889).

61. 98 U.S. 145, 25 L.Ed. 244 (1878), 250.

62. Leonard Levy, *The Establishment Clause: Religion and the First Amendment*, 2nd ed. (New York: Macmillan, 1994), 76.

63. The due-process clause of the Fourteenth Amendment, added to the Constitution in 1868, would ultimately empower the Court to selectively apply the protections of the Bill of Rights to the states. As it turned out, the free-exercise clause was not applied to state behavior until the Court so ruled in *Cantwell v. Connecticut*, 310 U.S. 296 (1940), and the establishment clause was not applied until *Everson v. Board of Education of Ewing Township, New Jersey*, 330 U.S. 1 (1947). Until the 1940s, in other words, the states were free to regulate religious conduct in any manner they chose that was consistent with their own constitutions and traditions, without legal regard for the First Ammendment.

64. Lawrence M. Friedman, *Total Justice* (Boston, Mass.: Beacon Press, 1985), 114.

65. Leonard Levy offers a striking example of judicial enforcement of the reading of the King James Version: "In 1845 . . . a Maine court upheld the expulsion of a Catholic child for refusing to read that Bible, even though the court acknowledged every religion as having equal rights." Levy, *The Establishment Clause*, 241. John J. Dinan notes, however, that some states, through the legislative process, would amend their Bible-reading laws to accommodate the religious liberty of Catholics. Dinan, *Keeping the People's Liberties: Legislators, Citizens, and Judges as Guardians of Rights* (Lawrence, Kans.: University Press of Kansas, 1998), 10–11, 41–42.

66. Actually, *local* governments carried much of the burden of administering governmental functions, not the states (and certainly not the national government). Martha Derthick, "The States in American Federalism: The Paradox of the Middle Tier," 1994. The point remains, in any event, that the U.S. Constitution's prohibition of any "law respecting an establishment of religion" was of far less importance in determining religion's role in American society and culture than were state and local norms and laws.

67. Thomas J. Curry, *The First Freedoms: Church and State in America to the Passage of the First Amendment* (New York: Oxford University Press, 1986), 219.

68. Robert Ingersoll was a notorious atheist in the latter decades of the nineteenth century. Martin E. Marty, *The Infidel: Freethought and American Religion* (New York: Meridian Books, 1961).

69. R. Pierce Beaver, *Church, State, and the American Indians* (St. Louis: Concordia, 1966), 178. As Indian commissioner Isaac Parker said, the goal of the policy was to elevate the Native Americans "toward that healthy Christian civilization in which are embraced the elements of material wealth and intellectual and moral development." Francis Paul Prucha, *American Indian Policy in Crisis: Christian Reformers and the Indians, 1865–1900* (Norman, Okla., 1976), 52; quoted in Robert M. Utley, *The Indian Frontier of the American West 1846–1890* (Albuquerque: University of New Mexico Press, 1984), 133.

70. John G. West Jr., *The Politics of Revelation and Reason: Religion and Civic Life in the New Nation* (Lawrence: University Press of Kansas, 1996), chapter 4.

71. Direct appropriations for sectarian education and civilization of the Native Americans by the national government ceased in 1896 after Roman Catholics started to

achieve success in converting Native Americans and their missionary competitors protested. *Quick Bear v. Luepp*, 210 U.S. 50 (1908).

72. Marty, *Modern American Religion*, vol. 1, *The Irony of It All, 1893–1919* (Chicago: University of Chicago Press, 1986), chapters 8 and 9.

73. Ibid., 148–49. The very presence in the nation of large numbers of religious minorities, however, contributed a great deal to the overall framework of American religious culture by forcing it to continue to value diversity as a central American characteristic.

74. Hudson, *Religion in America*, 13.

75. Michael Lienesch, "The Origins of the Christian Right: Early Fundamentalism as a Political Movement," in Corwin E. Smidt and James M. Penning, *Sojourners in the Wilderness: The Christian Right in Comparative Perspective* (Lanham, Md.: Rowman & Littlefield, 1997), 11; and Ernest Lee Tuveson, *Redeemer Nation: The Idea of America's Millennial Role* (Chicago: University of Chicago Press, 1968).

76. Lester D. Stephens, "Joseph Le Conte's Evolutional Idealism: A Lamarckian View of Cultural History," *Journal of the History of Ideas*, 39 (July–September 1978): 465–80; Cotkin, *Reluctant Modernism*, 22.

77. For a good explanation of these themes and their importance to Puritan thought, see Edmund S. Morgan, *Visible Saints: The History of a Puritan Idea* (Ithaca, N.Y.: Cornell University Press, 1963); and Francis J. Bremer, *The Puritan Experiment: New England Society from Bradford to Edwards*, rev. ed. (Hanover, N.H.: University Press of New England, 1995).

78. Marty, *Modern American Religion*, 1:33, and Cotkin, *Reluctant Modernism*, 14–16.

79. Richard Wightman Fox, "The Culture of Liberal Protestant Progressivism, 1875–1925," *Journal of Interdisciplinary History*, 23 (Winter 1993): 639–60.

80. Gerald Birney Smith, ed., *A Guide to the Study of the Christian Religion* (Chicago: University of Chicago Press, 1916), 570; quoted in Marty, *Modern American Religion*, 1:26.

81. Paul Carus, "Science a Religious Revelation," in Barrows, *World's Parliament of Religions*, 2:980–81; quoted in Marty, *Modern American Religion*, 1:20.

82. Fox, "Liberal Protestant Progressivism," 645. This is not to say that modernism's *theological* liberalism produced a concomitant commitment to *political* liberalism. To the contrary, the moralism resulting from the belief that worldly actions have divine implications resulted in profoundly conservative political beliefs and was manifested, for example, in the temperance movement.

83. Modernist theologians insisted that no specific style of scriptural interpretation was mandated by the Bible. Fundamentalists, they argued, had no basis for claiming that their way of reading the Bible was in any way superior or more accurate than any other way. Indeed, modernism's historicist hermeneutic rejected any interpretation of the Bible that might lead to conclusions that were not verified in the world.

84. Edward J. Larson, *Summer of the Gods: The Scopes Trial and America's Continuing Debate over Science and Religion* (New York: BasicBooks, 1997), esp. 3–85.

85. On the overall effort to accommodate evolution and revelation, see Menand, *Metaphysical Club*, 117–48.

86. William McGuire King, "An Enthusiasm for Humanity: The Social Emphasis in Religion and Its Accommodation in Protestant Theology," in Michael J. Lacey, *Religion in Twentieth Century American Intellectual Life* (New York: Cambridge University Press, 1991), 49–77.

87. Henry B. Metcalf, "A Nation's Crime against Her Own Soldiers: An Address before the National Temperance Society and Publication House" (Ocean Grove, N.J., 1899).

88. Ekirch, *Progressivism in America*, 52–55.

89. Cotkin, *Reluctant Modernism*, 14.

90. Tuveson, *Redeemer Nation*, ix–x; H. Richard Niebuhr, *The Kingdom of God in America* (New York: Willett, Clark, 1937), ix, 9, 25–27.

91. The Puritans adhered to a *providential* reading of history, but they were neither historicists, in the sense of thinking that meaning can be found within history, nor progressives, in the sense of believing that history is progressing.

92. See Hudson, *Nationalism and Religion in America*, xxi–xxix.

93. Robert N. Bellah, "The Kingdom of God in America: Language of Faith, Language of Nation, Language of Empire," in William Lee Miller et al., *Religion and the Public Good: A Bicentennial Forum* (Macon, Ga.: Mercer University Press, 1988), 51.

94. Garry Wills, *Under God: Religion and American Politics* (New York: Touchstone, 1990), 160; Michael Lienesch, *Redeeming America: Piety and Politics in the New Christian Right* (Chapel Hill: University of North Carolina Press, 1993), 224–46; Bellah, "The Kingdom of God in America," 51–52.

95. Wills, *Under God*, 167.

96. Lienesch, *Redeeming America*, 226–27.

97. Ibid., 226.

98. As H. Richard Niebuhr wrote, "The romantic [liberal] conception of the kingdom of God involved no discontinuities, no crises, no tragedies or sacrifices, no loss of all things, no cross and resurrection. . . . It was all fulfillment of promise without judgment." Niebuhr, *The Kingdom of God in America*, 191–93.

99. Frank H. Littell, "The Radical Reformation and the American Experience," in Thomas M. McFadden, ed., *America in Theological Perspective* (New York: Seabury Press, 1976), 84.

100. See Sidney Mead, "The Nation with the Soul of a Church," in Russell E. Richey and Donald G. Jones, *American Civil Religion* (New York: Harper & Row, 1974), 58–59.

101. John F. Wilson, "A Historian's Approach to Civil Religion," in Richey and Jones, *American Civil Religion*, 119; Niebuhr, *The Kingdom of God in America*, 178–79.

102. Hudson, *Nationalism and Religion in America*, 94.

103. See Walter Russell Mead, *Special Providence: American Foreign Policy and How It Changed the World* (New York: Alfred A. Knopf, 2001), chapter 5.

104. Beaver, *Church, State, and the American Indians*, 61.

105. William Radcliffe, "Presbyterian Imperialism," *Assembly Herald* (1899), 6; quoted in Moorhead, "The American Israel," in Hutchison and Lehmann, eds., *Many Are Chosen*, 156.

106. David Starr Jordan, "The Question of the Philippines" (Palo Alto, California: Graduate Club of Leland Stanford Junior University, 1899), 19. Jordan's argument is quite similar to James Madison's in his "Memorial and Remonstrance," which, along with Jefferson's "Virginia Statute for Religious Liberty," is one of the foundations of religious freedom in the United States.

107. Thus, disagreeing with Jordan, many held that missionary work was good for the country. As one writer of the times put it, "To save America, America must save the world." W. H. Price, "Expansion: Another View, or How It Saves America" (Chicago, 1899), 14.

108. Daniel J. Elazar, *Covenant and Constitutionalism: The Great Frontier and the Matrix of American Democracy* (New Brunswick, N.J.: Transaction, 1998); Conrad Cherry, *God's New Israel: Religious Interpretations of American Destiny*, revised and updated edition (Chapel Hill: University of North Carolina Press, 1998).

109. William M. Salter, *Imperialism* (Chicago, 1899), 15.

110. "Speech at Canton, Illinois, 6 October 1899," *Papers of William McKinley*, microfilm (hereafter, McK. microfilm).

111. *CR*, 55th Cong., 2d Sess., 3748 (April 12, 1898).

112. Jordan, "The Question of the Philippines," 16.

113. L. B. Hartman, *The Republic of America: Its Civil Polity as Outlined by the Prophets, Its Politico-Religious Mission in the World's Civilization, and Its Need of the Soldier* (New York, 1899), 9–10, 53.

114. Ibid., 31–33.

115. Ibid., 71.

116. Ibid., 34–36, 38, 93–94.

117. Rev. David Gregg, "Sermon Delivered at Lafayette Avenue Presbyterian Church on Sunday April 24, 1898: The National Crisis; or God's Purposes Worked Out Through International Relations" (Brooklyn, 1898), 5, 7.

118. Ibid., 2.

119. William Lee Miller, *The First Liberty: Religion and the American Republic* (New York: Paragon House, 1985), 142.

120. *CR*, 55th Cong., 3rd Sess., 432.

121. William Jennings Bryan, "Imperialism: Nomination Speech for the Democratic Candidacy for President of the United States, 8 August 1900," in William Jennings Bryan, *Imperialism: Extracts from Speeches, Interviews, and Articles* (1900?), 74.

122. For the best analysis of the inherent tension between liberalism's pretensions to universality and its logical inability actively to engage non-Western cultures on their own terms, see Uday Singh Mehta, *Liberalism and Empire: A Study in Nineteenth-Century British Liberal Thought* (Chicago: University of Chicago Press, 1999).

123. Francis A. Brooks, "An Examination of the Scheme for Engrafting the Colonial System of Government upon the United States Constitution" (Boston, Mass.: George H. Ellis, Printer, 1900), 24.

124. David J. Brewer, *The Spanish War: A Prophecy or an Exception?* Pamphlet of address before the Liberal Club, Buffalo, New York, February 16, 1899, 9, 12.

125. Carl Schurz, *American Imperialism*, pamphlet of convocation address at the University of Chicago, January 4, 1899, 4, 25; Jordan, "Lest We Forget," 36.

126. James Vernon Martin, *Expansion: Our Flag Unstained*, pamphlet (St. Louis, 1900), 9.

127. James W. Stillman, "A Protest against the President's War of 'Criminal Aggression,'" (Boston, Mass.: George H. Ellis, 1899), 11.

128. See, for example, Theodore W. Noyes, *Oriental America and Its Problems* (Washington, D.C., 1903).

129. George E. Adams, *McKinley and Bryan; Principles and Men*, pamphlet (Quincy, Ill., October 3, 1900), 16.

130. No less a defender of freedom than John Stuart Mill advanced this position when he qualified his defense of near-absolute individual liberty by declaring: "It is, perhaps, hardly necessary to say that this doctrine is meant to apply only to human beings in the maturity of their faculties. We are not speaking of children. . . . For the same reason we may leave out of consideration those backward states of society in which the race itself may be considered as in its nonage. . . . Despotism is a legitimate mode of government in dealing with barbarians." John Stuart Mill, *On Liberty*, ed. with introduction by Gertrude Himmelfarb (New York: Penguin Books, 1974), 69. Also, see Mehta, *Liberalism and Empire*, 1–115.

131. Nathan Matthews Jr., *Oration before the City Authorities of Boston on the Fourth of July, 1899* (Boston, Mass., 1899), 11.

132. Ibid., 11–12.

133. Ibid., 13.

134. Elihu Root, *Speech at Canton Ohio, October 24, 1900*, pamphlet (Canton, Ohio, 1900), 15.

135. Root, *Speech at Canton, Ohio*, 15.

136. Gladden, *Our Nation*, 32.

THREE. ENTERING THE WAR: THE GENERAL BACKGROUND

1. Richard Hofstadter, "Cuba, the Philippines, and Manifest Destiny," in *The Paranoid Style in American Politics and Other Essays* (Cambridge: Harvard University Press, 1996), 145–87.

2. H. Wayne Morgan, *America's Road to Empire: The War with Spain and Overseas Expansion* (New York: John Wiley & Sons, 1965), 5.

3. Philip S. Foner, *The Spanish-Cuban-American War and the Birth of American Imperialism, 1895–1902*, 2 vols. (New York: Monthly Review Press, 1972), 1:4–5.

4. All neutral countries patrolled their own waters to stop filibustering expeditions, and Britain captured two such vessels. But the United States, due to its proximity to Cuba and the fact that the Junta, a coordinating committee of pro-Cuban groups, was headquartered in New York, had by far the largest task in enforcing its neutrality laws.

5. That the United States considered its role in staunching the flow of contraband to be a hassle was made clear by President McKinley when he complained in his war address of April 11, 1898, that "the present revolution ... has subjected the United States to great effort and expense in enforcing its neutrality laws, caused enormous losses to American trade and commerce, [and] caused irritation, annoyance, and disturbance among our citizens." "Message of the President of the United States Communicated to the Two Houses of Congress on the Relations of the United States to Spain by Reason of Warfare on the Island of Cuba, 11 April 1898," McK. microfilm.

6. Trask reports that the United States intercepted thirty-three ships. David F. Trask, *The War with Spain in 1898* (New York: Macmillan, 1981), 5.

7. See Ivan Musicant, *Empire by Default: The Spanish-American War and the Dawn of the American Century* (New York: Henry Holt, 1998), 81–89.

8. See Ernest R. May, *Imperial Democracy: The Birth of America as a Great Power* (New York: Harcourt, Brace & World, 1961), 69–72, 87–88.

9. See John Dobson, *Reticent Expansionism: The Foreign Policy of William McKinley* (Pittsburgh, Pa.: Duquesne University Press, 1988), 42–43.

10. Stephen Grover Cleveland, "Annual Message of the President of the United States," December 7, 1896, in *Papers Relating to the Foreign Relations of the United States, 1896* (Washington, D.C.: Government Printing Office, 1897), xxix–xxxvi; quoted in Richard H. Miller, ed., *American Imperialism in 1898: The Quest for National Fulfillment* (New York: John Wiley & Sons, 1970), 53–59.

11. *CR*, 55th Cong., 1st Sess., 1036.

12. Bishop Las Casas, *An Historical and True Account of the Cruel Massacre and Slaughter of Twenty Millions of People in the West Indies by the Spaniards* [1620] (reprint, New York: JBoller, 1898).

13. Martí regarded the Junta as the true government of Cuba.

14. Jose Martí was killed shortly after the revolution began. Insisting on leading the rebellion in person, he left the safe confines of New York City and landed in Cuba, where he was ambushed and killed. Almost immediately he became a martyr to the Cuban cause. Martí has since come to be regarded as "the most beloved and important person in Cuban history." Walter LaFeber, *The Cambridge History of American Foreign Relations*, vol. 2, *The American Search for Opportunity, 1865–1913* (New York: Cambridge University Press, 1993), 129–30.

15. See John Tebbel, *America's Great Patriotic War with Spain: Mixed Motives, Lies, and Racism in Cuba and the Philippines, 1895–1915* (Manchester Center, Vt.: Marshall Jones, 1996), 1–43; Marcus M. Wilkerson, *Public Opinion and the Spanish-American War: A Study in War Propaganda* (Baton Rouge: Louisiana State University Press, 1932), passim.

16. Wilkerson, *Public Opinion*, 8; Tebbel, *America's Great Patriotic War*, 1–8.

17. *New York World*, May 17, 1896, 1; quoted in Wilkerson, *Public Opinion*, 32.

18. May, *Imperial Democracy*, 69.

19. George Gluyas Mercer, *Patriotism, Prestige, and the Flag* (1899), 3.

20. Edward A. Johnson, *History of the Negro Soldiers in the Spanish-American War* (Raleigh, N.C.: Capitol Printing, 1899; reprint, New York: Johnson Reprint, 1970), 6; Morgan, *America's Road to Empire*, 8–9.

21. Trask, *War with Spain*, 15.

22. For an excellent summary of Spanish politics and the domestic background leading up to the war in all of the countries, see John L. Offner, *An Unwanted War: The Diplomacy of the United States and Spain over Cuba, 1895–1898* (Chapel Hill: University of North Carolina Press, 1992), 1–36 and passim.

23. Though exaggerating the death toll, the following excerpt is representative of the situation as seen by Americans at the time: "In Cuba . . . by General Weyler's order, 500,000 miserable old men, women, children and babies had their homes burned to the ground, cattle, flour, everything eatable stolen, and they themselves were driven at the point of the bayonet into trochas or fortified fences put around the towns or villages, with sentinels posted with orders to shoot on the spot everyone who dared to try to creep through the fence to get a root to gnaw at, and so save himself from dying. These wretched people had no muskets, and were too weak to use them if they had. So, in cold blood, General Weyler and his men saw them die of starvation before their eyes. I doubt if all history can tell us of another horror as vast, which was as cold blooded as this." S. R. Calthrop, *The Wars of 1898*, pamphlet (1898), 6–7.

24. Joseph Smith, *The Spanish-American War: Conflict in the Caribbean and the Pacific, 1895–1902* (New York: Longman, 1994), 19.

25. Washington Gladden, *Our Nation and Her Neighbors* (Columbus, Ohio: Quinius & Ridenour, 1898), 6.

26. W. Edwin Priest, *Spain and Her Lost Colonies*, pamphlet (slide show presentation) (1898), 4.

27. B. Essex Winthrop, *Spain and the Spaniards* (New York: Street & Smith, 1899), 244–45.

28. Jenny Ward Hays, *The Echo of the Maine* (San Francisco, Calif., 1898).

29. Charles Henry Butler, *The Voice of the Nation, the President Is Right: A Series of Papers on Our Past and Present Relations with Spain* (New York: George Munro's Sons, 1898), 54.

30. Charles Francis Adams, *"Imperialism" and "The Tracks of Our Forefathers: A Paper Read before the Lexington, Massachusetts, Historical Society, December 20, 1898"* (Boston, Mass.: Dana Estes, 1899), 6–7.

31. May, *Imperial Democracy*, 73. May writes, "In all of these cities, the Cuban cause was taken up in the name of Republicanism, patriotism and Protestantism." *Imperial Democracy*, 74.

32. In another sermon, he called Roman Catholicism "Phariseeism" and held it responsible for the Dark Ages. Dixon, "The Bulwarks of the Nation," *Freelance*, October 1898, 82–83; and "Ingersoll's Mistakes," *Freelance*, November 1898, 143.

33. J. G. McCullough, *The Spanish War: An Address before the Reunion Society of Vermont Officers at Montpelier, October 26, 1898*, pamphlet (1898), 5–6.

34. Frank T. Reuter, *Catholic Influence on American Colonial Policies, 1898–1904* (Austin: University of Texas Press, 1967), 3.

35. W. S. Rainsford, *Our Duty to Civilization; or, Who Is My Neighbor* (New York, 1898), 6, 13, 16–17. Rainsford added, "We are pushed to do the work of God by elemental forces, which no politician, however shrewd, could not create, control or gainsay," 18.

36. *CR*, 54th Cong., 2d Sess., 162–68.

37. Herbert Welsh, *The Ethics of the War Viewed from the Christian Standpoint*, pamphlet of address before the Ethical Society in Philadelphia, June 19, 1898, 5, 7.

38. Ernest H. Crosby, *War from the Christian Point of View* (Boston, Mass., 1900), 6–7, 9.

39. Bacon, T. S. *A New Religion?* (Buskeystown, Md.: Self-published, 1898), 44.

40. See John Tebbel, *America's Great Patriotic War*, 60; Offner, *An Unwanted War*, 116–22; and David Traxel, *1898: The Tumultuous Year of Victory, Invention, Internal Strife, and Industrial Expansion that Saw the Birth of the American Century* (New York: Alfred A. Knopf, 1998), 98–99.

41. Morgan, *America's Road to Empire*, 43.

42. G. J. A. O'Toole, *The Spanish War: An American Epic–1898* (New York: W. W. Norton, 1984), 111–23.

43. For a description of the investigation of the court of inquiry, see Offner, *An Unwanted War*, 124–30; 135–38.

44. Charles S. Olcott, *The Life of William McKinley* (New York: Houghton Mifflin, 1916), 2:12–13.

45. Offner, *An Unwanted War*, 122. Offner argues that McKinley initially believed the explosion to be an accident.

46. Henry Watterson, *History of the Spanish-American War, Embracing a Complete Review of our Relations with Spain* (Philadelphia: Monarch, 1898), 24–25.

47. Traxel, *1898: The Birth of the American Century*, 111.

48. May, *Imperial Democracy*, 142.

49. Charles G. Dawes, *A Journal of the McKinley Years* (Chicago: Lakeside, 1950), 145.

50. The resolution began, "Whereas it is the established doctrine of the United States that the Western Hemisphere shall be dedicated to republican forms of government recognizing the political equality of human beings; . . . Whereas the island of Cuba, by reason of its location and close proximity to the United States, should, by right, be dedicated to a republican form of government; . . . Whereas the dictates of humanity require the intervention of the United States in such a case [of oppression] . . ." *CR*, 55th Cong., 2d Sess., 2069–74.

51. Foner, *Spanish-Cuban-American War*, 1:307–10.

52. May, *Imperial Democracy*, 144.

53. Offner, *An Unwanted War*, 130, 131.

54. Watterson, *War with Spain*, 45–46. See also Morgan, *America's Road to Empire*, 51. Julius Pratt cited reactions from the business community to Proctor's speech, including from the *Wall Street Journal* and the *American Banker*, that clearly demonstrate that when the business community did in fact begin to favor intervention, it did so not for reasons of economic gain but for the same humanitarian reasons that motivated everyone else. Julius Pratt, *Expansionists of 1898: The Acquisition of Hawaii and the Spanish Islands* (Baltimore: Johns Hopkins University Press, 1936), 246–47.

55. All passages are from "Proctor Report, 17 March 1898," *CR*, 55th Cong., 2d Sess., 2916–19.

56. Ibid., 3128–32.

57. Ibid., 3162–65.

58. Ibid., 3039.

59. David J. Brewer, *The Spanish War; A Prophecy or Exception? Address before the Liberal Club, Buffalo, New York, Feb. 16, 1899*, pamphlet (Anti-Imperialist League, 1899), 4.

60. Morgan, *America's Road to Empire*, 53.

61. James D. Richardson, *A Compilation of the Messages and Papers of the Presidents, 1789–1902*, vol. 10, revised and enlarged by George Raymond Devitt (Washington, D.C.: Bureau of Literature and Art, 1903), 55.

62. Watterson, *History of the Spanish-American War*, 42.

FOUR. MCKINLEY AND CONGRESS FRAME U.S. INTERVENTION IN THE WAR

1. To take one example of interpartisan hostility, Rep. Joseph W. Bailey (D-Tex.) stood up to declare, for no apparent reason, "If there is an idiot here, it is not on this side of the chamber, but on that." *CR*, 55th Cong., 2d Sess., 3442. The *Congressional Record* is littered throughout the debate with examples like this and with notations by the congressional reporter such as, "[Derisive laughter and jeers on the Republican side]" or "[Applause and laughter on the Democratic side]."

2. *CR*, 55th Cong., 2d Sess., 1578–85; 1581, 1585.

3. Ibid., 3193.

4. Ibid., 3211–12.

5. Ibid., 3255.

6. Ibid., 3412.

7. Ibid., 3968.

8. Ibid., 3283.

9. Ibid., 3672–73.

10. Ibid., 3985.

11. Ibid., 3463–64.

12. Ibid., 3465–66.

13. Kevin Phillips, *William McKinley* (New York: Henry Holt, 2003).

14. See John L. Offner, *An Unwanted War: The Diplomacy of the United States and Spain over Cuba, 1895–1898* (Chapel Hill: University of North Carolina Press, 1992). Offner characterizes McKinley as a strong leader in foreign affairs.

15. Walter LaFeber, *The Cambridge History of American Foreign Relations*, vol. 2, *The American Search for Opportunity, 1865–1913* (New York: Cambridge University Press, 1993), 126–27.

16. Quoted in H. W. Brands, *The Reckless Decade: America in the 1890s* (New York: St. Martin's Press, 1995), 260–61.

17. See Paul W. Glad, *McKinley, Bryan, and the People* (New York: J. B. Lippincott, 1964), 76–79, 113–42.

18. The Populist Party had already nominated Bryan as their standard bearer, and a fourth, unofficial party was also born from the mix–the Fusion Party, which fused populists and Democrats uncertain of their partisan identity.

19. See Margaret Leech, *In the Days of McKinley* (New York: Harper & Brothers, 1959), 85–87.

20. McK. microfilm.

21. "Speech to Delegation of Cleveland Workmen, October 31, 1896," McK. microfilm.

22. The American Protective Association, a nativist organization, hassled McKinley over his friendship with Ireland.

23. See A. James Reichley, *Religion in American Public Life* (Washington, D.C.: Brookings Institution, 1985), 209–13; Sidney M. Milkis and Michael Nelson *The American Presidency: Origins and Development, 1776–1990* (Washington, D.C.: CQ Press, 1990), 182–84; and Glad, *McKinley, Bryan, and the People*, passim.

24. See H. Wayne Morgan, *William McKinley and His America* (Syracuse: Syracuse University Press, 1963); and Leech, *In the Days of McKinley.*

25. Morgan, *William McKinley and His America*, 39.

26. The consensus that McKinley sought, however, was limited to whites. Although not a racist himself, at least not by the standards of the time, McKinley has come under warranted attack by scholars today, as he did by blacks at the time, as a result of his placing the goal of sectional unification above racial justice.

27. Charles S. Olcott, *The Life of William McKinley* (New York: Houghton Mifflin, 1916), 2:296.

28. Quoted in Ivan Musicant, *Empire by Default: The Spanish-American War and the Dawn of the American Century* (New York: Henry Holt, 1998), 614.

29. Charles G. Dawes, *A Journal of the McKinley Years* (Chicago: Lakeside, 1950), 144.

30. Morgan, *McKinley and His America*, 57, 104.

31. Offner, *An Unwanted War*, 38.

32. William McKinley, "First Inaugural Address," March 4, 1897; in Davis Newton Lott, *The Presidents Speak: The Inaugural Addresses of the American Presidents, from Washington to Clinton* (New York: Henry Holt, 1994).

33. Murat Halstead, a friend and supporter, extolled his virtue in this way: "In his family and social life, and in his personal habits, he commends himself to the friends of order, temperance, and good morals. In private life he is exemplary, in public life a patriotic Republican. . . . (H)e does not like stories that rest for their point upon some vulgarity. He never tells one himself, and has always avoided having to listen to them. McKinley is never profane." Halstead, *Life and Distinguished Services of the Honorable William McKinley*, 29, 100.

34. On itinerant preachers, see Nathan O. Hatch, *The Democratization of American Christianity* (New Haven: Yale University Press, 1989).

35. See Leech, *In the Days of McKinley*, 5–12, and H. Wayne Morgan, who wrote, "His own efforts to discover God's design produced a devout piety in William McKinley. His sincere lifelong adherence to Methodism in part reflected his deep attachment to his mother, for whom the church was a center of existence." Morgan, *William McKinley and His America*, 12.

36. "Speech of 22 February 1898, University of Pennsylvania," McK. microfilm.

37. Herman Hagedorn, *Leonard Wood*, 2 vols. (New York: Harper & Brothers, 1931), 1:141; quoted in Lewis Gould, *The Presidency of William McKinley* (Lawrence: Regents Press of Kansas, 1980), 78.

38. Morgan, *William McKinley and His America*, 31.

39. On McKinley's reluctance due to the military unpreparedness of the United States, see Trask, *War with Spain*, 474–76; and Olcott, *Life of William McKinley* 2:3.

40. See Leech, *In the Days of McKinley*, 133–40.

41. Alger wrote his own history of the war, which amounted to little more than a book-length apologia for himself. In his preface he wrote, for example: "Should war ever again come upon this country and find it so totally unprepared as it was in 1898, I hope that those who have been so profuse in their criticisms, and eager to discover faults, may have the patriotism and pride of country to rise above personalities, and, instead of striving to tear down, may endeavor to strengthen the hands of those upon whom the burden may fall and whose only hope of reward is that satisfaction which comes from the consciousness of having labored honestly and unremittingly to serve a government whose flag has never yet known defeat." Russell A. Alger, *The Spanish-American War* (New York: Harper & Brothers, 1901), vi–vii. Alger might have received greater sympathy from his countrymen had he not had so arrogant and disagreeable a personality, which was marked in particular by a stubborn refusal to recognize or acknowledge his own faults.

42. Trask, *War with Spain*, 58.

43. On the reluctance of the business community, see Julius W. Pratt, *Expansionists of 1898: The Acquisition of Hawaii and The Spanish Islands* (Baltimore: Johns Hopkins University Press, 1936), 230–79.

44. Morgan, *William McKinley and His America*, 372.

45. "Message to the Senate and House of Representatives Recommending Appropriation for the Relief of Destitute American Citizens in the Island of Cuba," May 17, 1897, McK. microfilm. McKinley quietly and anonymously gave $5,000 of his own money to the cause.

46. Cleveland had also resisted the congressional drive toward war.

47. Offner, *An Unwanted War*, 48.

48. "Message to Congress at Beginning of 55th Congress, 2d Session, 6 December 1897," McK. microfilm.

49. Trask, *War with Spain*, 21.

50. *CR*, 55th Cong., 2d Sess., 40.

51. This figure is from Smith, *Spanish-American War*, 23.

52. A good account of the syndicate's plan is in David Healy, *US Expansionism: The Imperialist Urge in the 1890s* (Madison: University of Wisconsin Press, 1970), 81–82. Healy notes that reasonable evidence ties the syndicate to the passage of the Teller Amendment, which profited the group handsomely. See also J. G. A. O'Toole, *The Spanish War: An American Epic* (New York: W. W. Norton, 1984), 84.

53. Interview in the *Pittsburgh Dispatch*, March 20, 1898, McK. microfilm.

54. *CR*, 55th Cong., 2d Sess., 1575.

55. "Mock Platform for the Republican Party in 1900," *CR*, 55th Cong., 2d Sess., 3748–51; excerpt from 3748–49.

56. *CR*, 55th Cong., 2d Sess., 3980.

57. Ibid., 3515.

58. Ibid., 3951–53.

59. Senator Donelson Caffery (D-La.) applied a racial interpretation to the belligerents' behavior: "They [the Cubans] are the same sort of people [as the Spaniards]. There is no difference between them in respect to cruelty and talent for destruction. They are mostly all of Spanish blood. They inherit all the virtues and vices of their parentage. They have shown as much cruelty in warfare, as much wanton waste and destruction of property, as the Spaniards themselves." *CR*, 55th Cong., 2d Sess., 3954.

60. Morgan, *William McKinley and His America*, 367.

61. David Traxel, *1898: The Birth of the American Century* (New York: Alfred A. Knopf, 1998) 121.

62. Trask, *War with Spain*, 53. See also Hofstadter, "Cuba, the Philippines, and Manifest Destiny," 156.

63. Offner, *An Unwanted War*, 181.

64. The McKinley papers include several drafts of the speech, all heavily edited in the president's hand, in which he inserted quotes from past presidents' addresses (or noted that such a reference would be useful), rearranged different sections of the speech to shift its emphasis to longer-term values, and generally gave excruciating attention to even its most minor details. The only other item to which he gave remotely similar attention was his instructions to the peace commission.

65. "Message of the President of the United States Communicated to the Two Houses of Congress on the Relations of the United States to Spain by Reason of Warfare on the Island of Cuba, 11 April 1898," McK. microfilm.

66. "Message of 11 April 1898," McK. microfilm.

67. Ibid.

68. Henry Cabot Lodge, *The War with Spain* (New York: Arno Press, 1970; reprint of Harper & Brothers, 1899), 35–36.

69. Henry Watterson, *History of the Spanish-American War* (Philadelphia: Monarch, 1898), 57.

70. *CR*, 55th Cong., 2d Sess., 3703.

71. Ibid.

72. As historian Paul S. Holbo demonstrates, McKinley used the message and the subsequent congressional debate that it launched to reassert his executive power. After letting himself get backed into the position of having to issue the message in the first place, McKinley had decided to seize control of the issue of Cuban intervention and, through it, U.S. foreign policy. Holbo's research shows that McKinley enlisted the support of his henchmen in Congress, including Senators Stephen Elkins (R-W.Va.), Henry Cabot Lodge (R-Mass.), and Charles Fairbanks (R-Iowa), to defend his position vigorously during the prolonged debate over the wording of the joint resolution declaring America's course of action in the Cuban affair. In the House, Speaker Thomas B. Reed (R-Maine) supported McKinley by taking the debate off the floor and enlisting *his* henchmen to persuade others to support nonrecognition. See Paul S. Holbo, "Presidential Leadership in Foreign Affairs: William McKinley and the Turpie-Foraker Amendment," *American Historical Review* 72 (July 1967): 1321–35.

73. "S.R. 149," *CR*, 55th Cong., 2d Sess., 3773.

74. "Report of the Committee on Foreign Relations Regarding S.R. 149," *CR*, 55th Cong., 2d Sess., 3773–74.

75. Ibid., 3774.

76. When seeking to find authorities that would acknowledge the merit of this claim, the report's authors admitted that "[t]he conflict of opinion and definition among the jurists upon the subject is very great." However, the committee cited several international lawyers whose arguments supported the American case, such as Vattel, who wrote, "As to those monsters who, under the title of sovereigns, render themselves the scourges and horror of the human race, they are savage beasts, whom every brave man may justly exterminate from the face of the earth." The authors concluded, "If these opinions state the correct rule, as we believe they do, the right of intervention by the United States in the present instance is indubitable." Ibid., 3775.

77. Ibid.

78. The Roosevelt Corollary, announced as a foreign policy principle of the United States, stated: "Chronic wrongdoing, or an impotence which results in a general loosening of the ties of civilized society, may in America, as elsewhere, ultimately require

intervention by some civilized nation, and in the Western Hemisphere the adherence of the United States to the Monroe Doctrine may force the United States, however reluctantly, in flagrant cases of wrongdoing or impotence, to the exercise of an international police power." In Thomas G. Patterson and Dennis Merrill, eds., *Major Problems in American Foreign Relations*, vol. 1, *To 1920* (Lexington, Mass: D. C. Heath, 1995), 507.

79. *CR*, 55th Cong., 2d Session. 3789–90.

80. Ibid., 3972.

81. Ibid., 3776.

82. Ibid., 3778.

83. For example, a Democrat, Senator Donelson Caffery of Louisiana, while disavowing any intention to use the war as a means of acquiring Cuba, offered this opinion: "I have no doubt in my mind that in the future the Island of Cuba will be ours. I do not say that we ought, in a spirit of aggression or greed for additional territory, to take any steps to bring about that result; but I do say that the finger of destiny itself points to it. . . . With its nearness to this great Republic, right under the shadow of our institutions and influence, with the commercial intercourse between us and Cuba so large and constantly increasing, it is the part of wisdom to forecast the time when the lone star of the Cuban banner will glitter in the constellation on the blue field of our own star-spangled banner." Ibid., 3958.

84. Ibid., 3983.

85. Ibid., 3781.

86. Walter Zimmerman, *First Great Triumph: How Five Americans Made Their Country a World Power* (New York: Farrar, Straus, Giroux, 2002), chapter 5.

87. *CR*, 55th Cong., 2d Sess., 3782–83.

88. "Report of the Minority of the House Committee on Foreign Relations," *CR*, 55th Cong., 2d Sess., 3816.

89. *CR*, 55th Cong., 2d Sess., 3817–19.

90. Ibid., 3945.

91. Ibid., 3960.

92. Senator Wilson expressed a similar sentiment using more visceral and insulting language: "Mr. President, Spain reached the height of her glory during a past age. Unwise and wasteful in her day of power and prosperity, when her splendor dazzled the world, she stands today, without art, without literature, without science, and without hope, a bankrupt and ruined nation. There can be no glory in war over such a carcass." Ibid., 3972.

93. Ibid., 3830–35.

94. Ibid., 3840.

95. Ibid., 3842.

96. Ibid., 3844–46.

97. Ibid., 3877–78.

98. Ibid., 3893.

99. Senator Samuel Pasco (D-Fla.), for instance, announced: "The people of Florida will accept the verdict which we will here render after a deliberate consideration of the situation as it has been presented, and will meet whatever result may follow calmly and courageously, and in full confidence that the God of Battles will give to us the ultimate victory." Ibid., 3970.

100. Ibid., 3959.

101. Ibid., 3943–44.

102. Ibid., 3879–80.

103. Ibid., 3891.

104. *Pamphlet of the Speech of Hon. John C. Spooner of Wisconsin in the Senate of the United States, Friday, April 15, 1898* (Washington, 1898), 1–47.

105. Ibid., 3898–99.

106. Ibid., 3954.

107. The debates were in *CR*, 55th Cong., 2d Sess., 3988–4064. The Senate vote is on p. 3993; the House vote is on pp. 4063–64. The dialogue that surrounded these votes contained little that substantively contributed to the resolution or to a clear understanding of its purpose, but it is interesting for revealing the dynamics of an angry legislative debate about an important issue. Speaker Reed, for instance, was ruthless (and successful) in silencing opposition to any Republican initiative, and senators started to call each other out by name, in violation of parliamentary procedure.

FIVE. "AMERICAN GREATNESS" IN POPULAR CULTURE AND POLITICAL ANALYSIS

1. David Traxel, *1898: The Birth of the American Century* (New York: Alfred A. Knopf, 1998), 137.

2. See Frank Freidel, *The Splendid Little War* (Boston, Mass.: Little, Brown, 1958), 3, 306.

3. William M. Salter, *A New Nation, and a New Duty* (Philadelphia, 1898), 185.

4. Of the 6,406 soldiers who died between May 1, 1898, and April 30, 1899, 5,438 died from disease, while only 968 were killed in combat or later died from war wounds. George M. Sternberg, *Sanitary Lessons of the War*, pamphlet reprinted from *Philadelphia Medical Journal*, June 10–17, 1899, 1. These numbers include those soldiers who died from combat or disease in the Philippines, which by then had become a separate war. Sternberg, the surgeon-general of the United States, was horrified by the diseases' impact.

5. "Sermon Preached in Madison Square Presbyterian Church by Dr. Charles H. Parkhurst, 27 February 1898," McK. microfilm.

6. Ivan Musicant, *Empire by Default: The Spanish-American War and the Dawn of the American Century* (New York: Henry Holt, 1998), 235.

7. The War Department received an allocation $19 million from this sum. Of this sum, $10 million was spent by the Ordnance Department on coastal defenses; the Engineer

Department spent $5.5 million, also for coastal defenses; the Medical, Quartermaster, and Signal Departments were given the remaining funds. David F. Trask, *The War with Spain in 1898* (New York: Macmillan, 1981), 149.

8. Walter Millis, *The Martial Spirit: A Study of Our War with Spain* (New York: Viking Press, 1931), 117–18.

9. Walter LaFeber, *The Cambridge History of American Foreign relations*, vol. 2, *The American Search for Opportunity, 1865–1913* (New York: Cambridge University Press), 113–18. For an interesting interpretation of the naval buildup of the 1890s, see Edward Rhodes, "Sea Change: Interest-Based vs. Cultural-Cognitive Accounts of Strategic Choice in the 1890s," *Security Studies*, 5 (Summer 1996): 73–124.

10. McKinley issued a call for 125,000 volunteers on April 22, 1898, the day after hostilities had begun (the April 25 declaration of war announced that hostilities had begun on April 21), and over the course of the war he requested a total of about 200,000 volunteers. By May, more than 750,000 men had responded to McKinley's initial call. Trask, *War with Spain*, 152–58; Henry Watterson, *History of the Spanish-American War, Embracing a Complete Review of Our Relations with Spain* (New York: Monarch, 1898), 77.

11. H. W. Brands, *The Reckless Decade: America in the 1890s* (New York: St. Martin's Press, 1995), 321; Musicant, *Empire by Default*, 640–47; Freidel, *Splendid Little War*, 295–300; Trask, *1898: The Birth of the American Century*, 159; Joseph Smith, *The Spanish-American War: Conflict in the Caribbean and the Pacific, 1895–1902* (New York: Longman, 1994), 159. Sternberg's tally, shown in n. 4 above, differs from Smith's and Musicant's (2,500 dead from disease, 243 from combat) because he included casualties from the Philippine-American War through April 30, 1899, whereas the two historians tallied only the deaths that took place during the official duration of the Spanish-American War, which ended August 12. For contemporary reactions to the conditions, see, for example, Arthur C. Andersen and Charles H. Briner, *"K" Company, 71st Regiment, New York Volunteers: A Record of Its Experience and Services and a Memorial to Its Dead*, pamphlet (New York, 1900); Massachusetts Reform Club, *Report of the Committee of the Massachusetts Reform Club Appointed to Collect Testimony in Relation to the Spanish-American War, 1898–1899*, pamphlet (Boston, Mass., 1899); W. B., *The Diary of a Rough Rider*, pamphlet (1898?).

12. The president pushed for the passage of a bill permanently enlarging the army to one hundred thousand men. Partisanship intruded, however, and McKinley was forced to settle for a temporary expansion of two years and sixty-five thousand men. As the Philippine War drew on until 1902, however, the enlargement gradually became permanent. Margaret Leech, *In the Days of McKinley* (New York: Harper & Brothers, 1959), 359–60.

13. David Axeen, "'Heroes of the Engine Room': American 'Civilization' and the War with Spain," *American Quarterly* 36 (Autumn 1984): 481–502. See also Trask, *War with Spain*, 485, and Olivier Zunz, *Why the American Century?* (Chicago: University of Chicago Press, 1998).

14. William Graham Sumner, *The Conquest of the United States by Spain: A Lecture before the Phi Beta Kappa Society of Yale University, January 16, 1899*, pamphlet (Boston, Mass., 1899), 3.

15. David Starr Jordan, *The Question of the Philippines*, pamphlet (Palo Alto, Calif., 1899); Hermann E. Von Holst, *The Annexation of Our Spanish Conquests*, pamphlet (Chicago, 1898); Clay McAuley, *A Straightforward Tale*, Anti-Imperialist League pamphlet (1899), reprinted from Boston, Mass., *Evening Transcript*, July 5, 1899.

16. Louis A. Pèrez Jr., *The War of 1898: The United States and Cuba in History and Historiography* (Chapel Hill: University of North Carolina Press, 1998), 1–22, 81–107; and Smith, *Spanish-American War*, 13–14, 21–22.

17. Watterson, *History of the Spanish-American War*, 119.

18. James Rankin Young, *History of Our War with Spain* (Philadelphia: Premier, 1898), 223.

19. "Speech to Congress of 9 May 1898," McK. microfilm.

20. Rev. James Marcus King, *The Situation and Justification of the Nation at War with Spain*, pamphlet (New York: Empire State Society, May 15, 1898), 14, 15.

21. Henry Van Dyke, *The Cross of War: A Sermon Preached on May 1st, 1898*, pamphlet, 5.

22. "Speech in Richmond, Virginia, 31 October 1898," McK. microfilm.

23. *CR*, 55th Cong., 2d Sess., 3193.

24. Ibid., 3954.

25. Ibid., 3763–64.

26. In Trask, *War with Spain*, 181.

27. See John Oldfield, "Remembering the *Maine*: the United States, 1898 and Sectional Reconciliation," in Angel Smith and Emma Dávila-Cox, eds., *The Crisis of 1898: Colonial Redistribution and Nationalist Mobilization* (New York: St. Martin's Press, 1999), 45–64.

28. William Andrews Pew, *The War with Spain and Its Aftermath* (Salem, Mass., 1927), 5.

29. Watterson, *History of the Spanish-American War*, 80.

30. Lodge drew an additional lesson from this reunification: "For thirty years the people of the United States had been absorbed in the development of their great heritage. They had been finishing the conquest of their continent, and binding all parts of it together with the tracks and highways of commerce. Once this work was complete, it was certain that the virile, ambitious, enterprising race which had done it would look abroad beyond their boundaries and seek to guard and extend their interests in other parts of the world." Lodge, *War with Spain*, 233–34.

31. "Speech at the Coliseum, St. Louis, Missouri, 14 October 1898," McK. microfilm.

32. "Speech at Denison, Iowa, 11 October 1898," McK. microfilm.

33. Frequently, McKinley would conjoin the themes of sectional reunification and expansion. In one speech in Savannah, Georgia, for example, he intoned, "My fellow

citizens, whatever covenants duty has made for us in the year 1898 we must keep. With a united country and the gathered wisdom of all the people, seeking only the right, inspired only by high purposes, moved only by duty and humanity, we cannot err. . . . If, following the clear precepts of duty, territory falls to us and the welfare of an alien people require our guidance and protection, who will shrink from the responsibility, grave though it may be? The chief consideration is one of duty; our actions must be controlled by it." "Speech at Savannah, Georgia, 17 December 1898," McK. microfilm.

34. Louis Menand, *The Metaphysical Club* (New York: Farrar, Straus, Giroux, 2001), esp. 3–69 and 235–442; see also Pèrez, *War of 1898*, 108–33.

35. Jeanne Abrams, "Remembering the Maine: The Jewish Attitude toward the Spanish-American War as Reflected in [the journal] *The American Israelite*," *American Jewish History* 76 (June 1987): 439–55. The quote is from *American Israelite* 44 (April 28, 1898): 4; quoted in Abrams, "Remembering the Maine," 443. There is certain irony in this claim, since the American self-characterization as being the "chosen people" was borrowed from the Bible's granting of that status to the Jews themselves. See Conrad Cherry, *God's New Israel: Religious Interpretations of American Destiny*, revised and updated (Chapel Hill: University of North Carolina Press, 1998).

36. "Speech to the Catholic Summer School, Cliff Haven, New York, 15 August 1898," McK. microfilm.

37. Frank T. Reuter, *Catholic Influence on American Colonial Policies, 1898–1904* (Austin: University of Texas Press, 1967), 10–11.

38. Reuter, *Catholic Influence*, 11–12. Reuter also notes that Catholics volunteered in large numbers for the war effort.

39. Reuter, *Catholic Influence*.

40. Champe S. Andrews, *Speech at Woolsey Hall, New Haven, Connecticut, 28 September 1903*, pamphlet reprinted from the *New Haven Leader*, September 29, 1903, 12.

41. "Speech at Georgia Agricultural and Mechanical College, Savannah Georgia, 18 December 1898," McK. microfilm.

42. According to one white writer, "[i]f it had not been for the Negro Cavalry the Rough Riders would have been exterminated. I am not a Negro Lover. My father fought with Mosby's Rangers, and I was born in the South, but the Negroes saved that fight, and the day will come when General Shafter will give them credit for their bravery." In Edward A. Johnson, *History of Negro Soldiers in the Spanish-American War* (Raleigh, N.C.: Capitol Printing, 1899; reprint, New York: Johnson Reprint, 1970), 55.

43. Hiram H. Thweatt, *What the Newspapers Say of the Negro Soldier in the Spanish-American War* (Thomasville, Ga., 1898).

44. Experiences recorded by Sergeant Major Frank W. Pullen of the Twenty-fifth U.S. Infantry can be found in Johnson, *History of Negro Soldiers in the Spanish-American War*, 22–31.

45. Matthew Frye Jacobson, *Barbarian Virtues: The United States Encounters Foreign Peoples at Home and Abroad, 1876–1917* (New York: Hill & Wang, 2000).

46. James Rankin Young, *History of the War with Spain* (Philadelphia: Premier, 1898), 658. Young was a Philadelphia Republican serving in the House of Representatives when he wrote his history of the war; previously, he had been clerk of the U.S. Senate.

47. Charles Morris, *The War with Spain* (Philadelphia: J. B. Lippincott, 1899), 6–7.

48. Marshall Everett, *Complete Life of William McKinley and Story of His Assassination* (Self-published, 1901), 261.

49. Henry Leo, *The Disaster to the Battleship* Maine *and the Cuban Warfare*, pamphlet (Chicago, 1898), 7.

50. Josiah Strong, *Expansion under New World Conditions* (New York: Baker & Taylor, 1900), 18–19, 212, 213.

51. Alden March, *The History and Conquest of the Philippines and Our Other Island Possessions* [1899] (reprint, New York: Arno Press, 1970), x.

52. Richmond P. Hobson, *Hobson's Story* (New York, 1898), 13–14.

53. Watterson, *History of the Spanish-American War*, 621–22.

54. Andrew S. Draper, *The Rescue of Cuba: An Episode in the Growth of Free Government* (New York: Silver, Burdett, 1899), 5–6. In his analysis of the war's events and outcome, Draper consistently adhered to his theme. Describing Dewey's victory, for instance, he wrote, "It was the triumph of skill and accurate marksmanship over mere daring without training, the victory of manly courage working through science over desperate valor without scientific direction," 79. His arguments supporting the position that the United States should retain the Philippines were even more pertinent and included the following: "The Gospel should be preached by representatives of all the denominations, and religious liberty must be enforced. This can be assured only by the United States. . . . We are bound to establish free institutions where American soldiers have, against armed resistance, carried the American flag; having the opportunity we must carry the means of intellectual and moral progress to the millions of Filipinos; it is the habit and the business of the Anglo-Saxon race to advance and aggressively exert its mighty influence in aid of mankind and in shaping the destiny of the world. . . . The time has come when our national interests require that we should take our place among the nations and assume our part in managing the affairs of the whole world." Draper's other reasons for holding on to the islands were more mundane: the islands were proper indemnity, were commercially valuable and necessary for military purposes, and the Europeans wanted us to hold them, in part because civil turmoil there would otherwise continue. *Rescue of Cuba*, 182–83.

55. "Speech by Postmaster-General Charles Emory Smith at the Exposition Banquet, St. Louis, 14 October 1898," McK. microfilm.

56. "Bishop C. H. Fowler, 'Abraham Lincoln and William McKinley,' Delivered: Auditorium, Chicago, 19 October, 1900; Crystal Palace Hall, New York, 30 October, 1900; Gray's Armory, Cleveland, 2 November, 1900," McK. microfilm.

57. Not all Protestants were expansionists, however. Presbyterians, Congregational Christians, and Methodists were "staunch supporters" of postwar imperialism; Unitarians,

Universalists, and Friends opposed imperialism; and Episcopalians and Baptists were split. Roman Catholics on the whole supported the policy, even if they disagreed with the efforts by some officials to Protestantize the colonies. Richard E. Welch Jr., *Response to Imperialism: The United States and the Philippine-American War, 1899–1902* (Chapel Hill, 1979), 94.

58. Winfred Lee Lyster, chairman, National Society of the Colonial Dames of America, *A Memorial to the Soldiers and Sailors of the United States Who Gave Up Their Lives for Their Country in the War of 1898 with Spain,* pamphlet preface (Springfield, Mass., 1902).

59. See Richard Hofstadter, "Cuba, the Philippines, and Manifest Destiny," in *The Paranoid Style in American Politics and Other Essays* (Cambridge: Harvard University Press, 1966), 167–70.

60. The "exception" imitated Edward Bellamy's enormously popular *Looking Backward* (1888). It described a futuristic society in the 1950s in which the United States was ruled by an emperor and money had replaced honor, justice, and truth: John Grosvenor Wilson, *The March of Millions; or, the Rise and Fall of the American Empire* (New York: Neely, 1900).

61. Alton B. Heimbach, *The Honorable Oluf Pederson on War with Spain and Expansion in the Philippines* (New York, 1899). In a similar vein, Thomas Cooper Deleon's, *Peace Issue! Being the Wonderful Scoop of Cipher Cablegrams about the Crowned Heads on Congress on the Fourth of July, 1898* (Atlanta, Ga., 1898), sought to parody the cultures and accents of many countries, among them Germany, France, Great Britain, China, Russia, and Spain.

62. Writing under the pseudonym Ensign Clarke Fitch, Sinclair wrote *A Gauntlet of Fire, Saved by the Enemy,* and *A Soldier Monk,* all of which were published by Street & Smith (New York) in 1898 and 1899. Each novel featured upright Americans, beautiful Hispanic women, and dastardly Spaniards.

63. The contrast between "good guy" Americans and "bad guy" Spaniards was especially sharply drawn in Douglas Wells, *Fighting against the Odds* and *For Spanish Gold* (both published by Street & Smith, New York, 1899), Leon Lewis, *The Avengers of the Maine: The Story of the Havana Assassins* (New York, 1898), and Ross M. Barclay, *Don Fernandez, the Spanish Spy: A Story of the War with Spain* (New York, 1899).

64. St. George Rathborne, *A Sailor's Sweetheart* (New York, 1898), 8.

65. St. George Rathborne, *A Chase for a Bride: A Romance of the Philippines* (New York, 1898), 50.

66. This theme was especially prominent in Charles Lester, *A Dangerous Mission: A Story of the Philippines* (Cincinnati, 1900).

67. Welch, *Response to Imperialism,* 123–28.

68. Frank Dumont, *The Scout of the Philippines: A Military Comedy Drama in Three Acts* (Chicago, 1899).

69. O. E. Young, *Back From the Philippines* (New York: Dick & Fitzgerald, 1905).

70. Thomas R. Beaty, *Old Glory in Cuba: A Drama in Four Acts* (Clyde, Ohio: Ames, 1898).

71. Beaty, *Old Glory in Cuba*, 24.

72. J. W. J. Marley, *Our Youthful Patriots: Patriotic Entertainment for Juvenile Performers* (New York, 1899).

73. W. V. Casey, *Accessional: A Victorious Ode* (Boulder, Colo., 1899).

74. Colonel Joseph A. Nunez, *The Fragmented* Maine *Shatters Proud Spain* (?, 1898).

75. For an informative discussion of the civil-religious, missionary importance of "The Battle Hymn of the Republic," see Ernest Lee Tuveson, *Redeemer Nation: The Idea of America's Millennial Role* (Chicago: University of Chicago Press, 1968).

76. Margaret Isabel Wolf, "The God of Battles," in *Songs of "Cuba Libre," a Remembrance of the Heroes of the Maine* (Dayton, Ohio, 1898), 13.

77. As, for example, with A. A. Hyde, *Dewey's Victory in Rhyme* (Buffalo Mills, Pa., 1898), and Jenny Ward Hays, *The Echo of the Maine* (San Francisco, 1898).

78. T. C. DeLeon, "As One," in *Peace Jubilee Souvenir: War Rhymes, Grave and Gay* (Atlanta, Ga., 1898).

79. Moody M. Watson, *A Poetical Tribute to Our Naval Heroes Who Fought the Battle of Manila* (Haverhill, Mass., 1901). See also H. N. Welch, *Dewey's Battle in Manila Bay* (Groton, Vt., 1899).

80. J. Milton Mason, *Armageddon* (Kansas City: Self-published, 1900), i–ii. The author's pen name, John Milton, is evidence enough of his ambitions.

81. Ibid., 60.

82. Florence Hooper Tilghman Baker, *Love Thoughts of the War, Composed during the War Between America and Spain in the Year 1898* (New York: G. W. Bowers, 1898).

83. Hofstadter, "Cuba, the Philippines, and Manifest Destiny," 158.

84. George Horton, *War and Mammon* (Wausau, Wisc., 1900), 7, 144–45.

85. W. H. Polhamus, "Bring Back the Fallen," in *Our Attitude Towards the Philippines: Does It Accord with Our View of Self-government*, pamphlet (1900), 27, 29.

86. Oscar Fay Adams, *Sicut Patribus* (Boston, Mass., 1902).

SIX. POWER AND EXPANSION

1. Walter LaFeber, *The Cambridge History of American Foreign Relations*, vol. 2, *The American Search for Opportunity, 1865–1913* (New York: Cambridge University Press, 1993), 115, 80.

2. Dumas Malone and Basil Rauch, *The New Nation, 1865–1917* (New York: Appleton-Century-Crofts, 1960), 56–57; LaFeber, *American Search for Opportunity*, 65.

3. See, for example, Charles Henry Butler, *There Is Something in the Air: Cuba Must Be Free: Why Do We Hesitate?* (New York, 1898), 12.

4. Andrew S. Draper, *The Rescue of Cuba: An Episode in the Growth of Free Government* (New York: Silver, Burdett, 1899), 43.

5. This was particularly the case whenever filibustering ships were captured by Spain during the 1895 insurrection. In April 1896, the *Competitor* was seized by Spanish officials under circumstances remarkably similar to those of the *Virginius* incident. Only high-level diplomacy, premised on the shared recognition that the American public would explode if the captives were executed, defused the situation. Ernest May, *Imperial Democracy: The Emergence of America as a Great Power* (New York: Harcourt, Brace & World, 1961), 84.

6. LaFeber, *American Search for Opportunity*, 26.

7. Harry Rubens, *The Dominion of the United States* (Chicago: Gunthorp-Warren, 1895), 8.

8. Fareed Zakaria, *From Wealth to Power: The Unusual Origins of America's World Role* (Princeton: Princeton University Press, 1998), 128–80.

9. James A. Field Jr., "American Imperialism: The Worst Chapter in Almost Any Book," *American Historical Review* 83 (June 1978): 644–68; John B. Hattendorf, editor's introduction to *Mahan on Naval Strategy: Selections from the Writings of Rear Admiral Alfred Thayer Mahan* (Annapolis: Naval Institute Press, 1991), and Walter Zimmerman, *First Great Triumph: How Five Americans Made Their Country a World Power* (New York: Farrar, Strauss & Giroux, 2002), 85–122.

10. Russian scholar I. Dementyev credits U.S. imperialism to the efforts of Lodge, John Hay, Senator Albert J. Beveridge, Whitelaw Reid (the head of the peace commission), Albert Shaw (editor of the *Review of Reviews*), Henry and Brooks Adams, Walter Hines Page (editor of *Atlantic Monthly*), and, above all, Theodore Roosevelt. These men, Dementyev argues, used their extraordinary influence in government and business to implement as government policies the theories of Mahan, Burgess, and others. I. Dementyev, *USA: Imperialists and Anti-Imperialists (The Great Foreign Policy Debate at the Turn of the Century)* (Moscow: Progress, 1979).

11. Daniel B. Schirmer, *Republic or Empire: American Resistance to the Philippine War* (Cambridge, Mass.: Schenkman, 1972), 44.

12. See, in particular, Philip S. Foner, *The Spanish-Cuban-American War and the Birth of American Imperialism*, 2 vols. (New York: Monthly Review Press, 1972), 2:240–41.

13. *Political Science Quarterly* (March 1894): 172; quoted in I. Dementyev, *USA: Imperialists and Anti-Imperialists*, 108.

14. Lodge, *War with Spain* [Harper & Brothers, 1899] (New York: Arno Press, 1970), 233–34.

15. Joseph Culbertson Clayton, *Some Earnest Words of an Old-Fashioned Democrat on the National Crisis* (New York: Patterson Press, 1900), 3. Clayton continued, "Henceforth, in all questions involving the international welfare of the world, America will speak with potent voice. And this is as it should be–it makes for a larger universal liberty, in the sense known only to the Anglo-Saxon peoples, and far outweighs mere trade interests."

16. Alfred T. Mahan, *Lessons of the War with Spain and Other Articles* [1899] (Freeport, N.Y.: Books for Libraries Press, 1970), 16.

17. For an interesting piece in which Mahan discusses the morality of power, see "The Peace Conference and the Moral Aspects of War," in his *Lessons of the War.*

18. Richard Hofstadter, "Cuba, the Philippines, and Manifest Destiny," in *The Paranoid Style in American Politics and Other Essays* (Cambridge: Harvard University Press, 1965), 145–87, 152–53.

19. Nathan Matthews Jr., *Oration before the City Authorities of Boston on the Fourth of July, 1899* (Boston, Mass.: Municipal Printing Office, 1899), 43.

20. Richard Olney, "International Isolation and the United States," *Atlantic* 81 (May 1898): 577–88; quoted in Ernest R. May, *American Imperialism: A Speculative Essay* (New York: Atheneum, 1968), 184–85.

21. Olney, "Richard Olney on Venezuela and U.S. 'Fiat' in the Hemisphere, 1895," in Thomas G. Paterson and Dennis Merrill, *Major Problems in American Foreign Relations,* vol. 1, *To 1920,* 4th ed. (Toronto: D. C. Heath, 1995), 356–58.

22. See May, *Imperial Democracy,* 33–55; LaFeber, *American Search for Opportunity,* 2:123–25.

23. Hofstadter, "Cuba, the Philippines, and Manifest Destiny," 158.

24. See I. Dementyev, *USA: Imperialists and Anti-Imperialists,* 12–20, and Robert Dallek, *The American Style of Foreign Policy* (New York: Alfred A. Knopf, 1982), 3.

25. Dallek, *American Style of Foreign Policy,* 10.

26. William Appleman Williams, *A William Appleman Williams Reader: Selections from His Major Historical Writings,* ed. with introduction and notes by Henry W. Berger (Chicago: Ivan R. Dee, 1992), 119–20.

27. David Healy, *U.S. Expansionism: The Imperialist Urge in the 1890s* (Madison: University of Wisconsin Press, 1970), 48; Hans Kohn, *American Nationalism: An Interpretive Essay* (New York: Macmillan, 1957), 22.

28. "The Historic Policy of the United States as to Annexation," by Simeon E. Baldwin, *Senate Document 102 of the 55th Congress, 2d Session,* January 31, 1898.

29. May, *Imperialism: A Speculative Essay,* 87.

30. George Cotkin, *Reluctant Modernism: American Thought and Culture, 1880–1900* (New York: Twayne, 1992), 123.

31. Albert Glanville, *War and the Good of It: The Dangers of Peace* (New York: W. B. Conkey, 1898), 107–8.

32. John Pettegew, "'The Soldier's Faith': Turn-of-the-century Memory of the Civil War and the Emergence of Modern American Nationalism," *Journal of Contemporary History* 31 (1996), 49–73, 61.

33. William James, "The Moral Equivalent of War," in *The Writings of William James: A Comprehensive Edition,* ed. with introduction and new preface by John J. McDermott (Chicago: University of Chicago Press, 1977), 660–71, 664.

34. Ibid., 668.

35. Ibid., 669.

36. William M. Salter, *The New Militarism* (Philadelphia, May 1899), 86–87, 100–101.

37. Professor Charles J. Bullock, *The Cost of War*, pamphlet (Anti-Imperialist League, June 1904), 9, reprinted from *Atlantic Monthly.*

38. David Starr Jordan, *The Question of the Philippines: A Speech before the Graduate Club of Leland Stanford, Junior University* (Palo Alto, Calif., 1899), 37–39.

39. David Starr Jordan, *Lest We Forget: An Address before the Graduating Class of 1898, Leland Stanford, Jr., University, 25 May 1898* (Palo Alto, Calif., 1898), 36.

40. William Graham Sumner, *The Conquest of the War with Spain: A Lecture before the Phi Beta Kappa Society of Yale University, January 16, 1899* (Boston, 1899), 3, 8–9.

41. Ibid., 30.

42. John Dobson, *Reticent Expansionism: The Foreign Policy of William McKinley* (Pittsburgh, Pa.: Duquesne University Press, 1988), 9; Matthew Frye Jacobson, *Barbarian Virtues: The United States Encounters Foreign Peoples at Home and Abroad, 1876–1917* (New York: Hill & Wang, 2000), 15–97; H. W. Brands, *The Reckless Decade: America in the 1890s* (New York: St. Martin's Press, 1995), 42–90; LaFeber, *American Search for Opportunity*, 28; 135.

43. Carman Randolph, *Notes on the Foreign Policy of the United States Suggested by the War with Spain* (New York: De Vinne Press, 1898), 11.

44. Healy, *U.S. Expansionism*, 159–60.

45. Matthews, *Oration*, 31.

46. Healy, *U.S. Expansionism*, 168.

47. Randolph, *Notes on Foreign Policy*, 12; James Vernon Martin, "Imperialism, Tyranny and Oppression," in James Vernon Martin, ed., *Expansion: Our Flag Unstained* (St. Louis, 1900), 6–8.

48. Matthews, *Oration*, 34. See also Healy, *U.S. Expansionism*, 163–65, 174.

49. See Norman A. Graebner, ed., *Manifest Destiny* (New York: Bobbs-Merrill, 1968), xix.

50. John L. O'Sullivan, "The Great Nation of Futurity," *United States Magazine and Democratic Review* 6 (November 1839): 426–30; quoted in Graebner, *Manifest Destiny*, 15–22.

51. Gilbert Chinard, *Thomas Jefferson* (Boston, Mass., 1929), 398; quoted in Albert K. Weinberg, *Manifest Destiny: A Study of Nationalist Expansionism in American History* (Baltimore: Johns Hopkins University Press, 1935), 29; and Weinberg, *Manifest Destiny*, 100–186.

52. See H. Wayne Morgan, *America's Road to Empire: The War with Spain and Overseas Expansion* (New York: John Wiley & Sons, 1965), 15.

53. Louis A. Pèrez, *The War of 1898: The United States and Cuba in History and Historiography* (Chapel Hill: University of North Carolina Press, 1998).

54. The phrase first appeared in an 1823 letter from John Quincy Adams to the U.S. minister to Spain, in which he wrote, "These islands from their local position are natural appendages to the North American continent, and one of them, Cuba, almost in sight of our shores, from a multitude of considerations has become an object of transcendent importance to the political and commercial interests of our Union." *Writings*

of John Quincy Adams, vol. 7, ed. W. C. Ford (New York, 1917), 372; quoted in Weinberg, *Manifest Destiny,* 65.

55. William Mills, *The Purpose of the Nation in the Present War* (San Francisco: Murdock Press, 1898), 9; Rubens, *The Dominion of the United States,* 6.

56. "The Late Cuban Expedition," *DeBow's Review* 9 (August 1850), 165–79; quoted in Graebner, *Manifest Destiny,* 252.

57. "Ostend Manifesto," in Graebner, *Manifest Destiny,* 285–88.

58. Graebner, *Manifest Destiny,* 290–91.

59. Mills, *Purpose of the Nation,* 20, 25.

60. All of the above citations are from H. E. Von Holst, *The Annexation of Our Spanish Conquests* (Chicago, 1898), 9–10.

61. Von Holst, *Annexation,* 11.

62. Brands, *Reckless Decade,* 41.

63. Frederick Jackson Turner, "The Significance of History," in Frederick Jackson Turner, *History, Frontier, and Section,* with introduction by Martin Ridge (Albuquerque: University of New Mexico Press, 1993), 49, 55.

64. Turner, "The Significance of the Frontier in American History," in *History, Frontier, and Section,* 61–88.

65. The equating of national power with economic success was reinforced by the Darwinian paradigm of survival of the fittest, applied by Herbert Spencer to the economic realm. See Healy, *U.S. Expansionism,* 174–77.

66. Hofstadter, "Cuba, the Philippines, and Manifest Destiny," 162–68.

SEVEN. MCKINLEY AND THE DECISION TO EXPAND

1. Philip S. Foner, *The Spanish-Cuban-American War and the Birth of American Imperialism, 1895–1902,* 2 vols. (New York: Monthly Review Press, 1972); Walter LaFeber, *The Cambridge History of American Foreign Relations,* vol. 2, *American Search for Opportunity, 1865–1913* (New York: Cambridge University Press, 1993); Daniel B. Schirmer, *Republic or Empire: American Resistance to the Philippine War* (Cambridge, Mass.: Schenkman, 1972); and William Appleman Williams, *A William Appleman Williams Reader: Selections of His Major Historical Writings,* ed. with introduction and notes by Henry W. Berger (Chicago: Ivan R. Dee, 1992).

2. Foner, *Spanish-Cuban-American War,* 307.

3. See, for example, Walter Millis, *The Martial Spirit: A Study of Our War with Spain* (New York: Viking Press, 1931); Julius W. Pratt, *Expansionists of 1898: The Acquisition of Hawaii and the Spanish Islands* (Baltimore: Johns Hopkins University Press, 1936); G. J. A. O'Toole, *The Spanish-American War: An American Epic–1898* (New York: W. W. Norton, 1984); Ernest R. May, *Imperial Democracy: The Emergence of America as a Great Power* (New York: Harcourt, Brace & World, 1961); and Barbara W. Tuchman, *The Proud Tower: A Portrait of the World before the War, 1890–1914* (New York: Macmillan, 1966).

4. John Dobson, *Reticent Expansionism: The Foreign Policy of William McKinley* (Pittsburgh, Pa.: Duquesne University Press, 1988); David Healy, *US Expansionism: The Imperialist Urge in the 1890s* (Madison: University of Wisconsin Press, 1970); David F. Trask, *The War with Spain in 1898* (New York: Macmillan, 1981); Margaret Leech, *In the Days of McKinley* (New York: Harper & Brothers, 1959); and, the best historiographical essay on the subject, Ephraim K. Smith, "William McKinley's Enduring Legacy: The Historiogaphical Debate on the Taking of the Philippine Islands," in James C. Bradford, ed., *Crucible of Empire: The Spanish-American War and Its Aftermath* (Annapolis: Naval Institute Press, 1993), 205–49.

5. Pratt, *Expansionists of 1898*, 314–16.

6. Charles S. Olcott, *The Life of William McKinley* (New York: Houghton Mifflin, 1916), 2:109–11. Olcott's source was an interview by General James F. Rusling with the head of the Methodist delegation, whose description of events was confirmed by others who were present.

7. Lewis L. Gould, *The Presidency of William McKinley* (Lawrence: Regents Press of Kansas, 1980), 141; Leech, *In the Days of McKinley*, 345.

8. Robert N. Bellah, "The Kingdom of God in America: Language of Faith, Language of Nation, Language of Empire," in William Lee Miller et al., *Religion and the Public Good: A Bicentennial Forum* (Macon, Ga.: Mercer University Press, 1988), 41–61, 49, 51.

9. James H. Moorhead, "The American Israel: Protestant Tribalism and Universal Mission," in William R. Hutchison and Hartmut Lehman, eds., *Many Are Chosen: Divine Elections and Western Nationalism* (Minneapolis, Minn.: Fortress Press, 1994), 145–66, 157.

10. *Christian and Missionary Alliance* 21 (August 3, 1898); quoted in Pratt, *Expansionists of 1898*, 291.

11. W. H. Price, *Expansion: Another View, or How It Saves America* (Chicago, 1899), 14.

12. Pratt, *Expansionists of 1898*, 312; and Richard E. Welch Jr., *Response to Imperialism: The United States and the Philippine-American War, 1899–1902* (Chapel Hill: University of North Carolina Press, 1979), 94.

13. Welch, *Response to Imperialism*, 97.

14. Quoted in Pratt, *Expansionists of 1898*, 296.

15. *Christian Advocate* 63 (September 1898), 1410; quoted in Frank T. Reuter, *Catholic Influence on American Colonial Policies, 1898–1904* (Austin: University of Texas Press, 1967), 13.

16. Quoted in Pratt, *Expansionists of 1898*, 303, 307.

17. YMCA International Committee, Women's Auxiliary, *Notes of Progress* 1 (New York, 1900), 18.

18. Ferdinand Blumentritt, *The Philippines: A Summary of Their Ethnographical, Historical, and Political Conditions*, trans. David J. Doherty (Chicago: Donohue Brothers, 1900), 28.

19. YMCA International Committee, Women's Auxiliary, *Notes of Progress* 2 (New York, 1900), 6. In another newsletter, the YMCA noted, "The more than one hundred

thousand young men in our Army and Navy usually have adequate provision made for their physical needs, but the peculiar conditions of life in the service leaves them almost entirely dependent upon outside agencies for the social, mental, moral, and religious influences which are to round out the life of the American young man." YMCA National Board, Armed Services Department, *Our Soldiers and Sailors*, pamphlet (1899), 3.

20. Healy, *US Expansionism*, 136.

21. Welch, *Response to Imperialism*, 90–91.

22. "Speech to Ecumenical Conference, New York, 21 April 1900," McK. microfilm.

23. On another occasion, he told a gathering of Christian educators, "He who serves the Master best serves man best; and he who serves truth serves civilization." "Speech at California Street Methodist Episcopal Church, San Francisco, 24 May 1901," McK. microfilm.

24. Cushman K. Davis, *The Treaty of Paris: A Speech before the Union League Club of Chicago, 22 February 1899*, pamphlet (1899).

25. H. Wayne Morgan, ed., *Making Peace with Spain: The Diary of Whitelaw Reid, September–December 1898* (Austin: University of Texas Press, 1965), 15.

26. "Instructions to the Peace Commission," McK. microfilm.

27. "Confidential Instructions to Major-General [John R.] Brooke, Rear Admiral [Winfield Scott] Schley, and Brigadier-General Gordon, 26 August 1898," *Senate Document No. 148 of the 56th Congress, 2d Session: Papers Relating to the Treaty with Spain*, 9–10.

28. Trask, *War with Spain*, 391–98.

29. The content of these meetings was widely discussed and debated, with the honor of the United States being directly implicated. It seems most likely that promises were indeed extended by the Americans to the Filipinos, but that these promises were not preapproved by responsible authorities.

30. "Proclamation of the Filipinos, Sent by Filipino Leaders from Hong Kong to Manila, April 1898," in Ora Williams, *Oriental America: Official and Authentic Records of the Dealings of the United States with the Natives of Luzon and Their Former Rulers* (Chicago: Oriental American Publishing, 1899), 25.

31. Ibid.

32. These meetings, which took place from September 27 through October 5, are recounted in Smith, "McKinley's Enduring Legacy," 234–35.

33. "Telegram from Mr. [William R.] Day [head of the peace commission] to Mr. [John] Hay [secretary of state], 7 October 1898," *Senate Document No. 148: Papers Relating to the Treaty with Spain*, 18.

34. Ibid., 18–21.

35. Commander R. B. Bradford's statement before the Paris commission; quoted in Julian W. Richards, *A Handbook of the Spanish-American War and the Insurrection in the Philippines* (Cedar Rapids, Iowa, 1899), 30–31.

36. Morgan, *Making Peace with Spain*, 64. Reid also notes that the commission's discussion with Foreman "revolutionized our views about Mindanao, showing it to be a far less difficult problem than had been supposed."

37. "Telegram from Mr. Day to Mr. Hay, 9 October 1898," *Senate Document No. 148: Papers Relating to the Treaty with Spain*, 24–26.

38. May, *Imperial Democracy*, 259.

39. "Speech at Kokomo, Indiana, 21 October 1898" McK. microfilm.

40. "Speech at Belle Plain, Iowa, 11 October 1898," McK. microfilm.

41. "Speech at the Auditorium, Chicago, Illinois, 18 October 1898," McK. microfilm. The reception was described in McKinley's papers as a religious function presided over by "a Jewish rabbi, a Roman Catholic priest, a Presbyterian clergyman, and a noted black orator." It seems McKinley sought to include a diversity of speakers as a way of symbolizing the spirit of national unity that he was cultivating on the tour, but the "noted black orator" was Booker T. Washington, who used the occasion to criticize pointedly McKinley's failure to defend the interests of African Americans during his administration.

42. "Speech to Cedar Rapids, Iowa, 11 October 1898," McK. microfilm.

43. "Speech at the Auditorium, Chicago, Illinois, 19 October 1898," McK. microfilm.

44. "Speech at Carroll, Iowa, 11 October 1898," McK. microfilm.

45. "Speech at the Trans-Mississippi Exposition, Omaha, Nebraska, 12 October 1898," McK. microfilm.

46. "Speech at the Merchant's Exchange, St. Louis, 14 October 1898," McK. microfilm.

47. "Speech at Indianapolis, Indiana, 21 October 1898," McK. microfilm.

48. "Banquet Speech at the Auditorium, Chicago, 19 October 1898," McK. microfilm.

49. "Telegram from Peace Commissioners to Mr. Hay, 25 October 1898," *Senate Document No. 148: Papers Relating to the Treaty with Spain*, 32–35.

50. Ibid.

51. "Telegram from Mr. Hay to Mr. Day, 26 October 1898." Ibid., 35.

52. "Telegram from Peace Commissioners to Mr. Hay, 11 November 1898." ibid., 45–48.

53. Ibid.

54. "Telegram from Mr. Hay to Mr. Day, 13 November 1898." ibid., 48–49.

EIGHT. DEBATING THE TREATY AND EXPANSION

1. *Journal of the Executive Proceedings of the Senate of the United States of America,* 55th Congress (vol. 31), part 2, 1161.

2. *CR*, 55th Cong., 3d Sess., 93–96, 96.

3. Ibid., 96.

4. Ibid., 288–97, 288–90.

5. Ibid., 295–96.

6. Ibid., 297.

7. Ibid., 502–3.

8. Other resolutions were introduced by Senators Will V. Sullivan (D-Miss.), William Lindsay (D-Ky.), William V. Allen (Pop-Neb.), Samuel McEnery (D-La.), and William E. Mason (R-Ill.).

9. "Senate Resolution 211," *CR*, 55th Cong., 3d Sess.; introduced on 561, discussed, 733–39.

10. Ibid., 735.

11. Ibid., 736.

12. Ibid., 1449.

13. Ibid., 1425, 1424.

14. Ibid., 921.

15. Ibid., 925.

16. *Speech of Senator William E. Mason, 10 January 1899*, pamphlet (Washington, D.C.: 1899), 9.

17. *CR*, 55th Cong., 3d Sess., 438.

18. Ibid., 789.

19. Ibid., 437–38.

20. *Speech of Senator Mason*, 11.

21. *CR*, 55th Cong., 3d Sess., 642.

22. Ibid., 1422.

23. Charles Francis Adams, *"Imperialism" and "Tracks of Our Forefathers": A Paper Read before the Lexington, Massachusetts, Historical Society, December 20, 1898* (Boston, Mass.: Dana Estes, 1899), 28, 35, 36.

24. Carl Schurz, *For the Republic of Washington and Lincoln*, pamphlet (Chicago, 1899), 28.

25. Carl Schurz, *American Imperialism: Convocation Address at the University of Chicago, January 4, 1899*, pamphlet (New York, 1900), 20.

26. Herman E. Von Holst, *The Annexation of Our Spanish Conquests* (Chicago, June 1898), 5.

27. Ibid., 12–13.

28. *CR*, 55th Cong., 3d Sess., 437–38.

29. Ibid., 639–42, 639. He also stated that "[u]niversal suffrage in the South long since degenerated into a race question, and as such led to the practical elimination of the Negro from politics; a policy that is today wisely advocated by the great leaders of the race like Professor Miller and Booker Washington, and which in time, without outside interference, under the guidance of the best thought of both races, will lead to a just and mutually satisfactory settlement of the gravest problem that has ever confronted any people of modern times. Conscious of the rectitude of purpose and feeling that the Negro was not responsible for the position into which he was thrust, the South, not defiantly, but by protestation, has patiently appealed to the nation to judge her righteously." Ibid., 639–42, 639.

30. Ibid., 927.

31. Von Holst, *Annexation*, 21, 23.

32. *CR*, 55th Cong., 3d Sess., 1416–22, 1419.

33. Ibid., 921–27, 922.

34. Ibid., 1422–32, 1424.

35. Ibid., 1430.

36. Ibid., 785.

37. David Starr Jordan, *The Question of the Philippines: An Address before the Graduate Club of Leland Stanford University*, pamphlet (Palo Alto, Calif., 1899), 62.

38. *CR*, 55th Cong., 3d Sess., 1446.

39. James Vernon Martin, *Expansion: Our Flag Unstained* (St. Louis: Self-published, 1900), 21.

40. George S. Boutwell, *In the Name of Liberty* (Boston, Mass.: Anti-Imperialist League, 1899), 2.

41. *CR*, 55th Cong., 3d Sess., 641.

42. Ibid., 924.

43. Jordan, *The Question of the Philippines*, 62.

44. Carl Schurz, *For American Principles and American Honor*, pamphlet (Anti-Imperialist League of New York, 1900), 11–12.

45. John White Chadwick, *The Present Distress: A Sermon upon Our Oriental War*, pamphlet (New York, 1899), 20–21.

46. Moorfield Storey, *The Importance to America of Philippine Independence: An Address Delivered before the Harvard Democratic Club at the Harvard Union, Cambridge, October 28, 1904*, pamphlet (Boston, Mass.: Anti-Imperialist League, 1904), 12.

47. Robert L. Beisner, *Twelve against Empire: The Anti-Imperialists, 1898–1900* (New York: McGraw-Hill, 1968), 139–64.

48. *CR*, 55th Cong., 3d Sess., 495.

49. Ibid., 496–503.

50. Ibid., 433–36.

51. *Speech of Senator Mason*, 4, 5.

52. *CR*, 55th Cong., 3d Sess., 565.

53. Foraker's most sustained criticism came from a supporter of the treaty (albeit a reluctant one), Senator William V. Allen, who railed in the final minutes before the treaty was to be voted on, "I can not resist the temptation of calling attention to a remarkable statement of the senior Senator from Ohio [Mr. Foraker] in his speech the other day, when he declared that the Declaration of Independence was simply a bill of complaint, or a bill enumerating certain grievances against the British Crown. . . . [T]he Declaration of Independence is the first great charter of American liberty. It was not the beginning of government; it was the first crystallization in the form of a written document of certain well-known and generally accepted doctrines held in this country in colonial days; it was the first defiance that was hurled in the face of England and

Continental Europe by the colonists who inhabited this country. It was not and is not simply a bill of complaint against the English Government. . . . It was the announcement of principles that are as deathless as the sun and as eternal as the rock-ribbed earth. I say in this splendid presence this day that I hold to the doctrine that every human being is born with the right to rule and control himself, if capable. I can not understand how, through the ages that have passed, any man could be found of such indifferent or weak intellect that he could have reached a different belief." *CR*, 55th Cong., 3d Sess., 1482–83.

54. Adams, *"Imperialism" and "The Tracks of Our Forefathers,"* 25.

55. William Graham Sumner, *The Predominant Issue*, pamphlet reprinted from *International Monthly*, November 1900 (Burlington, Vt., 1901), 10–12.

56. *CR*, 55th Cong., 3d session, 736–37.

57. Ibid., 642.

58. Ibid., 784–85.

59. Ibid., 1427.

60. Ibid., 965.

61. *Speech of Senator Mason*, 23.

62. Sumner, *The Predominant Issue*, 12–13.

63. Moorfield Storey, *"Marked Severities" in Philippine Warfare: An Analysis of the Law and Facts Bearing on the Action and Utterances of President Roosevelt and Secretary Root* (Boston, Mass., 1902), 118–19.

64. George S. Boutwell, "An Address," in *Free America, Free Cuba, Free Philippines: Addresses at Fanueil Hall* (Boston, Mass.: Anti-Imperialist League, 1901), 18–19.

65. Welch, *Response to Imperialism*, 36–42; and Schirmer, *Republic or Empire*, 225–41.

66. *CR*, 55th Cong., 3d Sess., 925.

67. Von Holst, *Annexation*, 18.

68. *CR*, 55th Cong., 3d Sess., 1448.

69. Ibid., 1417.

70. Ibid., 831–39.

71. Ibid., 960–61.

72. Teller's historical overview can be found in *CR*, 55th Cong., 3d Sess., 960–63.

73. Ibid., 1376–89, 1377. The case that Spooner cited was *American Insurance Company v. Canter*, 1 Peters 511.

74. Ibid., citing *Murphy v. Ramsey*, 114 U.S. 1.

75. Ibid., 1380.

76. Ibid., 13.

77. Ibid., 1383, 1384.

78. Ibid., 958–60, 959. Lodge continued, "I believe in the American people as they are today, and in the civilization they have created. I believe not merely in what they have done, but in what they are yet to do. To the American people and their Government I am ready to intrust my life, my liberty, my honor; and what is far dearer to me than

anything personal to myself, the lives of my children and my children's children. If I am ready thus to trust my children to the Government which the American people create and sustain, am I to shrink from intrusting to that same people the fate and fortune of the inhabitants of the Philippine Islands?" *CR*, 55th Cong., 3d Sess., 959.

79. Ibid., 958.

80. Ibid., 1242.

81. Ibid., 963.

82. Ibid., 1386–87.

83. Ibid., 959.

84. He continued, "We owe them a duty now, as in the case of the drowning child snatched from a watery grave. We have snatched them from the waves of their Spanish enslavement. It is not only our duty to snatch them from the waves, but it is our duty to see that they are restored to healthy municipal life. We must breathe into their nostrils the principles of law, order, and good government. . . . It would be the highest cruelty to turn them adrift today upon the political sea between a double danger–the danger of destruction form anarchy and chaos within and the danger of being swallowed up by some of the great powers of Europe." *CR*, 55th Cong., 3d Sess., 836.

85. Ibid., 1451.

86. Ibid., 327–29.

87. Ibid., 330.

88. Ibid., 959.

89. Ibid., 1242.

90. The following non-Republican senators voted for the treaty: Allen, Butler, Clay, Faulkner, Gray, Harris, Kenney, Kyle, Lindsay, McEnery, McLaurin, Mason, Morgan, Pettus, Sullivan, and Teller. Of these, Senators Gray, Clay, McEnery, McLaurin, Mason, and Allen had during the debates spoken strongly against the treaty. *Journal of the Executive Proceedings of the Senate of the United States of America*, 55th Cong., vol. 31, part 2, 1284.

91. *CR*, 55th Cong., 3d Sess., 1481.

NINE. SELLING IMPERIALISM

1. "Speech to the Home Market Club Banquet, Boston, 16 February 1898," McK. microfilm.

2. David Healy, *US Expansionism: The Imperialist Urge in the 1890s* (Madison: University of Wisconsin Press, 1970), 127–29.

3. In an undelivered speech that he drafted in October 1899, McKinley referred to the insurgents as "a single tribe in a single island, and not one-half of that tribe and not one-third of that territory," McK. microfilm.

4. "Speech at Pittsburgh, Pa., 28 August 1899," McK. microfilm.

5. "Speech at the Citizen's Banquet, Chicago, 19 October 1899," McK. microfilm.

6. "Speech at Watseka, Illinois, 11 October 1899," McK. microfilm.

7. "Speech at Minneapolis, Minnesota, 12 October 1899," McK. microfilm.

8. "Speech at Wadena, Minnesota, 13 October 1899," McK. microfilm.

9. "Speech at Fargo, North Dakota, 13 October 1899," McK. microfilm.

10. "Speech at Redfield, South Dakota, 14 October 1899," McK. microfilm.

11. "Speech at Huron, South Dakota, 14 October 1899," McK. microfilm.

12. "Speech at Sioux Falls, South Dakota, 14 October 1899," McK. microfilm.

13. "Speech at Iowa Falls, Iowa, 16 October 1899," McK. microfilm.

14. "Speech at Manchester, Iowa, 16 October 1899," McK. microfilm.

15. "Speech at Warren, Ohio, 18 October 1899," McK. microfilm.

16. "Speech at the Banquet of the Ohio Society, New York, 3 March 1899," McK. microfilm.

17. "President's Message to Congress, 5 December 1899," McK. microfilm.

18. Ibid.

19. Ibid.

20. John Savary, "Uncle Sam, the Real and the Ideal: A Dissertation" (Washington, D.C., 1899), 9.

21. Charles Henry Butler, *Our Treaty with Spain: Triumphant Diplomacy* (Washington, 1898), 9–10.

22. "Platform of the Anti-Imperialist League."

23. James Vernon Martin, *Expansion: Our Flag Unstained* (St. Louis, 1900), 3.

24. For more thorough treatments of the Anti-Imperialist League and the movement more generally, see Richard E. Welch Jr., *Response to Imperialism: The United States and the Philippine-American War, 1898–1902* (Chapel Hill: University of North Carolina Press, 1979); and Daniel B. Schirmer, *Republic or Empire: American Resistance to the Philippine War* (Cambridge, Mass.: Schenkman, 1972).

25. As he explained in one speech, "The ratification of the treaty, instead of committing the United States to a colonial policy, really clears the way for the recognition of a Philippine republic." "Speech at St. Paul, Minnesota, 14 February 1899," in William Jennings Bryan, *Imperialism: Extracts from Speeches, Interviews, and Articles* (New York, 1900), 16.

26. "Ratify the Treaty, Declare the Nation's Policy," *New York Journal*, January 9, 1899; reprinted in Bryan, *Imperialism*, 34–35.

27. "What Next?" *New York Journal*, February 12, 1899; reprinted in Bryan, *Imperialism*, 55.

28. Bryan, "Speech in Washington, D.C., 22 February 1899," in Bryan, *Imperialism*, 20.

29. "Will It Pay?" *New York Journal*, January 15, 1899; reprinted in Bryan, *Imperialism*, 42.

30. "Imperialism: Nomination Speech, 8 August 1900," in Bryan, *Imperialism*, 88–89.

31. "Speech in Washington, D.C., 22 February 1899," in Bryan, *Imperialism*, 21–22.

32. "Nomination Speech, 8 August 1900," 91.

33. "Speech in Denver, 17 January 1899," in Bryan, *Imperialism*, 15.

34. "Nomination Speech, 8 August 1900," 92.

35. Not all anti-McKinley pamphlets were associated with the Anti-Imperialist League. W. H. Scott, a black pastor at the St. John Baptist Church, urged blacks to vote against the incumbent because he had done nothing to support their interests during a period when blacks were being increasingly marginalized in society. W. H. Scott, *An Appeal to the Negroes in the Pivotal States* (Woburn, Mass., 1900). In another pamphlet, a Republican author complained that his party had been hijacked by the trusts, "an Imperialistic Oligarchy," for whom McKinley was their "weak and plastic figurehead." His ire was raised by U.S. Philippine policy, which he regarded as "un-Republican, un-Democratic, unconstitutional, un-Christian, and unjust." Henry Gratton Donnelly, *The Coming Empire: A Political Satire*, (1900), 7.

36. *Republican Policy Triumphs: Leaders of the Party Attest the Wisdom of the President's Administration*, anonymous pamphlet (New York, 1900).

37. "Speech of Senator C. W. Fairbanks at Canton, Ohio [Fairbanks was in Canton to tell McKinley he had won the Republican Party nomination at the Philadelphia convention], 12 July 1900," McK. microfilm.

38. See, for example, the Republican National Committee pamphlet *Commercial Expansion: Importance of Manila as a Market for Supplying the Needs of Eight Hundred Millions of People in its Immediate Vicinity* (New York, 1900); and George E. Adams, *McKinley and Bryan, Principles and Men: Issues of the Campaign*, pamphlet (Quincy, Ill., October 3, 1900).

39. See Republican National Committee, *Democratic Expansion*, pamphlet (New York, 1900).

40. Welch, *Response to Imperialism*, 69–70.

41. George E. Adams, *McKinley and Bryan and Their Paramount Issues*, pamphlet (Waukegan, Ill., October 25, 1900), 7.

42. "Formal Acceptance Speech for the Nomination of the Republican Party as President of the United States, 8 September 1900," McK. microfilm.

43. Davis Newton Lott, *The Presidents Speak: The Inaugural Addresses of the American Presidents, from Washington to Clinton* (New York: Henry Holt, 1994), 207–12.

44. "Speech at San Jose, California, 13 May 1901," McK. microfilm.

45. "Speech at Native Sons' Hall, San Francisco, California, 23 May 1901," McK. microfilm.

Bibliography

GOVERNMENT DOCUMENTS AND SPEECHES

Congress

Congressional Record
54th Congress, 2d Session, 1896–97.
55th Congress, 1st Session, 1897.
55th Congress, 2d Session, 1897–98.
55th Congress, 3d Session, 1898–99.
Journal of the Executive Proceedings of the Senate of the United States of America, 55th Congress (vol. 31), part 2.
Senate Document 102 of the 55th Congress, 2d Session. Printed January 31, 1898: Simeon E. Baldwin, "The Historic Policy of the United States to Annexation."
Senate Document 148 of the 56th Congress, 2d Session: Papers Relating to the Treaty with Spain

Presidents

Lott, Davis Newton. *The Presidents Speak: The Inaugural Addresses of the American Presidents, from Washington to Clinton.* New York: Henry Holt, 1994.
Papers of William McKinley, microfilm.
Richardson, James D. *A Compilation of the Messages and Papers of the Presidents, 1789–1902,* vol. 10. Revised and enlarged by George Raywood Devitt. Washington, D.C.: Bureau of National Literature and Art, 1903.

U.S. Supreme Court

Armstrong v. United States, 182 U.S. 243 (1901) (4th insular case).

Barron v. Baltimore, 7 Pet. 243 (1833).

Cantwell v. Connecticut, 310 U.S. 296 (1940).

Davis v. Beason, 133 U.S. 333 (1889).

DeLima v. Bidwell, 182 U.S. 1 (1901) (1st insular case).

Dooley v. United States, 182 U.S. 222 (1901) (3d insular case).

Downes v. Bidwell, 182 U.S. 244 (1901) (5th insular case).

Everson v. Board of Education of the Township of Ewing, 330 U.S. 1 (1947).

Goetze v. United States, 182 U.S. 221 (1901) (2d insular case).

Permoli v. New Orleans, 44 U.S. 589 (1845).

Plessy v. Ferguson, 163 U.S. 537 (1896).

Quick Bear v. Luepp, 210 U.S. 50 (1908).

Reynolds v. United States, 98 U.S. 145 (1878).

United States v. Curtiss-Wright, 299 U.S. 304 (1936).

Watson v. Jones, 13 Wall. (80 U.S.) 679 (1871).

West Virginia v. Barnette, 319 U.S. 624 (1943).

Youngstown Sheet and Steel Corporation v. Sawyer, 343 U.S. 579 (1952).

Other Government Sources

Comments of Rear-Admiral Pluddemann, German Navy, on the Main Features of the War with Spain. Washington, D.C.: Navy Department, Office of Naval Intelligence, 1898.

Root, Elihu. *Speech at Canton Ohio, October 24, 1900.* Pamphlet. 1900.

Spanish Treaty Claims Commission of 1901: Papers Printed for the Use of the Commission. Washington, D.C.: Government Printing Office, 1901.

BOOKS, ARTICLES, AND PAMPHLETS

Abrams, Jeanne. "Remembering the *Maine:* The Jewish Attitude toward the Spanish-American War as Reflected in the *American Israelite.*" *American Jewish History* 76 (June 1987): 439–55.

Acheson, Dean. *The Struggle for a Free Europe.* New York: W. W. Norton, 1971.

Adams, Brooks. *The Law of Civilization and Decay.* New York: Macmillan, 1896.

———. *The New Empire.* New York: Macmillan, 1904.

Adams, Charles Francis. *"Imperialism" and "Tracks of Our Forefathers."* New York: Dana Estes, 1899.

Adams, George E. *McKinley and Bryan and Their Paramount Issues.* Pamphlet. 1900.

———. *McKinley and Bryan: Principles and Men, Issues of the Campaign.* Pamphlet. 1900.

Adams, Oscar Fay. *Sicut Patribus.* Pamphlet. Boston, Mass., 1902.

Agoncilla, Felipe. *Letter to the American People.* Pamphlet. 1900.

Aguinaldo, Don Emilio. *True Version of the Philippine Revolution.* Pamphlet. 1899.

Albanese, Catherine. "Savage, Sinner, and Saved: Davy Crockett, Camp Meetings, and the Wild Frontier." *American Quarterly* 33 (Winter 1981): 482–501.

———. "Response to Miller." In *Religion and the Public Good: A Bicentennial Forum*, ed. William Lee Miller et al., 23–31. Macon, Ga.: Mercer University Press, 1988.

Alexander, Richard D. *Darwinism and Human Affairs.* Seattle: University of Washington Press, 1979.

Alger, Russell A. *The Spanish-American War.* New York: Harper & Brothers, 1901.

Alley, Robert S., ed. *James Madison on Religious Liberty.* Buffalo: Prometheus Books, 1985.

Ambrosius, Lloyd. "Woodrow Wilson and the Quest for Orderly Progress." In *Traditions and Values: American Diplomacy, 1865–1945*, ed. Norman A. Graebner, 73–100. New York: University Press of America, 1985.

Andersen, Arthur C., and Charles H. Briner. *"K" Company, 71st Regiment, New York Volunteers: A Record of Its Experience and Services during the Spanish-American War and a Memorial to Its Dead.* Pamphlet. New York, 1900.

Anderson, Benedict. *Imagined Communities: Reflections on the Origin and Spread of Nationalism.* Norfolk, Conn.: Thetford Press, 1986.

Andrews, Champe S. *Speech at Weilsey Hall, New Haven, Connecticut, September 28, 1903.* Pamphlet. Reprint from *New Haven Leader*, 1903.

Arasaratnam, Sinnappah. *Christianity, Traditional Cultures, and Nationalism: The South Asian Experience.* Ceylon: Bastian Press, 1978.

Atkinson, Edward. *The Cost of Criminal Aggression in the Philippine Islands to the People of Massachusetts.* Pamphlet. Boston, Mass., 1903.

Axeen, David. "'Heroes of the Engine Room': American 'Civilization' and the War with Spain." *American Quarterly.* 36 (Autumn 1984): 487–502.

Bacon, T. S. *A New Religion?* Pamphlet. Buskeystown, Md.: Self-published, 1898.

Baker, Florence Hooper Tilghman. *Love Thoughts of the War, Composed during the War between America and Spain.* Pamphlet. New York: G. W. Bowers, 1898.

Barber, Benjamin. *Jihad v. McWorld: How Globalism and Tribalism Are Reshaping the World.* New York: Ballantine Books, 1996.

Barclay, Ross M. *Don Fernandez, the Spanish Spy: A Story of the War with Spain.* Pamphlet. New York, 1899.

Beaty, Thomas R. *Old Glory in Cuba: A Drama in Four Acts.* Washington, D.C.: Ames, 1898.

Beaver, R. Pierce. *Church, State, and the American Indians.* St. Louis: Concordia, 1966.

Bedell, George C., et al. *Religion in America.* New York: Macmillan, 1975.

Beer, Samual H. *To Make A Nation: The Rediscovery of American Federalism.* Cambridge: Harvard University Press, 1993.

Beisner, Robert L. *Twelve against Empire: The Anti-Imperialists, 1898–1900.* New York: McGraw-Hill, 1968.

———. "Comments [on Field, "American Imperialism: The Worst Chapter in Almost Any Book"]." *American Historical Review* 83 (June 1978): 672–78.

Bell, Daniel. "'The Hegelian Secret': Civil Society and American Exceptionalism." In *Is America Different? A New Look at American Exceptionalism,* ed. Byron E. Shafer, 46–70. Oxford, Eng.: Clarendon Press, 1991.

Bellah, Robert N. "Civil Religion in America." In *American Civil Religion,* ed. Russell E. Richey and Donald G. Jones, 21–44. New York: Harper & Row, 1974.

———. 1988. "The Kingdom of God in America: Language of Faith, Language of Nation, Language of Empire." In *Religion and the Public Good: A Bicentennial Forum*, ed. William Lee Miller et al., 41–61. Macon, Ga.: Mercer University Press, 1988.

Bemis, Samuel Flagg. "American Foreign Policy and the Blessings of Liberty." *American Historical Review* 67 (January 1962): 291–305.

Berger, Peter F. "Globalism and Inclusion: Theoretical Remarks on the Non-Solidary Society." In *Religious Politics in Global and Comparative Perspective*, ed. William H. Swatos Jr., 39–54. Westport, Conn.: Greenwood Press, 1989.

Berger, Peter L. *The Sacred Canopy: Elements of a Sociological Theory of Religion*. New York: Anchor Books, 1967.

Berns, Walter. *The First Amendment and the Future of American Democracy*. New York: BasicBooks, 1976.

Blodgett, Geoffrey, Ronald P. Formisano, and William Lee Rose. "Comments [on Kelley, "Ideology and Political Culture from Jefferson to Nixon"]." *American Historical Review* 82 (June 1977): 563–82.

Bloomfield, Maxwell. "Dixon's 'The Leopard's Spots': A Study in Popular Racism." *American Quarterly* 16 (Autumn 1964): 387–401.

Blumentritt, Ferdinand. *The Philippines: A Summary Account of Their Ethnographical, Historical, and Political Conditions*. Trans. David J. Doherty. Chicago: Donohue Brothers, 1900.

Bonaparte, Charles J. *Can We Trust Our Army to Spoilsmen?* Pamphlet. Baltimore, 1898.

Boutwell, George S. *In the Name of Liberty*. Pamphlet. Boston, Mass.: Anti-Imperialist League, 1899.

Bradley, Gerard V. *Church-State Relationships in America*. Westport, Conn.: Greenwood Press, 1987.

Brands, H. W. *The Reckless Decade: America in the 1890s*. New York: St. Martin's Press, 1995.

———. *What America Owes the World: The Struggle for the Soul of Foreign Policy*. New York: Cambridge University Press, 1998.

———. *Bound to Empire: The United States and the Philippines*. New York: Oxford University Press, 1992.

Bratt, James D. "God, Tribe, and Nation: Ethno-Religious History at Middle Age." *Journal of the Comparative Study of Society and History* 33 (January 1991): 176–86.

Bremer, Francis J. *The Puritan Experiment: New England Society from Bradford to Edwards*. Hanover, N.H.: University Press of New England, 1995.

Breuilly, John. *Nationalism and the State*. 2d edition. Chicago: University of Chicago Press, 1994.

Brewer, David J. *The Spanish War: A Prophecy or an Exception? An Address before the Liberal Club, 16 February 1899*. Pamphlet. 1899.

Brill, Alida. "Response to Bellah." In *Religion and the Public Good: A Bicentennial Forum*, ed. William Lee Miller et al., 62- 66. Macon, Ga.: Mercer University Press, 1988.

Brooks, Francis A. *An Examination of the Scheme for Engrafting the Colonial System of Government upon the United States Constitution*. Boston, Mass.: George H. Ellis, 1900.

Bryan, William Jennings. *Imperialism: Extracts from Speeches, Interviews and Articles*. Pamphlet. 1900.

Buell, Charles Edward. *Industrial Liberty: Our Duty to Rescue the People of Cuba, Porto Rico, and the Philippine Islands from That Greatest of All Evils–Poverty*. Pamphlet. Plainfield, N.J., 1900.

Bull, Hedley. *The Anarchical Society: A Study of Order in World Politics*. 2d edition, with a foreword by Stanley Hoffmann. New York: Columbia University Press, 1995.

Bullock, Charles J. *The Cost of War*. Pamphlet. Anti-Imperialist League, 1904.

Bulman, Raymond F. "'Myth of Origin,' Civil Religion, and Presidential Politics." *Journal of Church and State* 33 (Summer 1991): 523–39.

Burke, E. A. *The War in the Far East*. Pamphlet. Cleveland, Ohio, 1901.

Burns, Edward McNall. *The American Idea of Mission: Concepts of National Purpose and Destiny*. New Brunswick, N.J.: Rutgers University Press, 1957.

Butler, Charles Henry. *Our Treaty with Spain: Triumphant Diplomacy*. Pamphlet. Washington, D.C., 1898.

——. *The Voice of the Nation: The President Is Right: A Series of Papers on our Past and Present Relations with Spain*. New York: George Munro's Sons, 1898.

——. *Cuba Must Be Free: There Is Something in the Air, Why Do We Hesistate?* Pamphlet. Self-published, 1898.

Butler, Jon. *Awash in a Sea of Faith: Christianizing the American People*. Cambridge: Harvard University Press, 1990.

Calthrop, S. R. *The Wars of 1898: A Sermon at the May Memorial Church, 1899*. Pamphlet. 1899.

Carey, Patrick W. "John Ireland and the American Catholic Church: Review Essay." *American Historical Review* 95 (October 1990): 1297–98.

Carson, H. R. *Recollections of a Chaplain in the Volunteer Army. Address before the Church Club of Louisiana*. Pamphlet. 1899.

Carwardine, Richard. "The Know-Nothing Party, the Protestant Evangelical Community, and American National Identity." In *Religion and National Identity*, ed. Stuart Mews, 449–63. Oxford, Eng.: Basil Blackwell, 1982.

Casey, W. V. *Accessional: A Victorious Ode*. Pamphlet. Boulder, Colo., 1899.

Ceaser, James. *Reconstructing America: The Symbol of America in Modern Thought*. New Haven, Conn.: Yale University Press, 1997.

Cellini, ed. *The American Republic and Ancient Israel* [1799]. New York: Arno Press, 1977.

Chadwick, John White. *The Present Distress: A Sermon upon Our Oriental War*. Pamphlet. New York, 1899.

Cherry, Conrad. *God's New Israel: Religious Interpretations of American Destiny*. Revised and updated edition. Chapel Hill: University of North Carolina Press, 1998.

Clayton, Joseph Culbertson. *Some Earnest Words of an Old-Fashioned Democrat on the National Crisis*. New York: Patterson Press, 1900.

Clinton, W. David. *The Two Faces of National Interest*. Baton Rouge: Louisiana State University Press, 1994.

Cobb, William W., Jr. *The American Foundation Myth in Vietnam: Reigning Paradigms and Raining Bombs*. New York: University Press of America, 1998.

Coleman, Ambrose. *The Friars in the Philippines*. Boston, Mass.: Marlier, Callanan, 1899.

Connor, Walker. *Ethnonationalism: The Quest For Understanding*. Princeton: Princeton University Press, 1994.

Cotkin, George. *Reluctant Modernism: American Thought and Culture, 1880–1900*. New York: Maxwell Macmillan International, 1992.

Croly, Herbert. *The Promise of American Life* [1909]. With an introduction by Scott R. Bowman. New Brunswick, N.J.: Transaction
Press, 1993.

Crosby, Ernest H. *The Absurdities of Militarism*. Boston, Mass.: American Peace Society, 1901.

———. *War Echoes*. Pamphlet. Philadelphia, 1898.

———. *War from the Christian Point of View*. Pamphlet. Boston, Mass., 1900.

Curry, Thomas J. *The First Freedoms: Church and State in America to
the Passage of the First Amendment*. New York: Oxford University
Press, 1986.

Dallek, Robert. *The American Style of Foreign Policy*. New York: Alfred
A. Knopf, 1982.

Darwin, Charles. *The Descent of Man and Selection in Relation to Sex*
[1871]. With an introduction by John Tyler Bonner and Robert M.
May. Princeton: Princeton University Press, 1981.

Daughton, Suzanne M. "Metaphorical Transcendence: Images of the
Holy War in Franklin Roosevelt's First Inaugural." *Quarterly Journal of Speech* 79 (1993): 427–46.

Davis, Charles. "The Political Use and Misuse of Religious Language." *Journal of Ecumenical Studies*. 26 (Summer 1989): 483–95.

Davis, Cushman K. *The Treaty of Paris. Speech before the Union
League Club of Chicago*. Pamphlet. 1989.

Dawes, Charles G. *A Journal of the McKinley Years*. Chicago: Lakeside, 1950.

DeLeon, Thomas Cooper. *Peace Issue! Being the Wonderful Scoop of
Cipher Cablegrams about the Crowned Heads Congress on the
Fourth of July, 1898*. Pamphlet. Atlanta, Ga., 1898.

———. *Peace Jubilee Souvenir: War Rhymes, Grave and Gay*. Pamphlet.
Atlanta, Ga., 1898.

Dinan, John J. *Keeping the People's Liberties: Legislators, Citizens, and
Judges as Guardians of Rights*. Lawrence: University Press of
Kansas, 1998.

Dixon, Thomas. *Dixon's Sermons, a Monthly Magazine* 1, nos. 1–3
(1898). With vol. 1, nos. 4–10 (1898–99) the title changed to *Freelance*.

Dmentyev, I. *USA: Imperialists and Anti-Imperialists (The Great Foreign Policy Debate at the Turn of the Century)*. Moscow: Progress
Publishers, 1979.

Dobson, John. *Reticent Expansionism: The Foreign Policy of William McKinley.* Pittsburgh, Pa.: Duquesne University Press, 1988.

Donnelly, Henry Gratton. *The Coming Empire: A Political Satire.* Pamphlet. 1900.

Doyle, Michael W. "Liberalism and World Politics." *American Political Science Review* 80 (December 1986): 1151–69.

Draper, Andrew S. *The Rescue of Cuba: An Episode in the Growth of Free Government.* New York: Silver, Burdett, 1899.

Dressel, C. M. F. *The Cuban-Spanish-American War.* Pamphlet. New York, 1898.

Duke, James T., and Barry L. Johnson. "Protestantism and the Spirit of Democracy." In *Religious Politics in Global and Comparative Perspective,* ed. Thomas M. McFadden, 131–46. Westport, Conn.: Greenwood Press, 1989.

Dulles, Foster Rhea. *America in the Pacific: A Century of Expansion,* 2d ed. New York: De Capo Press, 1969.

Dumont, Frank. *The Cuban Spy: A Comedy-Drama in Five Acts.* Pamphlet. Chicago, 1899.

———. *The Scout of the Philippines: A Military Comedy Drama in Three Acts.* Pamphlet. Chicago, 1899.

Dunn, Dennis J. "Nationalism and Religion in Eastern Europe." Introduction to *Religion and Nationalism in Eastern Europe and the Soviet Union,* ed. Dennis J. Dunn. Boulder, Colo.: Lynne Reinner, 1987.

Earley, Jay. *Transforming Human Culture: Social Evolution and the Planetary Crisis.* Albany: State University of New York Press, 1997.

Edwords, Frederick. "The Religious Character of American Patriotism." *Humanist* 47 (December 1987): 20–24+.

Ekirch, Arthur A., Jr. *Ideas, Ideals, and American Diplomacy: A History of Their Growth and Interaction.* New York: Appleton-Century-Crofts, 1966.

———. *Progressivism in America: A Study of the Era from Theodore Roosevelt to Woodrow Wilson.* New York: New Viewpoints, 1974.

Elazar, Daniel J. *Covenant and Constitutionalism: The Great Frontier and the Matrix of Federal Democracy.* New Brunswick, N.J.: Transaction, 1998.

Everett, Marshall. *Complete Life of William McKinley and Story of His Assassination.* Pamphlet. Self-published, 1901.

Field, James A., Jr. "American Imperialism: The Worst Chapter in Almost Any Book." *American Historical Review* 83 (June 1978): 644–68.

Field, James A., Jr., and George E. Mowry. "Comments [on Schlesinger, "America: Experiment or Destiny?"]." *American Historical Review* 82 (June 1977): 523–30.

Finke, Roger, and Rodney Stark. *The Churching of America 1776–1990: Winners and Losers in Our Religious Economy.* New Brunswick, N.J.: Rutgers University Press, 1992.

Finnemore, Martha. "Constructing Norms of Humanitarian Intervention." In *The Culture of National Security: Norms and Identity in World Politics*, ed. Peter J. Katzenstein, 153–85. New York: Columbia University Press, 1996.

Foner, Eric. *The Story of American Freedom.* New York: W. W. Norton, 1998.

Foner, Philip S. *The Spanish-Cuban-American War and the Birth of American Imperialism, 1895–1902.* 2 vols. New York: Monthly Review Press, 1972.

Fox, Richard Wightman. "The Culture of Liberal Protestant Progressivism, 1875–1925." *Journal of Interdisciplinary History* 23 (Winter 1993): 639–60.

Free America, Free Cuba, Free Philippines: Addresses at a Meeting in Faneuil Hall, March 30, 1901. Boston, Mass.: New England Anti-Imperialist League, 1901.

Freidel, Frank. *The Splendid Little War.* Boston, Mass.: Little, Brown, 1958.

Friedman, Lawrence J. *Inventors of the Promised Land.* New York: Alfred A. Knopf, 1975.

Friedman, Lawrence M. *Total Justice.* New York: Russell Sage Foundation, 1985.

Gadamer, Hans-Georg. *Truth and Method.* 2d edition. New York: Continuum, 1993.

Gastil, Raymond Duncan. *Progress: Critical Thinking about Historical Change.* Westport, Conn.: Praeger, 1993.

Gaston, Charles Robert, ed. *Washington's Farewell Address, Webster's First Bunker Hill Oration, Lincoln's Gettysburg Address* [1906]. New York: Ginn, 1919.

Gaustad, Edwin Scott. *A Religious History of America.* New York: Harper & Row, 1966.

Gellner, Ernest. "Homeland of the Unrevolution." *Daedalus* 122 (Summer 1993): 141–54.

———. "Nations and High Cultures." In *Nationalism,* ed. John Hutchinson and Anthony D. Smith, 63–70. New York: Oxford University Press, 1994.

Gentile, Emilio. "Fascism as Political Religion." *Journal of Contemporary History* 25 (1990): 229–51.

Germino, Dante. *The Inaugural Addresses of American Presidents: The Public Philosophy and Rhetoric.* Lanham, Md.: University Press of America, 1984.

Gerstle, Gary. "The Limits of American Universalism." *American Quarterly* 45 (June 1993): 230–36.

Giddens, Anthony. "The Nation as Power-Container." In *Nationalism,* ed. John Hutchinson and Anthony D. Smith, 34–35. New York: Oxford University Press, 1994.

Glad, Paul W. *McKinley, Bryan, and the People.* New York: J. B. Lippincott, 1964.

Gladden, Washington. *Our Nation and Her Neighbors.* Columbus, Ohio: Quinius & Ridenour, 1898.

Glanville, Albert. *War and the Good of It: The Dangers of Peace.* New York: W. B. Conkey, 1898.

Goudsblom, Johan, Eric Jones, and Stephen Mennell. *The Course of Human History: Economic Growth, Social Process, and Civilization.* Armonk, N. Y.: M. E. Sharpe, 1996.

Gould, Lewis L. *The Spanish-American War and President McKinley.* Lawrence: University Press of Kansas, 1982.

———. *The Presidency of William McKinley.* Lawrence: Regents Press of Kansas, 1980.

Graebner, Norman, ed. *Manifest Destiny.* New York: Bobbs-Merrill, 1968.

Gray, John. "Global Utopias and Clashing Civilizations: Misunderstanding the Present." *International Affairs* 74 (January 1998): 149–63.

Greeley, Andrew. "American Exceptionalism: The Religious Phenomenon." In *Is America Different? A New Look at American Exceptionalism,* ed. Byron E. Shafer, 94–115. Oxford, Eng.: Clarendon Press, 1991.

Greenfeld, Liah. *Nationalism: Five Roads to Modernity.* Cambridge: Harvard University Press, 1992.

——. "Transcending the Nation's Worth." *Daedalus* 122 (Summer 1993): 47–62.

Gregg, David. *Sermon Delivered at Lafayette Avenue Presbyterian Church on Sunday, April 24, 1898: The National Crisis; or God's Purposes Worked Out through International Relations.* Pamphlet. New York, 1898.

Hall, David D. *Worlds of Wonder, Days of Judgment: Popular Religious Belief in Early New England.* Cambridge: Harvard University Press, 1989.

Hall, John A. "Nationalisms: Classified and Explained." *Daedalus* 122 (Summer 1993): 1–28.

Halle, Louis J. *Men and Nations.* Princeton: Princeton University Press, 1962.

Halstead, Murat. *The Life and Distinguished Services of Honorable William McKinley and the Great Issues of 1896.* Philadelphia: Edgewood Publishing, 1896.

Hamilton, Alexander, John Jay, and James Madison. *The Federalist Papers.* With an introduction by Clinton Rossiter. New York: Mentor Books, 1961.

Hammersly, C. H. *"A Play" on the Spanish Cuban War.* Pamphlet. Lynchburg, Va., 1898.

Hanley, Thomas O'Brien, S. J. "Church/State Relations in the American Revolutionary Era." In *America in Theological Perspective*, ed. Thomas M. McFadden, 87–98. New York: Seabury Press, 1976.

Hann, Chris. "The Nation-State, Religion, and Uncivil Society: Two Perspectives From the Periphery." *Daedalus* 126 (September 1997): 27–45.

Hart, Roderick P. *The Political Pulpit.* West Lafayette, Ind.: Purdue University Press, 1977.

Hartman, L. B. *The People of America: Its Civil Polity as Outlined by the Prophets, Its Politico-Religious Mission in the World's Civilization, and Its Need of the Soldier.* Pamphlet. New York, 1899.

Hartz, Louis. *The Liberal Tradition in America* [1955]. With a new introduction by Tom Wicker. New York: Harcourt, Brace & World, 1991.

Hastings, Adrian. *The Construction of Nationhood: Ethnicity, Religion, and Nationalism.* New York: Cambridge University Press, 1997.

Hatch, Nathan O. *The Democratization of American Christianity.* New Haven, Conn.: Yale University Press, 1989.

Hawkins, Mike. *Social Darwinism in European and American Thought, 1860–1945: Nature as Model and Nature as Threat.* New York: Cambridge University Press, 1997.

Hays, Jenny Ward. *The Echo of the Maine.* Pamphlet. San Francisco, 1898.

Heald, Edward Thornton. *The William McKinley Story.* Stark County Historical Society, 1964.

Heald, Morrell, and Lawrence S. Kaplan. *Culture and Diplomacy: The American Experience.* Westport, Conn.: Greenwood Press, 1977.

Healy, David. *U.S. Expansionism: The Imperialist Urge in the 1890s.* Madison: University of Wisconsin Press, 1970.

Heath, Perry Sanford. *President McKinley's Share in the War with Spain.* Pamphlet. Chicago, 1899.

Heclo, Hugh. "The Sixties' False Dawn: Awakenings, Movements, and Post-Modern Policy-Making." *Journal of Policy History* 8 (1991): 34–63.

Heimbach, Alton B. *The Honorable Oluf Pedurson on War with Spain and Expansion in the Philippines.* Pamphlet. New York, 1899.

Henderson, John B. *Speech Delivered before the Pike County Colony of St. Louis, at Its Annual Dinner on February 25, 1899, in Reply to the Toast "Our Nation, State, and County."* Pamphlet. Washington, D.C., 1899.

Henkin, Louis. *Constitutionalism, Democracy, and Foreign Affairs.* New York: Columbia University Press, 1990.

———. "The Universal Declaration and the U.S. Constitution." *P.S.: Political Science and Politics* 31 (September 1998): 512–15.

———. "The Constitution and Other Holy Writ: Human Rights and Divine Commands." In *The Judeo-Christian Tradition and the United States Constitution,* 57–71. Philadelphia: Annenberg Research Institute, 1989.

Herberg, Will. "America's Civil Religion: What It Is and Whence It Comes." In *American Civil Religion,* ed. Russell E. Richey and Donald G. Jones, 76–88. New York: Harper & Row, 1974.

Hirschfeld, Charles. "Brooks Adams and American Nationalism." *American Historical Review* 69 (January 1964): 371–92.

Hertzke, Allen D. *Representing God in Washington: The Role of Religious Lobbies in the American Polity*. Knoxville: University of Tennessee Press, 1988.

Hobson, Richmond P. *Hobson's Story*. Pamphlet. New York, 1898.

Hofstadter, Richard. *Social Darwinism in American Thought, 1860–1915*. Philadelphia: University of Pennsylvania Press, 1944.

———. "Cuba, the Philippines, and Manifest Destiny." In *The Paranoid Style of American Politics and Other Essays*, 145–87. Cambridge: Harvard University Press, 1965.

Hogan, Michael J., and Thomas G. Paterson, eds. *Explaining the History of American Foreign Relations*. New York: Cambridge University Press, 1991.

Holbo, Paul S. "Presidential Leadership in Foreign Affairs: William McKinley and the Turpie-Foraker Amendment." *American Historical Review* 72 (July 1967): 1321–35.

Hollinger, David A. "National Solidarity at the End of the Twentieth Century: Reflections on the United States and Liberal Nationalism." *Journal of American History* 84 (September 1997): 559–69.

Horton, George. *War and Mammon*. Pamphlet. Wausau, Wisc., 1900.

Hudson, Winthrop. *Religion in America*, 4th ed. New York: Macmillan, 1987.

———, ed. *Nationalism and Religion in America: Concepts of American Identity and Mission*. New York: Harper & Row, 1970.

Humphrey, Edward Frank. *Nationalism and Religion in America, 1774–1789* [1924]. New York: Russell & Russell, 1965.

Hunt, Michael H. *Ideology and U.S. Foreign Policy*. New Haven, Conn.: Yale University Press, 1987.

Hunter, James Davison. *Culture Wars: The Struggle To Define America*. New York: BasicBooks, 1991.

Huntington, Samuel P. "The Clash of Civilizations?" *Foreign Affairs* 72 (Summer 1993): 22–49.

———. "American Ideals versus American Institutions." *Political Science Quarterly* 97 (Spring 1982).

Huntington, William R. *Duties of War Time: A Sermon Preached in Grace Church New York, on the Sunday after the Breaking Out of Hostilities between the United States and Spain, April 24th, 1898*. Pamphlet. New York, 1898.

Hutchison, William R. Introduction to *Many Are Chosen: Divine Elections and Western Nationalism*, ed. William R. Hutchison and Hartmut Lehman, 5–28. Minneapolis, Minn.: Fortress Press, 1994.

Hyde, A. A. *Dewey's Victory in Rhyme*. Pamphlet. Buffalo Mills, Pa., 1898.

Ikenberry, G. John. *After Victory: Institutions, Strategic Restraint, and the Rebuilding of Order after Major Wars*. Princeton: Princeton University Press, 2001.

In the Philippines: A Part of Greater America. Boston, Mass.: Perry Mason, 1901.

Iriye, Akira. "Exceptionalism Revisited." *Reviews in American History* 16 (June 1988): 291–97.

——. *The Cambridge History of American Foreign Relations*, vol. 3, *The Globalizing of America, 1913–1945*. New York: Cambridge University Press, 1993.

Jacobson, Matthew Frye. *Barbarian Virtues: The United States Encounters Foreign Peoples at Home and Abroad, 1876–1917*. New York: Hill & Wang, 2000.

James, William. *The Writings of William James, a Comprehensive Edition*. Edited with introduction and new preface by John J. McDermott. Chicago: University of Chicago Press, 1977.

——. *Writings, 1902–1910*. New York: Library of America, 1987.

Janes, Lewis G. *Our Nation's Peril: Social Ideals and Social Progress*. Pamphlet. Boston, Mass., 1899.

Jayne, Madison M. *Denby on Bryan*. Pamphlet. Bay St. Louis, Miss., 1900.

Jefferson, Thomas. *The Life and Selected Writings of Thomas Jefferson*. Edited and with introduction by Adrienne Koch and William Peden. New York: Modern Library, 1972.

Jepperson, Ronald L., Alexander Wendt, and Peter J. Katzenstein. "Norms, Identity, and Culture in National Security." In *The Culture of National Security: Norms and Identity in World Politics*, ed. Peter J. Katzenstein, 33–75. New York: Columbia University Press, 1996.

Jervis, Robert. *Perception and Misperception in International Politics*. Princeton: Princeton University Press, 1976.

John, Robert S. *The War in Brief*. Pamphlet. 1898.

Johnson, Edward A. *History of Negro Soldiers in the Spanish-American War, and Other Items of Interest* [Raleigh, N.C.: Capitol Printing, 1899]. Reprint, Johnson Reprint, 1970.

Johnston, Alastair Iain. *Cultural Realism: Strategic Culture and Grand Strategy in Chinese History*. Princeton: Princeton University Press, 1995.

Johnston, Douglas. "Beyond Power Politics." Introduction to *Religion, the Missing Dimension of Statecraft*, ed. Douglas Johnston and Cynthia Sampson, 3–7. Foreword by Jimmy Carter. New York: Oxford University Press, 1994.

Jordan, David Starr. *Lest We Forget: An Address before the Graduating Class of 1898, Leland Stanford University on May 25, 1898*. Pamphlet. Palo Alto, Calif., 1898.

———. *The Question of the Philippines: A Speech before the Graduate Club of Leland Stanford Junior University*. Pamphlet. Palo Alto, Calif., 1899.

Juergensmeyer, Mark. *The New Cold War? Religious Nationalism Confronts the Secular State*. Berkeley: University of California Press, 1993.

———. "Why Religious Nationalists Are Not Fundamentalists." *Religion* 23 (January 1993): 85–92.

Kammen, Michael. "The Problem of American Exceptionalism: A Reconsideration." *American Quarterly* 45 (March 1993): 1–43.

Katzenstein, Peter J. "Coping with Terrorism: Norms and Internal Security in Germany and Japan." In *Ideas and Foreign Policy: Beliefs, Institutions, and Political Change*, ed. Judith Goldstein and Robert O. Keohane, 265–95. Ithaca, N.Y.: Cornell University Press, 1993.

———. "Alternative Perspectives on National Security." Introduction to *The Culture of National Security: Norms and Identity in World Politics*, ed. Peter J. Katzenstein, 1–32. New York: Columbia University Press, 1996.

Kedourie, Elie. *Nationalism*, 4th ed. Cambridge, Mass.: Blackwell. 1993.

Kelley, Robert. "Ideology and Political Culture from Jefferson to Nixon." *American Historical Review* 82 (June 1977): 531–62.

Kidd, Benjamin. *Social Evolution*. New York: Macmillan, 1894.

King, Rev. James Marcus, *The Situation and Justification of the Nation at War with Spain: A Sermon at the Union Methodist Episcopal Church, New York*. Pamphlet. New York, 1898.

King, James McGuire. "An Enthusiasm for Humanity: The Social Emphasis on Religion and Its Accommodation in Protestant Theology."

In *Religion in Twentieth Century American Intellectual Life*, ed. Michael J. Lacey, 49–77. New York: Cambridge University Press, 1991.

Kissinger, Henry. *Diplomacy*. New York: Simon & Schuster, 1994.

Kitromilides, Paschalis M. "'Imagined Communities' and the Origins of the National Question in the Balkans." *European History Quarterly* 19 (1989): 149–94.

Klunk, Brian. *Consensus and the American Mission*. Lanham, Md.: University Press of America, 1986.

Koch, Adrienne. *Power, Morals, and the Founding Fathers: Essays on the Interpretation of the American Enlightenment*. Ithaca, N.Y.: Cornell University Press, 1961.

Kohn, Hans. *American Nationalism: An Interpretive Essay*. New York: Macmillan, 1957.

Koschmann, J. Victor. "The Nationalism of Cultural Uniqueness." *American Historical Review* 102 (June 1997): 758–68.

Kosmin, Barry A., and Seymour P. Lachman. *One Nation under God: Religion in Contemporary American Society*. New York: Harmony Books, 1993.

Kowert, Paul, and Jeffrey Legro. "Norms, Identity, and Their Limits: A Theoretical Reprise." In *The Culture of National Security*, ed. Peter J. Katzenstein, 451–97. New York: Columbia University Press, 1996.

Krakow, Knud. "Response [to Moorhead]." In *Many Are Chosen: Divine Elections and Western Nationalism*, ed. William R. Hutchison and Hartmut Lehman, 161–72. Minneapolis, Minn.: Fortress Press, 1994.

Kramnick, Isaac, ed. *The Portable Enlightenment Reader*. New York: Penguin Books, 1995.

Kramnick, Isaac, and R. Laurence Moore. *The Godless Constitution: The Case against Religious Correctness*. New York: W. W. Norton, 1996.

Krasner, Stephen D. "Westphalia and All That." In *Ideas and Foreign Policy: Beliefs, Institutions, and Political Change*, ed. Judith Goldstein and Robert O. Keohane, 235–64. Ithaca, N.Y.: Cornell University Press, 1993.

Krishna, Daya. "God and the National State." *Diogenes* 129 (September 1985): 91–100.

Kuklick, Bruce. "John Dewey, American Theology, and Scientific Politics." In *Religion and Twentieth Century American Intellectual Life*, ed. Michael J. Lacey, 78–93. New York: Cambridge University Press, 1991.

LaFeber, Walter. *The New Empire: An Interpretation of American Expansion, 1860–1898*. Ithaca, N.Y.: Cornell University Press, 1963.

———. "Comments [on Field, "American Imperialism: The Worst Chapter in Almost Any Book"]." *American Historical Review* 83 (June 1978): 669–72.

———. "The Constitution and United States Foreign Policy: An Interpretation." *Journal of American History* 74 (December 1987): 695–717.

———. *The Cambridge History of American Foreign Relations*, vol. 2, *The American Search for Opportunity, 1865–1913*. New York: Cambridge University Press, 1993.

Langan, John. "Nationalism, Ethnic Conflict, and Religion." *Theological Studies* 56 (March 1995): 122–36.

Laqueur, Walter, and Barry Rubin, eds. *The Human Rights Reader*. Revised edition. New York: Meridian Books, 1989.

Larson, Edward J. *Summer of the Gods: The Scopes Trial and America's Continuing Debate over Science and Religion*. New York: BasicBooks, 1997.

Las Casas, Bishop. *An Historical and True Account of the Cruel Massacre and Slaughter of Twenty Millions of People in the West Indies by the Spaniards* [1620]. New York: JBoller, 1898.

Leech, Margaret. *In the Days of McKinley*. New York: Harper & Brothers, 1959.

Leo, Henry. *The Disaster to the Battleship* Maine *and the Cuban Warfare*. Pamphlet. Chicago, 1898.

Lester, Charles. *A Dangerous Mission: A Story of the Philippines*. Pamphlet. Cincinnati, 1900.

Levy, Leonard W. *The Establishment Clause: Religion and the First Amendment*. 2d ed. New York: Macmillan, 1994.

Lewis, Leon. *The Avengers of the Maine: The Story of the Havana Assassins*. Pamphlet. New York, 1898.

Lienesch, Michael. *Redeeming America: Piety and Politics in the New Christian Right*. Chapel Hill: University of North Carolina Press, 1993.

———. "The Origins of the Christian Right: Early Fundamentalism as a Political Movement." In *Sojourners in the Wilderness: The Christian*

Right in Comparative Perspective, ed. Corwin E. Smidt and James M. Penning, 3–20. Lanham, Md.: Rowman & Littlefield, 1997.

Lindholm, Charles, and John A. Hall. "Is the United States Falling Apart?" *Daedalus* 126 (September 1997): 183–209.

Lipset, Seymour Martin. "American Exceptionalism Reaffirmed." In *Is America Different? A New Look at American Exceptionalism*, ed. Byron E. Shafer, 1–45. Oxford, Eng.: Clarendon Press, 1991.

———. *American Exceptionalism: A Double-Edged Sword*. New York: W. W. Norton, 1996.

Little, David. *From State Church to Pluralism: A Protestant Interpretation of Religion in American History*. Chicago: Aldine, 1962.

———. "The Origins of Perplexity: Civil Religion and Moral Belief in the Thought of Thomas Jefferson." In *American Civil Religion*, ed. Russell E. Richey and Donald G. Jones, 185–210. New York: Harper & Row, 1974.

Little, Frank H. "The Radical Reformation and the American Experience." In *America in Theological Perspective*, ed. Thomas M. McFadden, 71–86. New York: Seabury Press, 1976.

Loades, David. "The Origins of English Protestant Nationalism." In *Religion and National Identity*, ed. Stuart Mews, 297–307. Oxford, Eng.: Basil Blackwell, 1982.

Lodge, Henry Cabot. *The War with Spain*. New York: Harper & Brothers, 1899.

Long, Charles H. "Civil Rights–Civil Religion: Visible People and Invisible Religion." In *American Civil Religion*, ed. Russell E. Richey and Donald G. Jones, 211–21. New York: Harper & Row, 1974.

Luttwak, Edward. "The Missing Foundation." In *Religion: The Missing Dimension of Statecraft*, ed. Douglas Johnston and Cynthia Sampson, 8–19. Foreword by Jimmy Carter. New York: Oxford University Press, 1994.

Lyster, Winfred Lee, chairman, National Society of the Colonial Dames of America. *A Memorial to the Soldiers and Sailors of the United States Who Gave up Their Lives for Their Country in the War of 1898*. Pamphlet. Springfield, Mass., 1902.

Macauley, Clay. *A Straightforward Tale*. Pamphlet. Boston, Mass., 1899.

Maguire, Daniel C. "Catholic Ethics with an American Accent." In *America in Theological Perspective*, ed. Thomas M. McFadden, 13–36. New York: Seabury Press, 1976.

Mahan, Alfred T. *Lessons of the War with Spain and Other Articles* [1899]. Freeport, New York: Books for Libraries Press, 1970.

———. *Mahan on Naval Strategy: Selections from the Writings of Rear Admiral Alfred Thayer Mahan.* Edited with an introduction by John B. Hattendorf. Annapolis, Md.: Naval Institute Press, 1991.

Malone, Dumas, and Basil Rauch. *The New Nation, 1865–1917.* New York: Appleton-Century-Crofts, 1960.

Mandelbaum, Michael. *The Ideas That Conquered the World: Peace, Democracy, and Free Markets in the Twenty-first Century.* New York: Public Affairs, 2002.

Mann, Michael. "Nation-States in Europe and Other Continents: Diversifying, Developing, Not Dying." *Daedalus* 122 (Summer 1993): 115–40.

Mansfield, John H. "The Religious Clauses of the First Amendment and Foreign Relations." *DePaul Law Review* 36 (1986): 1–40.

Marburg, Theodore. *Expansion.* New York: John Murphy, 1900.

Marks, George P., III, ed. *The Black Press Views American Imperialism, 1898–1900* [1900]. With a preface by William Loren Katz. New York: Arno Press, 1971.

Marley, J. W. J. *Our Youthful Patriots: Patriotic Entertainment for Juvenile Performers.* Pamphlet. New York, 1899.

Marsden, George M. "Response to Miller." In *Religion and the Public Good: A Bicentennial Forum*, ed. William Lee Miller et al., 36–40. Macon, Ga.: Mercer University Press, 1988.

Martin, James Vernon. *Expansion: Our Flag Unstained.* St. Louis: Self-published, 1900.

Marty, Martin E. *The Infidel: Freethought and American Religion.* New York: Meridian Books, 1961.

———. "Two Kinds of Two Kinds of Civil Religion." In *American Civil Religion*, ed. Russell E. Richey and Donald G. Jones, 139–57. New York: Harper & Row, 1974.

———. *Modern American Religion*, vol. 1, *The Irony of It All, 1893–1919.* Chicago: University of Chicago Press, 1986.

———. *Modern American Religion*, vol. 3, *Under God, Indivisible, 1941–1960.* Chicago: University of Chicago Press, 1996.

———. *The One and the Many: America's Struggle for the Common Good.* Cambridge: Harvard University Press, 1997.

Mason, J. Milton. *Armageddon*. Pamphlet. Kansas City: Self-published, 1900.

Massachusetts Reform Club. *Report of the Committee of the Massachusetts Reform Club Appointed to Collect Testimony in Relation to the Spanish-American War, 1898–1899*. Pamphlet. Boston, Mass., 1899.

Matthews, Nathan, Jr. *Oration before the City Authorities of Boston on the Fourth of July*. Boston, Mass.: Municipal Printing Office, 1899.

Mawhinney, John J., S. J. "H. Richard Niebuhr and Reshaping American Christianity." In *America in Theological Perspective*, ed. Thomas M. McFadden, 140–62. New York: Seabury Press, 1976.

May, Ernest R. *Imperial Democracy: The Emergence of America as a Great Power*. New York: Harcourt, Brace & World, 1961.

———. *American Imperialism: A Speculative Essay*. New York: Atheneum, 1968.

McCormick, James M. *American Foreign Policy and American Values*. Itasca, Ill.: F. E. Peacock, 1985.

McCullough, J. G. *The Spanish War: Address before the Reunion Society of Vermont Officers at Montpelier*. Pamphlet. 1898.

McDougall, Walter A. *Promised Land, Crusader State: The American Encounter with the World since 1776*. New York: Houghton Mifflin, 1997.

McGerr, Michael. "The Price of a 'New Transnational History.'" *American Historical Review* 96 (October 1991): 1056–72.

McKim, Robert, and Jeff McMahan, eds. *The Morality of Nationalism*. New York: Oxford University Press, 1997.

McNamara, Robert S., and James G. Blight. *Wilson's Ghost: Reducing the Risk of Conflict, Killing, and Catastrophe in the Twenty-first Century*. New York: Public Affairs, 2001.

McWilliams, Wilson Carey. *The Idea of Fraternity in America*. Berkeley: University of California Press, 1973.

Mead, Sidney. *The Lively Experiment: The Shaping of Christianity in America*. New York: Harper & Row, 1963.

———. "The Nation with the Soul of a Church." In *American Civil Religion*, ed. Russell E. Richey and Donald G. Jones, 45–75. New York: Harper & Row, 1974.

———. *The Nation with the Soul of a Church*. Macon, Ga.: Mercer University Press, 1975.

Mead, Walter Russell. *Special Providence: American Foreign Policy and How It Changed the World*. New York: Alfred A. Knopf, 2001.

Mearshimer, John J. "The False Promise of International Institutions." *International Security* 19 (Winter 1994/1995): 5–49.

Merk, Frederick. *Manifest Destiny and Mission in American History: A Reinterpretation*. New York: Vintage Books, 1966.

Memorial to the United States Senate with Respect to the Spanish Treaty. Pamphlet. 1899.

Mercer, George Gluyas. *Patriotism, Prestige, and the Flag*. Pamphlet. Boston, Mass., 1899.

Metcalf, Henry B. *A Nation's Crime against Her Own Soldiers: An Address before the National Temperance Society and Publication House*. Pamphlet. Ocean Grove, N.J., 1899.

Milkis, Sidney M., and Michael Nelson. *The American Presidency: Origins and Development, 1776–1990*. Washington D.C.: CQ Press, 1990.

Mill, John Stuart. *On Liberty* [1859]. Edited with an introduction by Gertrude Himmelfarb. New York: Penguin Books, 1985.

Miller, Perry, ed. *The American Puritans: Their Prose and Poetry*. New York: Columbia University Press, 1956.

Miller, Richard H. *American Imperialism in 1898: The Quest for National Fulfillment*. New York: John Wiley & Sons, 1970.

Miller, William Lee. *The First Liberty: Religion and the American Republic*. New York: Alfred A. Knopf, 1986.

———. "Religion and the Constitution." In *Religion and the Public Good: A Bicentennial Forum*, ed. William Lee Miller et al., 1–22. Macon, Ga.: Mercer University Press, 1988.

———. *Arguing about Slavery: John Quincy Adams and the Great Battle in the United States Congress*. New York: Vintage Books, 1995.

Millis, Walter. *The Martial Spirit: A Study of Our War with Spain*. New York: Viking Press, 1931.

Mills, William H. *The Purpose of the Nation in the Present War*. San Francisco: Murdock Press, 1898.

Milosz, Czeslaw. "On Nationalism." *Partisan Review* 59 (Winter 1992): 14–20.

Moffat, James Stanley. *A Brief History of the Conflict between the United States and Spain*. Pamphlet. Eustice, Fla., 1899.

Montgomery, D. H. *The Leading Facts of American History*. Pamphlet. Boston, Mass., 1899.

Monroe Doctrine, The: A Political and Diplomatic Treatise. Pamphlet. New York, 1898.

Moore, R. Laurence. *Religious Outsiders and the Making of Americans*. New York: Oxford University Press, 1986.

Moorhead, James M. "The American Israel: Protestant Tribalism and Universal Mission." In *Many Are Chosen: Divine Elections and Western Nationalism*, ed. William R. Hutchison and Hartmut Lehman, 145–66. Minneapolis, Minn.: Fortress Press, 1994.

Morgan, Edmund S. *The Puritan Dilemma: The Story of John Winthrop*. Boston, Mass.: Little, Brown, 1958.

———. *Visible Saints: The History of a Puritan Idea*. Ithaca, N.Y.: Cornell University Press, 1963.

Morgan, H. Wayne. *William McKinley and His America*. Syracuse, N.Y.: Syracuse University Press, 1963.

———. *America's Road to Empire: The War with Spain and Overseas Expansion*. New York: John Wiley & Sons, 1965.

Morgan, Richard E. *The Supreme Court and Religion*. New York: Free Press, 1972.

Morgenthau, Hans J. *Politics among Nations: The Struggle for Power and Peace*. Brief edition, revised by Kenneth W. Thompson. New York: McGraw-Hill, 1985.

———. "The Mainsprings of American Foreign Policy." *American Political Science Review* 44 (December 1950): 833–54.

———. *The Purpose of American Politics*. With an introduction by Kenneth W. Thompson. Lanham, Md.: University Press of America, 1960.

Morris, Charles. *The War with Spain*. Philadelphia.: J. B. Lippincott, 1899.

Moss, Frank. *America's Mission to Save Humanity*. Boston, Mass.: Stratford, 1919.

Muller, Dorothea. "Josiah Strong and American Nationalism: A Reevaluation." *Journal of American History* 53 (December 1966): 487–503.

Musicant, Ivan. *Empire by Default: The Spanish-American War and the Dawn of the American Century*. New York: Henry Holt, 1998.

Musick, John R. *Lights and Shadows of Our War with Spain: A Series of Historical Sketches, Incidents, Anecdotes, and Personal Experiences in the Hispano-American War.* Pamphlet. New York, 1898.

Nairn, Tom. "Internationalism and the Second Coming." *Daedalus* 122 (Summer 1993): 155–70.

Nardin, Terry, and David R. Mapel, eds. *Traditions of International Ethics.* New York: Cambridge University Press 1992.

Nathan, James A., and James K. Oliver. *Foreign Policy Making and the American Political System.* 3rd ed. Baltimore: Johns Hopkins University Press, 1994.

National Society of the Colonial Dames of America. *A Memorial to the Soldiers and Sailors of the United States Who Gave Up Their Lives for Their Country in the War of 1898–1899 with Spain.* Pamphlet. Springfield, Mass., 1902.

Nau, Henry. *At Home Abroad: Identity and Power in American Foreign Policy.* Ithaca, N.Y.: Cornell University Press, 2002.

Neal, Marie Augusta, SND. "Civil Religion, Theology, and Politics in America." In *America in Theological Perspective*, ed. Thomas M. McFadden, 91–122. New York: Seabury Press, 1976.

Nelles, H. V. "American Exceptionalism: A Double-Edged Sword." *American Historical Review* 102 (June 1997), 749–57.

New England Anti-Imperialist League. *Free America, Free Cuba, Free Philippines: Addresses at a Meeting in Faneuil Hall, Saturday, March 30, 1901.* Pamphlet. Boston, Mass., 1901.

Niebuhr, H. Richard. *The Kingdom of God in America.* New York: Willett, Clark, 1937.

Niebuhr, Reinhold. *The Irony of American History.* New York: Charles Scribner's Sons, 1954.

——. *The Nature and Destiny of Man.* 2 vols. New York: Charles Scribner's Sons, 1964.

Nincic, Miroslav. *Democracy and Foreign Policy: The Fallacy of Political Realism.* New York: Columbia University Press, 1992.

Nolan, James L., Jr. *The American Culture Wars: Current Contests and Future Prospects.* Charlottesville: University Press of Virginia, 1996.

Nolan, Mary. "Against Exceptionalisms." *American Historical Review* 102 (June 1997): 769–74.

Norgren, Jill, and Serena Nanda. *American Cultural Pluralism and Law*, 2d ed. Westport, Conn.: Praeger, 1996.

Noyes, Theodore W. *Oriental America and Its Problems*. Pamphlet. Washington, D.C., 1903.

Nunez, Joseph A. *The Fragmented* "Maine" *Shatters Proud Spain*. Pamphlet. 1898.

O'Brien, Conor Cruise. *God Land: Reflections on Religion and Nationalism*. Cambridge: Harvard University Press, 1988.

Offner, John L. *An Unwanted War: The Diplomacy of the United States and Spain Over Cuba, 1895–1898*. Chapel Hill: University of North Carolina Press, 1992.

———. "United States Politics and the 1898 War over Cuba." In *The Crisis of 1898: Colonial Redistribution and Nationalist Mobilization*, ed. Angel Smith and Emma Dávila-Cox, 18–43. New York: St. Martin's Press, 1999.

Olcott, Charles S. *The Life of William McKinley*. 2 vols. New York: Houghton Mifflin, 1916.

Oldfield, John. "Remembering the *Maine:* The United States, 1898, and Sectional Reconciliation." In *The Crisis of 1898: Colonial Redistribution and Nationalist Mobilization*, ed. Angel Smith and Emma Dávila-Cox, 45–64. New York: St. Martin's Press, 1999.

Oomen, T. K. "The Shifting Salience of Religion in the Construction of Nationalism: The Indian Experience." Working paper for Conference on Nation, National Identity, and Nationalism, University of California at Berkeley, September 10–12, 1992.

O'Toole, G. J. A. *The Spanish War: An American Epic, 1898*. New York: W. W. Norton, 1984.

Paine, Thomas. *Common Sense and Other Writings* [1776]. Edited with an introduction by Nelson F. Adkins. New York: Macmillan, 1953.

Parenti, Michael. *The Anti-Communist Impulse*. New York: Random House, 1969.

Parker, George T. *Official Program of the National Peace Jubilee*. Washington, D.C.: Thomas W. Chadwick, 1899.

Pérez, Louis A., Jr. "Derailing Cuban Nationalism and Asserting U.S. Hegemony." In *Major Problems in American Foreign Relations*, vol. 1, *To 1920*. 4th edition, ed. Thomas G. Paterson and Dennis Merrill, 412–17. Lexington, Mass.: D. C. Heath, 1995.

——. *The War of 1898: The United States and Cuba in History and Historiography*. Chapel Hill: University of North Carolina Press, 1998.

Perkins, Dexter. *Foreign Policy and the American Spirit: Essays by Dexter Perkins*. Ed. Glyndon G. Van Deusen and Richard C. Wade. Ithaca, N.Y.: Cornell University Press, 1957.

——. *The Evolution of American Foreign Policy*. New York: Oxford University Press, 1966.

——. "Defense of Commerce and Ideals." In *Major Problems in American Foreign Relations*, vol. 1, *To 1920*. 4th edition, ed. Thomas G. Paterson and Dennis Merrill, 183–90. Lexington, Mass.: D. C. Heath, 1995.

Pettegew, John. "'The Soldier's Faith': Turn-of-the-Century Memory of the Civil War and the Emergence of American Nationalism." *Journal of Contemporary History* 31 (1996): 49–73.

Pew, William Andrews. *The War with Spain and Its Aftermath*. Pamphlet. Salem, Mass., 1927.

Pfaff, William. *Barbarian Sentiments: How the American Century Ends*. New York: Hill & Wang, 1989.

——. *The Wrath of Nations: Civilization and the Furies of Nationalism*. New York: Simon & Schuster, 1993.

Phillips, Kevin. *William McKinley*. New York: Henry Holt, 2003.

Piehler, G. Kurt. *Remembering War the American Way*. Washington, D.C.: Smithsonian Institution Press, 1995.

Polhamus, W. H. *Our Attitude toward the Philippines: Does It Accord with Our View of Self-Government?* Pamphlet. 1899.

Pratt, Julius W. *Expansionists of 1898: The Acquisition of Hawaii and the Spanish Islands*. Baltimore, Md.: Johns Hopkins University Press, 1936.

Price, W. H. Expansion: *Another View, or How It Saves America*. Pamphlet. Chicago, 1899.

Priest, W. Edwin. *Spain and Her Lost Colonies*. Pamphlet. Washington, D.C., 1898.

Raboteau, Albert J. "Exodus, Ethiopia, and Racial Messianism: Texts and Contexts of African-American Chosenness." In *Many Are Chosen: Divine Elections and Western Nationalism*, ed. William R. Hutchison and Hartmut Lehman, 175–201. Minneapolis, Minn.: Fortress Press, 1994.

Rainsford, W. S. *Our Duty to Civilization, or, Who Is My Neighbor.* Pamphlet. New York, 1898.

Rakove, Jack N. *Original Meanings: Politics and Ideas in the Making of the Constitution.* New York: Alfred A. Knopf, 1996.

Randolph, Carman F. *Constitutional Aspects of Annexation.* Pamphlet. 1899.

————. *Some Observations on the Status of Cuba.* Pamphlet. 1900.

Rathborne, St. George. *A Charge for a Bride: A Romance in the Philippines.* Pamphlet. New York, 1898.

————. *A Sailor's Sweetheart.* Pamphlet. New York, 1898.

Rawson, Jonathon A., Jr. *Our Army and Navy: What You Want to Know about Them.* Pamphlet. New York, 1898.

Reichley, A. James. *Religion in American Public Life.* Washington D.C.: Brookings Institution, 1985.

Reid, Whitelaw. *Making Peace with Spain: The Diary of Whitelaw Reid, September–December, 1898* [1898]. Edited by H. Wayne Morgan. Austin: University of Texas Press, 1965.

Renan, Ernest. "Qu'est-ce qu'une nation?" In *Nationalism*, ed. John Hutchinson and Anthony D. Smith, 17–18. New York: Oxford University Press, 1994.

Republican National Committee. *Commercial Expansion: Importance of Manila as a Market for Supplying the Needs of Eight Hundred Millions of People in Its Immediate Vicinity.* Pamphlet. New York, 1900.

————. *Democratic Expansion.* Pamphlet. New York, 1900.

————. *Shamming an Issue.* Pamphlet. New York, 1900.

Republican Policy Triumphs: Leaders of the Party Attest the Wisdom of the President's Administration. Anonymous pamphlet. New York, 1898.

Reuter, Frank T. *Catholic Influence on American Colonial Policies, 1898–1904.* Austin: University of Texas Press, 1967.

Rhodes, Edward. "Sea Change: Interest-Based vs. Cultural-Cognitive Accounts of Strategic Choice in the 1890s." *Security Studies* 5 (Summer 1996): 73–124.

Rice, W. H. *Expansion: Another View, or How It Saves America.* Pamphlet. Chicago, 1899.

Richards, Julian W. *A Handbook of the Spanish-American War of 1898 and the Insurrection in the Philippines.* Pamphlet. Cedar Rapids, Iowa, 1899.

Richey, Russell E., and Donald G. Jones. "The Civil Religion Debate." In *American Civil Religion*, ed. Russell E. Richey and Donald G. Jones, 3–18. New York: Harper & Row, 1974.

Rohrlich, Paul Egon. "Economic Culture and Foreign Policy: The Cognitive Analysis of Economic Policy Making." *International Organization* 41 (Winter 1987): 61–92.

Roof, Wade Clark. "The New Fundamentalism: Rebirth of Political Religion in America." In *Prophetic Religion and Politics: Religion and the Political Order*, ed. Jeffrey K. Hadden and Anson Shupe, 18–34. New York: Paragon House, 1986.

Roof, Wade Clark, and William McKinney. *American Mainline Religion: Its Changing Shape and Future*. New Brunswick, N.J.: Rutgers University Press, 1987.

Ross, Barclay M. *Don Fernandez, the Spanish Spy: A Story of the War with Spain*. Pamphlet. New York, 1899.

Rubens, Harry. *The Dominion of the United States*. Chicago: Gunthorp-Warren Printing, 1895.

Rudolph, Susanne Hoeber, and Lloyd I. Rudolph. "Modern Hate." *New Republic*, March 22, 1993, 24–29.

Ruggie, John Gerard. "What Makes the World Hang Together? Neoutilitarianism and the Social Constructivist Challenge. In *Essential Readings in World Politics*, ed. Karen Mingst and Jack Snyder, 91–119. New York: W. W. Norton, 2001.

Salter, William M. *A New Nation, and a New Duty*. Pamphlet. Philadelphia, 1898.

———. *Imperialism*. Pamphlet. Chicago: Anti-Imperialist League, 1899.

———. *The New Militarism*. Pamphlet. Philadelphia, 1899.

Saunders, Ernest C. *Suggestions to Christians: An Open Letter*. Pamphlet. New York, 1901.

Savage, Minot Judson. *Civilization and War*. Pamphlet. New York, 1898.

Savary, John. *Uncle Sam, the Real and the Ideal: A Dissertation*. Pamphlet. Washington, D.C., 1899.

Schaver, Frederick. "Forcing, Enforcing, and Reinforcing: The Problem of Religion and the State." In *Religion and Politics*, ed. Fred E. Bauman and Kenneth Jansen, 1–16. Charlottesville: University Press of Virginia, 1989.

Schirmer, Daniel B. *Republic or Empire: American Resistance to the Philippine War.* Cambridge, Mass.: Schenkman, 1972.

Schlesinger, Arthur M., Jr. "America: Experiment or Destiny." *American Historical Review* 82 (June 1977): 505–22.

Schneider, Mary L. "A Catholic Perspective on American Civil Religion." In *America in Theological Perspective*, ed. Thomas M. McFadden, 123–39. New York: Seabury Press, 1976.

Schurz, Carl. *American Imperialism: Convocation Address at the University of Chicago, January 4, 1899.* Pamphlet. Chicago, 1899.

———. *For American Principles and American Honor.* Pamphlet. New York, 1900.

———. *For the Republic of Washington and Lincoln.* Pamphlet. Chicago, 1900.

Schwartz, Benjamin. "Culture, Modernity, and Nationalism–Further Reflections." *Daedalus* 122 (Summer 1993): 207–26.

Schwartz, Regina M. "Nations and Nationalism: Adultery in the House of David." *Critical Inquiry* 19 (Autumn 1992): 131–50.

Scott, W. H. *An Appeal to the Negroes in the Pivotal States.* Pamphlet. Woburn, Mass., 1900.

Seaman, Abel. *In the Trenches: A Drama of the Cuban War.* Pamphlet. Chicago, 1898.

Selznick, Philip. *The Moral Commonwealth: Social Theory and the Promise of Community.* Berkeley: University of California Press, 1992.

Seward, George G. *The Treaty with Spain: Should It Be Ratified?* New York: Reform Club, 1898.

Shafer, Byron E. "What Is the American Way? Four Themes in Search of Their Next Incarnation." In *Is America Different? A New Look at American Exceptionalism*, ed. Byron E. Shafer, 222–61. Oxford, Eng.: Clarendon Press, 1991.

Shklar, Judith N. 1998. *Redeeming American Political Thought.* Ed. Stanley Hoffman and Dennis F. Thompson, with foreword by Dennis F. Thompson. Chicago: University of Chicago Press, 1998.

Simmons, H. M., Rev. *History of Our Philippine Relations as Told in Official Records: Address at the Anti-Imperialist Mass Meeting in Minneapolis, 12 December 1899.* Pamphlet. 1899.

Sinclair, Upton. *A Gauntlet of Fire.* New York: Street & Smith, 1899.

———. *A Soldier Monk*. New York: Street & Smith, 1899.

———. *Saved by the Enemy*. New York: Street & Smith, 1898.

Smith, Angel, and Emma Dávila-Cox. "1898 and the Making of the New Twentieth-Century World Order." In *The Crisis of 1898: Colonial Redistribution and Nationalist Mobilization*, ed. Angel Smith and Emma Dávila-Cox, 1–17. New York: St. Martin's Press, 1999.

Smith, Ephraim. "William McKinley's Enduring Legacy: The Historiographical Debate on the Taking of the Philippine Islands." In *Crucible of Empire: The Spanish-American War and Its Aftermath*, ed. James C. Bradford. Annapolis, Md.: Naval Institute Press, 1993.

Smith, Goldwin. *Commonwealth or Empire: A Bystander's View of the Question*. New York: Macmillan, 1902.

Smith, Joseph. *The Spanish-American War: Conflict in the Caribbean and the Pacific, 1895-1902*. New York: Longman, 1994.

Smith, Rogers M. *Civic Ideals: Conflicting Visions of Citizenship in U.S. History*. New Haven, Conn.: Yale University Press, 1997.

Smith, Tony. *America's Mission: The United States and the Worldwide Struggle for Democracy in the Twentieth Century*. Princeton: Princeton University Press, 1994.

Snyder, Jack. *Myths of Empire: Domestic Politics and International Ambition*. Ithaca, N.Y.: Cornell University Press, 1991.

Sorauf, Frank J. *The Wall of Separation: The Constitutional Politics of Church and State*. Princeton: Princeton University Press, 1976.

Stark, Rodney, and William Sims Bainbridge. *A Theory of Religion*. With a new foreword by Jeffrey K. Hadden. New Brunswick, N.J.: Rutgers University Press, 1987.

Stephanson, Anders. *Manifest Destiny: American Expansionism and the Empire of Right*. New York: Hill & Wang, 1995.

Stephens, Lester D. "Joseph Le Conte's Evolutional Idealism: A Lamarckian View of Cultural History." *Journal of the History of Ideas* 39 (July–September, 1978): 465–80.

Sternberg, George M. *Sanitary Lessons of the War*. Pamphlet. Philadelphia, 1899.

Stillman, James W. *A Protest against the President's War of "Criminal Aggression."* Boston, Mass.: George H. Ellis, 1899.

Storey, Moorfield. *'Marked Severities' in Philippine Warfare: An Analysis of the Law and Facts Bearing on the Action and Utterances of*

President Roosevelt and Secretary Root. Pamphlet. Boston, Mass., 1902.

———. *The Importance to America of Philippine Independence: Address before the Harvard Democratic Club, 24 October 1904.* Pamphlet. Boston, Mass.: New England Anti-Imperialist League, 1904.

Strathmore, Professor. *History of the United States and Spain.* Pamphlet. New York, 1898.

Street, George G. *Our Flag.* Pamphlet. Buffalo, N.Y., 1899.

Strong, Josiah. *The New Era; or, The Coming Kingdom.* New York: Baker & Taylor, 1893.

———. *Expansionism under New-World Conditions.* New York: Baker & Taylor, 1900.

Sumner, William Graham. *What the Social Classes Owe Each Other* [1884]. Caldwell, Idaho: Caxton Printers, 1961.

———. *The Conquest of the United States by Spain: A Lecture before the Phi Beta Kappa Society of Yale University, January 16, 1899.* Pamphlet. Boston, Mass., 1899.

———. *The Predominant Issue.* Pamphlet. Burlington, Vt., 1901.

———. *Social Darwinism: Selected Essays of William Graham Sumner.* Edited with an introduction by Stow Persons. Englewood Cliffs, N.J.: Prentice-Hall, 1963.

Swatos, William H., Jr. "The Kingdom of God and the World of Man: The Problem of Religious Politics." In *Religious Politics in Global and Comparative Perspective,* ed. William H. Swatos Jr., 1–11. Westport, Conn.: Greenwood Press, 1989.

———. "Ultimate Values in Politics: Problems and Prospects for World Society." In *Religious Politics in Global and Comparative Perspective,* ed. William H. Swatos Jr., 55–74. Westport, Conn.: Greenwood Press, 1989.

Tebbel, John. *America's Great Patriotic War with Spain: Mixed Motives, Lies, and Racism in Cuba and the Philippines, 1895–1915.* Manchester Center, Utah: Marshall Jones, 1996.

Thompson, Kenneth W. *Morality and Foreign Policy.* Baton Rouge: Louisiana State University Press, 1980.

———. *Traditions and Values in Politics and Diplomacy: Theory and Practice.* Baton Rouge: Louisiana State University Press, 1992.

———, ed. *Ethics and International Relations.* New Brunswick, N.J.: Transaction, 1985.

Thorne, Christopher. "American Political Culture and the End of the Cold War." *Journal of American Studies* 26 (1992): 303–30.

Thweatt, Hiram H. *What the Newspapers Say of the Negro Soldier in the Spanish-American War*. Pamphlet. Thomasville, Ga., 1898.

Tibi, Bassam. "Religious Fundamentalism and Ethnicity in the Crisis of the Nation-State in the Middle East: Superordinate Islamic and Pan-Arabic Identities and Subordinate Ethnic and Sectarian Identities." Working paper for Conference on Nation, National Identity, and Nationalism, University of California at Berkeley, September 10–12, 1992.

Tillich, Paul. *Christianity and the Encounter of World Religions*. New York: Columbia University Press, 1963.

Tilly, Charles. "National Self-Determination as a Problem for All of Us." *Daedalus* 122 (Summer 1993): 29–36.

Tocqueville, Alexis de. *Democracy in America* [1848]. Ed. J. P. Mayer, trans. George Lawrence. New York: Harper & Row, 1969.

Tracy, David. "Theology, Public Discourse, and the American Tradition." Afterword to *Religion in Twentieth Century American Intellectual Life*, ed. Michael J. Lacey, 193–203. New York: Cambridge University Press, 1991.

Trask, David F. *The War with Spain in 1898*. New York: Macmillan, 1981.

Traxel, David. *1898: The Birth of the American Century*. New York: Alfred A. Knopf, 1998.

Trubowitz, Peter. *Defending the National Interest: Conflict and Change in American Foreign Policy*. Chicago: University of Chicago Press, 1998.

———. "The Two Faces of Foreign Policy." *Clio: Newsletter of Politics and History, an Organized Section of the American Political Science Association* 10 (Spring/Summer 2000).

Tuchman, Barbara W. *The Proud Tower: A Portrait of the World before the War, 1890–1914*. New York: Macmillan, 1966.

Turner, Frederick Jackson. *History, Frontier, and Section*. With an introduction by Martin Ridge. Albuquerque: University of New Mexico Press, 1993.

Tuveson, Ernest Lee. *Redeemer Nation: The Idea of America's Millennial Role*. Chicago: University of Chicago Press, 1968.

Twain, Mark. *Collected Tales, Sketches, Speeches, and Essays, 1891–1910.* New York: Library Classics of America, 1992.

Tyrrell, Ian. "American Exceptionalism in an Age of International History." *American Historical Review* 96 (October 1991): 1031–55.

Utley, Robert M. *The Indian Frontier of the American West, 1846–1890.* Albuquerque: University of New Mexico Press, 1984.

Uyangoda, Jaydeva. "Understanding Ethnicity and Nationalism." *Ecumenical Review* 47 (April 1995): 190–94.

Vagts, Alfred. "The United States and the Balance of Power." In *Principles and Problems of International Politics*, ed. Hans J. Morgenthau and Kenneth W. Thompson, 178–209. New York: University Press of America, 1950.

Van Alstyne, Richard W. *Genesis of American Nationalism.* Toronto: Blaisdell, 1970.

Van Dyke, Henry. *The American Birthright and the Philippine Pottage: A Sermon Preached on Thanksgiving Day, 1898.* Pamphlet. New York, 1898.

———. *The Cross of War: A Sermon Preached on May First, 1898.* Pamphlet. New York, 1898.

Varshney, Ashutosh. "Contested Meanings: India's National Identity, Hindu Nationalism, and the Politics of Anxiety." *Daedalus* 122 (Summer 1993): 227–61.

Verdery, Katherine. "Whither 'Nation' and 'Nationalism'?" *Daedalus* 122 (Summer 1993): 37–46.

Volckmer, Otto. *Historical Sketch from the Destruction of the "Maine" to the Battle of Manila.* New York: M. F. Tobin, 1898.

Von Holst, H. E. *The Annexation of Our Spanish Conquests: Address Delivered before "The Sustaining Members of the National Association of Merchants and Travelers, Chicago, June 1898."* Pamphlet. 1898.

Vought, Hans. "Division and Reunion: Woodrow Wilson, Immigration, and the Myth of American Unity." *Journal of American Ethnic History.* 13 (Spring 1994): 24–50.

Wald, Kenneth D. "The Religious Dimension of American Anti-Communism." *Journal of Church and State* 36 (Summer 1994) 483–506.

Wall, Helena M. *Fierce Communion: Family and Community in Early America.* Cambridge: Harvard University Press, 1990.

Walls, A. F. "Carrying the White Man's Burden: Some British Views of National Vocation in the Imperial Era." In *Many Are Chosen: Divine*

Elections and Western Nationalism, ed. William R. Hutchison and Hartmut Lehman, 29- 50. Minneapolis, Minn.: Fortress Press, 1994.

Waltz, Kenneth. *Theory of International Politics*. Reading, Mass: Addison-Wesley, 1979.

———. "Political Structures." In *Neorealism and Its Critics*, ed. Robert O. Keohane, 70–97. New York: Columbia University Press, 1986.

Walzer, Michael. *Just and Unjust Wars: A Moral Argument with Historical Illustrations*. 2d ed. New York: BasicBooks, 1977.

Ward, Barbara. *Nationalism and Ideology*. New York: W. W. Norton, 1966.

Waring, Vechter. *The Enemy Has Surrendered*. Pamphlet. New York, 1898.

———. *The Flag of President McKinley*. Pamphlet. New York, 1898.

Warner, W. Lloyd. "An American Sacred Ceremony." In *American Civil Religion*, ed. Russell E. Richey and Donald G. Jones, 89–111. New York: Harper & Row, 1974.

Watson, Moody M. *A Poetical Tribute to Our Naval Heroes Who Fought the Battle of Manila*. Pamphlet. Haverhill, Mass., 1901.

Watterson, Henry. *History of the Spanish-American War*. Philadelphia: Monarch Book, 1898.

W.B. *The Diary of a Rough Rider*. Pamphlet. 1898.

Weeks, William Earl. "Decoding the Masquerade." *Diplomatic History* 21 (Summer 1997): 467–71.

Weinberg, Albert K. *Manifest Destiny: A Study of Nationalist Expansionism in American History*. Baltimore, Md.: Johns Hopkins University Press, 1935.

Welch, H. N. *Dewey's Battle in Manila Bay*. Pamphlet. Groton, Vt., 1899.

Welch, Richard E. *Response to Imperialism: The United States and the Philippine-American War, 1899–1902*. Chapel Hill: University of North Carolina Press, 1979.

———. 1985. "William McKinley: Reluctant Warrior, Cautious Imperialist." In *Traditions and Values: American Diplomacy, 1865–1945*, ed. Norman A. Graebner, 29–52. Lanham, Md.: University Press of America, 1985.

Wells, Douglas. *Fighting against the Odds*. New York: Street & Smith, 1899.

———. *For Spanish Gold*. New York: Street & Smith, 1899.

Welsh, Herbert. *The Ethics of the War Viewed from the Christian Standpoint: Address before the Ethical Society in Philadelphia, 19 June 1898.* Pamphlet. Philadelphia, 1898.

Wendt, Alexander. "Anarchy Is What States Make of It." *International Organization* 46 (Spring 1992): 391–425.

———. *Social Theory of International Politics.* New York: Cambridge University Press, 1999.

West, John G., Jr. *The Politics of Revelation and Reason: Religion and Civic Life in the New Nation.* Lawrence: University Press of Kansas, 1996.

Wheeler, Joseph. *The Santiago Campaign of 1898.* New York: Lamson, Wolffe, 1898.

Whitridge, Frederick Wallingford. *Our New National Policy: Address before the Laurel Hill Association, Stockbridge, Mass., 24 August 1898.* Pamphlet. 1898.

Wildavsky, Aaron. "Resolved, that Individualism and Egalitarianism be Made Compatible in America: Political-Cultural Roots of Exceptionalism." In *Is America Different? A New Look at American Exceptionalism,* ed. Byron E. Shafer, 116–37. Oxford, Eng.: Clarendon Press, 1991.

Wilkerson, Marcus M. *Public Opinion and the Spanish-American War: A Study in War Propaganda.* Baton Rouge: Louisiana State University Press, 1932.

Williams, Ora. *Oriental America: Official and Authentic Records of the Dealings of the United States with the Natives of Luzon and Their Former Rulers.* Chicago: Oriental America Publishing, 1899.

Williams, Rhys H., and Susan M. Alexander. "Religious Rhetoric in American Populism: Civil Religion as Movement Ideology." *Journal for the Scientific Study of Religion* 33 (March 1994): 1–15.

Williams, William Appleman. *A William Appleman Williams Reader: Selections from His Major Historical Writings.* Edited with introduction and notes by Henry W. Berger. Chicago: Ivan R. Dee, 1992.

Wills, Garry. *Under God: Religion and American Politics.* New York: Simon & Schuster, 1990.

Wilson, John F. "A Historian's Approach to Civil Religion." In *American Civil Religion,* ed. Russell E. Richey and Donald G. Jones, 115–38. New York: Harper & Row, 1974.

————. *Public Religion in American Culture*. Philadelphia: Temple University Press, 1979.

————. "Religion and Revolution in American History." *Journal of Interdisciplinary History* 23 (Winter 1993): 597–613.

Wilson, John Grosvenor. *The March of Millions; Or, The Rise and Fall of the American Empire*. New York: Neely, 1900.

Winthrop, Essex B. *Spain and the Spaniards*. New York: Street & Smith, 1899.

Wisner, J. A., and H. F. Humphrey. *Sketches from the Spanish-American War in the Philippine Islands, May to August 1898*. Pamphlet. Maryland, 1898.

Wolf, Margaret Isabel. *Songs of "Cuba Libre": A Remembrance of the Heroes of the "Maine."* Pamphlet. Dayton, Ohio, 1898.

Woodward, C. Vann. *The Strange Career of Jim Crow*. 2d ed. New York: Oxford University Press, 1957.

————. "The Age of Reinterpretation." In *Major Problems in American Foreign Relations*, vol. 1, *To 1920*. 4th edition, ed. Thomas G. Paterson and Dennis Merrill, 2–7. Lexington, Mass.: D. C. Heath, 1995.

Wuthnow, Robert. *The Restructuring of American Religion: Society and Faith since World War II*. Princeton: Princeton University Press, 1988.

————. *The Struggle for America's Soul: Evangelicals, Liberals, and Secularism*. Grand Rapids, Mich.: William B. Eerdmans, 1989.

Young Men's Christian Association (YMCA), International Committee, Women's Auxiliary. *Notes of Progress* (1). Pamphlet. New York, 1900.

————. *Notes of Progress* (2). Pamphlet. New York, 1900.

YMCA National Board, Armed Services Department. *Our Soldiers and Sailors*. Pamphlet. Brooklyn, 1899.

————. *A Growing Work*. Pamphlet. Brooklyn, 1900.

Young, James Rankin. *History of Our War with Spain*. Philadelphia: Premier, 1898.

Young, O. E. *Back from the Philippines*. New York: Dick & Fitzgerald, 1905.

Zakaria, Fareed. *From Wealth to Power: The Unusual Origins of America's World Role*. Princeton: Princeton University Press, 1998.

Zeiler, Thomas W. *Dean Rusk: Defending the American Mission Abroad*. Wilmington, Del.: Scholarly Resource, 2000.

Zelinsky, Wilbur. *Nation into State: The Shifting Symbolic Foundations of American Nationalism.* Chapel Hill: University of North Carolina Press, 1988.

Zimmerman, Walter. *First Great Triumph: How Five Americans Made Their Country a World Power.* New York: Farrar, Straus, Giroux, 2002.

Zuckert, Michael P. *Natural Rights and the New Republicanism.* Princeton: Princeton University Press, 1994.

Zunz, Olivier. *Why the American Century?* Chicago: University of Chicago Press, 1998.

Index

France, 200, 244

Franklin, Benjamin, 35

Free Exercise Clause, 66

French Revolution, 23

friars, Catholic in the Philippines, 208

Friends, 201–2

From Wealth to Power (Zakaria), 7

frontier thesis. *See* Turner, Frederick
  Jackson

Frye, William P., 101, 194, 218, 220–21; and
  peace commission, 205

fundamentalism, 72

Gallinger, Jacob H., 102

GAR. *See* Grand Army of the Republic
  (GAR)

General Convention of the Baptist
  Denomination for Foreign Missions,
  73

General Missionary Committee of the
  Methodist Episcopal Church, 200

Genesis, 69

George III (king), 39

Germany, 24, 25, 179, 184, 200

Giddens, Anthony, 23

Gladden, Washington, 49, 63, 85

"glut theory," 188–91

Goldstein, Judith, 16

Gomez, Máximo, 89

Gompers, Samuel, 267

Gould, Lewis L., 8, 201

Grand Army of the Republic (GAR),
  95

Grant, Ulysses S., 67

Gray, Asa, 49

Gray, George, 138, 205, 218–19, 221

Great Britain, 27, 89, 179, 181, 244

Greeley, Andrew, 20

Greene, Francis V., 210

Gregg, David, 76

Guam, 3, 174, 220

Halle, Louis J., 20

Hamilton, Alexander, 40, 42

Hanna, Marcus Alonzo, 115, 127

Harrison, Benjamin, 244

Hartman, Charles S., 124

Hartman, L. B., 75

Hastings, Adrian, 23

Havana, 4, 91

Hawaii, 4, 248

Hawley, Joseph R., 139

Hay, John, 146, 222

Healy, David, 189

Hearst, William Randolph, 91

Hegelianism, 19, 47

Herberg, Will, 157

Hitler, Adolf, 44

Hoar, George Frisbee, 137, 240–41, 248,
  250, 266–67

Hobbes, Thomas, 36, 37

Hobson, Richmond P., 159–60

Hofstadter, Richard, 88, 170, 182, 192

Holbach, Baron d', 36

Home Market Club (Boston), 258

Hudson, Winthrop, 67

Hume, David, 20

Humphreys, David, 28

Hunt, Michael H., 13

Hussein, Saddam, 1

imperialism, 5, 7, 80, 87, 172, 182, 188, 197,
  198, 238, 270, 274, 277

inaugural addresses, 28, 33–34, 119

Marshall, John, 249

Martí, Jose, 89

"martial spirit," 184–86

Marty, Martin, 33

Marx, Karl, 53

Mason, William E., 108, 109, 230–31, 242, 245

Mather, Cotton, 32

May, Ernest, 184, 194

McCook, John J., 123

McGee, W. J., 58

McKinley, Nancy Allison, 118

McKinley, William, 4, 7, 8, 60, 61, 74, 87, 89, 90, 97–100, 104, 107, 112, 121–25, 127, 129, 130, 137, 140, 142, 145, 146, 149, 154, 175, 178, 189, 190, 193, 204–8, 210–27, 252–54, 258–67, 269–70, 272–78; and the campaign of 1896, 114–16; and the campaign of 1900, 162, 269–71; and the Civil War, 120; conservatism of, 115–16; and the decision to annex the Philippines, 198–201, 219, 257, 271, 277; and the gold standard, 113, 115; popularity of, 116–17; religious beliefs of, 74, 118–19; and reluctance to enter war, 120; and speaking tours, 152, 163, 213

McLaurin, John L., 231, 235, 238, 243

McWilliams, Wilson Carey, 38

Mead, Sidney, 32

Mearshimer, John, 25

Menand, Louis, 152, 153

Merritt, Wesley, 210

Metaphysical Club, The (Menand), 152

Methodists, 202

Mexico, 191, 248

militarism, 2, 12, 188

millennialism, 12, 31, 70–73; postmillennialism, 71, 73; premillennialism, 71, 72

Miller, William Lee, 78

Mills, Roger Q., 134

Money, H. De Soto, 110, 232, 235, 247

Monroe Doctrine, 133, 179, 181, 205, 232, 250

Moorhead, James H., 41

Morgan, H. Wayne, 127

Morgan, John, 96

Morgenthau, Hans J., 17, 25

Mormons, 65

Mugwumps, 3

Napoleon Bonaparte. *See* Bonaparte, Napoleon

Nation, The, 194

national identity, American, 6, 11, 14, 17, 24–46, 47, 71, 77, 85, 138, 183, 196, 232; geographic sources of, 28–30; ideological nature of, 25–27; liberal sources of, 35–43, 77–79; origins of, 28–43; racist dimension of, 30, 39–40, 43, 58–59, 62, 81; religious sources of, 30–35, 65–67

nationalism, 23–24; Filipino, 82, 264; religion and, 30–32, 72

Native Americans, 30, 63, 67, 83

natural law, 112

natural rights, 110

Nau, Henry R., 17

naval expansion, 179

Nazism, 57

Nelson, Knute, 248, 253

neoliberalism, 15, 17

neorealism, 15

New Empire, The (Adams), 54
New York Journal, 91, 97
New York Tribune, 194
New York World, 91, 92
Niebuhr, Reinhold, 250
norms, 6, 12, 13, 19, 47, 102–4, 106–7; con-
stitutive versus prescriptive, 21–22

Olcott, Charles, 200
Olney, Richard, 180
Oregon Territory, 191
Ostend Manifesto, 193
O'Sullivan, John L., 191
Otey, Peter J., 150

Pacific Ocean, 3, 7, 227
pacifists, 96, 121
Paine, Thomas, 27, 240
Palma, Tomás Estrada, 91
Pamphlets of American History, 13, 164–
65
peace commission, 205, 218
Pearce, Charles E., 111
Peck, Harry Thurston, 55
peninsulares, 98
Pèrez, Louis A., Jr., 5–6
Perkins, George C., 111
Peters, Mason S., 109
Philippine-American War, 256, 260, 269,
272
Philippines, 3, 8, 12, 14, 44, 70, 73, 79, 84,
146, 158, 161–62, 175, 200, 204–13, 220,
222, 225–29, 231, 234–35, 237, 239, 243,
246–48, 250–53, 255, 258–63, 268, 271,
274
Pierce, Charles Sanders, 153

Pierce, Franklin, 193
Pittsburgh Dispatch, 123
Platt, Orville H., 225–27
Platt Amendment, 4
plays, patriotic, 163–66
Plessy v. Ferguson, 60
poems, 167–72; antiwar, 171–72; patriotic,
167–69
Politics among Nations (Morgenthau), 17
Populism, 3
Populist Party, 107, 125, 130, 135
Powell, John Wesley, 58
Pratt, Julius W., 48, 100, 200
Proctor, Redfield, 100–102, 105, 135
progress, 12, 47
Providence, 10, 28–29, 31, 34, 71, 73–76,
109, 110, 120, 122, 139, 143, 159, 161, 162,
191, 208, 216, 227, 233, 258, 261–62
Puerto Rico, 3, 8, 79, 174, 205, 207, 218,
220, 222, 250, 258
Pulitzer, Joseph, 91
Puritans, 27, 29, 31–33, 45, 69, 71, 74

Quakers. See Friends

racism, 5, 30, 57, 64, 80, 85, 245, 275; and
racial essentialism, 58; and racial paternalism, 58. See also lynching; national identity, American: racist dimension of; segregation; social
Darwinism
Randolph, Carman, 189
Rawls, John, 20
realism, 7, 8
"reconcentration Camps" / reconcentrados, 87, 93, 122, 246